Foundations of Real-World Intelligence

Foundations of Real-World Intelligence

edited by
Yoshinori Uesaka
Pentti Kanerva
Hideki Asoh

CSLI
PUBLICATIONS
Center for the Study of
Language and Information
Stanford, California

Copyright © 2001
CSLI Publications
Center for the Study of Language and Information
Leland Stanford Junior University
Printed in the United States
05 04 03 02 01   1 2 3 4 5

Library of Congress Cataloging-in-Publication Data

Foundations of real-world intelligence / edited by Yoshinori Uesaka,
Pentti Kanerva, Hideki Asoh.
    p. cm. -- (CSLI lecture notes ; no. 125)
    Includes bibliographical references and index.
    ISBN 1-57586-339-1 (acid-free paper) -- ISBN 1-57586-338-3 (pbk. :
acid-free paper)
    1. Artificial intelligence. 2. Neural networks (Computer science)
3. Evolutionary programming (Computer science) I. Uesaka, Yoshinori,
1936– . II. Kanerva, Pentti, 1937– . III. Asoh, Hideki, 1958– . IV. Series.
    Q335 .F685 2001
    006.3--dc21
                        2001043252

    ∞ The acid-free paper used in this book meets the minimum
requirements of the American National Standard for Information Sciences—
Permanence of Paper for Printed Library Materials, ANSI Z39.48-1984.

Please visit our web site at
http://cslipublications.stanford.edu/
for comments on this and other titles, as well as for changes
and corrections by the author and publisher.

Contents

v

Preface

As is well known, computers have become increasingly powerful and far exceed human ability to solve well-defined problems such as numerical computation, document processing, and logical inference in ideal worlds where all information is known and there is an algorithm for the solution that may be stated precisely in a programming language. Nevertheless, computers are still far inferior to humans in many other intellectual tasks such as pattern recognition, dealing with ill-posed problems, and learning. If computers are to develop to the point where they can perform humanlike, flexible processing in the real world—thus opening up a new horizon in information-processing technology—we must pursue the fundamentals of humanlike information-processing, come to terms with how humans process information at an intuitive level, and embody this theoretical knowledge in various developing hardware technologies. The development of advanced information systems that exhibit flexible, humanlike intelligence capable of dealing with real-world problems is one of the most important challenges shared by such diverse fields as pattern information processing, knowledge information processing, intelligent robots, and friendly human-machine interfaces.

With the aim of developing such information-processing systems, the Ministry of International Trade and Industry (MITI) of Japan launched a large-scale national program in Real World Computing (RWC) in 1992, with a ten-year budget of over 500 million dollars. The program is outlined in the general introduction to this book. Phase I of the RWC program (1992–1996) explored three general areas: novel functions for applications, theoretical foundations, and parallel and distributed computational bases. The research in Phase II (1997–2001) has been more integrated and focused, allotting resources to two projects: real-world intelligence (RWI) and parallel and distributed computing (PDC). The aim of the RWI program area is to broaden the application horizons of conventional information-processing technology to include flexible, real-world intelligence. To pursue this objective, we established six core areas of research and development: autonomous learning systems, multi-modal interaction systems, self-organizing information base systems, theoretical and algorithmic foundations, real-world adaptive devices, and intellectual resources.

This book is about the theoretical and algorithmic foundations of real-world intelligence. The objective of the research in this area has been to establish a theoretical foundation for two key technologies, information integration and learning, drawing ideas from neural networks, genetic algorithms, Bayesian networks, EM algorithms, hidden Markov models, and the like. Conventional artificial intelligence in a narrow sense is a top-down approach; it is too artificial, based on deductive formal logic and symbol manipulation. In contrast, neural networks—that is, connectionist AI—artificial life, genetic algorithms, complex systems, and emergent computation represent a bottom-up approach. They are based on pattern computing or subsymbolic dynamic computation, shifting the focus toward induction, learning, and self-learning. However, what is essential to developing systems with real-world intelligence is understanding the computational aspect of intelligence; that is, identifying and confirming the unifying principles of computation behind both these methods, to deepen them theoretically, and to implement them as a more powerful computational methodology.

We have classified the various themes investigated under theoretical and algorithmic foundation into the following six categories: models for representing knowledge, algorithms for inference and integration, algorithms for learning, system architectures for information integration and learning, frameworks of interaction for learning, and test-bed applications for empirical evaluation. The themes were researched by six research laboratories: NEC Laboratory, GMD Laboratory (German National Research Center for Information Technology), SNN Laboratory (Stichting Neurale Netwerken in the Netherlands), SICS Laboratory (Swedish Institute of Computer Science), Toshiba Laboratory, and ETL (Electrotechnical Laboratory) RWI Research Center.

To promote cooperative R&D among these laboratories, numerous workshops and meetings were held. As the research was drawing to a close, we faced the question of how to present the results because, in general, the fruits of theoretical research mature slowly and are not immediately demonstrated in practical systems or hardware. We finally decided to collect the results into a book, as well as try to exhibit them in more conventional ways such as prototypes. The introductory survey and the chapters in this book are the results of the research of five of the laboratories, each of which covers multiple research issues from representation of knowledge to test-bed applications.

We hope that this book will be of value to all who have at least a modest background in modern information-processing technology and a genuine interest in the fascinating possibilities that have motivated the research.

Finally, we want to express our thanks to all contributors to the book and to everybody who devoted themselves to the RWC program. In particular, we sincerely thank Professor Hidehiko Tanaka of the University of Tokyo, chairman of the promotion committee of the RWC program; Dr. Junichi Shimada, managing director of the RWC program and director of the Tsukuba Research Center of the Real World Computing Partnership (RWCP); Dr. Yoshikuni Okada, general manager of the research planning department of RWCP; and Dr. Nobuyuki Otsu, chief of the RWI Research Center of ETL. We also thank Dikran Karagueuzian and his staff at CSLI Publications for making it possible to produce and publish the book, and Judith Feldmann for diligent editing of the manuscript.

July 2001
The Editors

General Introduction†

RWI Research Center, Electrotechnical Laboratory

NOBUYUKI OTSU AND HIDEKI ASOH

This chapter provides a general introduction to the ideas discussed in this book. First, we introduce the concept of *real-world intelligence*. Then, we overview the Real-World Computing (RWC) program, a ten-year large-scale R&D program promoted by the Ministry of International Trade and Industry (MITI)† of the Japanese government since 1992. The program consists of two R&D domains, real-world intelligence (RWI) domain and the parallel distributed computing (PDC) domain. We briefly overview R&D activities in the RWI domain. Finally, we describe in greater detail R&D efforts in the theoretical and algorithmic foundation area of the RWI domain, which is the theme of this book, as introductions to the following chapters.

1 Real-World Intelligence and the Real-World Computing Program

NOBUYUKI OTSU

Supported by the remarkable development of computer and communication technologies, information technology is producing an innovative change in today's society, not only in industrial activities but also in the qualitative improvement of our way of life. The amount of information we handle will increase explosively because of the increasing needs of

---

†In a major reorganization, Electrotechnical Laboratory (ETL) became a part of the new National Institute of Advanced Industrial Science and Technology (AIST) in April 2001, while the Ministry of International Trade and Industry (MITI) was changed to Ministry of Economy, Trade, and Industry (METI) in January 2001.

Foundations of Real-World Intelligence.
Yoshinori Uesaka et al. (eds.).
Copyright © 2001, CSLI Publications.

multimedia information processing and the expansion of new application domains. This means not only an increase in quantity but also an increase in the quality and variety of information. Such social and technological needs are starting to require a new paradigm of information technology, not simply as a linear extension of the conventional one, but as an essentially new underlying framework. In other words, it is necessary to make computers more user-friendly and easy to use by providing them with humanlike flexible and intelligent capabilities in order to assist and collaborate with humans in the diverse information environment of the real world.

We call such intelligent capabilities *real-world intelligence* to stress the contrast with the conventional artificial intelligence technologies, which are mainly based on the explicit description of knowledge and logical inference in well-defined environments such as games, problem solving, and theorem proving.

Today, computers have come to possess enormous computing power that far surpasses human abilities to solve well-defined problems such as numerical computation, document processing, and logical inference in preassumed ideal information worlds where there are algorithms for the solution that can be stated clearly in programming languages. Nevertheless, computers are still inferior to humans in many areas such as pattern recognition, problem solving under incomplete information, and learning. The framework of the information processing done by modern computers is still not as flexible as that of the information processing done by humans in the real world, where many problems are illdefined and hard to describe in algorithms. It might be said that current information technology is still immature in the so-called intuitive or inductive aspect in contrast to the logical and deductive aspect of reasoning.

Therefore, to cope with such real-world problems and to open a new horizon in information processing technology, it is essential to pursue the more flexible ways that humans process information, by investigating the intuitive or subsymbolic level of human information processing and embodying these methods as new information processing technologies on the basis of the developing hardware technologies. The development of information systems that have humanlike, flexible intelligence and that can cope with real-world problems is one of the most important demands common to various fields such as pattern information processing, knowledge information processing, intelligent robotics, and friendly human–machine interface, all of which aim at advancing our methods of intelligent information processing.

1.1   Outline of the RWC Program

The Real World Computing (RWC) program started in 1992 as the successor to the Fifth Generation Computer project. This is the large-scale ten-year Japanese national project launched by MITI with a budget of over $500 million for ten years. Whereas the Fifth Generation project pursued the logical (symbol-based) aspect of information processing (or intelligence) of humans, the RWC program is rather pursuing the intuitive (pattern-based) aspect of information processing and also aiming at unifying both aspects in a bottom-up manner within a new framework and foundation for next-generation information processing.

The primary objective of the RWC program is to lay the theoretical foundation necessary to pursue the technological realization of human-like flexible, intelligent information processing, capable of directly and flexibly processing various kinds of information in the real world. The aim is to build a new paradigm of information processing for the highly information-based society of the twenty-first century (MITI, 1992; Otsu, 1993).

In July 1992 the *RWC partnership* (RWCP) was founded, and fifteen Japanese companies including almost all major electronics firms have since joined, with more than thirty contract research themes making it through the reviewing process. In October 1992, the RWCP founded its own central laboratory, Tsukuba Research Center (TRC), near ETL (Electrotechnical Laboratory) in Tsukuba City, expecting close cooperation with ETL and inviting about twenty researchers from laboratories of each company. The RWC program also opened the door to foreign counties, and four research institutes—GMD: German National Research Center for Information Technology, SNN: Stichting Neurale Netwerken (the Netherlands), SICS: Swedish Institute of Computer Science, and Kent Ridge Digital Laboratories (Singapore)—participate as contractors, and some others as subcontractors (details are available at http://www.rwcp.or.jp/home-E.html). ETL, which belongs to MITI and played an important role in the early conceptualization of the program, continues to support and lead the program, having sent some researchers to the main positions in TRC and also carrying out its own leading-edge research on RWC with a group of about fifty researchers.

In Phase I (1992–1996), exploratory research was done in three layered fields:

1. novel functions for application;
2. theoretical foundation; and
3. parallel and distributed computational bases.

Via the interim review in 1996, Phase II (1997–2001) has focused on more integrative and intensive R&D, allotting resources to two domains:

- RWI (real-world intelligence) and
- PDC (parallel and distributed computing).

The RWI domain, which is promoted by RWI Research Center in ETL/ MITI, aims to add real-world intelligence (learning and information integration capabilities) to the conventional information-processing technology in order to expand its application horizon. Main R&D topics include theoretical bases, application systems implementing novel functions (multi-modal computer–human interface systems, autonomous learning, mobile systems, etc.), and supporting hardware (adaptive devices such as evolvable hardware and smart pixels) and software (intellectual resources such as databases and library; Otsu, 1998). In the PDC domain, which is promoted by TRC/RWCP, aims to provide parallel and distributed computational bases (seamless computing systems) for improving general use of the currently expanding global computer network infrastructure. Main R&D topics include computer architecture (such as PC/WS cluster and optical interconnection), software environments (such as SCore, MPC++), and some PDC applications such as large-scale simulation, data retrieval, and parallel protein information analysis (PAPIA).

1.2 Real-World Intelligence

1.2.1 Objectives

As has already been stated, the goal of the research and development of real-world intelligence in the RWC program is to develop fundamental technologies for modeling and understanding humanlike flexible intelligence, including abilities of information integration and learning, and combining these with the conventional information technologies, thereby broadening the potential and application domain of information processing.

Unlike the computer, humans and other living creatures develop quite flexible intelligence that functions adaptively in the real world. The brain acquires such real-world intelligence through interactions with the real world via pattern information. Symbolic intelligence is actually formed on this real-world basis.

The essential functions of real-world intelligence are

- information integration, and
- learning/self-organization.

Information integration involves processing various kinds of information in the real world that contain ambiguity and uncertainty, such as images and sounds, in an integrated and parallel manner, so that such information can be used in recognition, understanding, overall judgment, and decision-making about behavior. *Learning/self-organization* involves systems' adapting or evolving their own functions by autonomously collecting information through interactions with the real world.

Information integration and learning/self-organization have been studied separately so far in theoretical contexts, but the special accomplishment of real-world intelligence lies in exercising these abilities in a consistent and integrated manner. In addition, information integration and learning/self-organization should be integrated with recognition and reasoning functions. Their integration in a theoretical framework requires stochastic and statistical methods to deal with uncertain information in the real world. Using these information integration and learning/self-organization functions as a common framework, we need a system that closely ties the research on theoretical foundations and research and development with actual applications of the theory.

1.2.2 Approach and Methodology

What kind of approach or methodology should we take in trying to realize real-world intelligence? To put it briefly and directly, we need to use the stochastic (probabilistic and statistical) and parallel/dynamic computing approach, in order to cope with large-scale but partial, uncertain, and incomplete information in the real world. Conventional methods of information processing are based on the computer's logic, i.e. procedural and serial processing (a linear method), whereby input information is converted into output information as an algorithm. This is a direct method with a rigid framework and is very efficient at handling well-defined problems; however, it lacks flexibility and often breaks down when dealing with real-world situations. In contrast, multilayer neural networks (Rumelhart et al., 1986) or multivariate data analysis are based on a feedback loop for optimization with evaluation by including degrees of freedom as parameters in the processing. With this, the method learns adaptively the optimal processing from examples. It is, in a sense, a forward adaptation method. On the other hand, model fitting (Geman and Geman, 1984; Hopfield and Tank, 1985) or regularization theory (Poggio and Koch, 1985) may be considered backward adaptation methods. These assume a parameterized model as an ideal output. With this, the method evaluates the discrepancy of the model, updating it based on input information, achieving optimal though implicit processing.

As we consider real-world intelligence, we must take such new techniques into account. Key issues are a mechanism for evaluation and a feedback loop for optimization, and both should be installed in the sys-

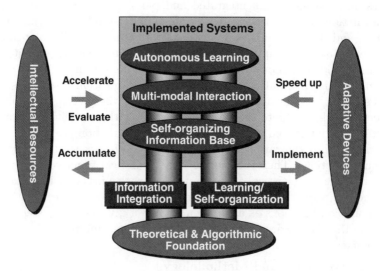

FIGURE 1.1. Scheme of R&D in the RWI domain.

tem if the system is to be adaptive and autonomous. It is also necessary to consider pattern recognition in thinking how the brain deals with pattern information in the real world. The basis for learning and inference, pattern recognition is very important for intelligence. It is located at the "front end" of intelligence, where it meets the real world, bridging patterns and symbols. From a logical perspective, pattern recognition has an inductive phase of learning and also a deductive phase of decision making. In addition, pattern recognition focuses essentially on parallel processing or overall judgment.

Behind the flexible and intelligent processing of information, in areas such as pattern recognition, neural computation, regularization, and stochastic inference, lies a Bayesian framework (Otsu, 1982, 1989; Geman and Geman, 1984). Multivariate data analysis represents such things most simply as a linear model; what allows for nonlinear functionality to some extent is a neural network. Its extremity is the Bayesian inference (Otsu, 1982).

1.2.3 Research and Development

For pursuing the above objectives, we have established six core areas for research and development (figure 1.1). Three of them are system oriented, covering basic information-processing abilities (such as recognition and understanding, reasoning, and control) and typical application domains, and the other three areas support the system-oriented areas.

To promote and encourage the cooperative R&D in those areas, workshops are being organized and meetings are often held within each area and across areas. Participants are researchers from contracted companies, university professors as subcontractors, and researchers from the RWI Research Center in ETL as chairs.

Autonomous Learning System. Autonomous learning system is a physical agent (e.g. a mobile robot) that moves around autonomously in real environments, acquires and learns information related to its environment (including people) by sensing and interacting with the environment, and can be developed into a system that offers services according to needs. This system is, in a sense, considered as a test bed for integrating various novel functions that are being developed. R&D topics include sensor- and vision-based navigation, map learning, vision for object recognition, understanding of speech and sounds in noisy environments, knowledge acquisition and representation, multi-agent architecture, action planning, and so on. A prototype system, Jijo2, is being developed in ETL.

Multi-modal Interaction System. A multi-modal interaction system is a personified agent-type computer–human interface that enables users to communicate with computers or information systems in a natural way, by integrating multi-modal information (speech, images, gestures, etc.). R&D topics are understanding and synthesis of images (in 2-D and 3-D), speech sounds, facial expressions, hand sign language, and inter-modal learning for concept formation by complementary use of imagery information and language (e.g. the way infants and children learn concepts of objects in the real world with assistance from mothers). It is hoped that this kind of system will become a next-generation interface system that will allow everybody to communicate easily with computers and information systems everywhere.

Self-organizing Information Base System. A self-organizing information base system is one that can retrieve, sort, summarize, and present diverse and vast amounts of information in the real world or in information networks in a self-organizing manner for supporting users' intellectual activities. This technology is urgently required in the current information society, especially given the flood of information typically encountered on the Internet. R&D topics are clustering of large-scale data such as contents of newspapers or TV, 3-D browsing and user interface, and mutual retrieval between different media such as texts, images, and speech sounds. Work is also being done to devlop a common format in which to represent and treat such multimedia information in a unified manner.

Theoretical and Algorithmic Foundations. Theoretical and algorithmic foundation is the target area of this volume. The area concerns the theoretical foundations of information integration, learning and self-organization, and optimization techniques that support RWI systems. The theoretical bases of the technology advances are of great importance in bringing about a true breakthrough and prevent the end result of these technologies from becoming a simple collection of heuristics. Extensive research is being carried out on neural networks, Bayesian networks, genetic algorithms, EM algorithm, HMM, ICA, and so on. A truly new technology will be created through the close interaction and collaboration of empirical work with application-oriented R&D.

Real-World Adaptive Devices. Systems in the real world need to operate adaptively in real time. It is often difficult to achieve this through only the application of software; hardware support is essential. This does not mean that we need supercomputers, but we may need certain specialized hardware devices (chips) that contribute to the realization of real-time and adaptive processing. New types of hardware are being developed, such as reconfigurable hardware (RHW: next generation FPGA), evolvable hardware (RHW+GA), and smart pixel (optical vision chip). Real-world application systems implemented with the adaptive devices are also being developed in ETL, for example, evolver (an autonomous mobile robot with gene), EMG-controlled prosthetic hands, and so on.

Intellectual Resources. Support from the software side is also important. That is, we need to provide and maintain various databases, benchmarks, and a library of software, in order to accelerate and evaluate the R&D of real-world intelligence technology. This area is called the intellectual resources for R&D. For instance, real-world databases such as images, speeches, and texts (corpus) are important for the design and evaluation of the real-world intelligence systems and techniques being developed. It is also important to archive acquired common techniques and programs in the software library; doing so will accelerate R&D and will also leave the results of R&D in a stable form for coming generations. Databases already developed are available in CD-ROM, and some of the software library will be open to the public on the Web.

1.3 Concluding Remarks

Conventional artificial intelligence in a narrow sense is a top-down approach. Based on deductive formal logic and symbol manipulation, it is too artificial to model human intelligence by itself. In contrast, the recent paradigm shift in neural networks (connectionist AI) and in artificial life (such as genetic algorithms, complex systems, and emergent computation) is a bottom-up approach, based on pattern recognition or subsymbolic dynamic computation, shifting the focus toward the inductive aspect of intelligence—toward learning and self-organization. However, what is essential to the project of modeling real-world intelligence is the computational (or cognitive) aspect of intelligence; we need to clarify and confirm the unified principle of computation behind these methods, to deepen them theoretically, and to implement them as more powerful computational paradigms. There already exists a framework of Bayesian inference, decision-making (Otsu, 1989), and other types of stochastic computation. The project also tends toward furthering this existing research.

A consequent and natural question is the following: how will AI research in the twenty-first century progress? An initial answer is that it will further investigate distributed and cooperative intelligence based on embedded systems, which corresponds to the further development of the global information network and of ubiquitous, wearable intelligent information appliances. The RWC program, in particular the R&D in the RWI domain, is actually providing technological bases for these future developments.

2 Theoretical and Algorithmic Foundations of Real-World Intelligence
HIDEKI ASOH

What are the theoretical and algorithmic foundations for realizing intelligent systems?

About ten to twenty years ago, the main answer was *symbolic logic* and *production rules*. Logic programming (declarative programming, constraint programming) and production systems were considered a very powerful tool for representing knowledges about the world and making inferences. Many kinds of logics, inference algorithms, and expert systems were investigated. The 5th Generation Computer Project developed special hardware that could handle very fast logical inference.

Logical statements are very powerful as representations of knowledge and rules that can be explicitly written down in language, and of the inferences we make with them. However, there are many types of implicit knowledge that are difficult to represent as logical statements or linguistic rules. For one thing, such knowledge often includes noise and contradictions. We human beings have huge amount of implicit knowledge that is indispensable to our surviving in the real world. For example, we can recognize a visual image of face, but we cannot explain why we can or just how we recognize it. Pattern recognition research has mainly been tackling such implicit knowledge. One of its major theoretical foundations is statistics.

Real-world intelligence systems should handle complex, uncertain, dynamic, multi-modal information in the real world. Both explicit and implicit types of knowledge are important here. Hence we need to develop a novel integrated framework that can represent our knowledge and inferential abilities using both types of knowledge. In addition, given the enormous complexity and variety of the real-world environment, it is impossible to preprogram all knowledge. Hence a learning capability is crucial to modeling real-world intelligence. Learning, like the process of evolution, is a kind of meta-programming strategy; instead of writing target programs themselves, we implement learning programs that themselves generate and modify target programs according to the interaction between system and environment.

2.1 Objective

The objective of the research activities in the area of the theoretical and algorithmic foundations of RWI is to establish the theoretical foundations of the two key technologies, *information integration* and *learning/self-organization*. Our aim is to provide novel schemes and algorithms for acquiring knowledge, representing knowledge, making inferences with that knowledge, and using that knowledge to interact with the environment and other users. Not only proposing new schemes and methods but also analyzing the performance of the methods theoretically and empirically, and efficiently implementing the methods and providing them to the researchers creating prototype systems of real-world intelligence are important objectives.

2.2 Approach

Approaches to the theoretical foundations of intelligent systems can be divided into two groups: rule-based and normative, or model-based. The former approach, based on symbolic logic, is used mainly in conventional AI in areas such as knowledge engineering, natural language processing, game playing, and so on. The latter is used in pattern recognition and is based on statistics and probability theory.

The two approaches are coming closer together recently, as the necessity of handling real-world information becomes consensus among the researchers of intelligent systems. Real-world information is multi-modal, noisy, uncertain, dynamic, and complex. To handle such information, both approaches need to be extended. For example, in some rule-based expert systems such as MYCIN, measures of certainty of information called certainty factor have been introduced. More recently, inductive logic inference is being investigated to try to make the systems learn logical statements from experiences.

Simple statistics based on Gaussian distributions or mixture of Gaussian distributions, which were major tools in statistical pattern recognition, turned to be not powerful enough to treat complex information such as speech signals or motion images. For example, in speech recognition systems, it seems that more complex probability models such as the hidden Markov model or neural networks play an important role. Probability distributions with combinatorial structure, called graphical models, have been investigated intensively in recent years.

The main approach we take here is the latter one: a normative approach based on statistics and probability theory. One reason to choose it is its theoretical soundness. At the same time, we remain open to novel alternatives. Explorative studies seeking new schemes of representing information, making inferences, and learning are also being done.

2.3 Research Issues

In order to review various research themes investigated in the RWI project, we will organize them in the following six categories and then briefly describe major research issues.

- Models for representing knowledge
- Algorithms for inference and integration
- Algorithms for learning/self-organization
- System architectures for information integration and learning
- Frameworks of interaction for learning
- Test-bed applications for empirical evaluation

2.3.1 Model

A model is a general scheme or language for representing various constraints between variables. It is also used to describe the generation process of observed data. Here we focus mainly on probabilistic relationships between variables and exploit as models families of probability distributions with graphical structure.

There is no universally superior model. Each model has its own characteristics. Hence our mission is to clarify the characteristics of models and make predictions of their performance in various specific but somehow general situations.

In addition to probabilistic models, we also investigate novel information representation schemes that are appropriate for information integration.

2.3.2 Algorithms for Inference and Integration

Since computations of probability using a structured probability distribution model is computationally intensive, efficient approximative algorithms are necessary to realize the real-time response of systems. Anytime algorithms, which can output approximate results at any requested moment, are preferable. The active control of the probability computing process is also important for the efficiency of the computation.

Integrating information from multiple sources can be considered a special case of inference. However, the vast variety of the information sources makes the problem more difficult.

2.3.3 Algorithms for Learning/Self-Organization

To learn is to acquire proper constraints to behave properly in environment. If a criterion for evaluating the appropriateness of constraints is given, the learning problem reduces to an optimization problem. A well-known criterion in statistics is maximum likelihood. However, the likelihood function is not appropriate as a criterion for selecting structure of models because it will always select the most complex model.

The models treated in this project have a graphical structure and so structure selection is indispensable for them to provide a good representation of knowledge. Hence we need to determine criteria for model selection and learning.

When the model is complex, the search for good representation tends to become computationally intractable. Thus we need heuristics that work in typical settings. Two of current major trends in machine learning research are distributed learning and active, explorative learning such as boosting. Genetic algorithms can be considered a kind of active distributed learning mechanism.

In many learning procedures, computing statistics from data is the most computationally costly part. Approximation techniques for statistical inference introduced from statistical mechanics are effective here, as well.

2.3.4 System Architecture

For the extensible systematic realization of a multi-modal information integration system, a flexible system architecture is necessary. Multi-agent software architecture is a candidate for implementing complex information processing.

2.3.5 Frameworks of Interaction for Learning

Although distributed learning or active learning is a powerful learning mechanism, acquiring the proper model structure is still a very difficult problem. To overcome this difficulty, we need to develop novel frameworks for learning.

2.3.6 Test-Bed Applications

To evaluate algorithms, we need test-bed applications. Several application problems are selected from various domains such as genetic information processing, decision support systems, natural language processing, and robotics. "Test-bed" does not mean just "toy problems" or "small-scale problems." Some of research issues are directly related to systems oriented research in other RWI research areas, and some of them treat large-scale real-world data.

2.4 Organization of R&D and This Book

As will be shown in the following chapters, various research issues in the theoretical and algorithmic foundations area have been investigated by five distributed laboratories in RWC partnership (RWCP) and one laboratory in RWI research center at ETL. Each laboratory covers multiple research issues from representation of knowledge to test-bed application. In what follows, we briefly summarize their goals and major results as an introduction to the following chapters.

2.4.1 Inference and Learning with Graphical Models (ETL Lab)

The ETL Lab aims to establish the foundations of learning and integrated information processing for real-world intelligence that can interact closely with the real world, including humans, and execute flexible information processing. Various models, such as Bayesian networks, probabilistic constraint programs (an extension of constraint program that can treat statements of the first order predicate logic with probability), and mixture of Gaussians, are explored by the lab.

A combination of Bayesian networks and neural networks developed by this lab is able to extend the applicability of the Bayesian networks to real-world continuous-valued data. The algorithm is also being implemented in Java language with an elegant graphical user interface and flexible data-base access capability. Another remarkable result is a new compilation mechanism for probabilistic constraint programs.

Another approach to graphical modeling, multivariate information analysis, is also being pursued. Several methods have been proposed to determine the relationship between random variables, including analyzing information-theoretic measures such as mutual entropy between variables. The methods are applied to the brain image data from functional MRIs, which describe the activity of the brain during cognitive tasks to reveal the relations between the activities of several parts of a brain.

Investigating novel learning schemes that interact more closely with the environment is another major research issue in this lab. Two new schemes have been proposed and are being implemented. The first is dialogue-based learning, or socially embedded learning, which uses communication between learning systems and human users intensively. The second is intermodal learning, which exploits the multimodality of the sensory-motor flow of real-world intelligent systems. There it is expected that integrating various parts of the structure that are acquired from different modalities of the sensory-motor flow will result in a complete structure of knowledge.

The performance and characteristics of the methods are analyzed theoretically and empirically. The developed methods are implemented efficiently and provided to the researchers to build prototypes of real-world intelligence.

In chapter I of this book, following an overview of the R&D in the ETL Lab, three major results, i.e. the combination of the Bayesian networks and neural networks, multivariate information analysis, and dialogue-based learning, are described in detail.

2.4.2 Probabilistic Knowledge Representation and Active Decision (SNN Lab)

Chapter II discusses the work of the SNN Lab. The aims of the research in this laboratory are to develop novel theory, techniques, and implementations for learning and reasoning in a complex dynamic multisensory environment. The approach to reasoning and learning is based on the axioms of probability theory and Bayesian statistics. Boltzmann Machines and Bayesian networks are investigated as main target models. The lab pursues efficient approximative algorithms for such graphical models, incorporating elegant methods from statistical mechanics such as mean field approximation. Efficient learning algorithms for Boltzmann Machines and Bayesian networks are developed and evaluated.

These novel methods are demonstrated in two real-world applications: medical diagnosis and music transcription. Large-scale probabilistic networks are constructed and applied to the diagnosis of anemia under the collaboration with University Hospital Utrecht.

2.4.3 Reflective Teams: Active Learning and Information Integration in Open Environments (GMD Lab)

The goal of the GMD Lab research on reflective teams (R-Teams) is to build complex artificial reality systems that provide new insights into real-world processes. This requires:

- building the theoretical foundations for real-world intelligent systems by developing new heuristics and algorithms based on soft computing embedded in R-Teams architecture;
- demonstrating the benefits of R-Teams architectures for the integration of real-world technologies; and
- implementing real-world applications like distributed problem solving in a network of computational agents, mobile radio networks, and city traffic simulations in R-Teams architectures.

The lab has proposed a new optimization algorithm. As a first step toward designing and evaluating decentralized heuristics for agents interconnected by a network, GMD Lab. has chosen a benchmark application—the optimization of decomposed discrete functions. They use two different agent types—probabilistic and intelligent—for generic decentralized solution methods. They have developed the probabilistic methods UMADA and FDA (factorized distribution algorithm), extensions of genetic algorithms. The lab has analyzed the dynamic behaviors of algorithms UMADA and FDA.

In a next step, the lab implements the R-Teams optimization method (*RTeam-Opt*) based on game theory. The agents are active and reflective. Each agent is responsible for a component of the fitness function. The global fitness function is unknown to the individual agent. The agents use local optimization, cooperation with neighbors, and reflection. RTeam-Opt more efficiently optimizes most of the fitness functions solved by FDA. This method is applied to the optimal antenna placement problem and its effectiveness is demonstrated.

Another result is multiagent-based distributed software architecture that has learning capabilities. The basic software units of the architecture are agents that are activated periodically and thus perform cycles as if they were making *ticks* like a clock. They can access tag boards for posting or reading messages, called tags. Moreover, they control when a tag board is to be *flipped*, i.e. turned over from the current display to an updated display. This collection of organizing principles and generic functional units is called the *flip-tick architecture* (FTA) for R-Teams applications. The architecture is cycle-based. It supports one of the most common operation principles of real-world intelligent systems: to efficiently perform cycles in large data spaces as well as in complex control loops. *R-Teams architecture* denotes the structure and design of application systems that are based on teams of reflective FTA agents. Such agents are able to assess their situation and the current context of operation and to draw conclusions for their future behavior, e.g. through adaptation or learning. This multiagent microsimulation architecture is applied to the problem of simulating city traffic in Bonn.

Based on the various activities of the GMD Lab described above, the theoretical foundation of evolutionary algorithms for optimization is fully described in chapter III.

2.4.4 Distributed and Active Learning (NEC Lab)

Chapter IV presents the work of the NEC Lab. Rigorous theoretical investigations on three topics, distributed cooperative Bayesian learning, learning specialist decision lists, and the lob-pass problem, are described. The goals of the research in this laboratory are to investigate and develop efficient and robust methods of distributed and active learning. New committee-based query learning methods and distributed cooperative Bayesian learning strategies are recognized as important progresses in this area. The performance of the methods is evaluated both theoretically and empirically, and rigorous theoretical analyses of the efficiency of the algorithms are given.

A new criterion, extended stochastic complexity, that extends the model selection criterion of MDL (minimum description length) from a Bayesian decision theoretic point of view has been applied to distributed cooperative learning strategies.

As a test-bed application, the development of the efficient word-clustering method and applications to syntactic disambiguation is a remarkable result. The method is applied to large scale tagged text corpus to show applicability to the real-world data and the world record performance are demonstrated. Probability distributions suited for natural language processing are explored. Another test-bed application is genetic information processing.

2.4.5 Stochastic Pattern Computing (SICS Lab)

Chapter V presents the research of the SICS Lab on computing with large random patterns and its application to natural language understanding. Goals of this laboratory are

- to understand natural (i.e. the brain's) mechanisms of intelligence, and
- to build computers that employ such mechanisms, based on holistic representation (combining syntax and semantics in a uniform representation) and on stochastic computing (combining the strengths of numeric and symbolic computing in a system that computes with very large pseudorandom patterns and achieves reliability by statistical laws of large numbers).

Sparse distributed representation is proposed and investigated. One major development is the *spatter code* and the *sparchunk code*. The spatter code is a method of forming analyzable holistic representations of higher-level concepts using dense binary vectors, i.e. vectors with roughly the same number of 1s as 0s. The sparchunk code solves the same problem with sparse codes. One advantage with this code is that the SDM memory can be used for breaking a concept down into its constituents. Both these methods can be used hierarchically. An algorithm for associating information represented by sparse vectors is proposed and applied to natural language understanding.

2.4.6   Symbol-Pattern Integration (Toshiba Lab)

The Toshiba Lab studies fundamental philosophical issues on the integration of symbols and patterns. Specifically, they aim at modeling the logical reasoning of patterns. Here a pattern is represented by a function and approximated by a neural network. Then the neural network is interpreted as a multilinear function. To make reasoning out of patterns, the lab investigates the logical structure embedded in the space of multilinear functions, collaborating with JAIST and Chiba University. Some fundamental relationships between multilinear function space and BCK logics have been revealed, and a complete many-valued logic with product-conjunction is selected as a suitable logic for making inferences with pattern information. The result is then applied to various real-world data such as financial time series.

2.5   Concluding Remark

This section provides an overview of the R&D in the theoretical and algorithmic foundations of the RWC program. Many important research topics have been covered by six distributed laboratories and five of them are described in more detail in the following chapters.

We hope that the readers will enjoy the following chapters and that the results of this project will become fundamental tools to open the door to the new world of information technology.

References

Geman, S. and Geman, D. (1984). Stochastic relaxation, Gibbs distributions, and the Bayesian restoration of images. *IEEE Transactions on Pattern Analysis and Machine Intelligence* PAMI-6:721–741.

Hopfield, J. and Tank, D. (1985). Neural computation of decisions in optimization problems. *Biological Cybernetics* 52:141–152.

MITI (1992). *The Master Plan of RWC Program.* Edited by Industrial Electronics Division, Machinery and Information Industries Bureau, Ministry of International Trade and Industry.

Otsu, N. (1982). Optimal linear and nonlinear solutions for least-square discriminant feature extraction. *Proceedings of 6th International Conference on Pattern Recognition*, pp. 557–560.

Otsu, N. (1989). Toward soft logic for the foundation of flexible information processing. *Bulletin of ETL* 53(10):75–95.

Otsu, N. (1993). Toward flexible intelligence: MITI's new program of real-world computing. *Proceedings of 13th International Joint Conference on Artificial Intelligence*, pp. 786–791.

Otsu, N. (1998). Project for fundamental information technology of the next generation: Real-world intelligence technology. RWC-98 Symposium (in RWC News 4-E, available at http://www.rwcp.or.jp/rwc-news/04e/ohtsu.html).

Poggio, T. and Koch, K. (1985). Ill-posed problems in early vision: From computational theory to analogue networks. *Proceedings of Royal Society of London* B226:303–323.

Rumelhart, D., Hinton, G., and Williams, R. (1986). Learning representations by back-propagating errors. *Nature* 323(9):533–536.

RWCP (1997). *Proceedings of 1997 Real World Computing Symposium.*, Tokyo: Real World Computing Partnership.

RWCP (1998). *Proceedings of 1998 Real World Computing Symposium.* Tokyo: Real World Computing Partnership.

RWCP (2000). *Proceedings of 2000 Real World Computing Symposium.* Tokyo: Real World Computing Partnership.

I

Inference and Learning with Graphical Models

RWI Research Center, Electrotechnical Laboratory

HIDEKI ASOH, YOICHI MOTOMURA, KAZUHISA NIKI, KOITI HASIDA, SHOTARO AKAHO, TATSUYA NIWA, SATORU HAYAMIZU, ISAO HARA, TOSHIHIRO MATSUI, MASARU TANAKA (*Saitama University*), KENJI FUKUMIZU (*The Institute of Statistical Mathematics*), IKUO TAHARA (*Science University of Tokyo*), JUNPEI HATOU (*Science University of Tokyo*), AND TOSHIAKI KAWAMATA (*Science University of Tokyo*)

Many researchers have pointed out that the conventional linear architecture of intelligence, which assumes that the system has complete knowledge about its environment and always makes correct inferences combining that knowledge with input information and then makes decisions and performs actions, does not work for building intelligent systems that can handle complex, uncertain, dynamic, multi-modal information in the real world. Instead, a more dynamical, situated, distributed architecture is necessary for these types of intelligent systems. Here an intelligent system is considered a collection of many situated behavior-based agents that have incomplete, behavior-specific knowledge, and that work very closely and dynamically with the environment and the system itself.

As theoretical foundations for such situated agents, two candidates are emerging as likely and are recently being investigated in more depth. One is dynamical systems and the other is probability models. Like symbolic logic, both have a long history as schemes for representing world knowledge and making inferences about the world. We do not think that these

Foundations of Real-World Intelligence.
Yoshinori Uesaka et al. (eds.).
Copyright © 2001, CSLI Publications.

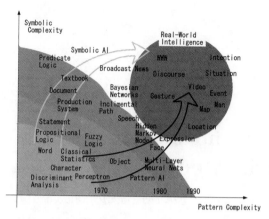

FIGURE I.1. Models and information in the real world.

three are mutually exclusive and instead are seeking a workable blend of them. To illustrate the history of the scheme for knowledge representation, figure I.1 depicts typical schemes used in intelligent system research with various kinds of information in the real world.

From the three candidates, we concentrate mainly on the probability models as the base of our investigation. In particular, probability distributions with graphical structure are our starting point. As is well known, probability models were born as a theory of gambling, came to be used widely in statistics, and have been highly successful in acquiring, representing and processing statistical knowledge extracted from data. They are also very popular in the study of pattern recognition and have become a foundation of current character recognition and speech recognition systems that have recently been commercialized.

In the history of probability models, various families of models have been proposed and applied to various kinds of data. To establish a theoretical foundation of real-world intelligence, we must deal with multimodal, complex, and structured information, not well-controlled, nonstationary information. For this purpose, many probability distribution models with combinatorial structure, such as hidden Markov models, Bayesian networks, probabilistic constraint programs, mixture models, and multivariate models, have been proposed and used in various research fields. Recently they are being called as *graphical models* and are starting to be investigated from a unified perspective (Jordan, 1998; Frey, 1998).

Because graphical models have a complex combinatorial structure, inference and learning procedures for the models tend to become difficult and computationally intensive. Efficient approximative algorithms are needed to apply such probability models to real-world problems. From this perspective, we have investigated efficient inference and learning algorithms for several kinds of typical graphical models. In particular, we focus on Bayesian networks, probabilistic constraint programs, multivariate models, and mixture models. We also consider neural network models and genetic algorithms as kinds of graphical model.

In addition to inference and learning algorithms, the framework of learning is another important research issue. In much conventional machine learning or statistics research, the data acquisition phase, learning phase, and the phase of using the learned result are separate. Real-world intelligence, however, is expected to work in the world in close interaction with the environment, and it does not separate the three phases of learning. More dynamic learning frameworks using this coupling with the evironment are necessary and may help to solve problems caused by shortage of training data or uncontrolled noisy training data.

In this chapter we describe three representative results of research on inference and learning of graphical models done in our laboratory. In the first section, the research activities of the theoretical foundation group in the RWI research center are overviewed. Then, in the following sections, three topics, namely Bayesian networks with neural networks, multivariate information analysis, and dialogue-based learning, are described in more detail.

3 An Overview of Theoretical Foundation Research in RWI Research Center

HIDEKI ASOH, KAZUHISA NIKI, KOITI HASIDA, SHOTARO AKAHO, MASARU TANAKA, YOICHI MOTOMURA, TATSUYA NIWA, AND KENJI FUKUMIZU

3.1 Models and Algorithms

3.1.1 Bayesian Networks on Neural Networks

A *Bayesian network* is recognized as a powerful tool for representing probabilistic knowledge of the real world. A Bayesian network consists of a directed acyclic graph and conditional probability distributions. Each node of the graph represents a random variable and a directed link represents conditional dependency (direct causal relation) between two variables connected by the link. A node that sends a link to another node is called a parent node of the target node. A conditional probability distribution of a random variable is assigned to the corresponding node, and the conditioning part of the distribution is composed of random variables represented by parent nodes of the node.

The whole structure defines a joint probability distribution of random variables represented by nodes. If all variables are statistically dependent, then the graph becomes fully connected and nothing varies from usual multinomial distributions. In many realistic cases, however, a random variable is conditionally independent of many of other variables, and the graph becomes rather sparse. In such cases, by representing the dependence structure explicitly with a graph and using the structure to control the computation process, an efficient inference process (i.e. a computation of a probability distribution of variables under a specific condition) can be realized.

Bayesian networks can be considered a generalization of major graphical models such as hidden Markov models and finite mixture models and are becoming a popular tools for treating incomplete and noisy information in the real world. One research issue is how to represent a conditional probability distribution assigned to each node. Normally a simple table is used. When the number of conditioning variables increases, however, the size of the table increases exponentially. In addition, if some of the conditioning variables take continuous values, the table is no longer able to represent the distribution.

Here we propose to use a neural network to represent a conditional probability of each Bayesian network node (Motomura, 1997). This idea leads to compact representation and efficient approximative probability computation. Learning the conditional probabilities from training examples is realized by learning algorithms for neural networks. Continuous-valued variables can also be treated by the proposed model. We applied the model to several experimental applications such as prediction of weather data, context-dependent handwritten character recognition, and localization of mobile robots to demonstrate the effectiveness of the model for situated probabilistic inferences (Motomura, 1998a).

We implemented a software environment for using our Bayesian network model easily. The software is written in Java and has a smart graphical user interface to build and edit the network structure, to run the inference procedure, and to acquire conditional probabilities from training examples. This is one of the first implementations of Bayesian Networks in Java and is listed in the Java Repository (Motomura, 1998b).

3.1.2 Probabilistic Constraint Program

Bayesian networks use causal structures (constraints) represented by predicate logic sentences such as "if (A and B) then C." Extending this to first-order logic is an interesting research issue. On the other hand, there is a tradition in logic programming and constraint-based programming (or declarative programming) of representing constraints in first-order logic sentences. In view of this tradition, the research issue concerns an extension of logic programming with probability.

Probabilistic constraint programming (PCP) is an attempt to combine constraint logic programming and probability theory. Its major feature is integration of symbol manipulation and probabilistic computation. A program (constraint) is a set of Horn clauses and a probability parameter is assigned to each clause, which derives a probability distribution over the program trees (candidates for proof trees).

The computational process is constraint satisfaction by program transformation to discard inconsistent program trees and obtain valid proof trees, seeking probable solutions (sets of value bindings). Learning probability values from examples is possible with maximum entropy estimation. The introduction of symbolic learning techniques like inductive logic programming is also within the scope of the method.

This representational and computational framework is a powerful one that can describe and processe complicated constraints such as the grammars of natural languages (Hasida, 1997). The major concern here is how to avoid huge computational costs in making inference and learning. The sophisticated control of the computation is indispensable. We have introduced several techniques to do so, such as structure sharing, using memo to avoid redundant computation, and a new general compilation method that subsumes some standard ones (Hasida, 1998).

3.1.3 Multivariate Information Analysis

In the context of Bayesian networks or probabilistic constraint programming, constraints are in principle written or designed by humans. A logic-based intuitive representation of the constraints is good for this purpose. However, determining the structural relationships between variables from observed data is also an important research issue. Historically this issue has been investigated in the domain of multivariate data analysis, such as causal analysis. Recently, researchers in the Bayesian network community and the KDD (knowledge discovery from data) community have shown interest in the causal analysis of data. *Multivariate information analysis* (Niki, 1999) includes methods for finding out information exchange or sharing between random variables by analyzing the mutual entropy between the variables. We formulate several methods and apply them to analyze the data of functional MRI brain imaging during experiments on cognitive functions of human brains. fMRI brain image data is composed of a huge number of time series, each of which represents

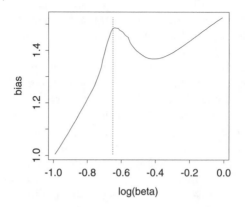

FIGURE 3.1. Generalization bias of mixture of Gaussians.

transient activities in a very small part of brain (voxel). By using the method we can determine relationships between voxels.

3.1.4 Mixture of Gaussians

A mixture of finite number of probability distributions is one of the simplest graphical models. In particular, *a mixture of Gaussian distributions* is an important target for theoretical analysis. We investigated the learning dynamics of the mixture of multiple Gaussians and clarify the structure of the learning curve around the bifurcation points.

Theories of learning and generalization tell us that the generalization bias, which is defined as the difference between the training error and the generalization error, increases on average with the number of adaptive parameters. In Akaho and Kappen (2000), however, we showed that this general tendency is violated for a Gaussian mixture model. For temperatures just below the first symmetry breaking point, the effective number of adaptive parameters increases and the generalization bias decreases (figure 3.1). We also applied mixture models and the EM algorithm to multiple object recognition (Akaho, 1995).

3.1.5 Mixture of Predictors

Mixture models are normally used to segment input signal space into several clusters. However, almost all real-world data, such as speech waveform or motion pictures, are multi-dimensional time series. For such data, not only segmenting the signal space but also segmenting the data along the time axis is an important research issue. Using a mixture of competitive dynamical predictors to segment time series data is a promising way to solve the problem. We investigated the property of the *mixture of Elman networks* using various kinds of data, such as data from mobile robot sensors, motion picture sequences from RWC multi-modal databases, and artificial chaotic time series, and clarified the relation between parameters of networks and convergence of learning (Horikawa et al., 1999).

3.1.6 Neural Network Models

A *neural network model*, in particular, a layered neural network model is often used as a pattern classifier or a function approximator. However, it is also possible to consider the learning in a neural network as an estimation of a probability distribution that generates the statistical training data. In that case, connection weights are parameters of the distribution and the learning of the network is its estimating the optimal parameter values. Here we investigate maximum likelihood estimation and Bayesian estimation of parameters.

In this framework, an important characteristic of the multilayer neural network model is its powerful description capability. As is well known, any continuous function can be approximated by a three-layer (one hidden layer) neural network with a proper number of hidden units. A drawback of the neural network model is the possibility that the Fisher information matrix at the true parameter may become singular. It may signify something special when such a singularity is satisfied. This singularity always occurs if we consider the model selection problem in neural networks. The limiting distribution of the MLE is not obtained by the ordinary statistical asymptotic theory in this case, and any methods based on the asymptotic theory such as AIC and MDL are not properly applicable.

We evaluated the generalization error of the linear neural network model as the simplest multilayer model, and explicitly showed that when the Fisher information matrix at the true parameter value is singular, the generalization error becomes larger than the generalization error derived from the usual asymptotic theory (Fukumizu, 1999). In addition, while the ordinary asymptotic theory asserts that the expectation of the generalization error depends only on the number of parameters, the generalization error in linear neural networks also depends on the rank of the target function.

3.1.7 Genetic Algorithms and Population Search

As has been pointed out by several researchers, optimization is closely related to probabilistic inference and learning. Let us suppose that an unknown black-box function is given and you are requested to find the maximum point of the function. If the target function is written as a continuous differentiable function, gradient-based methods can be used to solve the problem. However, in the real world the target function may be a very complicated black box. In such cases you can only input some sample points to the function and observe the outputs. Using this information you will revise your guess about the location of the maximum point. This process is very similar to an active learning process.

To represent the guess as a probability distribution is a natural idea. According to the distribution, the next sample points can be generated. Repeating these two processes, generating the population of sample points and revising the distribution, leads to population-based random search methods like genetic algorithms. Here two main research issues are how to select sample points and how to revise the guess using the observations at sample points. From this point of view, we are investigating the dynamics of some optimization methods.

Genetic algorithms (GAs) are optimization methods inspired by the process of biological evolution. These methods have been successful at solving difficult optimization problems. However, the dynamics of GAs is complex and is not yet thoroughly understood.

To understand the behavior of GAs, we analyzed the dynamics of a very simple and typical genetic process called the *Wright-Fisher model,* in the field of population genetics. We evaluated the mean convergence time of the model (with genetic drift, because of the finite population size) both theoretically and experimentally, and found a reference value of the most efficient mutation rate for canonical GAs (Niwa and Tanaka, 1995).

We then extended the model to a parallel island model. In this model, the global population is divided into several subpopulations and migration between them is introduced. We evaluated the mean convergence time with genetic drift in the model and derived a critical value of the efficient migration rate (Niwa and Tanaka, 1997; Niwa and Tanaka, 1998).

So far, a few optimization algorithms that use probability distributions to model guesses about the optimum point has been proposed. They use several kinds of statistical models, such as a special form of Bayesian networks, and the algorithms show performance superior to that of other random algorithms.

For the sake of simplicity of analysis we formalized an algorithm that uses a Gaussian distribution to model the guess and truncate selection to revise the guess. We analyzed the convergence property of the optimization process theoretically and found that the algorithm based on the explicit modeling of the elites' distribution tends to converge to local optima. We also proposed a modified algorithm to overcome the defect (Akaho, 1998).

3.2 Frameworks of Learning

3.2.1 Dialogue-based Learning

As mentioned in the introduction, conventional machine learning research is mainly investigating learning within the framework of *learning from examples*. Here it is assumed that a huge amount of training data is prepared and learning is executed off-line. The phase of training and the phase of task execution are separate.

To the contrary, intelligence systems of the real world must treat various kinds of multi-modal information, from sensor data to symbolic language in a dynamic environment. Here it is not possible to assume there is enough training data available beforehand. The systems are requested to gather the training data by themselves during the task execution phase. To be able to apply a learning system in the real world, we need it to solve many problems, such as learning from a small amount of data, learning from uncontrolled, not well-organized data, and so on. Hence in addition to the model and algorithms, investigating new frameworks of learning becomes very important.

A way to solve the problem of a small amount of training data is to use additional information such as heuristics, hints, and so on. Explanation-based learning is an example of this kind of learning, where domain knowledge represented by rules is used to assist the learning processes. Another kind of additional information comes from close interaction with the environment during learning. For example, children apparently have a very intense interaction with their surroundings, especially with their parents, and this helps the children's learning process very much. We call this kind of learning within social interaction between learning systems and the environment *socially embedded learning* (Asoh et al., 1997).

A powerful communication channel between learning systems and human users is dialogue using a natural or seminatural language. How effectively can this dialogue between systems and users be used in the learning process? How much does it help the system to learn?

We applied *dialogue-based learning,* to the problem of topological map learning in mobile autonomous robot navigation. The implemented system on a real mobile robot, Jijo-2, can engage in simple spoken dialogue with a human trainer and was able to acquire a graphical map of the environment (Asoh et al., 1996; Asoh et al., 1997). We are now extending the target to more general models of the environment, including various kinds of maps, task models, and user models. See section 6 for more on this issue.

3.2.2 Multiple-Attribute Learning

Interactions between users and intelligent systems should not be strongly controlled. This implies that the learning processes of the systems should also not be strongly controlled. Imagine that you will teach a system about your favorite mug. The mug is a large white one. You show the cup to the system and tell the agent: "This is white." Or you may tell the system: "This is large." The visual image of a mug has at least three attributes: color, size, and shape. Hence there are at least three ways of classification of a visual image: by color, by size, and by shape.

In the traditional research on pattern recognition, one way of classification is chosen in advance. However, in the real situation of the concept learning of interactive systems, training data relevant to multiple classification problems may be given to the system at once. The system needs to treat the uncontrolled data set and learn multiple classification rules from the data simultaneously.

Note that the system does not know in advance about what kinds of attribute the input signals have, and it will discover the attributes such as color, size, and shape during learning. Once the system discovers the attribute, adding a new category to the attribute, for example, adding "pink" to the color attribute, may become an easier task. We investigated this problem of *multiple attribute learning* and proposed a learning algorithm based on the EM algorithm (Akaho et al., 1997).

4 BAYONET: Bayesian Network on Neural Network
YOICHI MOTOMURA

In real-world environments, the robot's view of the world is filled with uncertainty caused by sensor noises, incomplete observations, and dynamic changes in its surroundings. Thus an autonomous intelligent system requires the ability to predict and estimate such uncertain factors. Probabilistic reasoning by Bayesian networks (Cowell et al., 1999; Castillo et al., 1997) is a promising approach to the problem.

Bayesian networks represent conditional dependencies among random variables as conditional probabilities. We have to give conditional probabilities to estimate uncertain variables. One possible approach is to determine probabilities from statistical data sampled in the real-world environment. Moreover, in the real world it becomes necessary to handle many kinds of variables. We propose using neural networks to represent conditional probabilities in Bayesian networks. Using neural networks can provide a general framework for representing and learning nonlinear conditional probabilities mixed with continuous, discrete, multivalued, and multidimensional variables.

In section 4.1, we propose a Bayesian network that learns conditional probabilities by feed-forward neural networks for real world applications. In section 4.2, we explain the implementation of this model as a Bayesian network learning system written in Java. To realize learning from a large database, the system uses JDBC (Java database connectivity) and it can connect to major SQL databases on an information network. Another feature of the system is its structure-finding functions introduced for Bayesian network learning. This strengthens the data-analyzing capability of the system. In section 4.3, an example of application in the field of autonomous learning robotics is described briefly.

4.1 Bayesian Networks Based on Neural Networks

4.1.1 Bayesian Networks

A Bayesian network (also called a belief network) is a probabilistic reasoning model that represents the dependency among random variables and gives a concise specification of joint probability distributions. This model is defined as a directed acyclic graph (DAG), which has conditional probabilities in each node. Nodes represent random variables in a domain. Directed links in the graph represent dependency between nodes.

To simplify, let us consider the simplest network $X \rightarrow Y$. X is called the *parent node* and Y is called the *child node*. The child node has a conditional probability $P(Y|X)$. When information about X is given, the *Belief* that $Y = y$ (or posterior probability distribution of Y given $P(X)$) is computed by a marginalizing operation over the sample space of X, Ω_X,

$$(4.1) \qquad \mathrm{Bel}(Y = y) \;\; = \;\; \alpha \int_{x \in \Omega_X} P(y|x)\, dP(x).$$

On the other hand, when we have $P(Y)$ at first, the *Belief* that $X = x$ is updated by,

$$\mathrm{Bel}(X = x) \;\; = \;\; \int_{y \in \Omega_Y} P(x|y)\, dP(y)$$
$$(4.2) \qquad\qquad\qquad = \;\; \beta \int_{y \in \Omega_Y} P(y|x)\, dP(y) \cdot P(x),$$

where α, β are normalizing constants. These calculations can be regarded as belief propagation through the links X and Y. For more complex Bayesian networks, probabilistic inference is executed by belief propagation through all links in the network (Cowell et al., 1999; Castillo et al., 1997; Frey, 1998; Jordan, 1998).

In most conventional Bayesian networks, random variables take discrete values and conditional probabilities are represented by a table of possible combinations of parent values and child values. For many kinds of variables such as continuous or multidimensional variables, however, we need a more flexible representation of conditional probabilities in Bayesian networks.

4.1.2 Bayesian Networks Based on Neural Networks

One solution for the problem of representing conditional probabilities with many kinds of variables is to use neural networks. We call this model a *Bayesian network based on neural networks* (BNNN). A neural network can handle both discrete variables and continuous variables in the same manner. Where Y is a discrete random variable, $Y = (y_1, y_2, \ldots, y_k)$, k neurons can represent the probability vector of Y, $P(y_1), P(y_2), \ldots, P(y_k)$ with normalization to make the sum equal to 1. Let's introduce a feed-forward neural network that has input neurons to represent X, output neurons to represent Y, and hidden neurons. Then we can represent a conditional probability $P(Y|X = x)$ as the following:

$$f_k(x) = g\left(\sum_j v_{jk} g\left(\sum_i w_{ij} x_i + b_j \right) + c_k \right)$$

$$g(x) = \frac{1}{1 + \exp(-x)}$$

$$P(y_k|x) = f_k(x) / \sum_k f_k(x).$$

Here v, w, b are connection weights of the neural network.

When Y is a continuous random variable, we approximate the probability distribution of Y as a Gaussian distribution parameterized by μ, σ, and represent $P(y|x)$ as

$$f_\mu(x) = \sum_j v_j^\mu g\left(\sum_i w_{ij}^\mu x_i + b_j^\mu \right) + c^\mu$$

$$f_\sigma(x) = \sum_j v_j^\sigma g\left(\sum_i w_{ij}^\sigma x_i + b_j^\sigma \right) + c^\sigma$$

$$P(y|x) = \frac{1}{\sqrt{2\pi} f_\sigma(x)} \exp\left(-\frac{(y - f_\mu(x))^2}{2 f_\sigma(x)^2} \right).$$

Using such neural networks to represent each conditional probability of each child node, we can construct a Bayesian network with neural networks. For example in figure 4.1, the child node C of the Bayesian network is represented by the output neurons, and the parent nodes A

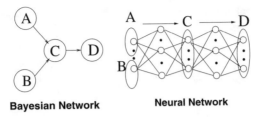

Bayesian Network   **Neural Network**

FIGURE 4.1. Structure of a Bayesian network based on a neural network.

and B are represented by the input neurons of the neural network(left side). Conditional dependency between C and D is also modeled by input and output neurons of another neural network (right side). Thus each child node of the Bayesian network has its own neural network. The number of input neurons of the neural network is determined by the dimension of the parent nodes, and the number of output neurons is determined by the dimension of the child node. The integral operations of equations (4.1) and (4.2) can be computed in the straight-forward way for discrete variables. For continuous variables, we can use Monte Carlo sampling and numerical integral operations to approximate.

4.1.3   Learning Conditional Probabilities

If we have enough data sets of parent nodes and child nodes, the neural network can be trained to approximate the conditional probability $P(Y|X)$ for the child node Y given X by the back-propagation method. Each neural network is trained with a corresponding data set of parent and child nodes. Learning the continuous conditional probability $P(Y|X)$ is regarded as an approximation of nonlinear functions, $\mu_Y(X)$ and $\sigma_Y(X)$. $\mu_Y(X)$ is given by mean of Y given X. The training set of $\sigma_Y(X)$ can be given by computing standard deviation of Y given X.

After successfully training the neural network, it can represent the conditional dependency between corresponding parent nodes and child nodes. If there is no conditional dependency between the nodes, learning will fail. This means that this training scheme can also be applied to detect conditional dependencies between the variables.

4.1.4   Finding Network Structure

Finding the structure of the Bayesian network is an important but hard problem. The difficulties are caused by the following reasons.

- The computation of searching graph structures is NP hard.
- To evaluate the quality of each structure, the learning of condi-

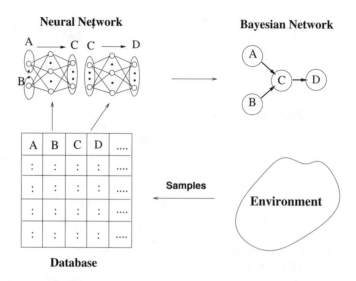

FIGURE 4.2. Learning of BNNN from a database.

tional probabilities has to be completed.

- Currently, a suitable evaluation criterion for this problem is being discussed, but still there are many controversial issues.

For the time being, we propose a method that keeps possible tree structures for each child node (local trees) and selects a better local tree structure with many kinds of algorithms using an information criterion like MDL (minimum description length). Tree-selecting algorithms decide appropriate local graph structure independently, and thus it can be assumed that this result makes the whole structure optimal.

4.2 Implementation

We have developed a system to implement the model described in the previous section. The name of our system is BAYONET.[1]

BAYONET is a probabilistic reasoning server in a network with a graceful graphical user interface (GUI; see figure 4.3). The server receives requests from a client program that requires probabilistic evaluation about uncertain variables. After probabilistic reasoning, the answer is sent back to the client. For example, a process that observes sensory information sends the sensor values to BAYONET. Then the other pro-

---

[1]The term *BAYONET* implies a powerful tool with two combined different functions.

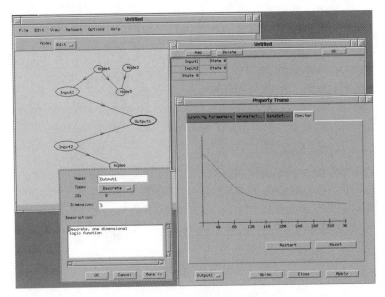

FIGURE 4.3. A screen snapshot of BAYONET.

cesses that need estimation (e.g. concerning the position of the robot) ask BAYONET and get the result based on probabilistic reasoning. In the same manner, a node in the BAYONET running on a machine can also connect to a node in another BAYONET running on another machine (figure 4.4). We define communication protocol messages as the following: "setEvidence", "getMAP", "getMean", "getVariance", "evalValue". The modules communicate with each other by using these messages.

Bayesian networks are essentially parallel processing models. The Monte Carlo method in each node can be executed independently. For these reasons, a development environment that has a multithread mechanism and object-oriented features is desirable for implementing this model. Therefore, our system is implemented in Java, which has multithread capability.

Java has database connectivity methods called JDBC. Using JDBC in the learning process, BAYONET can get data samples from major SQL databases like ORACLE, Postgress, and so on. The advantages of using SQL database include the following:

- There is a huge amount of data stored in major databases.
- It is possible to operate on large amounts of data with simple SQL commands.

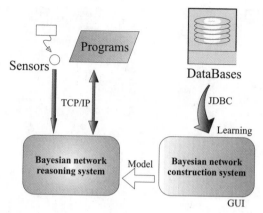

Figure 4.4. Connections.

- Computation with large amounts of data is optimized in such major databases.

Databases are specified by URL and particular items in the database are assigned to corresponding nodes by a drag and drop operation of the GUI (figure 4.5).

Moreover, users can make simple operations on the database using the GUI of BAYONET (figure 4.6). Repeating such operations, users can understand properties and tendencies of data. This helps to construct a suitable graph structure.

To realize the tree selection mechanism described in the previous section, we use object-oriented programming in Java. Each node is created as an instance of an object, and many other objects, datasets, and algorithms can be assigned to the node object.

For conditional probabilities in the system, there are two kinds of representations. One is a table-style conditional probability for discrete variables (figure 4.7). Connecting to a database, the system can calculate the corresponding conditional probability from frequencies under particular conditions in the database.

The other representation is a neural network style for both continuous and discrete variables. By connecting to a database, the neural network can be trained with a supervised dataset in the database. The system can also monitor the learning curve of the back propagation (see figure 4.3). If the learning converges with a small level of error, then the neural network is successfully approximating the corresponding conditional probability. Success in learning means the structure is justified by the way it fits

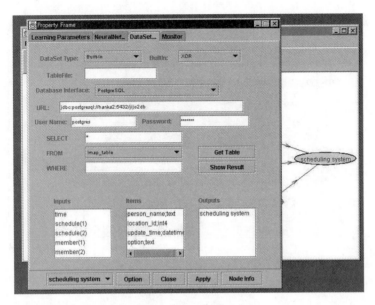

FIGURE 4.5. Assigning nodes to items in databases.

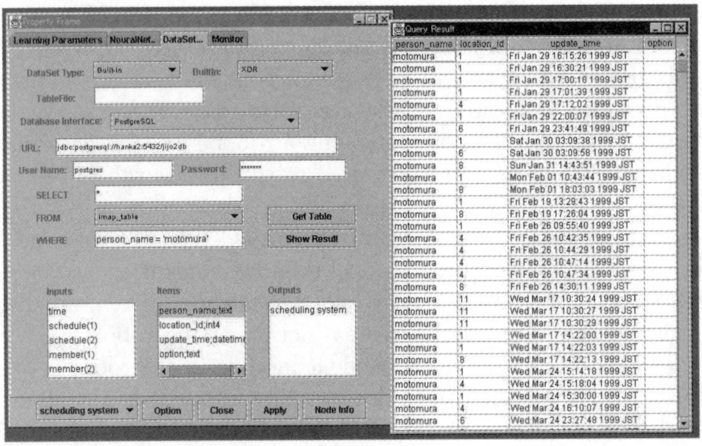

FIGURE 4.6. GUI operation for databases.

to the statistical data. Finally, we can model the data set including nonlinear conditional dependency. This can be regarded as an interactive data analysis.

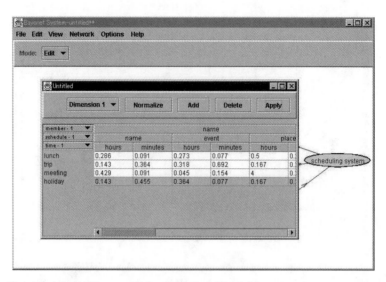

FIGURE 4.7. Editing conditional probability tables.

4.3 Application

After constructing the appropriate graph structure and acquiring the conditional probabilities of the Bayesian network, we can use the model to evaluate unknown random variables given observed variables. Therefore this model can work as an expert system. There are many real-world applications suitable for the use of Bayesian networks. We apply the model to the problem of controlling a robot in uncertain situations (PRASMA). The architecture required to control the robot is shown in figure 4.8.

The first layer of the architecture is BAYONET. The second layer consists of independent program modules to control the robot or to observe sensors. These are called *behavior modules*. The third layer is the decision maker to select the final action of the robot. Each module is designed as a situation-dependent module. If the robot is in some particular situation, then the corresponding situated behavior module designed for that situation can work well, and if the robot uses it, it receives a high utility value. However, when the actual situation cannot be determined exactly, the selection of which behavior module to use to get higher utility is a kind of a decision-making problem. In such a case, we can evaluate the probability of each situation on the BAYONET. Then a decision-theoretic selection can be made by maximizing the expected utility, which is, intuitively, the utility multiplied by the

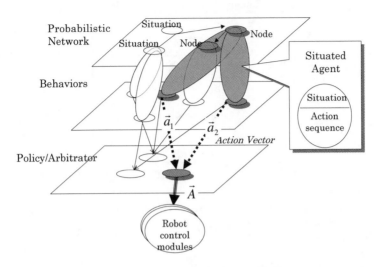

FIGURE 4.8. Robot control architecture PRASMA.

probability of each situation. By using this architecture, the robot can choose the optimal behavior in an uncertain environment.

4.4 Conclusion

In this section, we introduced a Bayesian network learning system based on neural networks. The system is written in Java, designed as a network server and can connect to major database systems. The system has a user-friendly GUI for interactive data analysis with the database. Conditional probabilities can be obtained from examples in the database. The advantage of the system is that neural networks are utilized to represent conditional probabilities of many kinds of variables including nonlinear continuous variables. To decide the most appropriate structure for the Bayesian network, the system can support the local tree-selecting mechanism. We can apply many different model-selection algorithms to the system.

The system will be used for controlling the robot moving in uncertain situations. Thanks to probabilistic evaluation using BAYONET, the robot can take the optimal action to maximize its expected utility. The GUI and learning properties in our system are useful for modeling state and situation transitions in the robotics domain with many continuous, nonlinear uncertain variables.

Table 5.1

Frequency List of Two Variables

X	Y						
	y_1	y_2	$\cdots$	y_j	$\cdots$	y_m	
x_1	n_{11}	n_{12}	$\cdots$	n_{1j}	$\cdots$	n_{1m}	n_{1*}
x_2	n_{21}	n_{22}	$\cdots$	n_{2j}	$\cdots$	n_{2m}	n_{2*}
$\vdots$	$\vdots$	$\vdots$	$\vdots$	$\vdots$	$\vdots$	$\vdots$	$\vdots$
x_i	n_{i1}	n_{i2}	$\cdots$	n_{ij}	$\cdots$	n_{im}	n_{i*}
$\vdots$	$\vdots$	$\vdots$	$\vdots$	$\vdots$	$\vdots$	$\vdots$	$\vdots$
x_n	n_{n1}	n_{n2}	$\cdots$	n_{nj}	$\cdots$	n_{nm}	n_{n*}
	n_{*1}	n_{*2}	$\cdots$	n_{*j}	$\cdots$	n_{*m}	N

5 Multivariate Information Analysis

Kazuhisa Niki, Junpei Hatou, Toshiaki Kawamata, and Ikuo Tahara

In this section, we introduce a new method for analyzing and extracting structures from data by using mutual information and interaction, based on Shannon's information theory. After defining information measurements, we present a structure analysis method that assumes a one-directional information flow schema: stimulus variate → state variate → response variate. Next, we present alternative structure analysis methods that focus on the common information in variates. We call these methods *multivariate information analysis*. These methods can be used in cases where the volume of data is not large enough and the direction of information flow is not obvious. We then apply our proposed structure analysis methods to two types of artificially generated data, and point out some classification errors of these methods. Intensive analysis that uses many kinds of information measurements can clarify information structure. Finally, we apply these methods to fMRI brain-imaging data and show how our methods are useful for this application.

5.1 Expression of Multivariate Analysis

5.1.1 Calculation of Information

First we make a frequency list of data in order to calculate information. The number of partitions in the list may be established freely, but it is necessary to pay close attention to it, because it relates to degrees of freedom of the analysis.

Table 5.1 is the frequency list in which data X is divided into n parts and Y into m. n_{ij} represents the frequency that x_i and y_j are observed in the same time interval. The relations that hold are:

$$\sum_{j=1}^{m} n_{ij} = n_{i*}$$

$$\sum_{i=1}^{n} n_{ij} = n_{*j}$$

$$\sum_{i=1}^{n} \sum_{j=1}^{m} n_{ij} = \sum_{i=1}^{n} n_{i*} = \sum_{j=1}^{m} n_{*j} = N,$$

where N is the number of observations. Estimated values of *entropy* are calculated as follows:

$$\hat{H}(X) = \log_2 N - \frac{1}{N} \sum_{i=1}^{n} n_{i*} \log_2 n_{i*}$$

$$\hat{H}(Y) = \log_2 N - \frac{1}{N} \sum_{j=1}^{n} n_{*j} \log_2 n_{*j}$$

$$\hat{H}(X,Y) = \log_2 N - \frac{1}{N} \sum_{i=1}^{n} \sum_{j=1}^{n} n_{ij} \log_2 n_{ij}.$$

Using these equations, an estimate for the value of *mutual information* $I(X : Y)$ can be calculated as

$$\hat{I}(X : Y) = \hat{H}(X) + \hat{H}(Y) - \hat{H}(X,Y).$$

Nearly the same extended result holds even if we consider the third variate Z. *Conditioned mutual information* $I(X : Y|Z)$ and interaction $R(X,Y,Z)$ are determined by:

$$\hat{I}(X : Y|Z) = \hat{H}(X,Z) + \hat{H}(Y,Z) \\ - \hat{H}(Z) - \hat{H}(X,Y,Z)$$

and

$$\hat{R}(X,Y,Z) = \hat{H}(X) + \hat{H}(Y) + \hat{H}(Z) \\ - \hat{H}(X,Y) - \hat{H}(Y,Z) - \hat{H}(Z,X) \\ + \hat{H}(X,Y,Z),$$

respectively. We can use χ^2 to check for significance. Figure 5.1 shows the relation between these types of information in a Venn diagram.

5.1.2 Structure Analysis with a Direction of Information Flow

Data, which is collected in order to analyze information processing in a living system, can be classified into three stages: stimulus variate, state variate, and response variate. This is true from the macroscopic and even

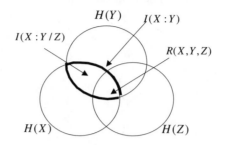

FIGURE 5.1. Relation of information.

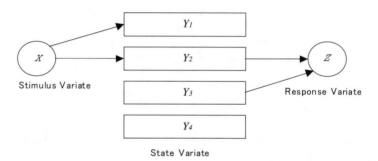

FIGURE 5.2. Relations of three variables.

the microscopic viewpoint. In a neural system, it is natural to assume an information flow from stimulus variate to response variate via a state variate. We apply the data to this schema: *stimulus variate* $(X) \rightarrow$ *state variate* $(Y) \rightarrow$ *response variate* (Z).

We pay close attention to state variate Y and then consider the relationship between stimulus variate X and response variate Z, through mediated effects of state variate Y.

Figure 5.2 represents the variety of state variates located between stimulus variate X and response variate Z. In this figure, the state variate Y_1 receives input from stimulus variate X and gives no influence to response variate Z. State variate Y_2 is influenced by stimulus variate X and influences the response variate Z. State variate Y_3 receives no input from stimulus variate, but influences the response variate. Finally, state variate Y_4 receives no input from stimulus variate X and does not influence the response variate Z. Here, we can show how to detect these four kinds of state variates by the information analysis method as follows (Tahara and Saito, 1978):

state variate Y_1 :

State variate Y_1 and response variate Z are both influenced by stimulus variate X thus they both have correlation

$$I(X : Y_1) \neq 0$$

and

$$I(Y_1 : Z) \neq 0.$$

Because state variate Y_1 is influenced directly by stimulus variate X and does not relate to response variate Z, we conclude that:

$$I(Y_1 : Z|X) = 0.$$

Then, we get

$$I(Y_1 : Z) = R(Y_1, X, Z) > 0.$$

state variate Y_2 :

As state variate Y_2 is influenced by stimulus variate X, we obtain

$$I(X : Y_2) \neq 0.$$

As state variate Y_2 has a direct link to response variate Z, we get

$$I(Y_2 : Z|X) \neq 0.$$

If state variate Y_2 is the only state variate that mediates a relation between stimulus variate X and response variate Z, the next expression holds:

$$I(X : Z|Y_2) = 0.$$

Then, we obtain

$$I(X : Z) = R(Y_2, X, Z) > 0.$$

But, in general, there are many variates that mediate relations between X and Z. Thus we get

$$I(X : Z|Y_2) > 0,$$

and the next expression holds in general:

$$R(Y_2, X, Z) \neq 0.$$

state variate Y_3 :

State variate Y_3 is independent of stimulus variate X. Thus we get

$$I(X : Y_3) = 0.$$

Then the next expression holds:

$$R(Y_3, X, Z) = -I(X : Y_3|Z) < 0.$$

state variate Y_4 :

State variate Y_4 has no relation to stimulus variate X nor response

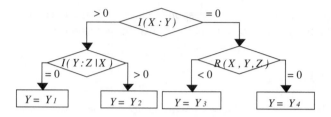

FIGURE 5.3. Structure analysis algorithm with information flow.

variate Z, so the following expressions also hold:

$$I(X : Y_4) = 0;$$
$$I(Z : Y_4) = 0;$$
$$R(X, Y_4, Z) = 0.$$

We can examine the structural relationship in variates X, Y, and Z, by using the above mentioned structure analysis algorithm that is shown in figure 5.3.

5.1.3 Structure Analysis with Focus on Common Information

There may be cases where it is difficult to know the direction of information flow in structure analysis, because the direction of information flow is not obvious or is bidirectional. To handle such cases, in this section we propose structure analysis methods that focuses on *common information* in variates, instead of on information flow. In other words, we think about bidirectional information flow or information share, as shown in figure 5.2.

Two structure analysis algorithms are possible, based on how the algorithm treats the influence of the third variate in calculating common information between two variates.

(1) This algorithm considers the third variate in calculating common information between two variates. That is known as mutual information. This algorithm is called *structure analysis algorithm with mutual information.*

(2) This algorithm ignores the third variate in calculating common information between two variates. That is conditioned mutual information. This algorithm is called *structure analysis algorithm with conditioned mutual information.*

Conditioned mutual information $I(X : Y|Z)$, which is used in algorithm (2), expresses common information that does not depend on Z

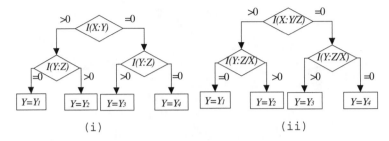

FIGURE 5.4. Structure analysis algorithm that focuses on common information. (i) With mutual information. (ii) With conditioned mutual information.

in calculating the relation between X and Y. The following expression holds for mutual information:

$$
\begin{aligned}
I(X:Y) &= I(X:Y|Z) + R(X,Y,Z) \\
&= H(X) + H(Y) - H(X,Y).
\end{aligned}
$$

This means that mutual information includes interaction R, which expresses the influence of the third variate in addition to the conditioned mutual information. This algorithm considers the third variate Z. But, as a matter of fact, it is important that only variates X and Y are used to calculate mutual information.

Two kinds of structure analysis algorithms are shown in figure 5.4. Mutual information of two variates is used for analysis when the influence of third variate is considered (figure 5.4(i)). Conditioned mutual information is used for analysis when the influence of third variate is ignored (figure 5.4(ii)).

In the structure analysis algorithm, which focuses on common information, the first decision does not influence analysis in the second stage.

5.2 Simulation

To examine the structure analysis algorithm proposed above, we artificially generate two kinds of time-series data: Data that has information flow just like a simple neural system; and data that shares information. Then we analyze the data by our proposed algorithm.

5.2.1 Data with a Flow of Information and Its Structure Analysis

We set up an input-output system that imitates a neural network, as shown in figure 5.5, in order to make artificial data with a direction of information flow in variates.

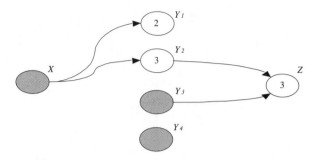

FIGURE 5.5. Structure data with a flow of information.

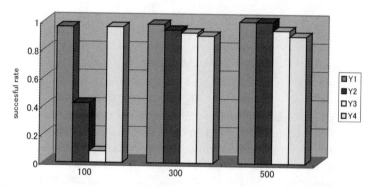

FIGURE 5.6. Success rate of algorithm with information flow.

At first, X, Y_3, and Y_4 are signal sources that output 0 and 1, randomly following different distributions. The output of X is the input of Y_1 and Y_2. The output of Y_2 and Y_3 are inputs of Z. Y_4 has no input nor output. When Y_1 gets two accumulated inputs, then it outputs 1, else its signal is 0. When Y_2 and Z have three accumulated inputs, then they output 1.

We made 50 sets of 100, 300, and 500 time-points data with this input-output model, then analyzed these data by the three proposed structure analysis algorithms. Each algorithm judges whether state variate Y is Y_1, Y_2, Y_3, or Y_4. Figure 5.6 shows success rates of the algorithm in each state Y and three different groups of data numbers. In the case of data number 100, the algorithm fails in the case of Y_2 and Y_3. But it is possible for the algorithm to distinguish the data when the data number increases to 300 or 500. That is, this algorithm can be applied precisely when there is enough data.

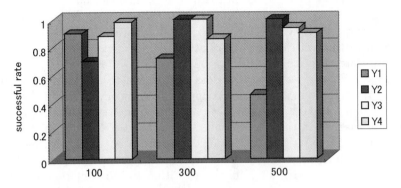

FIGURE 5.7. Success rate of algorithm with mutual information.

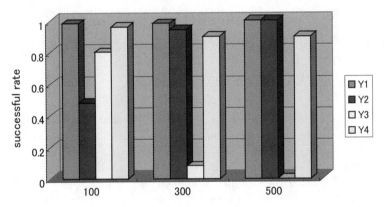

FIGURE 5.8. Success rate of algorithm with conditioned mutual information.

Figure 5.7 shows a result obtained when the algorithm with mutual information is applied to the neural-like generated data. This algorithm shows a high distinction rate in the case of 100 points data, but a lower distinction rate of Y_1 as the number of data points increases.

In this algorithm, influence of the remaining (X) variate is considered in calculating the relationship between Y and Z. Then, the relation between Y_1 and Z contains an indirect relation through X, even though there is no direct connection between Y_1 and Z.

This mismatching between analysis model and data model decreases success rate. In other words, there is mismatching between the structure of the data assumed by the algorithm and the actual structure of data.

But we should pay attention to all success rates, including Y_1, which in this algorithm is higher than in the algorithm with information flow that treats three variates for the case of 100 data points. This is why this algorithm with mutual information is simple enough to treat only two variates in calculation: It is robust against lack of data.

Figure 5.8 shows the result of data analysis where the algorithm with conditioned mutual information is applied to the neural-like data. When the amount of data increases in this case, the success rate for Y_3 falls. In the case where the distinction is wrong, almost all are misclassified into Y_2. That is, it fails to distinguish between X and Y, because of a mismatching between the data model and the analysis model. The classification criterion for Y_3 of the algorithm with information flow is

$$R(Y_3, X, Z) < 0.$$

Because there is no connection between X and Y_3, the following expression holds:

$$I(X : Y_3) = 0.$$

We then get the following expression:

$$R(Y_3, X, Z) = I(X : Y_3) - I(X : Y_3|Z) = -I(X : Y_3|Z).$$

This leads to

$$I(X : Y_3|Z) > 0.$$

This expression is equivalent to an expression that distinguishes the connection between X and Y using the algorithm with conditioned mutual information (see figure 5.4). If $I(Y_3 : Z|X)$ is not zero, then Y_3 should be mistaken for Y_2. In other words, when the algorithm with conditioned mutual information is applied to the neural-like data, the algorithm treats the relation between X and Y_3 as a matter of fact, instead of the relation between Y_3 and Z. Therefore, the success rate for Y_3 becomes remarkably low.

If data is sufficient and its flow is known, we can use the algorithm that treats data flow for structure analysis. But if there is not enough data for data analysis, it may be safer to use the algorithm with mutual information, which is simple and powerful for small amounts of data.

5.2.2 Data with Common Information and Structure Analysis

We construct data that shares common information in variates as shown in figure 5.9. There may be a next relation because common information exists in the variates. The data that X and Y share is D_1. The data that X and Y_2 share is D_{21}, and the data that X, Y and Z share is D_2. The data that Y_2 and Z share is D_{22}, and the data that D_{22}, Y_3 and Z share is D_3, just as in figure 5.9. The data volume of D_1 and D_3 is 25

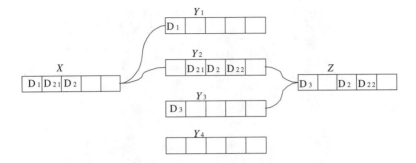

FIGURE 5.9. Structure of data with common information.

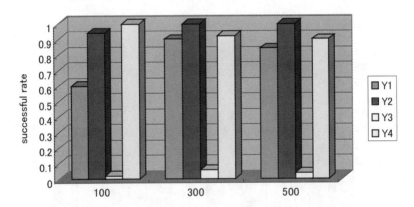

FIGURE 5.10. Success rate of algorithm with information flow.

percent of Y_1 and X. D_{21} and D_{22} is 13 percent, and D_2 is 12 percent of each variate. All the data of the remaining blank part are generated randomly.

We prepare 50 sets of 100, 300, and 500 points of time-series data generated by this input-output model, and then analyze these data by using three proposed structure analysis algorithms.

Figure 5.10 shows that the algorithm with information flow fails to predict Y_3 in most of the data sets. In this error phase, almost all data that originally belonged to Y_3 is identified as Y_4. The reason for this error is a reverse relation in subsection 5.2.1, where an algorithm with conditioned mutual information is applied to neuron-like flow data.

In other words, what happens when the algorithm with information

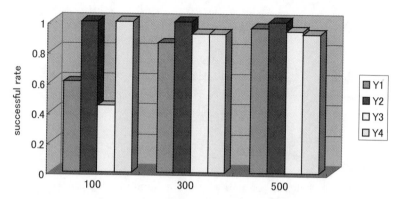

FIGURE 5.11. Success rate of algorithm with mutual information.

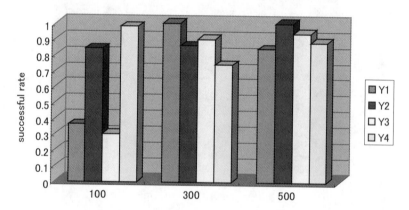

FIGURE 5.12. Success rate of algorithm with conditioned mutual information.

flow is applied to the data with common information in order to test the relationship between Y_3 and Z is that it actually tests the relation between X and Y_3.

Figures 5.11 and 5.12 show that both mutual information algorithms were successful in applying the common information data, if there was enough data. These results show us that both mutual information algorithms can be applied to data with common information with better performance than the algorithm with information flow.

In general, for small amounts of data, the algorithm with mutual information is superior to others because of its relatively simple calculation.

Finally, we conclude that data with information flow matches well with the algorithm with information flow, and data with common information matches well with both algorithms with mutual information, after combination tests of two types of data and three types of structure analysis algorithm. Mismatch between them evokes specific types of error, instead of random error. Therefore, detecting a mismatch provides useful information and helps us guess the true data type.

5.3 Structure Analyses of fMRI Data

So far, there are two kinds of well-known statistical analysis techniques for fMRI data. These are SPM (statistic parametric mapping), which is, from the viewpoint of Gaussian field theory, derived from t test, and ICA (independent component analysis), which looks for the origin of statistical independent signals. On the other hand, multivariate analysis was applied to data in living systems at the time when Shannon applied his information theory to communication systems. Mutual information was used for the analysis of psychology data (Attneave, 1959). This method was considered inapplicable for MRI data because of its computational complexity. However, recent developments in computer technology make it possible to apply the multivariate analysis method to MRI data.

We apply three structure analysis algorithms to real fMRI data. This fMRI data was gathered from a subject who performed a discriminate recognition task and was scanned 78 times in six-second intervals. Seventy-eight data points may be a small data set for statistic analysis.

First we apply the information flow algorithm to each voxel of fMRI data. Figure 5.13 shows the X voxel, Z voxel, and each Y voxel plotted onto an anatomical MR brain image. In this figure, we don't plot the Y_4 voxel onto the anatomical brain image. Figure 5.14 shows the result of algorithm with mutual information, and figure 5.15 shows the result of algorithm with conditioned mutual information. In this way, it is easy to use our algorithm to build the brain mapping image that reflects statistics of brain activity.

A common feature of the three kinds of structure analysis results is that neighborhood voxels of stimulus variate X and response variate Z have similar relations to X or Z, or both. This means that activity in the voxels is interconnected to some extent, rather than independent. A set of voxels in the left side of the brain that is judged as $Y_1(Y_1')$ may relate to X.

A difference between the algorithm with information flow (figure 5.13) and both mutual information algorithms (figure 5.14 and 5.15) is that a cluster of Y_3 voxels in the central and central bottom parts of the brain is found in figure 5.14 and 5.15, but the same voxels are identified as

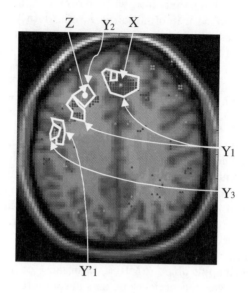

FIGURE 5.13. fMRI structure analysis by algorithm with information flow.

Y_4 in figure 5.13. This result was proved in previous section. That is, an information flow algorithm judges Y_4 instead of Y_3 if the data do not have a clear direction flow. Some clusters of voxels that were classified as Y_3 by the algorithm with mutual information were classified as Y_4 by the algorithm with conditioned mutual information. This mismatch was also predicated in previous section.

There are other kinds of differences in judgment when the algorithm with conditioned/nonconditioned mutual information analysis is applied to real fMRI data. Figure 5.16(left) shows a result of the algorithm with mutual information, and figure 5.16(right) shows a result of the algorithm with conditioned mutual information. A cluster of voxels that was classified as Y_2 by the mutual information algorithm was classified as Y_3 by the conditioned mutual information algorithm.

The relations that hold in this case are as follows:

$$I(X : Y) > 0;$$
$$I(X : Y | Z) = 0;$$
$$I(Y : Z) > 0;$$
$$I(Y : Z | X) > 0.$$

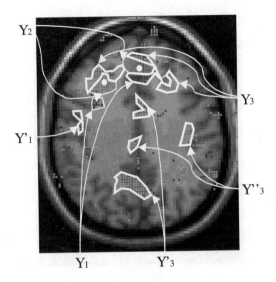

Y_2

Y_3

Y'_1

Y''_3

Y_1 Y'_3

FIGURE 5.14. fMRI structure analysis by algorithm with mutual information.

These expressions show that there is no common information between X and Y without the influence of Z. Moreover, there is common information between Y and Z even without the influence of X. In other words, common information between Y and Z includes common information between X and Y. We modify the definition of interaction as follows:

$$R(X,Y,Z) = I(X:Y) - I(X:Y|Z).$$

Interaction, then, is positive in this situation. We can check whether the voxel in this situation has a positive interaction. (A brain map of this interaction is easy to construct.) A judgment of this case shows us that the intensive structure analysis, which uses many kinds of information measurements, can make information structure clear.

5.4 Extended Functional Connectivity Analysis

In the previous section, we proposed the three models that described the logical relationships of voxels in the whole brain against the two fixed voxels we focused on. These three models have close relations, but they are different from each other in meaning and logic. From the viewpoint of logic, these three models share nearly the same logical form and each has the same specific logical parts.

In this section we try to combine the three models to arrive at a new

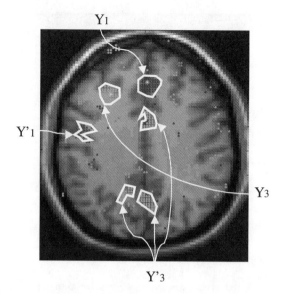

FIGURE 5.15. fMRI structure analysis by algorithm with conditioned information.

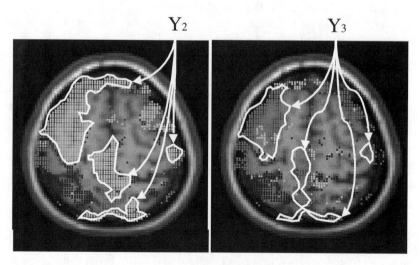

FIGURE 5.16. Other example of differences in judgment.

X→Y→Z				X←Y←Z				mutual information	conditional mutual information	the relation that can be supposed	the combination of all results
F	M	C	figure with a flow	F	M	C	figure with a flow				
1	1	1		4	3	3					
1	1	4		4	3	4					
1	2	1		2	2	3					
1	2	4		1	2	4					
2	1	2		3	3	2					
2	1	3		3	3	1					
2	2	2		2	2	2					
2	2	3		1	2	1					
3	3	1		2	1	3					
3	3	2		2	1	2					
3	4	1		4	4	3					
3	4	2		3	4	2					
4	3	3		1	1	1					
4	3	4		1	1	4					
4	4	3		3	4	1					
4	4	4		4	4	4					

Figure 5.17. Functional connectivity analysis by using a combination of three kinds of multivariate information analysis.

method (Niki et al. 2000). We call this method an *extended functional connectivity analysis.* The method uses many kinds of information measurements. In some cases, our method can detect mismatching between data and the analysis model and infer the true information flow in the brain. In another case, our method can detect a reverse flow of information without additional computation. In this way, our proposed method is better than previous models at providing a functional connectivity mapping of the brain. We hope that this new method clarifies the functional structure and connectivity in the brain.

5.4.1 Combining the Three Methods

A simple combination of the three methods introduces 64 possible results, because each algorithm includes four kinds of analysis. This is narrowed to 16 possibilities, however, as shown in figure 5.17, because there is a logical contradiction in some combinations.

In this summarized table in figure 5.17, analyzed results Y_1, Y_2, Y_3, and Y_4 are described simply as 1, 2, 3, and 4; C is used for the conditional mutual information algorithm, M is supposed for the mutual

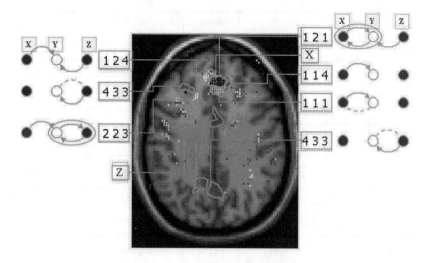

FIGURE 5.18. Functional connectivity analysis of fMRI brain image.

information algorithm, and F is used for the algorithm with direction of information flow. In addition to this summary, we can expand the power of inference as follows. One addition is the ability to detect the reverse information flow. Another is the ability to detect a mismatch between real data and the data structure assumed in analysis. We can get the reverse information flow without additional computation, because we have much information from 3 analysis methods (as discussed in the previous section). These summarized results are shown in figure 5.17.

Figure 5.18 shows one example of a functional connectivity analysis of fMRI brain data, which comes from a working memory task. Locations X, Y were selected, as SPM pointed them up as significant ($p < 0.001$) voxels in the same slice. Figure 5.18 shows that our proposed method is a new method that clarifies the functional connectivities in the brain.

5.5 Conclusion

In this section, we introduced a new brain mapping method that uses mutual information, interaction, and so on, and we applied it to fMRI brain data for its structure analysis (functional connectivity analysis). This preliminary trial shows that our proposed method promises to become a powerful tool for understanding brain connectivity and function, through an account and interpretation of well-defined information measurements.

6 Dialogue-based Map Learning in an Office Robot
Hideki Asoh, Yoichi Motomura, Toshihiro Matsui,
Satoru Hayamizu, and Isao Hara

Learning is an indispensable capability for autonomous intelligent systems that work in complex, unpredictable real-world environments. Many schemes and algorithms for modeling learning have been proposed and investigated so far. However, most of them are within the category of *learning from examples*, where a large amount of static learning examples are prepared in advance and fed into learning systems. We think that the learning systems that can behave robustly in real-world environments should exploit a more dynamical learning scheme. In other words, the system and the environment (or human users) should interact more closely.

The idea of *dialogue-based learning* that exploits dialogue in natural language for teaching is rather old. Although the idea is very simple and natural, understanding speech has been a bottleneck, and not much effort to realize a system has been made. Recently, as a result of the progress in AI and pattern-recognition research, the techniques of speaker-independent continuous speech recognition and natural-language understanding have reached an applicable level, and dialogue-based learning is becoming attractive for building real-world intelligent systems. More intimate human–machine interaction can also help the real-world intelligent systems collaborate with humans in daily life.

In the course of the RWC program, we developed and built a prototype of real-world intelligence: an autonomous learning mobile office robot, which moves autonomously in a real office environment, actively gathers information and acquires knowledge about the environment through sensing multi-modal data and engaging in dialogue with people (Matsui et al., 1995). In this section we describe our first step experiment where the dialogue-based learning was applied to the robot's map acquisition task.

6.1 Dialogue-based Map Acquisition
Map acquisition is an important research issue for mobile robots, and there has been extensive research on map learning. Typical research uses an occupancy grid, which discretizes the world into small cells, and the systems learn (estimate) whether or not each cell is occupied with an obstacle (Elfes, 1992; Buhmann, 1995). Another method is based on finite-state transition networks (Basye et al., 1989; Kuipers and Byun, 1988; Mataric, 1992; Tani, 1995).

Both approaches work well under certain assumptions, and their effectiveness has been confirmed by several autonomous mobile systems. However, these systems do not use closely coupled human–machine interaction. Here we apply the idea of dialogue-based learning to the map acquisition task. Our problem is how to utilize dialogue between humans and robots in the task. We found that designing a dialogue scenario with an appropriately articulated action space and introducing probabilistic descriptions of the map are very important in solving the problem.

6.1.1 Designing Scenario and Action Space

Our scenario for the dialogue was designed as the following (R: robot; H: human teacher):

R: Where am I?
H: You are in front of Dr. Nakashima's Office.
R: Where shall I go?
H: Please go to Dr. Hara's Office.
R: Sorry, I don't know how to go to Dr. Hara's Office.
H: OK. Please go straight.
R: OK.
(Goes straight until an end-of-action condition is satisfied.)
R: Where am I?
H: You are in front of Dr. Matsui's Office.

In designing the scenario, the most important point is designing the action elements of the robot. Designing the action elements is at the same time designing the articulation of the working space. The following criteria for the design were considered:

- The user (teacher) should easily be able to designate an elemental action. Commands with metrical information such as "go straight 5 m" are not convenient.

- The user (teacher) should easily be able to understand and predict the effect of elemental actions ("go straight," "right turn" etc.).

The office environment is characterized by its modular structure. Modules with a similar appearance make up the entire structure, and so it is difficult to attribute landmarks to specific locations. Figure 6.1 shows the floor plan of the ETL E-building, our field for experiments. Taking the modularity into account we exploited the compartment type articulation as in Naurbakhsh et al., (1995) and implemented as follows.

The space is articulated by the end of an elemental action. Each elemental action ends when the end-of-action condition is satisfied. Tentatively we implemented six elemental actions: go straight, right/left turn by free space following, right/left turn by wall following, turnover and go

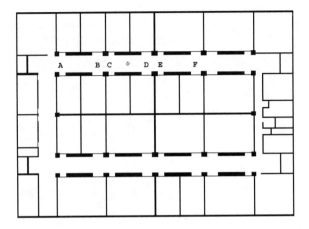

FIGURE 6.1. Map of ETL E-building.

straight. It is possible to add new elemental actions. The end-of-action conditions are tentatively the same for all actions, that is, an action ends when the system moves into an OPEN space from a CLOSE space. A CLOSE space is the hallway between two parallel walls. An OPEN space is either a doorway or an intersection of hallways. It is also possible to set different end-of-action conditions for each elemental action.

To discriminate OPEN space and CLOSE space, the following shift- and rotation-invariant features of the system were prepared, and a discriminant function was constructed with the simple discriminant analysis method:

- the number of detected walls around the system; and
- the spatial correlation, maximum, minimum of the sum of two distance values from sonars that are in opposite directions.

6.1.2 Probabilistic Map

The uncertainty of the real-world environment is caused mainly by unexpected noise. We introduced formal probabilistic model to cope with this uncertainty. Let us denote the system's status at time t by $D(t) \in D$, $S(t) \in S$, and $A(t) \in A$, where $D(t)$ is observed sensory information, $S(t)$ is the location state of the system that is not directly observable by the system, and $A(t)$ is the action executed at time t. Let G represent the goal that the system is aiming for. A stochastic process $\langle D(t), S(t), A(t), G \rangle$ is used to describe the whole probabilistic structure of the environment and system's behavior under the condition that the system is running to the goal G.

Like many researchers we assumed that the whole stochastic process is a Markov process, that is, the state transition probabilities $P(S(t)|S(t-1), A(t-1))$, observation probabilities $P(D(t)|S(t), S(t-1))$, and probabilistic plan $P(A(t)|S(t), G)$ to go to G do not depend on other past conditions. The equations

$$P(S(t)|S(t-1), A(t-1))$$
$$= P(S(t)|S(t-1), \ldots, S(0),$$
$$D(t-1), \ldots, D(1), A(t-1), \ldots, A(0), G),$$
$$P(D(t)|S(t), S(t-1))$$
$$= P(D(t)|S(t), S(t-1), \ldots, S(0),$$
$$D(t-1), \ldots, D(1), A(t-1), \ldots, A(0), G),$$

and

$$P(A(t)|S(t), G)$$
$$= P(A(t)|S(t), S(t-1), \ldots, S(0),$$
$$D(t), \ldots, D(1), A(t-1), \ldots, A(0), G)$$

hold for any combination of the conditional part.

This assumption implies that the result of an action $A(t-1)$ depends only on $S(t-1)$. This does not always hold. For example, when the robot enters into a state $S(t-1)$, its position and orientation are not uniquely determined. Hence the consequence or action $A(t-1)$ may differ depend on the position or orientation. To cancel the effect and to maintain the assumption we used potential-based motor control. This method makes a virtual valley of potential between walls, and the system moves along the bottom of the valley. The system normally keeps to the center of the corridor as long as there is no large obstacle. Even though there are obstacles, after avoiding the obstacle the system is expected to re-enter the potential valley with high probability and to keep the normal position and orientation.

According to the assumption, the probability $P(S(t), \ldots, D(t), \ldots, A(t-1), \ldots, G)$ can be computed from $P(S(t-1), \ldots, D(t-1), \ldots, A(t-2), \ldots, G)$ and the above two conditional probabilities. By the definition of the conditional probability,

$$P(S(t), \ldots, D(t), \ldots, A(t-1), \ldots, G)$$
$$= P(D(t)|S(t), \ldots, D(t-1), \ldots, A(t-1), \ldots, G)$$
$$\times P(S(t)|S(t-1), \ldots, D(t-1), \ldots, A(t-1), \ldots, G)$$
$$\times P(A(t-1)|S(t-1), \ldots, D(t-1), \ldots, A(t-2), \ldots, G)$$
$$\times P(S(t-1), \ldots, D(t-1), \ldots, A(t-2), \ldots, G)$$

holds, and with the Markov assumption we can show

$$P(S(t), \ldots, D(t), \ldots, A(t-1))$$
$$= P(D(t)|S(t), S(t-1))$$
$$\times P(S(t)|S(t-1), A(t-1))$$
$$\times P(A(t-1)|S(t-1), G)$$
$$\times P(S(t-1), \ldots, D(t-1), \ldots, A(t-2), \ldots, G).$$

In this framework, a probabilistic map is defined as:

Definition A *probabilistic map* is a probability distribution $P(S(t), D(t)|S(t-1), A(t-1))$, that is, a probability of staying at state $S(t)$ and observing $D(t)$ at time t conditioned by staying at state $S(t-1)$ and executing action $A(t-1)$ at time $t-1$.

The distribution $P(S(t), D(t)|S(t-1), A(t-1))$ is computed from two distributions $P(S(t)|S(t-1), A(t-1))$ and $P(D(t)|S(t), S(t-1))$.

In our tentative system $A(t)$ represents one of the six elemental actions, and $D(t)$ represents running distance $d(t)$ and accumulated steering angle $a(t)$ during an elemental action $A(t-1)$. If the system asks a question "Where am I?" the answer to the question is added to $D(t)$. S represents the position state where the system is. The representation is a kind of probabilistic finite automata. If we can get absolute coordinate information as a part of the observed data $D(t)$, we can easily incorporate the data into the probabilistic map, and the map becomes an integrated type of the finite automata and the occupancy grid.

To treat the continuous values from odometric sensors, we assume that the distribution $P(d(t), a(t)|S(t), S(t-1))$ is the product of two normal distributions:

$$P(d(t), a(t)|S(t), S(t-1))$$
$$= C \times \exp\left\{ -\frac{(d(t) - \mu_{d|S(t),S(t-1)})^2}{2\sigma^2_{d|S(t),S(t-1)}} \right\}$$
$$\times \exp\left\{ -\frac{(a(t) - \mu_{a|S(t),S(t-1)})^2}{2\sigma^2_{a|S(t),S(t-1)}} \right\}.$$

Here $\mu_{d|S(t),S(t-1)}$ and $\mu_{a|S(t),S(t-1)}$ are the mean values, $\sigma_{d|S(t),S(t-1)}$ and $\sigma_{a|S(t),S(t-1)}$ are the standard deviation of $d(t)$ and $a(t)$ under the condition of $S(t)$, and $S(t-1)$. C is a normalization constant. If there are enough examples, we can exploit nonparametric estimation of the distribution.

The current position (state) is estimated as follows. The probability $P(S(t)|S(t-1), D'(t), A(t-1))$ is computed from $P(D'(t)|S(t), S(t-1))$ and $P(S(t)|S(t-1), A(t-1))$ with Bayes's formula:

$$
\begin{aligned}
&P(S(t)|D'(t), S(t-1), A(t-1)) \\
&= \; C \times P(D'(t)|S(t), S(t-1)) \\
&\quad \times P(S(t)|S(t-1), A(t-1)),
\end{aligned}
$$

where $D'(t)$ denotes sensory information without asking questions, and C is a normalization factor.

The system estimates its location state as $S(t)$, which attains the maximum value of the probability

$$
P_{max} = \max_{S(t) \in S} P(S(t)|D'(t), S(t-1), A(t-1)).
$$

If this P_{max} is larger than a previously determined threshold, the system assumes that it is in the $S(t)$ that attains the maximum and executes the next action. If P_{max} becomes less than the previously determined threshold, the system confirms its current position. To confirm the position system asks teacher a question "Where am I?" Other confirmation methods such as vision-based position recognition can also be introduced. As a consequence, in both cases the system knows where it is with high confidence. It is very useful to avoid the accumulation of location uncertainty.

For the path planning, the usual shortest path finding algorithm in graph theory (Dijkstra's algorithm) is applied to the probabilistic map. The success rate of the path is evaluated and paths with a low success rate are discarded.

6.2 System and Experiment

We first use a Nomad 200 as a mobile robot platform (see figure 6.2 and 6.5) and then move to a Nomad XR4000. Here we describe our first system. It is equipped with 16 sonar distance sensors, 16 infrared proximity sensors, touch sensors, a compass, and odometric sensors that measure running distance and steering angle; it communicates with an external host computer (4 CPU Sparc Station 20) via a radio Ethernet link. All control software modules (shown in figure 6.3) are written in C language using the robot control library provided by Nomadic Co. and run on the external host.

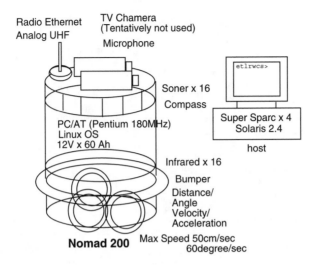

Radio Ethernet
Analog UHF

TV Chamera
(Tentatively not used)

Microphone

etlrwcs>

Soner x 16

Compass

PC/AT (Pentium 180MHz)
Linux OS
12V x 60 Ah

Super Sparc x 4
Solaris 2.4

host

Infrared x 16

Bumper

Distance/
Angle
Velocity/
Acceleration

Nomad 200   Max Speed 50cm/sec
60degree/sec

FIGURE 6.2. Hardware configuration.

As mentioned above, potential-based free space following and wall-following are used to implement elemental actions. An example trace of a moving robot with reports from sonar sensors during the move is shown in figure 6.4. The robot is moving from point "B" in figure 6.1 to point "D."

For the dialogue control we implemented a very simple pattern-matching-based module. The teacher's speech, collected by a microphone on Nomad 200, is sent to the host with analog UHF transmitter. A real-time continuous speaker-independent speech recognition module "niNja" developed in ETL (Itou et al. 1993) analyzes the speech signal and extracts key patterns such as "Dr. Nakashima" or "go straight."

Experiments are carried out on a floor of our laboratory's building (see figure 6.1 and 6.5). The system starts with no map information and acquires a probabilistic map through dialogue with human teachers. An example acquired map is shown in table 6.1. The map is acquired by moving in the corridor between "A" to "F" shown in figure 6.1. A part of the dialogue for acquiring the map is shown in appendix. Each row represents the start position, the goal position, the elemental action executed, mean and variance of distance and angle change, the number of trials, and the number of successes. Position is denoted by the label in figure 6.1. For example, "A:S" means staying position "A" in figure 6.1 facing the south (the right in figure 6.1). Distance is in inches and angles

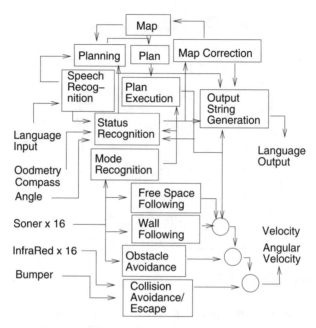

FIGURE 6.3. Software modules.

are in degrees. The compass is used to discriminate the direction that the system faces. Currently four directions—north (face left in figure 6.1), east, west, and south—are discriminated.

The map is modified after each execution of an elemental action. For example, suppose the system has been at "A:S". Then it executed the "go straight" action and arrived at a novel state. It asks "Where am I?" because it has no experience of the move "go straight from A:S". If the teacher answers "B", it knows the place is "B:S", combining the answer with signal from compass, and one new row that describes the move is added to the map. If the system executed this same move in the past, an existing row describing the move is modified.

Noise effects may make the robot halt in an unexpected position (e.g. at a nonbranching point). In such cases the teacher provides the robot with a special state, "on the way." This state is not used in the path planning. This trick is rather effective to discard confusing information.

This small map already includes some interesting events. First we can see that in some rows the standard deviation σ_d or σ_a is very large. For example, in rows 4 and 8, σ_d is 74.9 and 72.5 respectively. These large values suggest that the wheels slipped or obstacles (e.g. humans) dis-

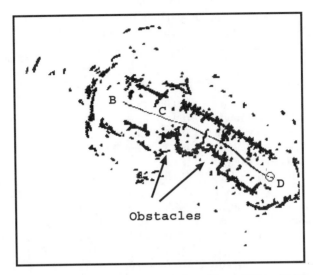

FIGURE 6.4. Trace of robot with sonar data (from "B" to "D" in figure 6.1).

FIGURE 6.5. Field of the experiment (on the way from "D" to "C" in figure 6.1).

Table 6.1

An Example of Acquired Probabilistic Map
T & G S = 'turnover and go straight' (see also figure 6.1).

Start	Goal	Action	μ_d	σ_d	μ_a	σ_a	Success	Trial
B:S	C:S	go straight	144.5	3.9	10.5	4.3	6	6
C:S	D:S	go straight	689.0	18.0	−8.3	4.2	5	5
D:S	E:S	go straight	169.0	41.0	−19.6	2.2	3	3
E:S	F:S	go straight	587.3	74.9	7.4	0.5	3	4
F:S	E:N	T & G S	494.3	17.6	165.7	8.2	3	3
E:N	D:N	go straight	88.0	31.2	26.5	50.3	3	3
D:N	C:N	go straight	779.0	24.8	−3.2	3.1	3	3
C:N	B:N	go straight	98.7	72.5	−3.9	3.8	4	5
B:N	A:N	go straight	644.7	37.9	−1.6	3.2	3	3
A:N	B:S	T & G S	476.3	6.9	172.7	12.1	7	7
C:S	B:N	T & G S	72.0	21.0	−167.3	1.3	2	2
E:S	E:S	go straight	16.0	0.0	−19.0	0.0	1	4
C:N	A:N	go straight	1375.0	0.0	5.4	0.0	1	5
C:S	B:N	T & G S	61.3	11.9	169.7	3.5	3	3
D:S	C:N	T & G S	529.7	16.4	174.3	2.5	3	3
C:N	D:S	T & G S	507.0	0.0	−179.6	0.0	1	1
B:S	A:N	T & G S	475.0	0.0	−179.4	0.0	1	1

turbed the system's path. Rows 8 and 13 show that the system missed point "B:N" once in five trials. Row 12 shows that the end-of-action condition happened to be satisfied by mistake. Using this sort of probabilistic map, we can keep track of such probabilistic information on the environment and utilize it for path planning and location estimation.

6.3 Discussion

The feasibility of the dialogue-based learning has been tested and confirmed. Although the dialogue capability of the system is very limited, the system can build a map without much effort on the part of human trainers. Our experiment provided insights into many features of the dialogue-based learning. Dialogue-based learning has the following advantages over sensor-based learning:

- *On the job supply and demand of information.* The system is always in learning mode and asks question autonomously. Combined with the context information that both teacher and system have in common, simple dialogue can have a rather large effect.
- *Enables the purposive design of dialogue.* Because the context of the dialogue is limited to a specific learning task, a rather small-

sized vocabulary and grammar can work well. To cope with multiple learning targets, switching small grammars and dictionaries is expected to be effective.

- *Users become intimate with the system.* The teaching effort is strongly motivated by the close interaction with the system. Estimating the knowledge status of the system becomes easy.
- *Provides structural information.* Information that has complex structure such as path plans can be conveyed through seminatural language dialogue.

The following points are possible defects:

- Frustration caused by the limited communication capability.
- Teaching is time-consuming.

The importance of the probabilistic model has also been confirmed. The major advantages of maintaining the probability information are:

- The system can reflectively assess the certainty of beliefs and can autonomously ask questions.
- The system can learn stochastic features of the environment such as frequently occupied space or a very slippery part of the hallway.
- The system becomes noise—or mistake—persistent.

6.4 Related Work

The state-transition automata map description is introduced by Kuipers and Byun, 1988) and used by some other researchers (Mataric, 1992; Tani, 1995). These are not probabilistic ones. Simmons and Koenig (Simmons, 1995) proposed a probabilistic map that is very similar to ours. The main difference between our map and theirs is in the design of S, A, and D. They used the assumption of perpendicularly crossing corridors and implemented three elemental actions: turning right 90 degrees, turning left 90 degrees, and going forward one meter. As a consequence their position state S is located every one meter. Our design is a little more flexible because it can cope with a less rigid layout of corridors, and it is more suitable to be combined with dialogue. As for D, we treat continuous-valued information whereas Simmons et al. treat discreet distance. Our design of S and A is inspired by the compartment-type quantization of the office environment used for the mobile robot DERVISH (Naurbakhsh et al., 1995).

The well-known intelligent robot SHAKEY developed by Nilsson (1969) is one of the earliest implementations of dialogue-based learning. Torrance (1994) has implemented a mobile robot that learns a map through natural-language dialogue.

Basye and Dean (1989) investigated the learnability of probabilistic map. They pointed out that avoiding the accumulation of uncertainty is very important for successful learning. Simmons and Koenig also reported the problem of the computational complexity in using their probabilistic map (Simmons, 1995). We have shown here that by introducing dialogue, this accumulation can be effectively avoided. The main contribution of our work is in combining the formal probabilistic map, the idea of dialogue-based learning, and real-time continuous spoken language understanding.

6.5 Conclusion and Future Work

We successfully applied dialogue-based learning to the task of map acquisition in mobile autonomous robot navigation. The implemented system can engage in simple dialogue with a human teacher through spoken seminatural language and can acquire a probabilistic map of the environment.

The implemented system has many points that can be improved. The most important one is reduction of the number of queries and teaching time. We tentatively assumed that the system can get responses from teacher at any time. However, in real situations, it may be the case that no person is around the system. To cope with this we are now planning:

- *Integrating with vision-based landmark navigation.*
- *Introducing reasoning capability on the map.* For example, in Torrance's system, reversing the acquired path is enabled. We are also planning to reconstruct a two-dimensional bird's-eye-view map from the topological state transition structure and the distance between neighboring states.
- *Dividing the problem into learning state transitions structure and learning states' name.* After autonomously learning the structure of the state transition, the system asks human teachers the name of the state.

As for the capability of dialogue, we are planning to implement a semantic analysis mechanism. To realize natural dialogue, the grammar and the dictionary should be tuned based on cognitive science research on man-machine dialogue. It is also necessary to improve the speech recognition module to cope with the noisy real-world environment.

Another interesting research issue is application of the dialogue-based learning to other tasks. In the project of building the office-conversant robot, we are also planning to apply the learning strategy to many other targets.

The design of an appropriate action space is the most important factor for successful learning. However, the design is heavily task- and environment-dependent. In our research, the action space is designed and implemented by humans. To make dialogue-based learning more effective, self-organization of action space will become an important and interesting research issue.

Appendix: A Part of the Dialogue for Acquiring the Map Shown in Table 6.1

R: Where am I?

H: You are in front of Dr. Matsui's Office (B:S).

R: Where shall I go?

H: Please go to Dr. Hara's Office (F:*).

R: Sorry, I don't know how to go to Dr. Hara's Office.

H: OK. Please go straight.

R: OK.

(Goes straight until an end-of-action condition is satisfied.)

R: Where am I?

H: You are in front of Dr. Onda's Office (C:S).

R: Where shall I go?

H: Go straight more.

R: OK.

(Goes straight again until an end-of-action condition is satisfied.)

R: Where am I?

H: You are in front of Dr. Ogasawara's Office (D:S).

$\vdots$

R: Where am I?

H: You are in front of Dr. Matsui's Office (B:S).

R: Where shall I go?

H: Please go to Dr. Ogasawara's Office (D:*).

R: OK.

(Goes straight and arrives at C:S.)

R: Where am I?

H: You are in front of Dr. Onda's Office (C:S).

R: OK. I'm on the right way.

(Goes straight and arrives at D:S.)

R: I'm at Dr. Ogasawara's Office (D:S).

R: Where shall I go?

H: Go to Dr. Matsui's Office (B:*).

R: OK. I'll turnover and go straight.

(Misses B and stop at A:N.)

R: Oh I'm lost. Where am I?

H: You are in front of Dr. Nakashima's Office (A:N).

R: Thank you. I'll turnover and go straight.

(Replans the path to Dr. Matsui's Office and executes it.)

R: I'm at Dr. Matsui's Office (B:S).

$$\vdots$$

(Here A:* means A:N or A:S.)

7 Conclusion

This chapter describes recent representative results from research in our laboratory on learning and inference with graphical models. Toward establishing theoretical and algorithmic foundations of real-world intelligence, we have been conducting wide variety of research from theoretical analysis to developing practical algorithms and implementing software.

One feature of our research is its wide variation in treating graphical models. We investigate simple graphical models such as Gaussian mixtures as well as very complex models such as probabilistic constraint programming.

Another feature of our research is that we will apply our practical algorithms and learning frameworks to the prototypes of real-world intelligence. Several prototypes such as mobile office robot Jijo-2 and a multi-modal interaction system are being developed in the project. We not only do theoretical work but also intensively apply our ideas to the systems and evaluate their effectiveness.

We believe that this hybrid style of research is crucial to finding which directions should be investigated and to keeping theoretical research sound.

References

Akaho, S. (1995). The EM algorithm for multiple object recognition. *Proceedings of 1995 IEEE International Conference on Neural Networks*, pp. 2426–2431.

Akaho, S., Hayamizu, S., Hasegawa, O., Yoshimura, T., and Asoh, H. (1997). Concept acquisition from multiple information sources by the EM algorithm. *Transactions of IEICE* J80-A:1546–1553 (in Japanese).

Akaho, S. (1998). Statistical learning in optimization: Gaussian modeling for population search. *Proceedings of 5th International Conference on Neural Information Processing*, pp. 675–678.

Akaho, S. and Kappen, B. (2000). Nonmonotonic generalization bias of Gaussian mixture models. *Neural Computation* 12(6):1411–1427.

Asoh, H., Motomura, Y., Hara, I., Akaho, S., Hayamizu, S., and Matsui, T. (1996). Combining probabilistic map and dialog for robust life-long office navigation. *Proceedings of 1996 IEEE/RSJ International Conference on Intelligent Robots and Systems*, pp. 807–812.

Asoh, H., Hayamizu, S., Hara, I., Motomura, Y., Akaho, S., and Matsui, T. (1997). Socially embedded learning of the office-conversant robot Jijo-2. *Proceedings of 15th International Joint Conference on Artificial Intelligence*, pp. 888–885.

Attneave, F. (1959). *Applications of Information Theory to Psychology.* New York: Holt, Rinehert, and Winston.

Basye, K., Dean, T., and Vitter, J. S. (1989). Coping with uncertainty in map learning. *Proceedings of 11th International Joint Conference on Artificial Intelligence*, pp. 663–668.

Buhmann, J. (1995). The mobile robot RHINO. *AI Magazine* summer 1995: 31–38.

Castillo, E., Gutierrez, J., and Hadi, A. (1997). *Expert Systems and Probabilistic Network Models.* New York: Springer-Verlag.

Cooper, G. and Herskovits, E. (1992). A Bayesian method for induction of probabilistic network from data. *Machine Learning* 9:309–347.

Cowell, R. G., Dawid A. P., Lauritzen, S. L., and Spiegelhalter, D. J. (1999). *Probabilistic Networks and Expert Systems.* New York: Springer-Verlag.

Elfes, A. (1992). Multi-source spatial data fusion using Bayesian reasoning. In M. A. Arbib and R. C. Gonzales (eds.), *Data Fusion in Robotics and Machine Intelligence* (pp. 137–163). Academic Press.

Friedman, N., Goldszmidt, M., Heckerman, D., and Russel, S. (1997). Challenge: What is the impact of Bayesian networks on learning? *Proceedings of 15th International Joint Conference on Artificial Intelligence*, pp. 10–15.

Frey, B. J. (1998). *Graphical Models for Machine Learning and Digital Communication.* Cambridge: MIT Press.

Fukumizu, K. (1999). Generalization error of linear neural networks in unidentifiable cases. *Proceedings of 10th International Conference on Algorithmic Learning Theory* (pp. 51–62). Springer-Verlag.

Geiger, D. and Heckerman, D. (1994). Learning Gaussian networks. *Uncertainty AI* 10:235–243.

Haddawy, P. (1999). An overview of some recent developments in Bayesian problem solving techniques. *AI Magazine* 20(1):11–19.

Hasida, K. (1997). Constraint-based derivation of cognitive model on parsing. *Proceedings of 1997 International Conference on Cognitive Science*, pp. 51–56.

Hasida, K. (1998). Parsing and generation with tabulation and compilation. *Proceedings of 1st Wrokshop on Tabulation in Parsing and Deduction (TAPD '98)* (pp. 26–35).

Horikawa, K., Asoh, H., Tani, J., Matsui, T., and Kakikura, M. (1998). Emergence of expert modules for mobile robot navigation from a mixture of Elman networks. *Proceedings of 5th International Conference on Neural Information Processing*, pp. 256–259.

ICA home page: http://www.cnl.salk.edu/~tewon/ica_cnl.html

Itou, K., Hayamizu, S., Tanaka, K., and Tanaka, H. (1993). System design, data collection, and evaluation of a speech dialogue system, *IEICE Transactions on Information & Systems* E76-D:121–127.

Jordan, M. I. (ed.) (1998). *Learning in Graphical Models*. Kluwer Academic.

Kuipers, G. J. and Byun, Y.-T. (1988). A robust, qualitative method for robot spatial reasoning. *Proceedings of the AAAI-88*, pp. 774–779.

Mataric, M. (1992). Integration of representation into goal-driven behavior-based robot. *IEEE Transactions on Robotics and Automation* 8:304–312.

Matsui, T., Hayamizu, S., Asoh, H., Hara, I., and Motomura, Y. (1995). Office-Conversant mobile robot project. *Proceedings of 1995 Annual Conference of the Robotics Society of Japan* (in Japanese).

Motomura, Y., Hara, I., Asoh, H., and Matsui, T. (1997). Bayesian network that learns conditional probabilities by neural networks. In *The Progress in Connectionist-Based Information Systems* (pp. 584–587). New Youk: Springer-Verlag.

Motomura, Y. (1998). Integration of situated prior probability and neural network classifier in a handwritten recognition task. *Proceedings of 5th International Conference on Neural Information Processing*, pp. 283–286.

Motomura, Y. (1998). BAYONET: Probabilistic reasoning system with learning from database. *Proceedings of 12th Annual Conference of Japanese Society for Artificial Intelligence*, pp. 632–633 (in Japanese).

Motomura, Y. and Hara, I. (2000). *Probabilistic Network based Multi Agent Model*. Technical report 2000-MPS-28, pp. 17–20. Information Processing Society of Japan.

Naurbakhsh, I., Powers, R., and Birchfield, S. (1995). DERVISH: An office-navigating robot. *AI Magazine* 16(2):53–60.

Niki, K., Hatou, J., and Tahara, I. (1999). Structure analysis and activity mapping of fMRI by using multivarable information. *Proceedings of 1999 Annual Conference of Japanese Neural Network Society*, pp. 140–141 (in Japanese).

Niki, K., Hatou, J., Luo, J., and Tahara, I. (2000). Functional connectivity analysis for fMRI data using mutual information and interaction. *NeuroImaging* 11(5):484.

Nilsson, J. (1969). A mobile automaton: An application of artificial intelligence techniques. *Proceedings of the First International Joint Conference on Artificial Intelligence*, pp. 509–520.

Niwa, T. and Tanaka, M. (1995). On the mean convergence time for simple genetic algorithms. *Proceedings of 1995 International Conference on Evolutionary Computing*, pp. 373–377.

Niwa, T. and Tanaka, M. (1997). Analysis of simple genetic algorithms and island model parallel genetic algorithms. *Proceedings of International Conference on Artificial Neural Nets and Genetic Algorithms*, pp. 224–228.

Niwa, T. and Tanaka, M. (1998). Analysis on the island model parallel genetic algorithms for the genetic drifts. *Proceedings of 2nd Asia-Pacific Conference on Simulated Evolution and Learning*, pp. 349–356.

Russell, S. and Norvig, P. (1994). *Artificial Intelligence: A modern approach.* Upper Saddle River, NJ: Prentice Hall.

Simmons, R. and Koenig, S. (1995). Probabilistic robot navigation in partially observable environments. *Proceedings of 14th International Joint Conference on Artificial Intelligence*, pp. 1080–1087.

SPM home page: http://www.fil.ion.bpmf.ac.uk/spm/

Tahara, I. and Saito, M. (1978). Application of multivariate information theory to the analysis of neural interaction. *Proceedings of International Conference on Signals and Images in Medicine and Biology (BIOSIGMA '78)*, pp. 27–32.

Tahara, I. (1980). Multi-variate analysis of information transmit function in neural system. *BioMedical Engineering* 18(4):295–296.

Tani, J. (1995). Dynamical systems approach in learnable autonomous robots. *Proceedings Information Integration Workshop 95*, pp. 241–249.

Torrance, M. C. (1994). *Natural Communication with Robots.* Masters thesis, Massachusetts Institute of Technology, Department of Electrical Engineering and Computer Science.

II

Approximate Reasoning: Real-World Applications of Graphical Models

RWC Theoretical Foundation SNN Laboratory

BERT KAPPEN, STAN GIELEN, WIM WIEGERINCK, ALI TAYLAN CEMGIL,
TOM HESKES, MARCEL NIJMAN, AND MARTIJN LEISINK

In the 1990s, the use of probabilistic methods in artificial intelligence (AI) and machine learning has gained enormous popularity. In particular, probabilistic graphical models have become the preferred method for knowledge representation and reasoning. However, the drawback of the probabilistic approach is that its methods are intractable. This means that the typical computation increases exponentially with the problem size, which prevents large-scale applications.

A popular approximation scheme is provided by mean field theory, developed originally in the statistical physics community. In section 8, we present an introduction to mean field theory and an overview of our contributions to this research.

Subsequently, we sketch two applications of graphical models: medical diagnosis (section 9) and automatic music transcription (section 10). The medical diagnostic system is based on a probabilistic model and features inference with missing values and reasoning with multiple causes. The system provides a differential diagnosis and insight into underlying mechanisms of illness and disease. In addition, it can advise the physician on the optimal selection of actions (based on the diagnostic interests of the physician) and to assist in the diagnostic process. The system is being developed and evaluated in close collaboration with the Department of Internal Medicine of the University Hospital Utrecht.

Foundations of Real-World Intelligence.
Yoshinori Uesaka et al. (eds.).
Copyright © 2001, CSLI Publications.

The second application, the automatic music transcriber, automatically generates an acceptable music score from onsets obtained from a MIDI keyboard. There are two problems in automatic transcription: tracking tempo fluctuations and "filtering out" expressive timing deviations. If these fluctuations are not filtered out, the resulting notation would be very complicated and useless. This is a shortcoming of current commercial transcription software. We developed a dynamic Bayesian network that jointly tracks the tempo and quantizes the events. This model closely resembles human performance on this task.

This overview of probabilistic methods is far from complete, but it is hoped that the selected topics will give the reader an impression of the usefulness and generality of the approach. There are of course many other interesting applications of graphical models not discussed here, such as genetic modeling, data mining, and human machine interfaces.

8 Mean Field Approximations

As mentioned earlier, probabilistic graphical models have recently become the preferred method for knowledge representation and reasoning in the fields of AI and machine learning. (Jordan, 1996). The advantage of this approach is that all assumptions are made explicit in the modeling process and consequences, such as predictions on novel data, are assumption-free and follow from mechanistic computations. The drawback of the probabilistic approach is that the method is intractable: the typical computation scales exponentially with the problem size.

Recently, a number of authors have proposed methods for approximate inference in large graphical models. The approach attempts to find an approximating, tractable, distribution q that is as close as possible to the original distribution p. The simplest approach uses as a distance measure between p and q the Kullback-Leibler divergence and minimizes this distance with respect to the parameters in q (Saul et al., 1996). The marginals computed from the approximate probability distribution q give a lower bound on the true probabilities. This method is also referred to as the *naive mean field theory*. The method can be applied to a large class of probability models, such as sigmoid belief networks, directed acyclic graphical models (DAGs), and Boltzmann Machines (BM).

Our approach extends this standard method in two novel directions. The first extension is the inclusion of structure in the approximating distribution (section 8.1). Using variational approximations with structure results in significant improvements to the naive approach and scales well with the problem size.

The second extension is the consideration of higher-order approximations. This method is also called the TAP approximation, after the authors that introduced this method (Thouless et al., 1977). In particular, in section 8.2 we introduce the TAP approximation and the linear response theory for a simple class of probability models, the Boltzmann distributions. We compare the performance of the exact BM learning algorithm with the naive mean field theory and second-order (TAP) mean field theory. We conclude that the contributions of the linear response correction and the TAP correction significantly improve learning (Plefka, 1982; Kappen and Rodríguez, 1998).

For probability distributions that are not Boltzmann-Gibbs distributions, it is not obvious how to obtain the second-order approximation. However, there is an alternative way to compute the higher-order corrections, based on an information-theoretic argument. Recently, this argument was applied to stochastic neural networks with asymmetric connectivity (Kappen and Spanjers, 1999). In section 8.3 we apply the same idea to directed graphical models (Kappen and Wiegerinck, 2001b).

8.1 Mean Field Approximation with Structure

The problem of probabilistic inference is to find the conditional probability distribution of a set of variables (representing the inference) given the values of some other set of variables (representing the evidence). More formally, let $s = (s_1, \ldots, s_n)$ denote the unknown variables, and let $e = (e_1, \ldots, e_k)$ denote the evidence variables. Let $p(s, e)$ denote the probability distribution on the total set of variables. We wish to compute $p_e(s) = p(s|e)$, or more specifically $p(s_i|e)$ of each of the nodes $i = 1, \ldots, n$ given the evidence e.

In the variational method, the intractable probability distribution $p_e(s)$ is approximated by a tractable distribution $q(s)$ (on the nonevidential nodes). Then q is used to compute the single node marginals $q(s_i)$, which is a tractable operation. To construct q, one first has to define a tractable graphical structure for q: $q(s) = \prod_\gamma q(s_\gamma | \pi_\gamma)$ (Barber and Wiegerinck, 1999; Wiegerinck and Barber, 1998a,b). The next step is to optimize the parameters of q such that the Kullback-Leibler (KL) divergence between q and p_e,

$$(8.1) \qquad D(q, p_e) = \sum_{\{s\}} q(s) \log \frac{q(s)}{p_e(s)},$$

is minimized.

The KL-divergence is related to the difference of the marginals of q

and p_e:

$$(8.2) \qquad \max_i |p(s_i|e) - q(s_i)| \leq \sqrt{\frac{1}{2}D(q, p_e)}$$

(see Whittaker, 1990). The KL-divergence satisfies $D(q, p_e) \geq 0$, and $D(q, p_e) = 0 \Leftrightarrow q = p_e$. Using $p(s|e) = p(s, e)/p(e)$ and substituting the graphical structures for p and q, we can rewrite D as

$$D(q, p_e) = \sum_{\{s\}} q(s) \left(\sum_\gamma \log q(s_\gamma|\pi_\gamma) - \sum_i \log p(s_i|\pi_i) \right) + \text{constant}.$$

(8.3)

Parent sets π_γ and π_i are understood with respect to the probability distribution in which they appear and are in principle distinct. As a consequence of the factorization of $p(s, e)$ into conditionals, the average $\langle \log p(s, e) \rangle_q$ reduces to a sum of local averages $\sum_i \langle \log(p(s_i|\pi_i)) \rangle_q$. This reduces the complexity of computing D from exponential in the size of n to exponential in the size of the conditional probability tables of p and q.

$D(q, p_e)$ depends on the numerical values of the conditional probability tables $q(s_i|\pi_i)$. Setting the gradient of D equal to zero with respect to these parameters yields the equations

$$q(s_i|\pi_i) = \frac{1}{Z_i} \exp \langle \log p(s, e) - \log q(s) \rangle_{q(s|s_i, \pi_i)}$$

$$(8.4) \qquad = \frac{1}{Z_i} \exp \left\langle \sum_k \log p(s_k|\pi_k) - \sum_\gamma \log q(s_\gamma|\pi_\gamma) \right\rangle_{q(s|s_i, \pi_i)},$$

where $\langle \cdot \rangle_{q(s|s_i, \pi_i)}$ denotes the average with respect to q with node i and its parents clamped to s_i and π_i, respectively. Z_i is a normalization factor. Eqs. (8.4) are a coupled set of nonlinear equations that must be solved for $q(s_i|\pi_i)$. For each i, the right hand side of eqs. (8.4) does not depend on the parameters $q(s_i|\pi_i)$. This means that asynchronous iteration of eqs. (8.4) is guaranteed to converge to a local minimum of the KL-divergence.

The quality of the approximation depends strongly on the structure of q. The simplest approach is the so-called (naive) mean field approach, in which the graph of q is completely disconnected, i.e. $q(s) = \prod_i q(s_i)$. Then eqs. (8.4) reduces to the standard mean field equation:

$$q(s_i) = \frac{1}{Z_i} \exp \left\langle \sum_k \log p(s_k|\pi_k) \right\rangle_{q(s|s_i)}.$$

The more complicated approach is to factorize q according to a triangulated graph (Lauritzen and Spiegelhalter, 1988; Castillo et al., 1997) of p. In this case, iteration of eqs. (8.4) leads to the solution $q = p_e$ and $D = 0$. This solution is of interest only theoretically, since its computational complexity is equal to that of the original inference problem. However, it does indicate that the variational structural approach will interpolate between the standard mean field theory and the exact solution. In general one must choose a structure for q that is a reasonable compromise between approximation error and complexity.

The complexity of the variational method is at least exponential in the parent size of the original model p, since it requires the computation of averages of the form $\langle \log p(s_k|\pi_k)\rangle$. This is also true for noisy-OR gates. This means that a computational advantage is obtained if the parent size is much smaller than the clique size of p (Lauritzen and Spiegelhalter, 1988; Castillo et al., 1997). For large parent sets, one can use additional approximations. For instance, for the noisy-OR gates with positive findings, we can use the approximation proposed in Jaakkola (1997):

$$(8.5) \qquad \langle\log(1 - \exp(-z_f))\rangle \approx -\sum_{\kappa=0}^{K} \log(\langle 1 + \exp(-2^{\kappa} z_f)\rangle),$$

which is tractable if q is tractable.

8.1.1 Numerical Results

We illustrate the theory with two toy problems. The first one is inference in the chest clinic model (see Lauritzen and Spiegelhalter, 1988, for more details). We compared exact marginals with approximate marginals using the approximating models shown in figure 8.1. We found that even the fully disconnected mean field approximation is qualitatively correct (maximum error between marginals $p(s_i)$ and $q(s_i)$ is 0.214). Adding structure to the approximating network decreases the error in the approximation to 0.065. We will use the chest clinic model again in section 8.3.3, when we demonstrate the TAP approximation.

In the second toy problem we simulated inference in networks with a structure that is similar to the structure encountered in medical diagnosis, as discussed in section 9.1. We generated models with graphical structure as shown in figure 8.2. The upper node is a mixture node with m mixture components. The next layer consists of $n_d + 1$ binary nodes. These two layers represent prior probabilities and hidden pathophysiological mechanisms. The third layer of n_d binary nodes s_d represents the diseases. Each of these nodes has two parents in the preceding layer. Up to this layer the network is tractable. We refer to this part of the net-

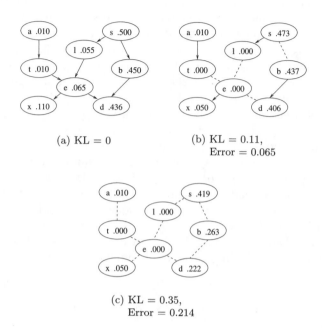

(a) KL = 0

(b) KL = 0.11,
Error = 0.065

(c) KL = 0.35,
Error = 0.214

Figure 8.1. Chest clinic model. Arrows: links in the exact model (a): exact model with marginal probabilities. (b-c): approximating models with approximated marginal probabilities. Arrows indicate the graphical structure of the approximating models. Dashed lines indicate the underlying links in the exact model. KL is the KL-divergence $D(q,p)$ between the approximating model q and the true model p. Error is the maximal absolute difference between the exact and approximate marginals.

work as $\mathcal{N}_1$. Finally, there is a layer of n_f findings s_f. These are modeled as noisy-OR gates, receiving inputs from all the nodes of the preceding disease layer. In the simulations, the findings are all clamped on positive values $s_f = 1$. This makes the network intractable for large n_d and n_f.

We chose $m = 10$, $n_f = n_d$, and varied $n_d = 7,\ldots,13$. Networks of this size are still tractable for exact computation. The values in the entries in the probability tables of $\mathcal{N}_1$ were drawn uniformly at random between zero and one. We computed exact and approximated marginals for the diseases s_d. As approximating models we used the model with structure $\mathcal{N}_1$ (fig 8.2b) and a factorized model (fig 8.2c).

In figure 8.3 we plotted the maximal error $\max_d |q(s_d) - p(s_d|s_f)|$ as a function of the network size. We also plotted the required computer

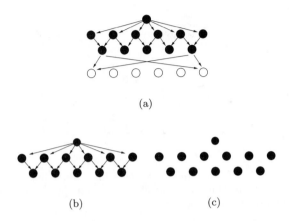

(a)

(b)   (c)

FIGURE 8.2. (a): Graphical structure of artificially generated probability distribution p. Nonevidential nodes are black. White nodes are positive findings. (b) and (c): Graphical structure on the nonevidential nodes of the approximating distributions q.

time for exact and approximate inference as a function of the network size.

We conclude that variational methods using structure significantly improve the quality of approximation, within feasible computer time. In a network with tractable substructures, as can be expected in medical diagnosis, these substructures provide a useful starting point for the approximating model. The choice of optimal structure for Q is a topic for further investigation.

8.2 Boltzmann Machine Learning Using Mean Field Theory and Linear Response Correction

Boltzmann Machines (BMs), discussed in Ackley et al. (1985), are networks of binary neurons with a stochastic neuron dynamics known as Glauber dynamics. Assuming symmetric connections between neurons, the probability distribution over neuron states $\mathbf{s}$ becomes stationary and is given by the Boltzmann-Gibbs distribution $p(\mathbf{s})$. The Boltzmann distribution is a known function of the weights and thresholds of the network. However, computation of $p(\mathbf{s})$ or any statistics involving $p(\mathbf{s})$, such as mean firing rates or correlations, requires exponential time in the number of neurons. This is owing to the fact that $p(\mathbf{s})$ contains a normalization term Z, which involves a sum over all states in the network,

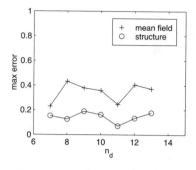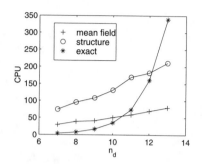

FIGURE 8.3. Left: The maximal error as a function of the network size. Right: CPU-time in Matlab seconds for exact and approximate inference as a function of the network size.

of which there are exponentially many.

The learning problem for the Boltzmann Machine is to estimate the weights and thresholds from data, using gradient ascent on a maximum likelihood scoring function. The gradients are simple analytical expressions, but they involve the computation of the mean firing rates and correlations of the neurons in the network (see eq. (8.8)). Since these quantities are computationally intractable, BM learning is intractable.

When Boltzmann Machines were first proposed as an abstract framework for neural network learning (Ackley et al., 1985), the authors proposed to use a statistical statistical sampling technique (Itzykson and Drouffe, 1989) to overcome issue of intractability. However, the method has rather poor convergence and can be applied only to small networks.

Peterson and Anderson (1987) and Hinton (1989) first proposed to use mean field theory for learning in BMs. More specifically, they computed the mean firing rates approximately using mean field theory and ignoring correlations. It can be shown, however, that such a naive mean field approximation does not work well for learning in general (Kappen and Rodríguez, 1998). Furthermore, we argue that it is rather easy to compute the correlations approximately within the naive mean field approximation using the linear response theorem (Parisi, 1988).

In Saul et al. (1996) and Kappen and Rodríguez (1998), the mean field approximation is derived by making use of the properties of convex functions (Jensen's inequality and tangential bounds). Here, we present an alternative derivation that uses a Legendre transformation and a small coupling expansion (Plefka, 1982). It has the advantage that higher-order contributions (TAP and higher) can be computed systematically.

8.2.1 Boltzmann Machine Learning

The Boltzmann Machine is defined as follows. The possible configurations of the network can be characterized by a vector $\mathbf{s} = (s_1, \ldots, s_i, \ldots, s_n)$, where $s_i = \pm 1$ is the state of the neuron i, and n is the total number of the neurons.

Let us define the energy of a configuration $\mathbf{s}$ as

$$-E(\mathbf{s}) = \frac{1}{2} \sum_{i,j} w_{ij} s_i s_j + \sum_i s_i \theta_i.$$

The probability of finding the network in a state $\mathbf{s}$ is given by the Boltzmann distribution

(8.6)
$$p(\mathbf{s}) = \frac{1}{Z} \exp\{-E(\mathbf{s})\}.$$

$Z = \sum_{\mathbf{s}} \exp\{-E(\mathbf{s})\}$ is the partition function, which normalizes the probability distribution.

The network consists of a visible and a hidden part, $\mathbf{s} = (\mathbf{v}, \mathbf{h})$. Learning consists of adjusting the weights and thresholds in such a way that the Boltzmann distribution approximates a target distribution $q(\mathbf{v})$ as closely as possible on the visible neurons (Ackley et al., 1985). A suitable measure of the difference between the distributions $p(\mathbf{v})$ and $q(\mathbf{v})$ is the Kullback divergence (Kullback, 1959):

(8.7)
$$K = \sum_{\mathbf{v}} q(\mathbf{v}) \log \frac{q(\mathbf{v})}{p(\mathbf{v})}.$$

When $q(\mathbf{v})$ is given in terms of a data set, minimization of K is equivalent to maximization of the log likelihood.

Learning consists of minimizing K using gradient descent (Ackley et al., 1985):

(8.8) $$\Delta w_{ij} = \eta \Big(\langle s_i s_j \rangle_c - \langle s_i s_j \rangle \Big), \quad \Delta \theta_i = \eta \Big(\langle s_i \rangle_c - \langle s_i \rangle \Big).$$

The parameter η is the learning rate. The brackets $\langle \cdot \rangle$ denote the "free" expectation values, i.e. the expectation under the model p:

$$\langle s_i \rangle = \sum_{\mathbf{s}} s_i p(\mathbf{s})$$

and $\langle \cdot \rangle_c$ denote the "clamped" expectation values, where the visible neurons are clamped to the target distribution:

$$\langle s_i \rangle_c = \sum_{\mathbf{v}} \sum_{\mathbf{h}} s_i q(\mathbf{v}) p(\mathbf{h}|\mathbf{v}).$$

The computation of both the free and the clamped expectation values is intractable, because it consists of a sum over all unclamped states.

As a result, the BM learning algorithm cannot be applied to practical problems.

8.2.2 The Mean Field Approximation

We derive the mean field free energy using the small γ expansion as introduced by Plefka (1982). The energy of the network is given by

$$E(s, w, h, \gamma) = \gamma E_{\text{int}} - \sum_i \theta_i s_i$$

$$E_{\text{int}} = -\frac{1}{2} \sum_{ij} w_{ij} s_i s_j$$

for $\gamma = 1$. The free energy is given by

$$F(w, \theta, \gamma) = -\log \sum_s e^{-E(s, w, \theta, \gamma)}$$

and is a function of the independent variables w_{ij}, θ_i and γ. We perform a Legendre transformation on the variables θ_i by introducing $m_i = -\frac{\partial F}{\partial \theta_i}$. The Gibbs free energy

$$G(w, m, \gamma) = F(w, \theta, \gamma) + \sum_i \theta_i m_i$$

is now a function of the independent variables m_i and w_{ij}, and θ_i is given implicitly by $\langle s_i \rangle_\gamma = m_i$. The expectation $\langle \cdot \rangle_\gamma$ is computed with respect to the full model with interaction γ.

We expand

$$G(\gamma) = G(0) + \gamma G'(0) + \frac{1}{2} \gamma^2 G''(0) + \mathcal{O}(\gamma^3).$$

We obtain directly from Plefka (1982):

$$G'(\gamma) = \langle E_{\text{int}} \rangle_\gamma$$

$$G''(\gamma) = \langle E_{\text{int}} \rangle_\gamma^2 - \langle E_{\text{int}}^2 \rangle_\gamma + \left\langle E_{\text{int}} \sum_i \frac{\partial \theta_i}{\partial \gamma} (s_i - m_i) \right\rangle_\gamma.$$

For $\gamma = 0$ the expectation values $\langle \cdot \rangle_\gamma$ become the mean field expectations, which we can compute directly:

$$G(0) = \frac{1}{2} \sum_i \left((1 + m_i) \log \frac{1}{2} (1 + m_i) + (1 - m_i) \log \frac{1}{2} (1 - m_i) \right)$$

$$G'(0) = -\frac{1}{2} \sum_{ij} w_{ij} m_i m_j$$

$$G''(0) = -\frac{1}{2} \sum_{ij} w_{ij}^2 (1 - m_i^2)(1 - m_j^2).$$

Thus

$$G(1) = \frac{1}{2} \sum_i \left((1 + m_i) \log \frac{1}{2}(1 + m_i) + (1 - m_i) \log \frac{1}{2}(1 - m_i) \right)$$

$$- \frac{1}{2} \sum_{ij} w_{ij} m_i m_j$$

(8.9) $$- \frac{1}{4} \sum_{ij} w_{ij}^2 (1 - m_i^2)(1 - m_j^2) + \mathcal{O}(w^3 f(m)),$$

where $f(m)$ is some unknown function of m.

The mean field equations are given by the inverse Legendre transformation

(8.10) $$\theta_i = \frac{\partial G}{\partial m_i} = \tanh^{-1}(m_i) - \sum_j w_{ij} m_j + \sum_j w_{ij}^2 m_i (1 - m_j^2),$$

which we recognize as the mean field equations.

The correlations are given by

$$\langle s_i s_j \rangle - \langle s_i \rangle \langle s_j \rangle = -\frac{\partial^2 F}{\partial \theta_i \partial \theta_j} = \frac{\partial m_i}{\partial \theta_j} = \left(\frac{\partial \theta}{\partial m} \right)_{ij}^{-1} = \left(\frac{\partial^2 G}{\partial m^2} \right)_{ij}^{-1}.$$

We therefore obtain from eq. (8.9):

$$\langle s_i s_j \rangle - \langle s_i \rangle \langle s_j \rangle = A_{ij}$$

with

$$(A^{-1})_{ij} = \delta_{ij} \left(\frac{1}{1 - m_i^2} + \sum_k w_{ik}^2 (1 - m_k^2) \right) - w_{ij} - 2 m_i m_j w_{ij}^2.$$

(8.11)

Thus, for given w_{ij} and θ_i, we obtain the approximate mean firing rates m_i by solving eqs. (8.10) and the correlations by their linear response approximations eqs. (8.11).

The inclusion of hidden units is straightforward. One applies the above approximations in the free and the clamped phase separately (Kappen and Rodríguez, 1998). The complexity of the method is O(n^3), owing to the matrix inversion.

8.2.3 Learning Without Hidden Units

We now assess the accuracy of the above method for networks with no hidden units. Let us define $C_{ij} = \langle s_i s_j \rangle_c - \langle s_i \rangle_c \langle s_j \rangle_c$, which can be computed directly from the data. The fixed point equation for $\Delta \theta_i$ gives

(8.12) $$\Delta \theta_i = 0 \Leftrightarrow m_i = \langle s_i \rangle_c.$$

The fixed point equation for Δw_{ij}, using eq. (8.12), gives

(8.13) $\qquad \Delta w_{ij} = 0 \Leftrightarrow A_{ij} = C_{ij}, i \neq j.$

From eq. (8.13) and eq. (8.11) we can solve for w_{ij}, using a standard least squares method. In our case, we used `fsolve` from Matlab. Subsequently, we obtained θ_i from eq. (8.10). We refer to this method as the *TAP approximation*.

To assess the effect of the TAP term, we also computed the weights and thresholds in the same way as described above, but without the terms of order w^2 in eqs. (8.11) and (8.10). This method is the mean field approximation.

The fixed point equations are imposed only for the off-diagonal elements of Δw_{ij} because the Boltzmann distribution eq. (8.6) does not depend on the diagonal elements w_{ii}. In Kappen and Rodríguez (1998), we explored a variant of the naive mean field approximation where we included diagonal weight terms. As discussed there, if we were to impose eq. (8.13) for $i = j$ as well, we would have $A = C$. If C is invertible, we therefore have $A^{-1} = C^{-1}$. However, we now have more constraints than variables. Therefore, we introduce diagonal weights w_{ii} by adding the term $w_{ii}m_i$ to the right-hand side of eq. (8.10) in the naive mean field approximation. Thus

$$w_{ij} = \frac{\delta_{ij}}{1 - m_i^2} - (C^{-1})_{ij},$$

and θ_i is given by eq. (8.10) in the naive mean field approximation. Clearly, this method is computationally simpler: it gives an explicit expression for the solution of the weights involving only one matrix inversion.

8.2.4 Numerical Results

For the target distribution $q(s)$ in eq. (8.7) we chose a fully connected Ising spin-glass model with equilibrium distribution

$$q(s) = \frac{1}{Z} \exp\{-\frac{1}{2}\sum_{ij} J_{ij}s_i s_j\},$$

with J_{ij} i.i.d. Gaussian variables with mean $\frac{J_0}{n-1}$ and variance $\frac{J^2}{n-1}$. This model is known as the Sherrington-Kirkpatrick (SK) model (Sherrington and Kirkpatrick, 1975). Depending on the values of J and J_0, the model displays a paramagnetic (unordered), ferromagnetic (ordered), and a spin-glass (frustrated) phase. For $J_0 = 0$, the paramagnetic (spin-glass) phase is obtained for $J < 1$ ($J > 1$). We assess the effectiveness of our approximations for finite n, for $J_0 = 0$, and for various values of J. Since this is a realizable task, the optimal KL divergence is zero, which is indeed observed in our simulations.

We measure the quality of the solutions by means of the Kullback divergence. Therefore, this comparison is feasible only for small networks. The reason is that the computation of the Kullback divergence requires the computation of the Boltzmann distribution, eq. (8.6), which requires exponential time owing to the partition function Z.

We present results for a network of $n = 10$ neurons. For $J_0 = 0$, we generated for each value of $0.1 < J < 3$, 10 random weight matrices J_{ij}. For each weight matrix, we computed the $q(\mathbf{s})$ on all 2^n states. For each of the 10 problems, we applied the TAP method, the naive mean field method, and the mean field method with diagonal weights. In addition, we applied the exact Boltzmann Machine learning algorithm using conjugate gradient descent and verified that it gives KL divergence equal to zero, as it should. We also applied a factorized model $p(\mathbf{s}) = \prod_i \frac{1}{2}(1 + m_i s_i)$ with $m_i = \langle s_i \rangle_c$ to assess the importance of correlations in the target distribution. In figure 8.4a, we show for each J the average KL divergence over the 10 problem instances as a function of J for the TAP method, the naive mean field method, the mean field method with diagonal weights, and the factorized model. We observe that the TAP method gives the best results, but that its performance deteriorates in the spin-glass phase ($J > 1$).

Note that the performance of the exact method is absolutely insensitive to the value of J. Naively, one might have thought that for highly multimodal target distributions, any gradient based learning method would suffer from local minima. Apparently, this is not the case: the exact KL divergence has just one minimum, but the mean field approximations of the gradients may have multiple solutions.

8.3 Second-order Approximations for Probability Models

In the previous section, we saw how to derive a TAP approximation for Boltzmann-Gibbs distributions. The method is based on an expansion of free energy. Free energy occurs naturally in Boltzmann-Gibbs distributions and typically does not exist for other distributions. Therefore, for probability distributions that are not Boltzmann-Gibbs distributions, it is not obvious how to obtain the second-order approximation. However, there is an alternative way to compute the higher-order corrections, based on an information-theoretic argument. Recently, this argument was applied to stochastic neural networks with asymmetric connectivity (Kappen and Spanjers, 1999). Here we apply the same idea to directed graphical models (Kappen and Wiegerinck, 2001b).

Let $x = (x_1, \ldots, x_n)$ be an n-dimensional vector, with x_i taking on discrete values. Let $p(x)$ be a directed graphical model on x. We will as-

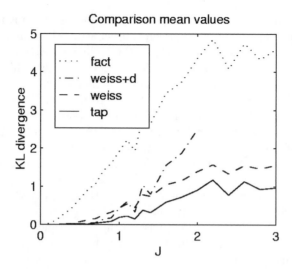

FIGURE 8.4. Mean field learning of paramagnetic ($J < 1$) and spin-glass ($J > 1$) problems for a network of 10 neurons. Comparison of mean KL divergences for the factorized model (fact), the mean field approximation with and without diagonal weights (weiss+d and weiss), and the TAP approximation, as a function of J. The exact method yields zero KL divergence for all J.

sume that $p(x)$ can be written as a product of potentials in the following way:

$$(8.14) \qquad p(x) = \prod_{k=1}^{n} p_k(x_k|\pi_k) = \exp \sum_{k=1}^{n} \phi_k(x^k).$$

Here, $p_k(x_k|\pi_k)$ denotes the conditional probability table of variable x_k given the values of its parents π_k; $x^k = (x_k, \pi_k)$ denotes the subset of variables that appear in potential k and $\phi_k(x^k) = \log p_k(x_k|\pi_k)$. Potentials can overlap, $x^k \cap x^l \neq \emptyset$, and $x = \cup_k x^k$.

We wish to compute the marginal probability that x_i has some specific value s_i in the presence of some evidence. We therefore let $x = (e, s)$, where e denotes the subset of variables that constitute the evidence and s denotes the remainder of the variables. The marginal is given as

$$(8.15) \qquad p(s_i|e) = \frac{p(s_i, e)}{p(e)}.$$

Both numerator and denominator contain sums over hidden states. These sums scale exponentially with the size of the problem, and therefore the computation of marginals is intractable.

We propose to approximate this problem by using a mean field approach. Consider a factorized distribution on the hidden variables s:

$$(8.16) \qquad q(s) = \prod_i q_i(s_i).$$

We wish to find the factorized distribution q that best approximates $p(s|e)$. Consider as a distance measure

$$(8.17) \qquad KL = \sum_s p(s|e) \log \left(\frac{p(s|e)}{q(s)} \right).$$

It is easy to see that the q that minimizes KL satisfies:

$$(8.18) \qquad q(s_i) = p(s_i|e)$$

We now consider the manifold of all probability distributions of the form eq. (8.14), spanned by the coordinates $\phi_k(x^k), k = 1, \ldots, m$. For each k, $\phi_k(x^k)$ is a table of numbers, indexed by x^k. This manifold contains a submanifold of factorized probability distributions in which the potentials factorize: $\phi_k(x^k) = \sum_{i,i \in k} \phi_{ki}(x_i)$. When, in addition, $\sum_{k,i \in k} \phi_{ki}(x_i) = \log q_i(x_i), i \in h$, $p(s|e)$ reduces to $q(s)$.

Assume now that $p(s|e)$ is close to the factorized submanifold. The difference $\Delta p(s_i|e) = p(s_i|e) - q_i(s_i)$ is then small, and we can expand this small difference in terms of changes in the parameters $\Delta \phi_k(x^k) = \phi_k(x^k) - \log q(x^k), k = 1, \ldots, m$:

$$
\begin{aligned}
\Delta \log p(s_i|e) \;=\; & \sum_{k=1}^{n} \sum_{\bar{x}^k} \left(\frac{\partial \log p(s_i|e)}{\partial \phi_k(\bar{x}^k)} \right)_q \Delta \phi_k(\bar{x}^k) \\
& + \frac{1}{2} \sum_{kl} \sum_{\bar{x}^k, \bar{y}^l} \left(\frac{\partial^2 \log p(s_i|e)}{\partial \phi_k(\bar{x}^k) \partial \phi_l(\bar{y}^l)} \right)_q \Delta \phi_k(\bar{x}^k) \Delta \phi_l(\bar{y}^l)
\end{aligned}
$$

$$(8.19) \qquad\qquad\qquad + \text{ higher-order terms.}$$

The differentials are evaluated in the factorized distribution q. The left-hand side of eq. (8.19) is zero because of eq. (8.18). We then solve for $q(s_i)$. This factorized distribution gives the desired marginals up to the order of the expansion of $\Delta \log p(s_i|e)$.

It is straightforward to compute the derivatives:

$$
\frac{\partial \log p(s_i|e)}{\partial \phi_k(\bar{x}^k)} = p(\bar{x}^k|s_i, e) - p(\bar{x}^k|e)
$$

$$
\frac{\partial^2 \log p(s_i|e)}{\partial \phi_k(\bar{x}^k) \partial \phi_l(\bar{y}^l)} = p(\bar{x}^k, \bar{y}^l|s_i, e) - p(\bar{x}^k, \bar{y}^l|e)
$$

$$(8.20) \qquad\qquad - p(\bar{x}^k|s_i, e) p(\bar{y}^l|s_i, e) + p(\bar{x}^k|e) p(\bar{y}^l|e).$$

We introduce the notation $\langle \ldots \rangle_{s_i}$ and $\langle \ldots \rangle$ as the expectation values for the factorized distributions $q(x|s_i, e)$ and $q(x|e)$, respectively. We define $\langle\langle \ldots \rangle\rangle_{s_i} \equiv \langle \ldots \rangle_{s_i} - \langle \ldots \rangle$. We obtain

$$
\begin{aligned}
\Delta \log p(s_i|e) &= \sum_k \langle\langle \Delta\phi_k \rangle\rangle_{s_i} + \frac{1}{2} \sum_{k,l} (\langle\langle \Delta\phi_k \Delta\phi_l \rangle\rangle_{s_i} \\
&\quad - \langle \Delta\phi_k \rangle_{s_i} \langle \Delta\phi_l \rangle_{s_i} + \langle \Delta\phi_k \rangle \langle \Delta\phi_l \rangle) \\
&\quad + \text{higher-order terms.}
\end{aligned}
$$
(8.21)

To the first order, setting eq. (8.21) equal to zero, we obtain

$$
(8.22) \qquad 0 = \sum_k \langle\langle \Delta\phi_k \rangle\rangle_{s_i} = \langle \log p(x) \rangle_{s_i} - \log q(s_i) + \text{const.},
$$

where we have absorbed all terms independent of i into a constant. Thus we arrive at the solution

$$
(8.23) \qquad q(s_i) = \frac{1}{Z_i} \exp\left(\langle \log p(x) \rangle_{s_i} \right)
$$

in which the constants Z_i follow from normalization. The first-order term is equivalent to the standard mean field equations, obtained from Jensen's inequality.

The correction with second-order terms is obtained in the same way, again dropping terms independent of i:

$$
\begin{aligned}
q(s_i) &= \frac{1}{Z_i} \exp\left(\langle \log p(x) \rangle_{s_i} \right. \\
&\qquad \left. + \frac{1}{2} \sum_{k,l} \left(\langle \Delta\phi_k \Delta\phi_l \rangle_{s_i} - \langle \Delta\phi_k \rangle_{s_i} \langle \Delta\phi_l \rangle_{s_i} \right) \right)
\end{aligned}
$$
(8.24)

where, again, the constants Z_i follow from normalization. These equations, which form our main result, are a generalization of the mean field equations with TAP corrections for directed graphical models. Both the left- and right-hand sides of eqs. (8.23) and (8.24) depend on the unknown probability distribution $q(s)$ and can be solved by fixed point iteration.

8.3.1 Complexity and Single-overlap Graphs

The complexity of the first-order equations eq. (8.23) is exponential in the number of variables in the potentials ϕ_k of P: if the maximal clique size is c, then for each i we need of the order of $n_i \exp(c)$ computations, where n_i is the number of cliques that contain node i.

The second term scales worse, because we must compute averages over the union of two overlapping cliques and also because of the double sum. However, the situation is not so bad. First of all, notice that the sum over k and l can be restricted to overlapping cliques $(k \cap l \neq \emptyset)$ and that i must be in either k or l or both $(i \in k \cup l)$. Denote by n^k the number of cliques that have at least one variable in common with clique k and that denote by $n_{\text{overlap}} = \max_k n_k$. Then, the sum over k and l contains no more than $n_i n_{\text{overlap}}$ terms.

Each term is an average over the union of two cliques, which can be in the worst case of size $2c-1$ (when only one variable is shared). However, since $\langle \Delta\phi_k \Delta\phi_l \rangle_{s_i} = \langle\langle \Delta\phi_k \rangle_{k \cap l} \Delta\phi_l \rangle_{s_i}$ ($\langle \cdot \rangle_{k \cap l}$ means expectation wrt q conditioned on the variables in $k \cap l$), we can precompute $\langle \Delta\phi_k \rangle_{k \cap l}$ for all pairs of overlapping cliques k, l, for all states in $k \cap l$. Therefore, the worst-case complexity of the second-order term is less than $n_i n_{\text{overlap}} \exp(c)$. Thus we see that the second-order method has the same exponential complexity as the first-order method, but with a different polynomial prefactor. Therefore, the first- or second-order method can be applied to directed graphical models as long as the number of parents is reasonably small.

The fact that the second-order term has a higher complexity than the first-order term is in contrast to Boltzmann Machines, in which the TAP approximation has the same complexity as the standard mean field approximation. This phenomenon also occurs for a special class of DAGs, which we call *single-overlap graphs*. These are graphs in which the potentials ϕ_k share at most one node. Figure 8.5 shows an example of a single-overlap graph.

For single overlap graphs, we can use the first-order result eq. (8.22) to simplify the second-order correction. The derivation is rather tedious so we just present the result:

$$
q(s_i) = \frac{1}{Z_i} \exp\left(\langle \log p(x) \rangle_{s_i} + \frac{1}{2} \sum_{l, i \in l} \left(\langle (\Delta\phi_l)^2 \rangle_{s_i} - \langle \Delta\phi_l \rangle_{s_i}^2 \right) \right.
$$

$$
(8.25) \qquad \left. - \sum_{l, i \in l} \sum_{j \neq i} \langle \langle\langle \Delta\phi_l \rangle\rangle_{s_j} \Delta\phi_l \rangle_{s_i} \right),
$$

which has a complexity of order $n_i(c-1) \exp(c)$. For probability distributions with many small potentials that share nodes with many other potentials, eq. (8.25) is more efficient than eq. (8.24). For instance, for Boltzmann Machines $n_i = n_{\text{overlap}} = n - 1$ and $c = 2$. In this case, eq. (8.25) is identical to the TAP equations (Thouless et al., 1977).

8.3.2 Sigmoid Belief Networks

In this section, we consider sigmoid belief networks as an interesting class of directed graphical models. In these networks one can expand in terms of the couplings instead of the potentials, which is more efficient.

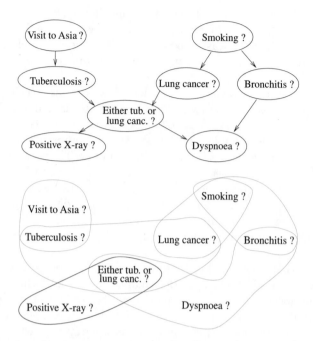

FIGURE 8.5. An example of a single-overlap graph. Upper: The chest clinic model (ASIA) (Lauritzen and Spiegelhalter, 1988). Lower: Nodes within one potential are grouped together, showing that potentials share at most one node.

The sigmoid belief network is defined as

$$(8.26) \qquad p(x) = \prod_i \sigma(x_i h_i),$$

where $\sigma(x) = (1 + \exp(-2x))^{-1}$, $x_i = \pm 1$ and h_i is the local field: $h_i(x) = \sum_{j=1}^n w_{ij} x_j + \theta_i$.

We separate the variables into evidence variables e and hidden variables s: $x = (s, e)$. When couplings from hidden nodes to either hidden or evidence nodes are equal to zero, $w_{ij} = 0$, $i \in e, s$, and $j \in s$, the probability distributions $p(s|e)$ and $p(e)$ reduce to

$$(8.27) \qquad p(s|e) \quad \rightarrow \quad q(s) = \prod_{i \in s} \sigma\left(s_i \theta_i^q\right)$$

$$(8.28) \qquad p(e) \quad \rightarrow \quad r(e) = \prod_{i \in e} \sigma\left(e_i \theta_i^q\right),$$

where $\theta_i^q = \sum_{j \in e} w_{ij} e_j + \theta_i$ depends on the evidence.

We expand to the second-order around this tractable distribution and obtain

$$
\begin{aligned}
m_i \;=\; \tanh\Bigg(& \sum_{k\in s,e} m_j w_{ik} + \theta_i + 2\sum_{k\in e} r(-e_k)e_k w_{ki} \\
& - m_i \sum_{k\in s}(1 - m_k^2)w_{ik}^2 + 4m_i \sum_{k\in e} r(e_k)r(-e_k)w_{ki}^2 \\
& - 4 \sum_{k\in e, l\in s} r(e_k)r(-e_k)m_l w_{kl} w_{ki} \\
& + 2 \sum_{k\in s, l\in e} (1 - m_k^2)r(-e_l)e_l w_{lk} w_{ki} \Bigg)
\end{aligned}
$$

(8.29)

where $m_i = \langle s_i \rangle_q \approx \langle s_i \rangle_p$ and r is given by eq. (8.28).

The terms that appear in this equation can be interpreted easily. The first term describes the lowest-order forward influence on node i from its parents. Parents can be either evidence or hidden nodes (fig. 8.6a). The second term is the bias θ_i. The third term describes to the lowest-order the effect of Bayes's rule: it affects m_i such that the observed evidence on its children becomes most probable (fig. 8.6b). Note that this term is absent when the evidence is explained by the evidence nodes themselves: $r(e_k) = 1$. The fourth and fifth terms are the quadratic contributions to the first and third terms, respectively. The sixth term describes "explaining away." It describes the effect of hidden node l on node i, when both have a common observed child k (fig. 8.6c). The last term describes the effect on node i when its grandchild is observed (fig. 8.6d).

Note that these equations are different from eq. (8.23). Applying eq. (8.23) to sigmoid belief networks requires additional approximations to compute $\langle \log \sigma(x_i h_i) \rangle$ (Saul et al., 1996).

Since only feed-forward connections are present, we can order the nodes such that $w_{ij} = 0$ for $i < j$. Then the first-order mean field equations can be solved in one single sweep starting with node 1. The full second-order equations can be solved by iteration, starting with the first-order solution.

8.3.3 Numerical Results

We illustrate the theory with two toy problems. The first one is the chest clinic model, also used in section 8.1.1. We computed exact marginals and approximate marginals using the approximating methods up to the first (eq. 8.23) and second-order (eq. 8.24), respectively. The approximate marginals are determined by sequential iteration of (8.23) and

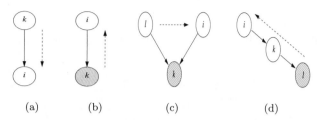

FIGURE 8.6. Interpretation of different interaction terms appearing in eq. (8.29). The open and shaded nodes are hidden and evidence nodes, respectively (except in (a), where k can be any node). Solid arrows indicate the graphical structure in the network. Dashed arrows indicate interaction terms that appear in eq. (8.29).

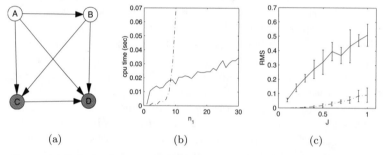

FIGURE 8.7. Second-order approximation for fully connected sigmoid belief network of n nodes. (a) Nodes $1, \ldots, n_1$ are hidden (white) and nodes $n_1 + 1, \ldots, n$ are clamped (grey), $n_1 = n/2$; (b) CPU time for exact inference (dashed) and second-order approximation (solid) versus n_1 ($J = 0.5$); (c) RMS of hidden node exact marginals (solid) and RMS error of second-order approximation (dashed) versus coupling strength J ($n_1 = 10$).

(8.24), starting at $q(x_i) = 0.5$ for all variables i. The maximal error in the marginals using the first- and second-order method is 0.214 and 0.065, respectively. We verified that the single-overlap expression eq. (8.25) gives similar results.

In figure 8.7, we assess the accuracy and CPU time of the second-order approximation eq. (8.29) for sigmoid belief networks. We generate random fully connected sigmoid belief networks with w_{ij} from a normal distribution with mean zero and variance J^2/n and $\theta_i = 0$. We observe in figure 8.7b that the computation time is very fast: For $n_1 = 500$,

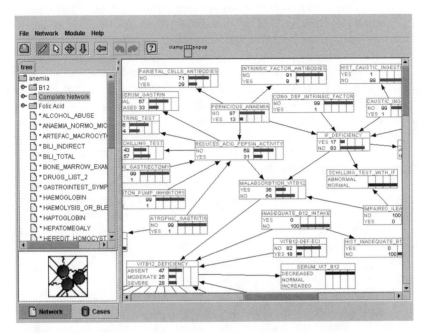

FIGURE 8.8. BayesBuilder graphical software for construction of Bayesian networks and for efficient computation can be downloaded from http://www.mbfys.kun.nl/snn/Research/bayesbuilder. The figure shows a small part of a model for medical diagnosis. Nodes represent variables and arrows represent conditional dependencies. The histograms show the (marginalized) probabilities of the variables and the externally provided values (clamped nodes). Computation is intractable in such networks. Our approximate methods allow these models to be applied to practical problems.

we obtain convergence in 37 seconds on a Pentium 300 Mhz processor. The accuracy of the method depends on the size of the weights and is computed for a network of $n_1 = 10$ (fig. 8.7c). In Kappen and Wiegerinck (2001a), we compare this approach to Saul's variational approach (Saul et al., 1996) and show that our approach is much faster and slightly more accurate.

8.4 Discussion

We have introduced the problem of intractable inference in probability models. We have described a first method that can formulate approximate inference as a variational problem from which one can obtain the approximate marginal probabilities. The simplest approximation is obtained by using a factorized distribution, in which case the naive mean field result is reproduced. One can extend the variational approximation by using a more complex approximating distribution, such as a tree structure, as long as the structure allows for tractable computation.

Subsequently, we have shown that the variational method can be seen as the first-order term in a Taylor series expansion in terms of "couplings" between variables. This expansion can in principle be computed to an arbitrary order. We computed the second-order mean field approximation for the special case of the Boltzmann distributions as well as for directed graphical models. We showed that the second-order approximation is a significant improvement over the first-order result.

Our numerical experiments on the Asia problem show that the naive mean field approximation (which is identical to the factorized variational approximation) is qualitatively correct in the sense that it correctly estimates whether probabilities are high or low. However, the numerical errors can be rather large.

Using the variational approximations with structure or using the TAP approximation results in significant improvements. On the chest clinic model, both extensions yield similar improvements. Our results seem to indicate that this improvement is independent of the problem size.

Some of the above methods have been implemented in our public domain software BayesBuilder (see fig. 8.8), which is freely available for noncommercial use.

9 Medical Diagnosis

Health care will change profoundly with the introduction of clinical diagnostic decision support systems (DSSs), preferably integrated with electronic patient data together with on-line computer communication (Reisman, 1996). However, such systems have not yet entered daily clinical practice for a variety of reasons (Brigl et al., 1998). Some of the reasons are the lack of adequate computer infrastructure in hospitals, the lack of standardized terminology, and the poor performance of current medical diagnostic systems. In this paper we focus on this last issue.

Diagnostic reasoning in the medical domain is a typical example of reasoning with uncertainty. This uncertainty has several sources: missing patient information, uncertainty in medical tests results or observations, and uncertainty about the physiological processes involved. A model on which a DSS is based should be able to deal with these uncertainties. The different systems that have been developed so far use a variety of modeling approaches that can be divided roughly into two categories: rule-based approaches and probabilistic approaches. The large systems, which attempt to cover the whole of internal medicine, use a rule-based approach that relies on some heuristic method to quantify the uncertainty. These methods perform poorly in practice (Berner et al., 1994, 1996), mainly because they model the relations between diseases and findings at a very coarse level. Therefore, the diagnoses suggested by these systems are too superficial for clinical use. Moreover, the diagnostic process requires reasoning from causes to effects (diseases → finding) and vice versa simultaneously. The rule-based approach, together with the heuristics for uncertainty, is not well suited for such bidirectional reasoning.

Smaller systems typically use the probabilistic approach. The probabilistic approach has the important advantage of mathematical consistency and correctness. In particular, Bayesian networks (see e.g. Lauritzen and Spiegelhalter, 1988; Pearl, 1988; Castillo et al., 1997) provide a powerful and conceptual transparent formalism for probabilistic modeling. In addition, they allow for easy integration of domain knowledge and learning from data. Systems based on detailed modeling have been restricted to a relatively small domain (Heckerman et al., 1992; Heckerman and Nathwani, 1992). The reason for this restriction is that Bayesian networks become intractable for exact computation when modeling a large medical domain in detail. To proceed one must therefore rely on *approximate* computations, such as Monte Carlo sampling or mean field approximations. See section 8 for an introduction to these methods.

Although the formalism of Bayesian networks is very powerful, the construction of networks for medical diagnosis is not straightforward. A learning approach depends crucially on the availability of high-quality patient data. In particular, rare disorders should be well covered. In general, unfortunately, this is rather the exception than the rule (Wiegerinck et al., 1997). Therefore, reaching a successful diagnostic DSS requires explicit modeling effort by human experts. The existing medical literature is not sufficient to define the probabilistic model. Not all probabilistic relations between variables have been documented. But existing literature provides a useful starting point for model design. Once a minimal performance is thus obtained, the model can be improved by learning from patient data.

9.1 Probabilistic Modeling in the Medical Domain

We here outline the typical structure of a broad and detailed Bayesian network. This is based on an extrapolation of our current modeling experiences. Details of the medical domain are beyond the scope of this paper and are discussed elsewhere (ter Burg et al., 1999).

The variables to consider in the network are of different types. There are diseases variables, which are typically of the binary type, signaling whether a disease is present or not. The findings encode the results from laboratory measurements, physical examinations, and so on. As a simplification, these variables are discretized, with medically relevant cut-off points. In practice, such discretization does not lead to significant loss of information. In addition, there are prior variables that describe the patient, such as sex and age.

In constructing the graph for the Bayesian network, human experts use mostly "causal" relationships between variables as a guideline (the arrows in fig. 9.1). Often, the expert can relate (large numbers of) variables via additional hidden variables. These hidden variables may represent pathophysiological variables that are known to have certain relations to the observable variables, but which are themselves not accessible during clinical investigation. Often, the use of hidden variables results in a simplified and more transparent network.

The majority of probabilistic relations between the variables involve only a small number of parents. Consequently, modeling using explicit probability tables is feasible. These are estimated on the basis of data in the literature, or on "educated guesses" based on local statistics or experience if no data from the literature are available.

Medical experts tend to divide knowledge concerning a medical domain into subdomains with relatively small overlap. Therefore, the network will typically have a modular structure (see fig. 9.1). Each module represents a disease with its relevant findings. In practice, the modules are rather small, containing between twenty and fifty variables. The modules are connected via shared variables (e.g. pathophysiological variables that are relevant in different modules), common prior nodes, and/or common findings nodes. The computational complexity of the network $\mathcal{N}_1$ consisting of the modules and their parents (black nodes in fig. 9.1) can be assumed to be tractable.

The probabilistic relations for the findings require somewhat more care. For example, "hemoglobin level" (Hb) is a variable whose value is affected by many diseases. Such nodes may have parents in many subdomains. This makes the use of a conditional probability table infeasible, as the size of the table grows exponentially in the number of parents. Fortunately, this is not necessary, since medical experts are likely to agree with a "sum of univariate relations" between this finding and its parents. This can be modeled by a noisy-OR gate (Pearl, 1988). Assuming binary variables for convenience, the noisy-OR gate for finding $f = 0, 1$

given its parents $S_k = 0, 1, k = 1, \ldots, n_f$ is

(9.1)
$$p(f = 0|S_1, \ldots, S_{n_f}) = \exp(-z_f),$$

where $z_f \equiv \sum_k^{n_f} \theta_{fk} S_k + \theta_{f0}$, with parameters satisfying $0 < \theta_{fk} < \infty$. The total model on all variables is given as $p(S_1, \ldots, S_n) = \prod_k^n p(S_k|\pi_k)$, where the conditional probability distributions are either tables or noisy-ORs. π_k denotes the state of the parent nodes of node k. Thus, if node k has n_k parents, π_k can take on 2^{n_k} values.

Even though the findings are modeled in a compact way, instantiated findings are likely to cause computational problems in inference. Let $\{f_{+,-}\}$ denote the subset of instantiated positive and negative findings, respectively. The marginal probability of the findings is

$$\sum_{\{S_H\}} p(S_H, S_{\{f_+\}} = 1, S_{\{f_-\}} = 0)$$

(9.2)
$$= \sum_{\{S_H\}} \prod_k p(S_k|\pi_k) \prod_{f_+} (1 - \exp z_{f_+}) \prod_{f_-} \exp z_{f_-},$$

where S_H is the set of states of the remaining nodes in $\mathcal{N}_1$. As a result of the linearity of z_f in S_k, $\exp z_{f_-}$ factorizes as a product over parent states. Thus the negative findings can be absorbed in $\mathcal{N}_1$ via the transformation $P \rightarrow R$, where $R(S_k|\pi_k) = \exp(-\theta_{fk} S_k) p(S_k|\pi_k)$ $(k \in \mathcal{N}_1)$. These terms can be summed efficiently in linear time. This is not possible with positive findings. Therefore the computational costs will grow exponentially in the number of positive findings f_+ (Jaakkola and Jordan, 1997; Jaakkola, 1997), and the total network will be intractable.

9.2 Promedas, a Demonstration DSS

Promedas (PRObabilistic MEdical Diagnostic Advisory System)[1] is a DSS we are developing for the problem of anemia. The aim is to use Promedas to assess the usefulness of approximate methods for a DSS in practice. The problem domain, anemia, is chosen because we expect that the computational problems described in the previous sections will be encountered in this domain. For instance, anemia can be subdivided in a large number of subdomains, each of which share a large number of findings. Furthermore, anemia is a common medical problem. This facilitates evaluation in practice. To cover the domain completely, we expect that approximately 1000 nodes are needed. To develop Promedas, we will use our internally developed software environment, called BayesBuilder. BayesBuilder has graphical tools for network construction, evaluation, and maintenance. So far, Promedas covers megaloblastic anemia. It is

---

[1]A demonstration version of Promedas is available on CD-ROM. See www.mbfys.kun.nl/snn/Research/promedas

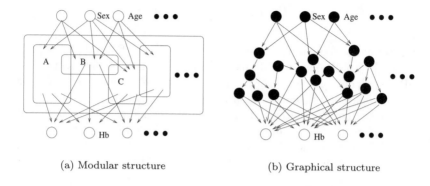

(a) Modular structure   (b) Graphical structure

FIGURE 9.1. Modular and graphical network structure. Left: modular structure of the network. A, B, C, ... represent (overlapping) subdomains. Each subdomain is modeled by a number of nodes (see right figure) representing variables that are relevant in that domain. The upper nodes, e.g. "sex" and "age" represent common ancestors of nodes in several subdomains. The lower nodes, e.g. "Hb" represent common children of nodes in several subdomains (e.g. related to anemia). Right: underlying bipartite graphical structure of same network. Filled circles: nodes in subdomains and their common ancestors. Open circles: common children.

currently based on a network of 91 variables and is still tractable for exact algorithms.

Promedas consists of a graphical user interface (GUI) to enter patient data and for diagnostic consultation. It provides a differential diagnosis, i.e. the probabilities of potentially relevant diagnoses and the probabilities of potentially involved underlying mechanisms (e.g. pathophysiology) as percentages (ranked in descending order). These probabilities are computed on the basis of the available findings entered into the system. In addition, Promedas computes which additional tests it expects to be most informative when deciding on a diagnosis, specified by the user. This information is computed given the values of the variables previously entered and is defined as

$$I(D, T) = \sum_{D,T} p(D, T) \ln(p(D, T)/p(D)p(T)),$$

with $p(D, T)$ the joint probability of diagnosis and test result, and $p(D)$ and $p(T)$ the marginal probabilities of diagnoses and tests, respectively. These probabilities are computed by marginalizing over all the missing

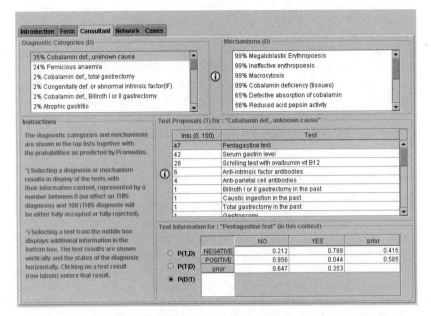

FIGURE 9.2. Results of the decision support of Promedas. After an initial visit, a small number of patient findings are entered into the system. Promedas displays the most likely diagnoses. After selecting "Cobalamin deficiency due to unknown cause," Promedas computes the expected information for all unknown tests. It finds that "Pentagastine test" is expected to be most informative to rule in or out the selected diagnosis. When selecting this test, the probability table of the diagnosis (d) given the possible test outcomes (t) is displayed, as well as the probability of each of the test outcomes. All this information is computed in the context of the particular patient information that is entered into the system.

variables in the network and are conditioned on the evidence present. The information is normalized between 0 and 100 and displayed in descending order (see fig. 9.2). In addition, Promedas provides helpful information, medical background information, and pointers to the literature.

9.3 Discussion

The development of a DSS for comprehensive medical diagnosis in internal medicine represents a great challenge for AI. A broad and detailed probabilistic network is intractable for exact inferences in this context. It is currently unknown whether variational or other approximate methods are sufficiently powerful to provide a practical solution. The "quality of approximation" is to a large extent a user-defined (medical) issue, since (1) comparison with exact inference is not possible owing to the size of the networks and (2) errors in the approximation will be judged as acceptable not just on the basis of their numerical values but, more important, on the basis of their medical implications. The only way to assess the usefulness of approximate methods for modeling medical domains is by actually building such a system and having users evaluate it. The Promedas model must be extended to several hundred variables in order to be able to address this issue properly.

10 Automatic Music Transcription

An important and interesting subtask in automatic music transcription is tempo tracking: how to follow the tempo in a performance that contains expressive timing and tempo variations. When these tempo fluctuations are identified correctly it becomes much easier to separate the continuous expressive timing from the discrete note categories (i.e. quantization). The sense of tempo seems to be carried by the beats and thus tempo tracking is related to the study of beat induction, i.e. the perception of beats or pulse while listening to music (see Desain and Honing, 1994). However, it is still unclear what precisely constitutes tempo and how it relates to the perception of rhythmical structure. Tempo is a perceptual construct and cannot be measured directly in a performance.

There is a significant body of research on the psychological and computational modeling aspects of tempo tracking. Early work by Michon (1967) describes a systematic study on the modeling of human behavior in tracking tempo fluctuations in artificially constructed stimuli. Longuet-Higgins (1976) proposes a musical parser that produces a metrical interpretation of performed music while tracking tempo changes. Knowledge about meter helps the tempo tracker to quantize a performance.

Desain and Honing (1991) describe a connectionist model of quantization, a relaxation network based on the principle of steering adjacent time intervals toward integer multiples. Here as well, a tempo tracker helps the listener to arrive at a correct rhythmical interpretation of a performance. Neither model, however, has been tested systematically on empirical data. Still, quantizers can play a important role in addressing the difficult problem of what is a correct tempo interpretation by defining it as the one that results in a simpler quantization (Cemgil et al., 2000).

Large and Jones (1999) describe an empirical study on tempo tracking, interpreting the observed human behavior in terms of an oscillator model. A peculiar characteristic of this model is that it is insensitive (or becomes so after enough evidence is gathered) to material in between expected beats, suggesting that the perception of tempo change is indifferent to events in this interval. Toiviainen (1999) discusses some problems regarding phase adaptation.

Another class of models makes use of prior knowledge in the form of an annotated score (Dannenberg, 1984; Vercoe, 1984; Vercoe and Puckette, 1985). These models match the known score to incoming performance data. Vercoe and Puckette (1985) use a statistical learning algorithm to train the system with multiple performances. Even with this information at hand tempo tracking stays a nontrivial problem.

More recently, attempts have been made to deal directly with the audio signal (Goto and Muraoka, 1998; Scheirer, 1998) without using any prior knowledge. However, these models assume constant tempo (albeit timing fluctuations may be present), and thus are in fact not tempo trackers but beat trackers. Although successful for music with a steady beat (e.g. popular music), they have problems with syncopated data (e.g. reggae or jazz music).

All tempo-tracking models assume an initial tempo (or beat length) as known in order to begin the tempo-tracking process (e.g. Longuet-Higgins, 1976; Large and Jones, 1999). There is little research addressing how to arrive at a reasonable first estimate. Longuet-Higgins and Lee (1982) propose a model based on score data, and Scheirer (1998) proposes one for audio data. A complete model should incorporate both aspects.

In this paper we formulate a tempo-tracking model in a probabilistic framework, modeling the tempo tracker as a stochastic dynamical system. The tempo is modeled as a hidden state variable of the system and is estimated by Kalman filtering. The Kalman filter operates on a multiscale representation of a real performance. We call the filter a *tempogram*. In this respect the tempogram is analogous to a wavelet transform (Rioul and Vetterli, 1991). In the context of tempo tracking, wavelet analysis and related techniques have already been investigated by various researchers (Smith, 1999; Todd, 1994). A similar comb filter basis is used by Scheirer (1998). The tempogram is also related to the periodicity transform proposed by Sethares and Staley (1999) but uses a time-localized basis. Kalman filters have already been applied in the music domain, for example in polyphonic pitch tracking (Sterian, 1999) and audio restoration (Godsill and Rayner, 1998). From the modeling point of view, the framework discussed in this paper also bears some resemblance to the work of Sterian (1999), who views transcription as a model-based segmentation of a time-frequency image.

The outline of the paper is as follows: We first consider the problem of tapping along a "noisy" metronome and introduce the Kalman filter and its extensions. Subsequently, we introduce the tempogram representation to extract beats from performances and we discuss the probabilistic interpretation. We then discuss issues of parameter estimation from data. Finally, we report simulation results of the system on a systematically collected data set, solo piano performances of two Beatles songs, "Yesterday" and "Michelle."

10.1 Dynamical Systems and the Kalman Filter

Mathematically, a dynamical system is characterized by a set of *state variables* and a set of *state transition equations* that describe how state variables evolve over time. For example, a perfect metronome can be described as a dynamical system with two state variables: a beat $\hat{\tau}$ and a period $\hat{\Delta}$. Given the values of the state variables at the $j-1$'th step as $\hat{\tau}_{j-1}$ and $\hat{\Delta}_{j-1}$, the next beat occurs at $\hat{\tau}_j = \hat{\tau}_{j-1} + \hat{\Delta}_{j-1}$. The period of a perfect metronome is constant so $\hat{\Delta}_j = \hat{\Delta}_{j-1}$. By using vector notation and by letting $\mathbf{s}_j = [\hat{\tau}_j, \hat{\Delta}_j]^T$ we can write a linear state transition model as

$$(10.1) \qquad \mathbf{s}_j = \begin{pmatrix} 1 & 1 \\ 0 & 1 \end{pmatrix} \mathbf{s}_{j-1} = \mathbf{A}\mathbf{s}_{j-1}.$$

When the initial state $\mathbf{s}_0 = [\hat{\tau}_0, \hat{\Delta}_0]^T$ is given, the system is fully specified. For example, if the metronome clicks at a tempo of 60 beats per minute ($\hat{\Delta}_0 = 1$ sec.) and the first click occurs at time $\hat{\tau}_0 = 0$ sec., the next beats occur at $\hat{\tau}_1 = 1$, $\hat{\tau}_2 = 2$, and so on. Since the metronome is perfect, the period stays constant.

Such a deterministic model is not realistic for natural music performance, as it cannot be used for tracking the tempo in presence of tempo fluctuations and expressive timing deviations. Tempo fluctuations may be modeled by introducing a noise term that "corrupts" the state vector

$$(10.2) \qquad \mathbf{s}_j = \mathbf{A}\mathbf{s}_{j-1} + \mathbf{v}_j,$$

where $\mathbf{v}$ is a Gaussian random vector with mean 0 and diagonal covariance matrix $\mathbf{Q}$, i.e. $\mathbf{v} \sim \mathcal{N}(0, \mathbf{Q})$.[2] The tempo will drift from the initial tempo quickly if the variance of $\mathbf{v}$ is large. When $\mathbf{Q} \to 0$, we have the constant tempo case.

---

[2] A random vector $\mathbf{x}$ is said to be Gaussian with mean μ and covariance matrix $\mathbf{P}$ if it has the probability density

$$p(\mathbf{x}) = |2\pi\mathbf{P}|^{-1/2} \exp -\frac{1}{2}(x - \mu)^T \mathbf{P}^{-1}(x - \mu).$$

In this case we write $\mathbf{x} \sim \mathcal{N}(\mu, \mathbf{P})$.

In a musical performance, the actual beat $\hat{\tau}$ and the period $\hat{\Delta}$ cannot be observed directly. By "actual beat" we mean the beat interpretation that coincides with human perception when listening to music. For example, suppose an expert drummer is tapping along with a performance at the beat level and we assume her beats as the correct tempo track. If the task were repeated on the same piece, we would observe a slightly different tempo track. As an alternative, suppose we know the score of the performance and can identify onsets that coincide with the beat. However, owing to small-scale expressive timing deviations, these onsets will also be noisy, i.e. we can at best observe "noisy" versions of actual beats. We will denote this noisy beat by τ in contrast with the actual but unobservable beat $\hat{\tau}$. Mathematically we have

$$(10.3) \qquad \tau_j \;=\; \hat{\tau}_j + \mathbf{w}_j,$$

where $\mathbf{w}_j \sim \mathcal{N}(0, \mathbf{R})$. Here, τ_j is the beat at step j that we get from a (noisy) observation process. In this formulation, tempo tracking corresponds to the estimation of hidden variables $\hat{\tau}_j$ given observations up to the jth step. We note that in a "blind" tempo tracking task, i.e. when the score is not known, the (noisy) beat τ_j cannot be observed directly since there is no expert drummer tapping along and no score to guide us. The noisy beat itself has to be *induced* from events in the music. In the next section we will present a technique to estimate both a noisy beat τ_j as well a noisy period Δ_j from a real performance.

Equations (10.2) and (10.3) define a *linear dynamical system*, because all noises are assumed to be Gaussian and all relationships between variables are linear. Hence all state vectors $\mathbf{s}_j$ have Gaussian distributions. A Gaussian distribution is characterized fully by its mean and covariance matrix, and in the context of linear dynamical systems, these quantities can be estimated efficiently by a *Kalman filter* (Kalman, 1960; Roweis and Ghahramani, 1999). The operation of the filter is illustrated in figure 10.1.

10.1.1 Extensions

The basic model can be extended in several directions. First, we can relax the linearity constraint on the Kalman filter. Indeed, in tempo tracking such an extension is necessary to ensure that the period $\hat{\Delta}$ is always positive. Therefore we define the state transition model in a warped space defined by the mapping $\omega = \log_2 \Delta$. This warping also ensures the perceptually more plausible assumption that tempo changes are relative rather than absolute. For example, under this warping, a deceleration from $\Delta \to 2\Delta$ has the same likelihood as an acceleration from $\Delta \to \Delta/2$.

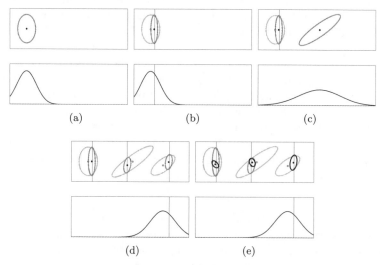

Figure 10.1. Operation of the Kalman filter and smoother. The system is given by equations (10.2) and (10.3). In each subfigure, the above coordinate system represents the hidden state space $[\hat{\tau}, \hat{\Delta}]^T$ and the below coordinate system represents the observable space τ. In the hidden space, the x and y axes represent the phase $\hat{\tau}$ period $\hat{\Delta}$ of the tracker. The ellipse and its center correspond to the covariance and the mean of the hidden state estimate $p(\mathbf{s}_j|\tau_1, \ldots, \tau_k) = \mathcal{N}(\mu_{j|k}, P_{j|k})$ where $\mu_{j|k}$ and $P_{j|k}$ denote the estimated mean and covariance given observations $\tau_1, \ldots, \tau_k$. In the observable space, the vertical axis represents the predictive probability distribution $p(\tau_j|\tau_{j-1}, \ldots, \tau_1)$. (a) The algorithm starts with the initial state estimate $\mathcal{N}(\mu_{1|0}, P_{1|0})$. In presence of no evidence this state estimate gives rise to a prediction in the observable τ space. (b) The beat is observed at τ_1, The state is updated to $\mathcal{N}(\mu_{1|1}, P_{1|1})$ according to the new evidence. Note that the uncertainty "shrinks." (c) On the basis of current state a new prediction $\mathcal{N}(\mu_{2|1}, P_{2|1})$ is made. (d) Steps are repeated until all evidence is processed to obtain filtered estimates $\mathcal{N}(\mu_{j|j}, P_{j|j})$, $j = 1, \ldots, N$. In this case $N = 3$. (e) Filtered estimates are updated by backtracking to obtain smoothed estimates $\mathcal{N}(\mu_{i|N}, P_{i|N})$ (Kalman smoothing).

The state space $\mathbf{s}_j$ can be extended with additional dynamic variables $\hat{\mathbf{a}}_j$. Such additional variables store information about the past states (e.g. in terms of acceleration) and introduce inertia to the system. Inertia reduces the random walk behavior in the state space and renders smooth state trajectories more likely. Moreover, this can result in more accurate predictions.

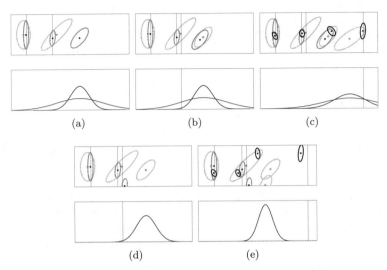

FIGURE 10.2. Comparison of a standard Kalman filter with a switching Kalman filter. (a) Based on the state estimate $\mathcal{N}(\mu_{2|2}, P_{2|2})$ the next state is predicted as $\mathcal{N}(\mu_{3|2}, P_{3|2})$. When propagated through the measurement model, we obtain $p(\tau_3|\tau_2, \tau_1)$, which is a mixture of Gaussians where the mixing coefficients are given by $p(c)$. (b) The observation τ_3 is way off the mean of the prediction, i.e. it is highly likely an outlier. Only the broad Gaussian is active, which reflects the fact that the observations are expected to be very noisy. Consequently, the updated state estimate $\mathcal{N}(\mu_{3|3}, P_{3|3})$ is not much different than its prediction $\mathcal{N}(\mu_{3|3}, P_{3|3})$. However, the uncertainty in the next prediction $\mathcal{N}(\mu_{4|3}, P_{4|3})$ will be higher. (c) After all observations are obtained, the smoothed estimates $\mathcal{N}(\mu_{j|4}, P_{j|4})$ are obtained. The estimated state trajectory shows that the observation τ_3 is correctly interpreted as an outlier. (d) In contrast with the switching Kalman filter, the ordinary Kalman filter is sensitive to outliers. In contrast to (b), the updated state estimate $\mathcal{N}(\mu_{3|3}, P_{3|3})$ is way off the prediction. (e) Consequently a very "jumpy" state trajectory is estimated. This is simply owing to the fact that the observation model does not account for presence of outliers.

The observation noise $\mathbf{w}_j$ can be modeled as a mixture of Gaussians. This choice has the following rationale: To follow tempo fluctuations the observation noise variance $\mathbf{R}$ should not be too "broad." A broad noise covariance indicates that observations are not very reliable, and so have less effect on the state estimates. In the extreme case, when $\mathbf{R} \to \infty$, practically all observations are missing so the observations have no effect on state estimates. On the other hand, a narrow $\mathbf{R}$ makes the filter sensitive to outliers, since the same noise covariance is used regardless of the distance of an observation from its prediction. Outliers can be modeled explicitly using a mixture of Gaussians—for example, one "narrow" Gaussian for normal operation and one "broad" Gaussian for outliers. Such a switching mechanism can be implemented by using a discrete variable c_j that indicates whether the jth observation is an outlier or not. In other words, the noise covariance depends on the value of c_j. Mathematically, we write this statement as $\mathbf{w}_j | c_j \sim \mathcal{N}(0, \mathbf{R}_c)$. Since c_j cannot be observed, we define a prior probability $c_j \sim p(c)$ and sum over all possible settings of c_j, i.e. $p(\mathbf{w}_j) = \sum_{c_j} p(c_j) p(\mathbf{w}_j | c_j)$. In figure 10.2 we compare a switching Kalman filter and a standard Kalman filter. A switch variable makes a system more robust against outliers, and consequently more realistic state estimates can be obtained. For a review of more general classes of switching Kalman filters, see Murphy (1998).

To summarize, the dynamical model of the tempo tracker is given by

$$(10.4) \qquad \hat{\tau}_j = \hat{\tau}_{j-1} + 2^{\hat{\omega}_{j-1}}$$

$$(10.5) \qquad \begin{pmatrix} \hat{\omega}_j \\ \hat{\mathbf{a}}_j \end{pmatrix} = \mathbf{A} \begin{pmatrix} \hat{\omega}_{j-1} \\ \hat{\mathbf{a}}_{j-1} \end{pmatrix} + \mathbf{v}_j$$

$$(10.6) \qquad \begin{pmatrix} \tau_j \\ \omega_j \end{pmatrix} = \begin{pmatrix} \hat{\tau}_j \\ \hat{\omega}_j \end{pmatrix} + \mathbf{w}_j,$$

where $\mathbf{v}_j \sim \mathcal{N}(0, \mathbf{Q})$, $\mathbf{w}_j | c_j \sim \mathcal{N}(0, \mathbf{R}_c)$ and $c_j \sim p(c_j)$. We take c_j as a binary discrete switch variable. Note that in eq. (10.6) the observable space is two-dimensional (includes both τ and ω), in contrast with the one-dimensional observable τ in figure 10.2.

10.2 Tempogram Representation

In the previous section, we assumed that the beat τ_j is observed at each step j. In a real musical situation, however, the beat cannot be observed directly from performance data. The sensation of a beat emerges from a *collection* of events rather than, say, single onsets. For example, a syncopated rhythm induces beats that do not necessarily coincide with an onset.

In this section, we will define a probability distribution that assigns probability masses to all possible beat interpretations given a performance. The Bayesian formulation of this problem is

$$(10.7) \qquad p(\tau, \omega | \mathbf{t}) \propto p(\mathbf{t} | \tau, \omega) p(\tau, \omega),$$

where $\mathbf{t}$ is an onset list. In this context, a *beat interpretation* is the tuple τ (local beat) and ω (local log-period).

The first term $p(\mathbf{t} | \tau, \omega)$ in eq. (10.7) is the probability of the onset list $\mathbf{t}$ given the tempo track. Since $\mathbf{t}$ is actually observed, $p(\mathbf{t} | \tau, \omega)$ is a

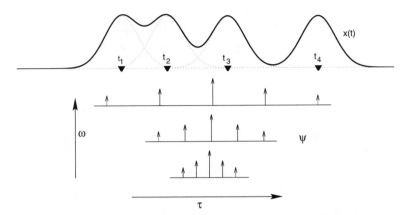

FIGURE 10.3. Tempogram calculation. The continuous signal $x(t)$ is obtained from the onset list by convolution with a Gaussian function. Below, three different basis functions ψ are shown. All are localized at the same τ and at different ω. The tempogram at (τ, ω) is calculated by taking the inner product of $x(t)$ and $\psi(t; \tau, \omega)$. Owing to the sparse nature of the basis functions, the inner product operation can be implemented very efficiently.

function of τ and ω and is thus called the *likelihood* of τ and ω. The second term $p(\tau, \omega)$ in eq. (10.7) is the *prior* distribution. The prior can be viewed as a function that weights the likelihood on the (τ, ω) space.

It is reasonable to assume that the likelihood $p(\mathbf{t}|\tau, \omega)$ is high when onsets $[t_i]$ in the performance coincide with the beats of the tempo track. To construct a likelihood function with this property we propose a similarity measure between the performance and a *local* constant tempo track. First we define a continuous time signal $x(t) = \sum_{i=1}^{I} G(t - t_i)$, where we take $G(t) = \exp(-t^2/2\sigma_x^2)$, a Gaussian function with variance σ_x^2. We represent a local tempo track as a pulse train $\psi(t; \tau, \omega) = \sum_{m=-\infty}^{\infty} \alpha_m \delta(t - \tau - m2^\omega)$, where $\delta(t - t_0)$ is a Dirac delta function, which represents an impulse located at t_0. The coefficients α_m are positive constants such that $\sum_m \alpha_m$ is a constant. (See fig. 10.3.) In real-time applications, where causal analysis is desirable, α_m can be set to zero for $m > 0$. When α_m is a sequence of form $\alpha_m = \alpha^m$, where $0 < \alpha < 1$, we adopt the infinite impulse response (IIR) comb filters used by Scheirer (1998). We define the *tempogram* of $x(t)$ at each (τ, ω) as the inner product:

$$(10.8) \qquad \mathrm{Tg}_x(\tau, \omega) = \int dt\, x(t)\psi(t; \tau, \omega).$$

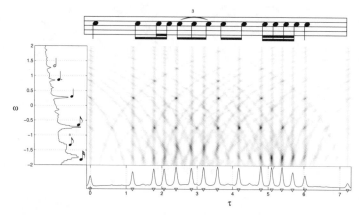

FIGURE 10.4. A simple rhythm and its tempogram. x and y axes correspond to τ and ω respectively. The bottom part of the figure shows the onset sequence (triangles). Assuming flat priors on τ and ω, the curve along the ω axis is the marginal $p(\omega|\mathbf{t}) \propto \int d\tau \exp(\mathrm{Tg_x}(\tau, \omega))$. We note that $p(\omega|\mathbf{t})$ has peaks at ω, which correspond to quarter, eight, and sixteenth note level, as well as dotted quarter and half note levels of the original notation. This distribution can be used to estimate a reasonable initial state.

The tempogram representation can be interpreted as the response of a comb filter bank and is analogous to a multiscale representation (e.g. the wavelet transform), where τ and ω correspond to transition and scaling parameters (Rioul and Vetterli, 1991; Kronland-Martinet, 1988).

The tempogram parameters have simple interpretations. The filter coefficient α adjusts the time locality of basis functions. When $\alpha \to 1$, basis functions ψ extend to infinity and locality is lost. When $\alpha \to 0$, the basis degenerates to a single Dirac pulse, and the tempogram is effectively equal to $x(t)$ for all ω and thus gives no information about the local period.

The variance parameter σ_x corresponds to the amount of small-scale expressive deviation in an onset's timing. If σ_x is large, the tempogram gets "smeared out" and all beat interpretations become almost equally likely. When $\sigma_x \to 0$, a very "spiky" tempogram results, where most beat interpretations have zero probability.

Figure 10.4 shows a tempogram obtained from a simple onset sequence. We define the likelihood as $p(\mathbf{t}|\tau, \omega) \propto \exp(\mathrm{Tg_x}(\tau, \omega))$. When combined with the prior, the tempogram gives an estimate of likely beat interpretations (τ, ω).

TABLE 10.1

Summary of Conditional Distributions and Their Parameters

Model	Distribution	Parameters
State transition (eq. 10.5)	$p(\mathbf{s}_{j+1}|\mathbf{s}_j)$	$\mathbf{A}, \mathbf{Q}$
(Switching) Observation (eq. 10.6)	$p(\tau_j, \omega_j|\mathbf{s}_j, c_j)$	$\mathbf{R}_c$
Switch prior (eq. 10.6)	$p(c_j)$	p_c
Tempogram (eq.10.8)	$p(\mathbf{t}|\tau_j, \omega_j)$	σ_x, α

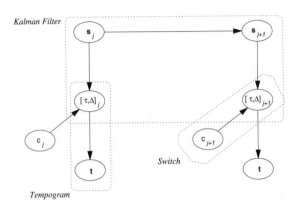

FIGURE 10.5. The graphical model.

10.3 Model Training

In this section, we review the techniques for parameter estimation. First, we summarize the relationships between variables by using a *graphical model*. A graphical model is a directed acyclic graph, where nodes represent variables and missing directed links represent conditional independence relations. The distributions that we have specified so far are summarized in table 10.1.

The resulting graphical model is shown in figure 10.5. Links in the model represent probabilities. For example, the directed link from $\mathbf{s}_j$ to $\mathbf{s}_{j+1}$ encodes $p(\mathbf{s}_{j+1}|\mathbf{s}_j)$. Other links toward $\mathbf{s}_{j+1}$ are missing.

In principle, we could jointly optimize all model parameters. However, such an approach would be computationally very intensive. Instead, at the expense of getting a suboptimal solution, we assume that we observe the noisy tempo track τ_j. This observation effectively "decouples" the model into two parts (see fig. 10.5), (i) the Kalman filter (State transition model and Observation [Switch] model) and (ii) the tempogram. We will train each part separately.

10.3.1 Estimation of τ_j from Performance Data

In our studies, we make use of the score and extract τ_j from a performance $\mathbf{t}$ by matching the notes that coincide with the beat (quarter note) level and the bar (whole note). If there is more than one note per beat, we take the median of the onset times[3]. For each performance, we compute $\omega_j = \log_2(\tau_{j+1} - \tau_j)$ from the extracted noisy beats $[\tau_j]$. We denote the resulting tempo track $\{\tau_1, \omega_1, \ldots, \tau_j, \omega_j, \ldots, \tau_J, \omega_J\}$ as $\{\tau_{1:J}, \omega_{1:J}\}$.

10.3.2 Estimation of State Transition Parameters

We estimate the state transition model parameters $\mathbf{A}$ and $\mathbf{Q}$ using an EM algorithm (Ghahramani and Hinton, 1996) that learns a linear dynamics in the ω space. The EM algorithm monotonically increases $p(\{\tau_{1:J}, \omega_{1:J}\})$, i.e. the likelihood of the observed tempo track. Put another way, the parameters $\mathbf{A}$ and $\mathbf{Q}$ are adjusted in such a way that, at each j, the probability of the observation is maximized under the predictive distribution $p(\tau_j, \omega_j | \tau_{j-1}, \omega_{j-1}, \ldots, \tau_1, \omega_1)$. The likelihood is simply the height of the predictive distribution evaluated at the observation (see fig. 10.1).

10.3.3 Estimation of Switch Parameters

The observation model is a Gaussian mixture with diagonal $\mathbf{R}_c$ and prior probability p_c. We could estimate $\mathbf{R}_c$ and p_c jointly with the state transition parameters $\mathbf{A}$ and $\mathbf{Q}$. However, the noise model would then be totally independent from the tempogram representation. Instead, the observation noise model should reflect the uncertainty in the tempogram, for example the expected amount of deviations in (τ, ω) estimates due to spurious local maxima. To estimate the "tempogram noise" by standard EM methods, we sample from the tempogram around each $[\hat{\tau}_j, \hat{\omega}_j]$, i.e. we sample τ_j and ω_j from the posterior distribution $p(\tau_j, \omega_j | \hat{\tau}_j, \hat{\omega}_j, \mathbf{t}; \mathbf{Q}) \propto p(\mathbf{t} | \tau_j, \omega_j) p(\tau_j, \omega_j | \hat{\tau}_j, \hat{\omega}_j; \mathbf{Q})$. Note that $[\hat{\tau}_j, \hat{\omega}_j]$ is estimated during the E step of the EM algorithm when finding the parameters $\mathbf{A}$ and $\mathbf{Q}$.

10.3.4 Estimation of Tempogram Parameters

We have already defined the tempogram as a likelihood $p(\mathbf{t} | \tau, \omega; \theta)$ where θ denotes the tempogram parameters (e.g. $\theta = \{\alpha, \sigma_x\}$). If we assume a

---

[3]The scores do not have notes on each beat. We interpolate missing beats by using a switching Kalman filter with parameters $\mathbf{Q} = \mathrm{diag}([0.01^2, 0.05^2])$, $\mathbf{R}_1 = 0.01^2$, $\mathbf{R}_2 = 0.3^2$, $\mathbf{A} = 1$ and $p(c) = [0.999, 0.001]$.

uniform prior $p(\tau, \omega)$ then the posterior probability can be written as

$$(10.9) \qquad p(\tau, \omega | \mathbf{t}; \theta) = \frac{p(\mathbf{t} | \tau, \omega; \theta)}{p(\mathbf{t} | \theta)},$$

where the normalization constant is given by $p(\mathbf{t} | \theta) = \int d\tau d\omega p(\mathbf{t} | \tau, \omega; \theta)$. We can at this point estimate tempogram parameters θ using a maximum likelihood approach. We write the log-likelihood of an observed tempo track $\{\tau_{1:J}, \omega_{1:J}\}$ as

$$(10.10) \qquad \log p(\{\tau_{1:J}, \omega_{1:J}\} | \mathbf{t}; \theta) = \sum_j \log p(\tau_j, \omega_j | \mathbf{t}; \theta).$$

Note that the quantity in equation (10.10) is a function of the parameters θ. If we have k tempo tracks in the dataset, the complete data log-likelihood is simply the sum of all individual log-likelihoods, i.e.

$$(10.11) \qquad \mathcal{L} = \sum_k \log p(\{\tau_{1:J}, \omega_{1:J}\}^k | \mathbf{t}^k; \alpha, \sigma_x),$$

where $\mathbf{t}^k$ is the kth performance and $\{\tau_{1:J}, \omega_{1:J}\}^k$ is the corresponding tempo track.

10.4 Evaluation

Many tempo trackers described in the introduction have been tested with ad hoc examples. However, to validate tempo-tracking models, more systematic data and rigorous testing are necessary. A tempo tracker can be evaluated by systematically modulating the tempo of the data, for instance by applying instantaneous or gradual tempo changes and comparing the models responses to human behavior (Michon, 1967; Dannenberg, 1993). Another approach is to evaluate tempo trackers on a systematically collected set of natural data, monitoring piano performances in which the use of expressive tempo change is free. This type of data has the advantage of reflecting the type of data one expects automated music transcription systems to deal with. We adopt the latter approach in this study.

10.4.1 Data

For the experiment 12 pianists were invited to play arrangements of two Beatles songs, "Michelle" and "Yesterday." Both pieces have a relatively simple rhythmic structure with ample opportunity to add expressiveness by fluctuating the tempo. The subjects consisted of four professional jazz players (PJ), four professional classical performers (PC), and four amateur classical pianists (AC). Each arrangement had to be played in three tempo conditions, three repetitions per tempo condition. The tempo conditions were normal, slow, and fast tempo (all in a musically

Table 10.2

Optimal Tempogram Parameters

	α	σ_x
Noncausal	0.55	0.017
Causal	0.73	0.023

realistic range and all according to the judgment of the performer). We present here the results for twelve subjects (12 subjects × 3 tempi × 3 repetitions × 2 pieces = 216 performances). The performances were recorded on a Yamaha Disklavier Pro MIDI grand piano using Opcode Vision. To be able to derive tempo measurements related to the musical structure (e.g. beat, bar) the performances were matched with the MIDI scores using the structure matcher of Heijink et al. (2000) available in POCO (Honing, 1990). This MIDI data, as well as related software, will be made available at http://www.mbfys.kun.nl/~cemgil and http://www.nici.kun.nl/mmm (under the heading Download).

10.4.2 Kalman Filter Training Results

We use the performances of "Michelle" as the training set and "Yesterday" as the test set. To find the appropriate filter order (dimensionality of s) we trained Kalman filters of several orders on two rhythmic levels: the beat (quarter note) level and the bar (whole note) level. Figure 10.6 shows the training and testing results as a function of filter order.

Extending the filter order, i.e. increasing the the size of the state space, loosely corresponds with looking further into the past. At bar level, using higher-order filters results merely in overfitting as indicated by decreasing test likelihood. In contrast, on the beat level, the likelihood on the test set also increases and has a jump around order of 7. Effectively, this order corresponds to a memory that can store state information from the past two bars. In other words, tempo fluctuations at beat level have some structure that a higher-dimensional state transition model can use to produce more accurate predictions.

10.4.3 Tempogram Training Results

We use a tempogram model with a first-order IIR comb basis. This choice leaves two free parameters that need to be estimated from data, namely α, the coefficient of the comb filter, and σ_x, the width of the Gaussian window. We obtain optimal parameter values by maximizing of the log-likelihood in equation (10.11) on the "Michelle" dataset. The resulting likelihood surface is shown in figure 10.7. The optimal parameters are shown in table 10.2.

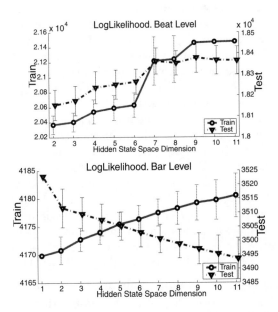

FIGURE 10.6. Kalman filter training. Training set: "Michelle," test set: "Yesterday."

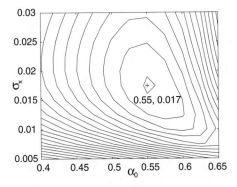

FIGURE 10.7. Log-likelihood surface of tempogram parameters α and σ_x on "Michelle" dataset.

10.4.4 Initialization

To have a fully automated tempo tracker, the initial state s_0 has to be estimated from data as well. In the tracking experiments, we initialized the filter to the beat level by computing a tempogram for the first 5 seconds of each performance. By assuming a flat prior on τ and ω we compute the posterior marginal $p(\omega|\mathbf{t}) = \int d\tau p(\omega, \tau|\mathbf{t})$. Note that this operation is equivalent to summation along the τ dimension of the tempogram (see fig. 10.4). For our Beatles dataset, we observed that for all performances of a given piece, the most likely log-period $\omega^* = \arg\max_\omega p(\omega|\mathbf{t})$ always corresponds to the same level, i.e. the ω^* estimate was always consistent. For "Michelle," this level is the beat level and for "Yesterday" the half-beat (eighth note) level. The latter piece begins with an arpeggio of eighth notes; based on onset information only, and without any other prior knowledge, half-beat level is also a reasonable solution. For "Yesterday," to test the tracking performance, we corrected the estimate to the beat level.

We could have estimated τ^* using a similar procedure; however since all performances in our dataset started "on the beat," we chose $\tau^* = t_1$, the first onset of the piece. All the other state variables $\hat{\mathbf{a}}_0$ were set to zero. We chose a broad initial state covariance, $P_0 = 9\mathbf{Q}$.

10.4.5   Evaluation of Tempo Tracking Performance

Here we evaluated the accuracy of the tempo-tracking performance of the complete model. The accuracy of tempo tracking is measured by using the following criterion:

$$\rho(\psi, \mathbf{t}) = \frac{\sum_i \max_j W(\psi_i - t_j)}{(I+J)/2} \times 100,$$

where $[\psi_i]$ $i = 1, \ldots, I$ is the target (true) tempo track, $[t_j]$ $j = 1, \ldots, J$ is the estimated tempo track, and W is a window function. In the following results we use a Gaussian window function $W(d) = \exp(-d^2/2\sigma_e^2)$. The width of the window is chosen as $\sigma_e = 0.04$ sec., which corresponds roughly to the spread of onsets from their mechanical means during performance of short rhythms (Cemgil et al., 2000).

It can be shown that $0 \leq \rho \leq 100$ and $\rho = 100$ if and only if $\psi = \mathbf{t}$. Intuitively, this measure is similar to a normalized inner product (as in the tempogram calculation); the difference is in the max operator, which merely avoids double counting. For example, if the target is $\psi = [0, 1, 2]$ and we have $\mathbf{t} = [0, 0, 0]$, the ordinary inner product would still give $\rho = 100$, whereas only one beat is correct ($t = 0$). The proposed measure gives $\rho = 33$ in this case. The tracking index ρ can be interpreted roughly as percentage of "correct" beats. For example, $\rho = 90$ effectively means that about 90 percent of estimated beats are in the near vicinity of their targets.

Table 10.3

Average Tracking Performance ρ and Standard Deviations on
"Yesterday" Dataset Using a Noncausal Tempogram
+ denotes the case when we have the switch prior $p(c) = [0.8, 0.2]$.
− denotes the absence of a switching, i.e. the case when $p(c) = [1, 0]$.

Filter order	Switching	Tempogram	No tempogram
10	+	92 ± 7	75 ± 21
2	+	91 ± 9	75 ± 21
10	−	91 ± 6	73 ± 21
2	−	90 ± 9	73 ± 22

10.4.6 Results

To test the relative relevance of model components, we designed an experiment where we evaluate the tempo-tracking performance under different conditions. We varied the filter order and enabled or disabled switching. For this purpose, we trained two filters, one with a large (10) and one with a small (2) state space dimension on beat level (using the "Michelle" dataset). We tested each model with both causal and noncausal tempograms. To test whether a tempogram is necessary, we propose a simple onset-only measurement model. In this alternative model, the next observation is taken as the nearest onset to the Kalman filter prediction. In the case where no onsets are within 1σ of the prediction, we declare the observation as missing (note that this is an implicit switching mechanism).

Table 10.3 shows the tracking results averaged over all performances in the "Yesterday" dataset. The estimated tempo tracks are obtained by using a noncausal tempogram and Kalman filtering. In this case, Kalman smoothed estimates are not significantly different. The results suggest that for the "Yesterday" dataset, a higher-order filter or a (binary) switching mechanism does not improve the tracking performance. However, the presence of a tempogram makes the tracking performance both more accurate and consistent (note the lower standard deviations). As a "base line" performance criteria, we also compute the best constant tempo track (by a linear regression to estimated tempo tracks). In this case, the average tracking index obtained from a constant tempo approximation is rather poor ($\rho = 28 \pm 18$), confirming that there is indeed a need for tempo tracking.

We repeated the same experiment with a causal tempogram and computed the tracking performance for predicted, filtered, and smoothed estimates. Table 10.4 shows the results for a switching Kalman filter. The results without switching are not significantly different. As one would

Table 10.4

Average Tracking Performance ρ on "Yesterday" Dataset
Figures indicate tracking index ρ followed by the standard deviation. The label "noncausal" refers to a tempogram calculated using noncausal comb filters. The labels predicted, filtered and smoothed refer to state estimates obtained by the Kalman filter/smoother.

Filter order	Causal		
	predicted	filtered	smoothed
10	74 ± 12	86 ± 9	91 ± 8
2	73 ± 12	85 ± 8	90 ± 8

expect, the tracking index with predicted estimates is lower. In contrast with a noncausal tempogram, smoothing improves the tempo tracking and results in a performance comparable to that of a noncausal tempogram.

Naturally, the performance of the tracker depends on the amount of tempo variations introduced by the performer. For example, the tempo tracker fails consistently for a subject who tends to use quite a bit of tempo variation.[4]

We find that the tempo tracking performance is not significantly different among different groups (table 10.5). However, when we consider the predictions, we see that the performances of professional classical pianists are less predictable. For different tempo conditions (table 10.6) the results are also similar. As one would expect, for slower performances, the predictions are less accurate. This has two potential explanations. First, the performance criteria ρ is independent of the absolute tempo, i.e. the window W is always fixed. Second, for slower performances there is more room for adding expression.

10.5 Discussion and Conclusions

In this section, we have introduced the problem of building a tempo-tracking model in a probabilistic framework. The proposed model consist of a dynamical system (a Kalman filter) and a measurement model (tempogram). Although many of the methods proposed in the literature can be viewed as particular choices of a dynamical model and a measurement model, a Bayesian formulation exhibits several advantages over other models for tempo tracking. First, components in our model have natural probabilistic interpretations. An important and practical consequence of such an interpretation is that uncertainties can be easily quantified and integrated into the system. Moreover, all desired quan-

---

[4]This subject claimed to have never heard the Beatles songs before.

TABLE 10.5

Tracking Averages on Subject Groups
PJ, AC, and PC stand for Professional Jazz, Amateur Classical and
Professional Classical pianists. As a reference, the right most column
shows the results obtained by the best constant tempo track. The label
"noncausal" refers to a tempogram calculated using noncausal comb
filters. The labels predicted, filtered, and smoothed refer to state
estimates obtained by the Kalman filter/smoother.

Subject group	Noncausal filtered	Causal			Best const.
		predicted	filtered	smoothed	
PJ	95 ± 3	81 ± 7	92 ± 4	94 ± 3	34 ± 22
AC	92 ± 8	74 ± 7	88 ± 5	92 ± 4	24 ± 19
PC	89 ± 7	66 ± 14	82 ± 11	86 ± 11	27 ± 12

TABLE 10.6

Tracking Averages on Tempo Conditions
As a reference, the right most column shows the results obtained by the
best constant tempo track. The label "noncausal" refers to a tempogram
calculated using noncausal comb filters. The labels predicted, filtered, and
smoothed refer to state estimates obtained by the Kalman filter/smoother.

Condition	Noncausal filtered	Causal			Best const.
		predicted	filtered	smoothed	
fast	94 ± 5	79 ± 9	90 ± 6	93 ± 6	39 ± 21
normal	92 ± 8	74 ± 9	88 ± 6	92 ± 4	25 ± 13
slow	90 ± 7	68 ± 14	84 ± 10	87 ± 11	21 ± 14

tities can be inferred consistently. For example, once we quantify the
distribution of tempo deviations and expressive timing, the actual behavior of the tempo tracker results automatically from these a priori
assumptions. This contrasts with other models where one has to invent
ad hoc methods to avoid undesired or unexpected behavior on real data.

Additionally, prior knowledge (such as smoothness constraints in the
state transition model and the particular choice of measurement model)
are explicit and can be changed as needed. For example, the same state
transition model can be used for both audio and MIDI; only the measurement model needs to be elaborated. Another advantage is that for a
large class of related models, efficient inference and learning algorithms
are already well understood (Ghahramani and Hinton, 1996). This is
appealing since we can train tempo trackers with different properties
automatically from data. Indeed, we have demonstrated that all model
parameters can be estimated from experimental data.

We have investigated several potential directions in which the basic dynamical model can be improved or simplified. We have tested the relative relevance of the filter order, switching, and the tempogram representation on a systematically collected set of natural data. The dataset consists of polyphonic piano performances of two Beatles songs ("Yesterday" and "Michelle") and contains a lot of tempo fluctuation as indicated by the poor constant tempo fits.

The test results on the Beatles dataset suggest that using a high-order filter does not improve tempo tracking performance. Although beat level filters capture some structure in tempo deviations (and hence can generate more accurate predictions), this additional precision does not seem very important in tempo tracking. This indifference may be because training criteria (maximum likelihood) and testing criteria (tracking index), while related, are not identical. However, one can imagine scenarios where accurate prediction is crucial. An example would be a real-time accompaniment situation, where the application needs to generate events for the next bar.

The test results also indicate that a simple switching mechanism is not very useful. It seems that a tempogram already gives a robust local estimate of likely beat and tempo values so the correct beat can unambiguously be identified. The indifference of switching could also be an artifact of the dataset, which lacks extensive syncopations. Nevertheless, the switching noise model can be elaborated further to replace the tempogram with a rhythm quantizer (Cemgil et al., 2000).

To test the relevance of the proposed tempogram representation on tracking performance we compared it to a simpler, onset-based alternative. The results indicate that in the onset-only case, tracking performance decreases significantly, suggesting that a tempogram is an important component of the system.

Note that the choice of a comb basis set for tempogram calculation is rather arbitrary. In principle, one could formulate a "richer" tempogram model, for example by including parameters that control the shape of basis functions. The parameters of such a model can similarly be optimized by likelihood maximization on target tempo tracks. Unfortunately, such an optimization (e.g. with a generic technique such as gradient descent) requires the computation of a tempogram at each step and is thus computationally quite complex. Moreover, a model with many adjustable parameters might eventually overfit.

We have also demonstrated that the model can be used both on-line (filtering) and off-line (smoothing). On-line processing is necessary for real-time applications, such as automatic accompaniment, and off-line processing is desirable for transcription applications.

References

Ackley, D., Hinton, G., and Sejnowski, T. (1985). A learning algorithm for Boltzmann Machines. *Cognitive Science* 9:147–169.

Barber, D. and Wiegerinck, W. (1999). Tractable variational structures for approximating graphical models. In Kearns, M. S., Solla, S. A., and Cohn, D. A., (eds.), *Advances in Neural Information Processing Systems*, vol. 11 (pp. 183–189). Cambridge, MA: MIT Press.

Berner, E. S,, Jackson, J. R., and Algina, J. (1996). Relationships among performance scores of four diagnostic decision support systems. *J. Am. Med. Inform. Assoc.* 3(3):208–215.

Berner, E. S., Webster, G. D., Shugerman, A. A., Jackson, J. R., Algina, J., Baker, A. L., Ball, E. V., Cobbs, C. G., Dennis, V. W., Frenkel, E. P., Hudson, L. D., Mancall, E. L., Racley, C. E., and Taunton, O. D. (1994). Performance of four computer-based diagnostic systems. *N. Engl. J. Med.* 330(25):1792–1796.

Brigl, B., Ringleb, P., Steiner, T., Knaup, P., Hacke, W., and Haux, R. (1998). An integrated approach for a knowledge-based clinical workstation: Architecture and experience. *Methods of Information in Medicine* 37:16–25.

Castillo, E., Gutierrez, J. M., and Hadi, A. S. (1997). *Expert Systems and Probabilistic Network Models*. Berlin: Springer-Verlag.

Cemgil, A. T., Desain, P., and Kappen, H. (2000). Rhythm quantization for transcription. *Computer Music Journal* 24(2)60–76.

Dannenberg, R. B. (1984). An on-line algorithm for real-time accompaniment. In *Proceedings of ICMC* (pp. 193–198). San Francisco: International Computer Music Association.

Dannenberg, R. B. (1993). Music understanding by computer. In *Proceedings of the International Workshop on Knowledge Technology in the Arts* (pp. 41–56). Osaka: Laboratories of Image Information Science and Technology.

Desain, P. and Honing, H. (1991). Quantization of musical time: a connectionist approach. In Todd, P. M. and Loy, D. G., (eds.), *Music and Connectionism* (pp. 150–167). Cambridge, MA: MIT Press.

Desain, P. and Honing, H. (1994). A brief introduction to beat induction. In *Proceedings of ICMC* (pp. 78–79). San Francisco: International Computer Music Association.

Ghahramani, Zoubin and Hinton, Goeffrey E. (1996). Parameter estimation for linear dynamical systems (crg-tr-96-2). Technical report, Dept. of Computer Science, University of Totronto.

Godsill, Simon J. and Rayner, Peter J. W. (1998). *Digital Audio Restoration— A Statistical Model-Based Approach*. Berlin: Springer-Verlag.

Goto, M. and Muraoka, Y. (1998). Music understanding at the beat level: Real-time beat tracking for audio signals. In Rosenthal, David F. and Okuno, Hiroshi G., (eds.), *Computational Auditory Scene Analysis* (pp. 68–75). Mahweh, NJ: Lawrence Erlbaum Associates.

Heckerman, D. E., Horvitz, E. J., and Nathwani, B. N. (1992). Towards normative expert systems: part I, the Pathfinder project. *Methods of Information in Medicine* 31:90–105.

Heckerman, D. E. and Nathwani, B. N. (1992). Towards normative expert systems. Part II, Probability-based representations for efficient knowledge acquisition and inference. *Methods of Information in Medicine* 31:106–116.

Heijink, H., Desain, P., and Honing, H. (2000). Make me a match: An evaluation of different approaches to score-performance matching. *Computer Music Journal* 24(1):43–56.

Hinton, G. E. (1989). Deterministic Boltzmann learning performs steepest descent in weight-space. *Neural Computation* 1:143–150.

Honing, H. (1990). Poco: An environment for analysing, modifying, and generating expression in music. In *Proceedings of ICMC* (pp. 364–368). San Francisco: International Computer Music Association.

Itzykson, C. and Drouffe, J-M. (1989). *Statistical Field Theory.* Cambridge monographs on mathematical physics. Cambridge: Cambridge University Press.

Jaakkola, T. (1997). *Variational Methods for Inference and Estimation in Graphical Models.* Ph.D. thesis, Massachusetts Institute of Technology.

Jaakkola, T. S. and Jordan, M. I. (1997). Variational methods and the QMR-DT database. MIT Computational Cognitive Science Technical Report 9701, Massachusetts Institute of Technology.

Jordan, M., (ed.) (1996). *Learning in Graphical Models.* London: Kluwer Academic Publishers.

Kalman, R. E. (1960). A new approach to linear filtering and prediction problems. *Transactions of the ASME—Journal of Basic Engineering* 82:35–45.

Kappen, H. J. and Rodríguez, F. B. (1998). Efficient learning in Boltzmann Machines using linear response theory. *Neural Computation* 10:1137–1156.

Kappen, H. J. and Spanjers, J. J. (1999). Mean field theory for asymmetric neural networks. *Physical Review E* 61:5658–5663.

Kappen, H. J. and Wiegerinck, W. (2001a). Mean field theory for graphical models. In Opper, M. and Saad, D. (eds.), *Advanced Mean Field Theory.* Cambridge, MA: MIT Press.

Kappen, H. J. and Wiegerinck, W. A. J. J. (2001b). Second order approximations for probability models. In Leen, Todd et al. (eds.), *Advances in Neural Information Processing Systems 13.* Cambridge, MA: MIT Press. In press.

Kronland-Martinet, R. (1988). The wavelet transform for analysis, synthesis and processing of speech and music sounds. *Computer Music Journal* 12 (4):11–17.

Kullback, S. (1959). *Information Theory and Statistics.* New York: Wiley.

Large, E. W. and Jones, M. R. (1999). The dynamics of attending: How we track time-varying events. *Psychological Review* 106:119–159.

Lauritzen, S. L. and Spiegelhalter, D. J. (1988). Local computations with probabilties on graphical structures and their application to expert systems. *J. Royal Statistical society B* 50:154–227.

Longuet-Higgins, H. C. and Lee, C. S. (1982). Perception of musical rhythms. *Perception* 11:115–128.

Longuet-Higgins, H. C. (1976). The perception of melodies. *Nature* 263: 646–653.

Michon, J. A. (1967). *Timing in Temporal Tracking*. Ph.D. thesis, Institute of Sensory Physiology, Human Fectors Research Institute (RVO TNO), Soesterberg, The Netherlands.

Murphy, Kevin (1998). Switching Kalman filters. Technical report, Dept. of Computer Science, University of California, Berkeley.

Parisi, G. (1988). *Statistical Field Theory*. Cambridge, MA: Addison-Wesley.

Pearl, J. (1988). *Probabilistic Reasoning in Intelligent Systems: Networks of Plausible Inference*. San Francisco: Morgan Kaufmann.

Peterson, C. and Anderson, J. R. (1987). A mean field theory learning algorithm for neural networks. *Complex Systems* 1:995–1019.

Plefka, T. (1982). Convergence condition of the TAP equation for the infinite-range Ising spin glass model. *Journal of Physics A* 15:1971–1978.

Reisman, Y. (1996). Computer-based clinical decision aids: A review of methods and assessment of systems. *Med. Inform.* 21(3):179–197.

Rioul, Oliver and Vetterli, Martin. (1991). Wavelets and signal processing. *IEEE Signal Processing Magazine* October:14–38.

Roweis, Sam and Ghahramani, Zoubin. (1999). A unifying review of linear gaussian models. *Neural Computation* 11(2):305–345.

Saul, L. K., Jaakkola, T., and Jordan, M. I. (1996). Mean field theory for sigmoid belief networks. *Journal of artificial intelligence research* 4:61–76.

Scheirer, E. D. (1998). Tempo and beat analysis of acoustic musical signals. *Journal of Acoustical Society of America* 103:1:588–601.

Sethares, W. A. and Staley, T. W. (1999). Periodicity transforms. *IEEE Transactions on Signal Processing* 47(11):2953–2964.

Sherrington, D. and Kirkpatrick, S. (1975). Solvable model of Spin-Glass. *Physical Review Letters* 35:1792–1796.

Smith, Leigh. (1999). *A Multiresolution Time-Frequency Analysis and Interpretation of Musical Rhythm*. Ph.D. thesis, University of Western Australia.

Sterian, A. (1999). *Model-Based Segmentation of Time-Frequency Images for Musical Transcription*. Ph.D. thesis, University of Michigan, Ann Arbor.

ter Burg, W. J. P. P., Lucas, P., and ter Braak, E. W. M. T. (1999). A diagnostic advice system based on pathophysiological models of diseases. In P. Kokol et al. (eds.) *Medical Informatics Europe* (pp. 654–659). Amsterdam: IOS Press.

Thouless, D. J., Anderson, P. W., and Palmer, R. G. (1977). Solution of "Solvable Model of a Spin Glass". *Phil. Mag.* 35:593–601.

Todd, Neil P. McAngus. (1994). The auditory "primal sketch": A multiscale model of rhythmic grouping. *Journal of New Music Research* 23:25–70.

Toiviainen, P. (1999). An interactive midi accompanist. *Computer Music Journal* 22(4):63–75.

Vercoe, B. (1984). The synthetic performer in the context of live performance. In *Proceedings of ICMC* (pp. 199–200). San Francisco: International Computer Music Association.

Vercoe, B. and Puckette, M. (1985). The synthetic rehearsal: Training the synthetic performer. In *Proceedings of ICMC* (pp. 275–278), San Francisco: International Computer Music Association.

Whittaker, J. (1990). *Graphical Models in Applied Multivariate Statistics.* Chichester: Wiley.

Wiegerinck, W. and Barber, D. (1998a). Mean field theory based on belief networks for approximate inference. In L. Niklasson, M. Boden, and T. Ziemke (eds.) *Proceedings of the 8th International Conference on Artificial Neural Networks* (ICANN '98, Skövde, Sweden, pp. 499–504). London: Springer.

Wiegerinck, W. and Barber, D. (1998b). Variational belief networks for approximate inference. In La Poutre, H. and van den Herik, J., (eds.), *Proceedings of the Tenth Netherlands/Belgium Conference on Artificial Intelligence (NAIC'98)* (pp. 177–183). Amsterdam: CWI.

Wiegerinck, W., ter Burg, W., ter Braak, E., van Dam, P., O, Y., J., Neijt, and Kappen, H. (1997). Inference and advisory system for medical diagnosis. Report TR-SNN-97-348, SNN, Univerity of Nijmegen, The Nehterlands.

III

Evolutionary Computation and Beyond

RWC Theoretical Foundation GMD Laboratory

Heinz Mühlenbein and Thilo Mahnig

Simulating evolution as seen in nature has been identified as one of the key computing paradigms for the new decade. Today evolutionary algorithms have been used successfully in a number of applications. These include discrete and continuous optimization problems, synthesis of neural networks, synthesis of computer programs from examples (also called genetic programming), and even evolvable hardware. But all application areas have encountered problems where evolutionary algorithms performed badly. Therefore a mathematical theory of evolutionary algorithms is urgently needed. Theoretical research so far has evolved from two opposing ends: from the theoretical approach there are theories emerging that are getting closer to practice, and from the applied side ad hoc theories have arisen that often lack theoretical justification.

In this chapter we concentrate on the analysis of evolutionary algorithms for optimization. The first section introduces the most popular algorithm, the *simple genetic algorithm*. This algorithm has many degrees of freedom, especially in the choice of recombination scheme. We show the shortcomings of the traditional *schema analysis*. We prove that all genetic algorithms behave very similarly, if recombination is done without selection a sufficient number of times before the next selection step. We approximate this conceptual algorithm by the *univariate marginal distribution algorithm* (UMDA), which is analyzed in section 12. We compute the difference equation for the univariate marginal distribu-

Foundations of Real-World Intelligence.
Yoshinori Uesaka et al. (eds.).
Copyright © 2001, CSLI Publications.

tions under the assumption of proportionate selection. This equation has been proposed in population genetics by Sewall Wright as early as 1937 (Wright, 1970). This is an independent confirmation of our claim that UMDA approximates any genetic algorithm. Using *Wright's equation* we show that UMDA solves a *continuous optimization problem*. The function to be optimized is given by the average fitness of the population.

Proportionate selection is far too weak for optimization. This was recognized very early in the breeding of livestock. *Artificial selection* as done by breeders is a much better model for optimization than *natural selection* modeled by proportionate selection. Unfortunately an exact mathematical analysis of efficient artificial selection schemes seems impossible. Therefore breeders have developed an approximate theory, using the concepts of regression of offspring to parent, heritability, and response to selection. This theory is discussed in section 13. At the end of the section we represent numerical results that show the strength and the weakness of UMDA as a numerical optimization method.

UMDA optimizes very efficiently some difficult optimization problems, but it fails on some simple problems. These problems require higher-order marginal distributions that capture the nonlinear dependency between variables. In section 14 UMDA is extended to the *factorized distribution algorithm* (FDA). We prove convergence of the algorithm to the global optima if *Boltzmann selection* is used. The theory of factorization connects FDA with the theory of *graphical models* and *Bayesian networks*. We derive a new adaptive Boltzmann selection schedule SDS using ideas from the science of breeding.

In section 15 we use results from the theory of Bayesian networks for the *learning factorized distribution algorithm* (LFDA), which computes a factorization from the data. We make a preliminary comparison between the efficiency of FDA and LFDA.

In section 16 we describe the *system dynamics approach to optimization*. The difference equations obtained for UMDA are iterated until convergence. Thus the continuous optimization problem is solved mathematically without using a population of points. We present numerical results for three system dynamics equations: Wright's equation, the *diversified replicator equation,* and a modified version of Wright's equation that converges more quickly.

In the final section we classify the various evolutionary computation methods presented. The classification criterion is whether the method uses a microscopic or a macroscopic model for selection and/or recombination.

11 Analysis of the Simple Genetic Algorithm

In this section we investigate the standard genetic algorithm, also called the simple genetic algorithm (SGA). The algorithm has been described by Holland (1975/1992) and Goldberg (1989). It consists of

- fitness proportionate selection
- recombination/crossover, and
- mutation.

Here we will analyze only selection and recombination. Mutation is considered to be a background operator. It can be analyzed by known techniques from stochastics (Mühlenbein and Schlierkamp-Voosen, 1994; Mühlenbein, 1997).

There have been many claims concerning the optimization power of SGA. Most of them are based on a rather qualitative application of the *schema theorem*. We will show the shortcomings of this approach. Our analysis is based on techniques used in population genetics. The analysis reveals that an exact mathematical analysis of SGA is possible only for small problems. For a binary problem of size n the exact analysis needs the computation of 2^n equations. But we propose an approximation, often used in population genetics, that assumes that the gene frequencies are in *linkage equilibrium*. The main result is that *any genetic algorithm can be approximated by an algorithm using only n parameters, the univariate marginal gene frequencies.*

11.1 Definitions

Let $\mathbf{x} = (x_1, \ldots, x_n)$ denote a binary vector. For notational simplicity we restrict the discussion to binary variables $x_i \in \{0, 1\}$. We use the following conventions. Capital letters X_i denote variables, small letters x_i assignments.

Definition 11.1. *Let a function $f : \boldsymbol{X} \to R^{\geq 0}$ be given. We consider the optimization problem*

$$(11.1) \qquad \mathbf{x}_{\mathrm{opt}} = \operatorname{argmax} f(\mathbf{x}) .$$

We will use $f(\mathbf{x})$ as the fitness function for the SGA. We will investigate two widely used recombination/crossover schemes.

Definition 11.2. *Let two strings $\mathbf{x}$ and $\mathbf{y}$ be given. In* one-point crossover *the string $\mathbf{z}$ is created by randomly choosing a crossover point $0 < l < n$ and setting $z_i = x_i$ for $i \leq l$ and $z_i = y_i$ for $i > l$. In* uniform crossover *z_i is randomly chosen with equal probability from $\{x_i, y_i\}$.*

Definition 11.3. *Let $p(\mathbf{x}, t)$ denote the probability of $\mathbf{x}$ in the population at generation t. Then $p_i(x_i, t) = \sum_{\mathbf{x}, X_i = x_i} p(\mathbf{x}, t)$ defines a univariate marginal distribution.*

We will often write $p_i(x_i)$ for simplicity if just one generation is discussed. In this notation the average fitness of the population and the variance is given by

$$\bar{f}(t) = \sum_x p(\mathbf{x}, t) f(\mathbf{x})$$

$$V(t) = \sum_x p(\mathbf{x}, t) \left(f(\mathbf{x}) - \bar{f}(t) \right)^2.$$

The *response to selection $R(t)$* is defined by

$$(11.2) \qquad R(t) = \bar{f}(t+1) - \bar{f}(t)$$

11.2 Proportionate Selection

Proportionate selection changes the probabilities according to

$$(11.3) \qquad p(\mathbf{x}, t+1) = p(\mathbf{x}, t) \frac{f(\mathbf{x})}{\bar{f}(t)}.$$

Lemma 11.1. *For proportionate selection the response is given by*

$$(11.4) \qquad R(t) = \frac{V(t)}{\bar{f}(t)}.$$

Proof. We have

$$(11.5) \qquad R(t) = \sum_x p(\mathbf{x}, t) \frac{f(\mathbf{x})^2}{\bar{f}(t)} - \bar{f}(t) = \frac{V(t)}{\bar{f}(t)}.$$

$\square$

With proportionate selection the average fitness never decreases. This is true for every rational selection scheme.

11.3 Recombination

For the analysis of recombination we introduce a special distribution.

Definition 11.4. *Robbins's proportions are given by the distribution π:*

$$(11.6) \qquad \pi(\mathbf{x}, t) := \prod_{i=1}^{n} p_i(x_i, t).$$

A population in Robbins's proportions is also said to be in linkage equilibrium.

Geiringer (1944) has shown that all reasonable recombination schemes lead to the same limit distribution.

Theorem 11.1 (Geiringer). *Recombination does not change the univariate marginal frequencies, i.e.* $p_i(x_i, t+1) = p_i(x_i, t)$. *The limit distribution of any complete recombination scheme is Robbins's proportions* $\pi(\mathbf{x}, 0)$.

Complete recombination means that for each subset S of $\{1, \ldots, n\}$, the probability of an exchange of genes by recombination is greater than zero. Convergence to the limit distribution is very fast. We will prove this for $n = 2$ loci.

Theorem 11.2. *Let* $D(t) = p(0, 0, t)p(1, 1, t) - p(0, 1, t)p(1, 0, t)$. *If there is no selection then we have for two loci and uniform crossover:*

$$(11.7) \qquad D(t) = (-1)^{|x|^2} \big(p(\mathbf{x}, t) - p_1(x_1, 0)p_2(x_2, 0)\big).$$

$|x|^2$ *denotes the number of ones in* $\mathbf{x}$. $p_i(x_i, 0)$ *denotes the univariate marginal frequency at* $t = 0$. *The factor* $D(t)$ *is halved each generation:*

$$(11.8) \qquad\qquad D(t+1) = \frac{1}{2}D(t).$$

Proof. Without selection the univariate marginal frequencies are independent of t, because in an infinite population they are unchanged by a recombination operator. Then from

$$p(1, 1, t) - p_1(1, 0)p_2(1, 0)$$
$$= p(1, 1, t) - \big(p(1, 0, t) + p(1, 1, t)\big)\big(p(0, 1, t) + p(1, 1, t)\big)$$
$$= p(1, 1, t) - p(0, 1, t)p(1, 0, t) - p(1, 1, t)(1 - p(0, 0, t))$$
$$= D(t)$$

we obtain equation (11.7) for $\mathbf{x} = (1, 1)$. The other cases are proven in the same way.

The gene frequencies after recombination are obtained as follows. We consider only $p(1, 1, t)$. The probability of $p(1, 1, t+1)$ can be computed from the probability that recombination generates string $(1, 1)$. The probability is given by

$$p(1, 1, t+1) = p(1, 1, t) \cdot \left(\tfrac{1}{2}p(0, 0, t) + p(0, 1, t) + p(1, 0, t) + p(1, 1, t)\right)$$
$$+ \frac{1}{2}p(0, 1, t)p(1, 0, t)$$
$$= p(1, 1, t) - \tfrac{1}{2}\big(p(1, 1, t)p(0, 0, t) - p(0, 1, t)p(1, 0, t)\big)$$
$$= p(1, 1, t) + (-1)^{|x|^2+1}\frac{1}{2}D(t).$$

By computing D(t+1) equation (11.8) is obtained. □

We will use as a measure for the deviation from Robbins's proportions the mean square error DSQ(t):

$$(11.9) \qquad \text{DSQ}(t) = \sum_{\mathbf{x}} \big(p(\mathbf{x}, t) - p_1(x_1, t)p_2(x_2, t)\big)^2.$$

From the above theorem we obtain the following corollary.

Corollary 11.1. *For two loci the mean square error is reduced each step by one fourth:*

$$\text{DSQ}(t + 1) = \frac{1}{4}\text{DSQ}(t).$$

For more than two loci the equations for uniform crossover and one-point crossover get more complicated. Uniform crossover converges faster to linkage equilibrium because it "mixes" the genes much more than does one-point crossover.

In a finite population linkage equilibrium cannot be achieved exactly. Consider as an example the uniform distribution. Here linkage equilibrium is given by $p(\mathbf{x}) = 2^{-n}$. This value can be obtained only if the size of the population is substantially larger than 2^n. In a finite population we observe first a fast decrease of linkage disequilibrium. Then DSQ slowly increases owing to stochastic fluctuations by *genetic drift*. Ultimately the population will consist of only one genotype. Genetic drift has been analyzed by Asoh and Mühlenbein (1994b). It will not be considered here.

11.4 Selection and Recombination

We have shown that the average $\bar{f}(t)$ never decreases after selection and that any complete recombination scheme rearranges the genetic population to Robbins's proportions. Now the difficult question arises: What happens if recombination is applied *after* selection? This problem is still a puzzle in population genetics (Nagylaki, 1992). Formally, the difference equations can be easily written. Let a recombination distribution R be given. $R_{x,yz}$ denotes the probability that y and z produce x after recombination. Then

$$(11.10) \qquad p(\mathbf{x}, t + 1) = \sum_{y,z} R_{x,yz}p^s(\mathbf{y}, t)p^s(\mathbf{z}, t),$$

where $p^s(x)$ denotes the probability of string x after selection. For n loci the recombination distribution R consists of $2^n \times 2^n$ parameters. Recently Christiansen and Feldman (1998) have written a survey about the mathematics of selection and recombination from the viewpoint of population genetics. A new technique to obtain the equations has been developed by Vose (1999). In both frameworks one needs a computer program to compute the equations for a given fitness function.

We discuss the problem only for a special case, uniform crossover for $n = 2$ loci.

Theorem 11.3. *For proportionate selection and uniform crossover the gene frequencies obey the following difference equation:*

$$(11.11) \quad p(\mathbf{x}, t+1) = p(\mathbf{x}, t)\frac{f(\mathbf{x})}{\bar{f}(t)} + (-1)^{|\mathbf{x}|^2+1}\frac{1}{2}\frac{D_s(t)}{\bar{f}(t)^2} \, .$$

$|\mathbf{x}|$ *denotes the number of ones in* $\mathbf{x}$. $\bar{f}(t) = \sum_{\mathbf{x}} p(\mathbf{x}, t) f(\mathbf{x})$ *is the average fitness of the population; and* $D_s(t)$ *is defined as*

$$D_s(t) = f(0,0)f(1,1)p(0,0,t)p(1,1,t)$$
$$(11.12) \qquad\qquad - f(0,1)f(1,0)p(1,0,t)p(0,1,t) \, .$$

Proof. For proportionate selection the gene frequencies $p^s(\mathbf{x}, t)$ after selection are given by

$$p^s(\mathbf{x}, t) = p(\mathbf{x}, t)\frac{f(\mathbf{x})}{\bar{f}(t)} \, .$$

Now we pair randomly between the selected parents and count how often genotype $\mathbf{x}$ arises after uniform crossover. Taking $\mathbf{x} = (0,0)$ as an example, and computing the probabilities of mating, we obtain

$$p(0,0,t+1)$$
$$= \ p^s(0,0,t)\left(p^s(0,0,t) + p^s(0,1,t) + p^s(1,0,t) + \tfrac{1}{2}p^s(1,1,t)\right)$$
$$+ \tfrac{1}{2}p^s(0,1,t)p^s(1,0,t) \, .$$

Using the fact that $p^s(0,0,t) + p^s(0,1,t) + p^s(1,0,t) + p^s(1,1,t) = 1$ we obtain the theorem for $\mathbf{x} = (0,0)$. The remaining equations are obtained in the same manner. □

A rigorous analysis of the mathematical properties of n loci systems is difficult. For a problem of size n we have 2^n equations. Furthermore the equations depend on the recombination operator used. If the gene frequencies remain in linkage equilibrium, then only n equations are needed for the marginal frequencies. Thus the crucial question is: Does the optimization process get worse because of this simplification? The answer is no. Evidence for this statement is found in a theorem from Mühlenbein (1997). It shows that the univariate marginal frequencies are the same for all recombination schemes if applied to the same distribution $p(\mathbf{x}, t)$.

Theorem 11.4. *For any complete recombination/crossover scheme used after proportionate selection the univariate marginal frequencies are determined by*

$$(11.13) \qquad\qquad p_i(x_i, t+1) = \sum_{\mathbf{x}|X_i=x_i} \frac{p(\mathbf{x}, t)f(\mathbf{x})}{\bar{f}(t)} \, .$$

Proof. After selection the univariate marginal frequencies are given by

$$p_i^s(x_i, t) = \sum_{\mathbf{x}|X_i=x_i} p^s(\mathbf{x}, t) = \sum_{\mathbf{x}|X_i=x_i} \frac{p(\mathbf{x}, t)f(\mathbf{x})}{\bar{f}(t)}.$$

Now the selected individuals are paired randomly. Since complete recombination does not change the allele frequencies, these operators do not change the univariate marginal frequencies. Therefore

$$p_i(x_i, t+1) = p_i^s(x_i, t).$$

$\square$

11.5 Schema Analysis Demystified

Many of the more intuitive arguments about the behavior of genetic algorithm are based on the analysis of "schemata" and their evolution in a population. The theory has been developed by Holland (1975/1992). By using probability distributions and an ideal schema equation we demonstrate by a simple example that the popular conclusions about the proliferation of schemata are wrong. Our analysis is based on an exact solution of the probability distribution for proportionate selection.

Definition 11.5. *Let $p(\mathbf{x}, t)$ denote the probability of $\mathbf{x}$ in the population at generation t. Let $\mathbf{x}_s = (x_{s_1}, \ldots, x_{s_i}) \subset \{x_1, \ldots, x_n\}$. Thus $\mathbf{x}_s$ denotes a sub vector of $\mathbf{x}$ defined by the indices $s_1, \ldots, s_i$. Then the probability of schema $H(\mathbf{s})$ is defined by*

$$(11.14) \qquad p(H(\mathbf{s}), t) = \sum_{X|X_s=x_s} p(\mathbf{x}, t).$$

The summation is done by fixing the values of $\mathbf{x}_s$. Thus the probability of a schema is just the corresponding marginal distribution $p(\mathbf{x}_s)$. If $\mathbf{x}_s$ consists of only a single element, we have a univariate marginal distribution.

SGA uses fitness proportionate selection, which means that the probability of $\mathbf{x}$ being selected is given by

$$(11.15) \qquad p^s(\mathbf{x}, t) = p(\mathbf{x}, t)\frac{f(\mathbf{x})}{\bar{f}(t)}.$$

$\bar{f}(t) = \sum_x p(\mathbf{x}, t)f(\mathbf{x})$ is the average fitness of the population. Let us now assume that we have an algorithm that generates new points according to the distribution of selected points, or more formally:

$$(11.16) \qquad p(\mathbf{x}, t+1) = p(\mathbf{x}, t)\frac{f(\mathbf{x})}{\bar{f}(t)}.$$

$p(\mathbf{x}, t+1)$ can be seen as the ideal probability distribution of SGA.

Definition 11.6. *The fitness of schema $H(s)$ is defined by*

$$(11.17) \qquad f(H(s),t) = \sum_{X|X_s=x_s} \frac{p(\mathbf{x},t)}{p(H(s),t)} f(\mathbf{x}).$$

Theorem 11.5 (Schema Theorem). *The probability of schema $H(s)$ is given by*

$$(11.18) \qquad p(H(s),t+1) = p(H(s,t)) \frac{f(H(s),t)}{\bar{f}(t)}.$$

Holland (1975/1992, Theorem 6.2.3) computed for SGA the following inequality:

$$(11.19) \qquad p(H(s),t+1) \geq (1-\delta)p\big(H(s,t)\big)\frac{f(H(s),t)}{\bar{f}(t)},$$

where δ is a small factor that captures the loss by mutation and crossover. The inequality only complicates the analysis. Equation (11.17) is obviously an ideal case for Holland's analysis. The mathematical difficulty of using the inequality (11.19) to estimate the distribution of schemata lies in the fact that the fitness of a schema depends on $p(\mathbf{x},t)$, i.e. the distribution of the genotypes of the population. This is a defining fact of Darwinian *natural selection*. The fitness is always relative to the current population. To cite a proverb: *the one-eyed is the king of the blind.*

Thus an application of the inequality (11.19) is not possible without computing $p(\mathbf{x},t)$. Goldberg (1989) circumvented this problem by assuming

$$(11.20) \qquad p(H(s),t) \geq (1+c)\bar{f}(t).$$

With this assumption we estimate $p(H(s),t) \geq (1+c)^t p(H(s),0)$. But the assumption can never be fulfilled for all t. When approaching an optimum, the fitness of all schemata in the population will be only $1 \pm \epsilon$ away from the average fitness. Here proportionate selection meets difficulties.

The typical folklore that arose from the schema analysis is nicely summarized by Ballard (1997, page 270). He is not biased toward or against genetic algorithms. He just cites the commonly used arguments:

- *Short schemata have a high probability of surviving the genetic operations.*
- *Focusing on short schemata that compete shows that, over the short run, the fittest are increasing at an exponential rate.*
- *Ergo, if all of the assumptions hold (we cannot tell whether they do, but we suspect they do), GAs are optimal.*

We will not investigate the optimality argument, but will show that the basic conclusion of exponential increasing schemata does not hold.

It turns out that equation (11.16) for proportionate selection admits an analytical solution.

Theorem 11.6 (Convergence). *The distribution $p(\mathbf{x}, t)$ for proportionate selection is given by*

$$(11.21) \qquad p(\mathbf{x}, t) = \frac{p(\mathbf{x}, 0) f(\mathbf{x})^t}{\sum_y p(\mathbf{y}, 0) f(\mathbf{y})^t} .$$

Let $\mathcal{M}$ be the set of global optima, then

$$(11.22) \qquad \lim_{t \to \infty} p(\mathbf{x}, t) = \begin{cases} 1/|\mathcal{M}| & \mathbf{x} \in \mathcal{M} \\ 0 & \text{otherwise.} \end{cases}$$

Proof. The proof is by induction. The assumption is fulfilled for $t = 1$. Then

$$p(\mathbf{x}, t+1) = \frac{p(\mathbf{x}, 0) f(\mathbf{x})^{t+1}}{\sum_y p(\mathbf{y}, 0) f(\mathbf{y})^{t+1}}$$

$$= \frac{p(\mathbf{x}, 0) f(\mathbf{x})^t}{\bar{f}(t)} \cdot \frac{f(\mathbf{x})}{\sum_y \frac{p(\mathbf{y}, 0) f(\mathbf{y})^t \cdot f(\mathbf{y})}{\bar{f}(t)}}$$

$$= \frac{p(\mathbf{x}, 0) f(\mathbf{x})^{t+1}}{\sum_y p(\mathbf{y}, 0) f(\mathbf{y})^{t+1}} .$$

Let $\mathbf{x}_{\max} \in \mathcal{M}$ and $f(\mathbf{x}) < f(\mathbf{x}_{\max})$. Then

$$\frac{p(\mathbf{x}, t)}{p(\mathbf{x}_{\max}, t)} = \frac{p(\mathbf{x}, 0) f(\mathbf{x})^t}{p(\mathbf{x}_{\max}, 0) f(\mathbf{x}_{\max})^t} \to 0 .$$

$\square$

This shows that our algorithm is ideal in the sense that it converges even to the set of global optima. Equation (11.21) was already used by Goldberg and Deb (1991).

By using equation (11.21) we can make a correct schema analysis. We compute the probabilities of all schemata. We discuss only the interesting case of a *deceptive function*. We take the 3-bit deceptive function defined by

$$\text{Decep}(\mathbf{x}) = 0.9 - 0.1(x_1 + x_2 + x_3)$$
$$- 0.7(x_1 x_2 + x_2 x_3 + x_1 x_3) + 2.5 x_1 x_2 x_3 .$$

The function is called *deceptive* because the global optimum $(1, 1, 1)$ is isolated, whereas the local optimum $(0, 0, 0)$ is surrounded by strings of high fitness. We now look at the behavior of some schemata.

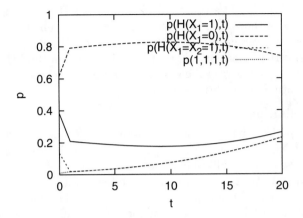

FIGURE 11.1. Evolution of some schemata.

Definition 11.7. *A schema is* optimal *if its defining string s is contained in an optimal string.*

For the deceptive function, $H(X_1 = 1)$ and $H(X_1 = X_2 = 1)$ are optimal schemata. These are displayed in figure 11.1. We see that the probability of the optimal schema $p(H(X_1 = 1))$ decreases for about 8 generations, then it increases fairly slowly. This behavior is contrary to the folklore arising from Holland's schema analysis. Schema $H(X_1 = X_2 = 1)$ decreases dramatically at the first generation; then its probability is almost identical to the probability of the optimum $(1, 1, 1)$.

To summarize the results: All complete recombination schemes lead to the same univariate marginal distributions after one step of selection and recombination. If recombination is used a number of times without selection, then the genotype frequencies converge to linkage equilibrium. This means that *all genetic algorithms are identical if after one selection step recombination is done without selection a sufficient number of times.* This fundamental algorithm keeps the population in linkage equilibrium.

12 The Univariate Marginal Distribution Algorithm (UMDA)

The univariate marginal distribution algorithm UMDA generates new points according to $p(\mathbf{x}, t) = \prod_{i=1}^{n} p_i^s(x_i, t)$. Thus UMDA keeps the gene frequencies in linkage equilibrium. This makes a mathematical analysis possible. We derive a difference equation for proportionate selection. This equation has already been proposed by Sewall Wright in 1937 (Wright, 1970). Wright's equation shows that UMDA is trying to solve a continuous optimization problem. The continuous function to be optimized is the average fitness of the population $W(\mathbf{p})$. The variables are the univariate marginal distributions. In a fundamental theorem we show the relation between the attractors of the continuous problem and the local optima of the fitness function $f(\mathbf{x})$.

12.1 Definition of UMDA

Instead of performing recombination a number of times in order to converge to linkage equilibrium, one can achieve this in one step by *gene pool recombination* (Mühlenbein and Voigt, 1996). In gene pool recombination a new string is computed by randomly taking for each locus a gene from the distribution of the selected parents. This means that gene x_i occurs with probability $p_i^s(x_i)$ in the next population. $p_i^s(x_i)$ is the distribution of x_i in the selected parents. New strings $\mathbf{x}$ are generated according to the distribution

$$(12.1) \qquad p(\mathbf{x}, t+1) = \prod_{i=1}^{n} p_i^s(x_i, t).$$

One can simplify the algorithm by directly computing the univariate marginal frequencies from the data. Then equation (12.1) can be used to generate new strings. This method is used by UMDA.

UMDA

- STEP 0: Set $t \Leftarrow 1$. Generate $N \gg 0$ points randomly.
- STEP 1: Select $M \leq N$ points according to a selection method. Compute the marginal frequencies $p_i^s(x_i, t)$ of the selected set.
- STEP 2: Generate N new points according to the distribution $p(\mathbf{x}, t+1) = \prod_{i=1}^{n} p_i^s(x_i, t)$. Set $t \Leftarrow t+1$.
- STEP 3: If termination criteria are not met, go to STEP 1.

For proportionate selection we need the average fitness of the population $\bar{f}(t)$. We consider $\bar{f}(t)$ as a function that depends on $p(x_i)$. To emphasize this dependency we write

$$(12.2) \qquad W(p_1(X_1 = 0), p_1(X_1 = 1), \ldots, p_n(X_n = 1)) := \bar{f}(t).$$

W depends formally on $2n$ parameters. $p_i(X_i = 1)$ and $p_i(X_i = 0)$ are considered to be two independent parameters despite the constraint $p_i(X_i = 0) = 1 - p_i(X_i = 1)$. We abbreviate $p_i := p_i(X_i = 1)$. If we insert $1 - p_i$ for $p_i(X_i = 0)$ into W, we obtain $\tilde{W}$. $\tilde{W}$ depends on n parameters. Now we can formulate the main theorem.

Theorem 12.1. *For infinite populations and proportionate selection the difference equations for the gene frequencies used by UMDA are given by*

$$(12.3) \qquad p_i(x_i, t+1) = p_i(x_i, t) \frac{\bar{f}_i(x_i, t)}{W(t)} = p_i(x_i, t) \frac{\frac{\partial W}{\partial p_i(x_i)}}{W(t)}$$

with

$$(12.4) \qquad \bar{f}_i(x_i, t) := \sum_{\mathbf{x}, X_i = x_i} f(\mathbf{x}) \prod_{j \neq i}^{n} p(x_j, t).$$

The equation can also be written as

$$(12.5) \qquad p_i(t+1) = p_i(t) + p_i(t)(1 - p_i(t)) \frac{\frac{\partial \tilde{W}}{\partial p_i}}{\tilde{W}(t)}.$$

The response $R(t)$ is given by

$$R(t) = \frac{\mathrm{VA}(t)}{\tilde{W}} + \frac{1}{2} \sum_{i \neq j} \frac{\alpha_i \cdot \alpha_j}{\tilde{W}^2} \frac{\partial^2 \tilde{W}}{\partial p_i \partial p_j}$$

$$(12.6) \qquad + \frac{1}{3!} \sum_{i \neq j, j \neq k, i \neq k} \frac{\alpha_i \cdot \alpha_j \cdot \alpha_k}{\tilde{W}^3} \frac{\partial^3 \tilde{W}}{\partial p_i \partial p_j \partial p_k} + \cdots,$$

$$(12.7) \qquad \mathrm{VA}(t) = \sum_i p_i(1, t)\big(f_i(1, t) - W\big)^2 + p_i(0, t)\big(f_i(0, t) - W\big)^2$$

$$\alpha_i = p_i(t)\big(1 - p_i(t)\big) \frac{\partial \tilde{W}}{\partial p_i}.$$

$\mathrm{VA}(t)$ *is called the* additive genetic variance. *The average fitness never decreases:*

$$(12.8) \qquad W(t+1) \geq W(t).$$

Proof. Equation (12.3) has been proven in Mühlenbein (1997). We have to prove equation (12.5). Note that

$$p_i(t+1) - p_i(t) = p_i(t) \frac{\bar{f}_i(x_i = 1, t) - \tilde{W}(t)}{\tilde{W}(t)}.$$

Obviously we have

$$\frac{\partial \tilde{W}}{\partial p_i} = \bar{f}(x_i = 1, t) - \bar{f}(x_i = 0, t).$$

From $p_i(t)\bar{f}_i(x_i = 1, t) + (1 - p_i(t))\bar{f}_i(x_i = 0, t) = \tilde{W}(t)$, we obtain

$$\bar{f}(x_i = 1, t) - \tilde{W}(t) - \big(1 - p_i(t)\big)\bar{f}(x_i = 1, t) + \big(1 - p_i(t)\big)\bar{f}(x_i = 0, t) = 0.$$

This gives

$$\bar{f}_i(x_i = 1, t) - \tilde{W}(t) = \left(1 - p_i(t)\right)\frac{\partial \tilde{W}}{\partial p_i}.$$

Inserting this equation into the difference equation yields equation (12.5). Equation (12.6) is just the multidimensional Taylor expansion. The first term follows from

$$\sum_i (p_i(t+1) - p_i(t))\frac{\partial \tilde{W}}{\partial p_i}$$

$$= \sum_i p_i(t)(1 - p_i(t))\left(\frac{\partial \tilde{W}}{\partial p_i}\right)^2$$

$$= \sum_i p_i(t)(f_i(1,t) - \tilde{W})(f_i(1,t) - \tilde{W} + \tilde{W} - f_i(0,t))$$

$$= \sum_i p_i(t)(f_i(1,t) - \tilde{W})^2 + (1 - p_i(t))(f_i(0,t) - \tilde{W})$$

$$= \text{VA}(t).$$

□

The above equations completely describe the dynamics of UMDA with proportionate selection. Mathematically UMDA performs gradient ascent in the landscape defined by W or $\tilde{W}$.

Equation (12.5), Wright's equation, is especially suited for the theoretical analysis. Wright's (1970, p. 8) remarks are still valid today:

> The appearance of this formula is deceptively simple. Its use in conjunction with other components is not such a gross oversimplification in principle as has sometimes been alleged. ... Obviously calculations can be made only from rather simple models, involving only a few loci or simple patterns of interaction among many similarly behaving loci. ... Apart from application to simple systems, the greatest significance of the general formula is that its form brings out properties of systems that would not be apparent otherwise.

The restricted application lies in the following fact. In general the difference equations requite the evaluation of 2^n terms. The computational complexity can be reduced drastically if the fitness function has a special form.

Example 12.1. $f(\mathbf{x}) = \sum_i a_i x_i, \quad x_i \in \{0, 1\}$.

After some tedious manipulations one obtains:

$$W(\mathbf{p}) = \sum_i a_i p_i(1)$$

$$\frac{\partial W}{\partial p_i(1)} = a_i + \sum_{j \neq i} a_j p_j(1).$$

This gives the difference equation:

$$(12.9) \qquad \Delta p_i(1) = p_i(1,t)\big(1 - p_i(1,t)\big) \frac{a_i}{\sum_i a_i p_i(1,t)}.$$

Given that $\frac{\partial \tilde{W}}{\partial p_i(1)} = a_i$, we have proven nothing other than Wright's equation. This equation has been solved approximately in Mühlenbein and Mahnig (1999a).

This example shows that the expressions for W and its derivatives can be surprisingly simple. $W(\mathbf{p})$ can be obtained from $f(\mathbf{x})$ by exchanging x_i with $p_i(1)$. But the formal derivation of $W(\mathbf{p})$ cannot be obtained from the simplified $W(\mathbf{p})$ expression.

Another interesting example is a multiplicative function.

Theorem 12.2. *For a multiplicative function* $f(\mathbf{x}) = \prod_{i=1}^{n} f_i(x_i)$ *we have*

$$(12.10) \qquad\qquad R(t) = \frac{V(t)}{\tilde{W}} = S(t)$$

Proof. The proof is technically somewhat complicated. We just sketch the proof for $n = 2$. We set $p_1 = p_1(x_1, t)$ and $p_2 = p_2(x_2, t)$. Using equation (12.3) we obtain

$$p(\mathbf{x}, t+1) = \frac{p_1 \bar{f}_1(x_1,t) p_2 \bar{f}(x_2,t)}{W^2}$$
$$\bar{f}_1(x_1,t) = p_2 f(x_1, x_2) + (1 - p_2) f(x_1, 1 - x_2)$$
$$\bar{f}_2(x_2,t) = p_1 f(x_1, x_2) + (1 - p_1)) f(1 - x_1, x_2).$$

After some manipulations we obtain

$$\bar{f}_1(x_1,t) \bar{f}_2(x_2,t) = f(x_1, x_2) W,$$

and finally

$$p(\mathbf{x}, t+1) = p(\mathbf{x}, t) \frac{f(\mathbf{x})}{W}.$$

From lemma 11.1 we obtain $R(t) = V(t)/W$. □

12.2 Computing the Average Fitness

In the this section we investigate the computation of W and its gradient. Wright is also the originator of the landscape metaphor now popular in evolutionary computation and population genetics. Unfortunately

Wright used two quite different definitions for the landscape, apparently without realizing the fundamental distinction between them. The first landscape describes the relation between the genotypes and their fitness, whereas the second describes the relation between the allele frequencies in a population and its mean fitness.

The first definition is just the fitness function $f(\mathbf{x})$ used in evolutionary computation; the second is the average fitness $\tilde{W}(\mathbf{p})$. The second definition is much more useful, because it lends itself to a quantitative description of the evolutionary process, i.e. Wright's equation.

For notational simplicity we derive only the relation between $f(\mathbf{x})$ and $\tilde{W}$ for binary alleles. Let $\alpha = (\alpha_1, \ldots, \alpha_n)$ with $\alpha_i \in \{0, 1\}$ be a multi-index. We define with $0^0 := 1$:

$$\mathbf{x}^\alpha := \prod_i x_i^{\alpha_i}.$$

Definition 12.1. *The representation of a binary discrete function using the ordering according to function values is given by*

$$f(\mathbf{x}) = f(0, \ldots, 0)(1 - x_1) \cdots (1 - x_n) + \cdots + f(1, \ldots, 1)x_1 \cdots x_n.$$

The representation using the ordering according to variables is

$$(12.11) \qquad\qquad f(\mathbf{x}) = \sum_\alpha a_\alpha x^\alpha.$$

$\max\{|\alpha|_1 = \sum_i \alpha_i : a_\alpha \neq 0\}$ *is called the* order *of the function.*

In both representations the function is linear in each variable x_i. The following lemma is obvious.

Lemma 12.1. *The two representations are unique. There exists a unique matrix A of dimension $2^n \times 2^n$ such that*

$$a_\alpha = (Af)_\alpha.$$

We now use this result for $\tilde{W}$.

Lemma 12.2. $\tilde{W}(\mathbf{p}) := \bar{f}(t)$ *is an extension of $f(x)$ to S. There exist two representations for $\tilde{W}(p)$. These are given by*

$$(12.12)$$
$$\tilde{W}(\mathbf{p}) = f(0, \ldots, 0)(1 - p_1) \cdots (1 - p_n) + \cdots + f(1, \ldots, 1)p_1 \cdots p_n$$

$$(12.13) \qquad\qquad \tilde{W}(\mathbf{p}) = \sum_\alpha a_\alpha p^\alpha.$$

The proofs in this section have been informal. The above lemma can be proven rigorously by Moebius inversion. If the function is given in analytical form (equation (12.11)) and the order of the function is bounded by a constant independent of n, $\tilde{W}(\mathbf{p})$ can be computed in polynomial time. The equation can also be used to compute the derivative of $\tilde{W}$, which is needed for Wright's equation. It is given by

(12.14) $$\frac{\partial \tilde{W}(p)}{\partial p_i(1)} = \sum_{\alpha | \alpha_i = 1} a_\alpha p^{\alpha'}$$

with $\alpha_i' = 0, \alpha_j' = \alpha_j$.

We will now characterize the attractors of UMDA. Let $S_i = \{q_i | \sum_{k \in \{0,1\}} q_i(x_k) \le 1; \ 0 \le q_i(x_k) \le 1\}$ and $S = \prod_i S_i$ the Cartesian product. Then $S = [0,1]^n$ is the unit cube.

Theorem 12.3. *The stable attractors of Wright's equation are at the corners of S, i.e. $p_i \in \{0,1\}$, $i = 1, \ldots, n$. In the interior there are only saddle points or local minima where* grad $W(p)) = 0$. *The attractors are local maxima of $f(x)$ according to one bit changes. Wright's equation solves the continuous optimization problem* argmax$\{\tilde{W}(\mathbf{p})\}$ *in S by gradient ascent.*

Proof. W is linear in p_i; therefore it cannot have any local maxima in the interior. Points with grad $W(p) = 0$ are unstable fix points of UMDA.

We next show that boundary points that are not local maxima of $f(x)$ cannot be attractors. We prove the conjecture indirectly. Without loss of generality, let the boundary point be $\hat{p} = (1, \ldots, 1)$. We now consider an arbitrary neighbor, i.e. $p^* = (0, 1, \ldots, 1)$. The two points are connected at the boundary by

$$p(z) = (1 - z, 1, \ldots, 1) \qquad z \in [0,1].$$

We know that $\tilde{W}$ is *linear* in the parameters p_i. Because $\tilde{W}(p^*) = f(0, 1, \ldots, 1)$ and $\tilde{W}(\hat{p}) = f(1, \ldots, 1)$ we have

(12.15) $\quad \tilde{W}(p(z)) = f(1, \ldots, 1) + z \cdot [f(0, 1, \ldots, 1) - f(1, \ldots, 1)].$

If $f(0, 1, \ldots, 1) > f(1, \ldots, 1)$ then $\hat{p}$ cannot be an attractor of UMDA. The mean fitness increases with z. $\qquad \square$

The extension of the above lemma to multiple alleles and multivariate distributions is straightforward, but the notation becomes difficult.

13   The Science of Breeding

Fitness proportionate selection is the undisputed selection method in population genetics. It is considered a model for *natural selection*. But for proportionate selection the following problem arises. When the population approaches an optimum, selection gets weaker and weaker because the fitness values become similar. Therefore breeders of livestock use other selection methods. These are called *artificial selection* methods. For large populations they mainly apply *truncation selection*. It works as follows. A truncation threshold τ is fixed. Then the τN best individuals are selected as parents for the next generation. These parents are then randomly mated.

The science of breeding is the domain of *quantitative genetics*. The theory is based on macroscopic variables. Because an exact mathematical analysis is impossible, many statistical techniques are used. In fact, the concepts of regression, correlation, heritability, and decomposition of variance were first developed and applied in quantitative genetics.

13.1 Single Trait Theory

For a single trait the theory is easily summarized. Starting with the fitness distribution, the *selection differential* $S(t)$ is introduced. It is the difference between the average of the selected parents and the average of the population:

$$(13.1) \qquad S(t) = W(\mathbf{p}^s(t+1)) - W(\mathbf{p}(t)).$$

Similarly, the response $R(t)$ is defined:

$$(13.2) \qquad R(t) = W(\mathbf{p}(t+1)) - W(\mathbf{p}(t)).$$

Next a linear regression is performed:

$$(13.3) \qquad R(t) = b(t)S(t).$$

$b(t)$ is called *realized heritability*. The most difficult part of applying the theory is predicting $b(t)$. The first estimate uses the *regression of offspring to parent*. Let f_i, f_j be the phenotypic values of parents i and j. Then

$$\bar{f}_{i,j} = \frac{f_i + f_j}{2}$$

is the mid-parent value. Let the stochastic variable $\bar{F}$ denote the mid-parent value.

Theorem 13.1. *Let $P(t) = (f_1, \dots, f_N)$ be the population at generation t, where f_i denotes the phenotypic value of individual i. Assume that an offspring generation $O(t)$ is created by random mating, without selection. If the regression equation*

$$(13.4) \qquad o_{ij}(t) = a(t) + b_{\bar{P}O}(t) \cdot \frac{f_i + f_j}{2} + \epsilon_{ij}$$

with

$$E(\epsilon_{ij}) = 0$$

is valid, where o_{ij} is the fitness value of an offspring of i and j, then

$$(13.5) \qquad b_{\bar{P}O}(t) \approx b(t).$$

Proof. From the regression equation we obtain for the expected averages:

$$E(O(t)) = a(t) + b_{\bar{P}O}(t)M(t).$$

Because the offspring generation is created by random mating without selection, the expected average fitness remains constant:

$$E(O(t)) = M(t).$$

Let us now select a subset as parents. The parents will be randomly mated, producing the offspring generation. If the subset is large enough, we may still use the regression equation and obtain for the averages:

$$M(t+1) = a(t) + b_{\bar{P}O}(t) \cdot M_s(t).$$

Here $M(t+1)$ is the average fitness of the offspring generation produced by the selected parents. Subtracting the above equations we obtain

$$M(t+1) - M(t) = b_{\bar{P}O}(t) \cdot (M_s(t) - M(t)).$$

This proves $b_{\bar{P}O}(t) = b(t)$. $\qquad\square$

The importance of regression for estimating the heritability was discovered by Galton and Pearson at the end of the nineteenth century. They computed the regression coefficient intuitively, using scatter diagrams of mid-parent and offspring (Freedman et al., 1991). The problem of computing a good regression coefficient is solved mathematically by the theorem of Gauss-Markov. Here we just cite the theorem. The proof can be found in any textbook on statistics (e.g. Rao, 1973).

Theorem 13.2. *A good estimate for the regression coefficient of mid-parent and offspring is given by*

$$(13.6) \qquad b_{\bar{P}O}(t) = \frac{\text{cov}(O(t), \bar{P}(t))}{\text{var}(\bar{P}(t))}.$$

The covariance of O and $\bar{P}$ is defined by

$$\text{cov}(O(t), \bar{P}(t)) = \frac{1}{N} \sum_{i,j} (o_{i,j} - \text{av}(O(t))) \cdot (\bar{f}_{i,j} - \text{av}(\bar{P}(t))),$$

where *av* denotes the average and *var* the variance. Closely related to the regression coefficient is the correlation coefficient $\text{cor}(\bar{F}, O)$. It is given by

$$\text{cor}(\bar{P}(t), O(t)) = b_{\bar{P}O}(t) \cdot \left(\frac{\text{var}(\bar{P}(t))}{\text{var}(O(t))} \right)^{1/2}.$$

The concept of covariance is restricted to parents producing offspring. It cannot be used for UMDA. Here the *analysis of variance* helps. We will decompose the fitness value $f(\mathbf{x})$ recursively into an additive part and interaction parts. Recall the definition of conditional probability:

Definition 13.1. *Let $p(\mathbf{x})$ denote the probability of $\mathbf{x}$. Then the conditional probability $p(\mathbf{x}|y)$ of $\mathbf{x}$ given y is defined by*

$$(13.7) \qquad p(\mathbf{x}|y) = \frac{p(\mathbf{x}, y)}{p(y)}.$$

The decomposition works as follows. First we extract the average:

$$(13.8) \qquad f(\mathbf{x}) = \bar{f} + r_0(\mathbf{x}).$$

Then we extract the first-order (additive) part from the residual $r_0(\mathbf{x})$:

$$(13.9) \qquad r_0(\mathbf{x}) = \sum_{i=1}^{n} f_{(i)}(x_i) + r_1(\mathbf{x}),$$

where $f_{(i)}(x_i)$ is given by

$$f_{(i)}(x_i) = \sum_{\mathbf{x}|x_i} p(\mathbf{x}|x_i) r_0(\mathbf{x}) = \sum_{\mathbf{x}|x_i} p(\mathbf{x}|x_i) f(\mathbf{x}) - \bar{f}.$$

Here $\sum_{\mathbf{x}|x_i}$ means that the ith locus is fixed to the value x_i. The $f_{(i)}(x_i)$ minimize the quadratic error $\sum_{\mathbf{x}} p(\mathbf{x}) r_1(\mathbf{x})^2$.

If $r_1(\mathbf{x}) \neq 0$, we can proceed further to extract the second-order terms from $r_1(\mathbf{x})$:

$$(13.10) \qquad r_1(\mathbf{x}) = \sum_{\substack{(i,j) \\ i<j}} f_{(i,j)}(x_i, x_j) + r_2(\mathbf{x}),$$

where

$$\begin{aligned}
f_{(i,j)}(x_i, x_j) &= \sum_{\mathbf{x}|x_i,x_j} p(\mathbf{x}|x_i, x_j)\, r_1(\mathbf{x}) \\
&= \sum_{\mathbf{x}|x_i,x_j} p(\mathbf{x}|x_i, x_j)\, f(\mathbf{x}) - f_{(i)}(x_i) - f_{(j)}(x_j).
\end{aligned}$$

If we have n loci, we can iterate this procedure $n - 1$ times recursively and finally get the decomposition of f as

$$\begin{aligned}
f(\mathbf{x}) &= \bar{f} + \sum_{i} f_{(i)}(x_i) + \sum_{(i,j)} f_{(i,j)}(x_i, x_j) + \cdots \\
&\quad + \sum_{\substack{(i_1,\dots,i_{n-1}) \\ i_1 < \cdots < i_{n-1}}} f_{(i_1,\dots,i_{n-1})}(x_{i_1}, \dots, x_{i_{n-1}}) + r_{n-1}(\mathbf{x}).
\end{aligned}$$

Let V_k for $k = 1$ to $n - 1$ be defined as

$$(13.11) \quad V_k = \sum_{\substack{(i_1,\dots,i_k) \\ i_1 < \cdots < i_k}} \sum_{x_{i_1},\dots,x_{i_k}} p(x_{i_1}, \dots, x_{i_k}) f_{(i_1,\dots,i_k)}(x_{i_1}, \dots, x_{i_k})^2,$$

and

(13.12)
$$V_n = \sum_{\mathbf{x}} p(\mathbf{x}) r_{n-1}(\mathbf{x})^2.$$

If the population is in linkage equilibrium, the reader can easily verify that V_1 is the *additive genetic variance* defined by equation (12.7). $p(x_{i_1}, \ldots, x_{i_k})$ is a marginal probability distribution defined by $p(\mathbf{x})$. We are now able to formulate the theorem.

Theorem 13.3. *Let the population be in linkage equilibrium, i.e.*

(13.13)
$$p(\mathbf{x}) = \prod_{i=1}^{n} p_i(x_i).$$

Then the variance of the population is given by

(13.14)
$$V = V_1 + V_2 + \cdots + V_{n-1} + V_n.$$

The covariance of mid-parent and offspring can be computed from

(13.15)
$$\mathrm{cov}(\bar{P}, O) = \frac{1}{2} V_1 + \frac{1}{4} V_2 + \cdots + \frac{1}{2^n} V_n = \sum_{k=1}^{n} \frac{1}{2^k} V_k.$$

The proof can be found in Asoh and Mühlenbein (1994a). We now compare the estimates for heritability. For proportionate selection, we have from theorem 12.1:

$$R_{\mathrm{UMDA}}(t) = \frac{\mathrm{VA}(t)}{V(t)} S(t) + \mathrm{error}_1(t).$$

For two-parent recombination (TPR), Mühlenbein (1997) has shown for $n = 2$ loci:

$$R_{\mathrm{TPR}}(t) = 2 \frac{\mathrm{cov}(\bar{P}(t), O(t))}{V(t)} S(t) + \frac{1}{2} \mathrm{error}_2(t).$$

If the population is in linkage equilibrium we have $\mathrm{error}_1 = \mathrm{error}_2$. Using the covariance decomposition we can write

$$R_{\mathrm{TPR}}(t) = \frac{\mathrm{VA}(t)}{V(t)} S(t) + \frac{1}{2} \frac{V_2(t)}{V(t)} S(t) + \frac{1}{2} \mathrm{error}(t).$$

Thus the first term of the expansion is identical to the UMDA term. This shows again the similarity between two-parent recombination and the UMDA method.

Breeders typically use the expression $b(t) = \mathrm{VA}(t)/V(t)$ as an estimate. This is called *heritability in the narrow sense* (Falconer, 1981). But note that the variance decomposition seems to be true only for Robbins's proportions.

The selection differential is not suitable for mathematical analysis. For truncation selection it can be approximated by

$$(13.16) \qquad S(t) \approx I_\tau V^{\frac{1}{2}}(t),$$

where I_τ is called the *selection intensity*. Combining the two equations we obtain the famous *equation for the response to selection*:

$$(13.17) \qquad R(t) = b(t)I_\tau V^{\frac{1}{2}}(t).$$

These equations are discussed in depth by Mühlenbein (1997). The theory of breeding uses macroscopic variables, the average and the variance of the population. But we have derived only one equation, the *response-to-selection equation*. We need a second equation connecting the average fitness and the variance in order to be able to compute the evolution over time of the average fitness and the variance. There have been many attempts in population genetics to find a second equation. But all equations assume that the variance of the population decreases continuously. This is not the case for arbitrary fitness functions. Prügel-Bennet and Shapiro (1997) have proposed to use moments for describing genetic algorithms. They apply methods of statistical physics to derive equations for higher moments for special fitness functions.

13.2 Tournament Selection

Besides proportionate and truncation selection, *tournament selection of size k* is another popular selection method. Here k individuals are chosen randomly. The best individual is taken as parent. Here we model binary tournament selection ($k = 2$) as a game. Two individuals with genotype **x** and **y** "play" against each other. The one with the larger fitness gets a payoff of 2. If the fitness values are equal, both will win half of the games. This gives a payoff of 1. The game is defined by a *payoff matrix* with coefficients as follows:

$$a_{xy} = \begin{cases} 2 & f(\mathbf{x}) > f(\mathbf{y}) \\ 1 & f(\mathbf{x}) = f(\mathbf{y}) \\ 0 & f(\mathbf{x}) < f(\mathbf{y}) . \end{cases}$$

With some effort one can show that

$$(13.18) \qquad \sum_{\mathbf{x}} \sum_{\mathbf{y}} p(\mathbf{x}, t) a_{xy} p(\mathbf{y}, t) = 1.$$

After a round of tournaments the genotype frequencies are given by

$$(13.19) \qquad p^s(\mathbf{x}, t+1) = p(\mathbf{x}, t) \sum_{\mathbf{y}} a_{xy} p(\mathbf{y}, t).$$

If we set
$$b(\mathbf{x}, t) = \sum_{\mathbf{y}} a_{xy} p(\mathbf{y}, t),$$

then the above equation is similar to proportionate selection using the function $b(\mathbf{x}, t)$. But b depends on the genotype frequencies. Furthermore the average $\bar{b}(t) = \sum p(\mathbf{x}, t) b(\mathbf{x}, t)$ remains constant, $\bar{b}(t) \equiv 1$.

The difference equations for the univariate marginal frequencies can be derived in the same manner as for proportionate selection. They are given by

(13.20) $$p_i(x_i, t+1) = p_i(x_i, t) \cdot \bar{B}_i(t)$$

(13.21) $$\bar{B}_i(t) = \sum_{\mathbf{x}, X_i = x_i} b(\mathbf{x}, t) \prod_{\substack{j=1 \\ j \neq i}}^{n} p_j(x_j, t).$$

The difference equation for binary tournament selection is more difficult than the equation for proportionate selection. $\bar{B}_i$ is quadratic in $p(x_j)$. The fitness value of $\mathbf{x}$ is given by $\sum_y a_{xy} p(\mathbf{y}, t)$. This is called called *frequency dependent fitness* in population genetics.

Tournament selection uses only the order relation of the fitness values. The fitness values themselves do not change the outcome of a tournament. Therefore the evolution of the univariate marginal frequencies depends only on the order relation. The same is true for truncation selection. It can be seen that tournament selection can be approximated by truncation selection. For each k there exists a selection intensity I_k with

$$S(t) = I_k V^{\frac{1}{2}}(t).$$

For $k = 2$ we have $I_2 = 1/\sqrt{\pi} \approx 0.564$ (Mühlenbein, 1997).

13.3 Analytical Results for Linear Functions

For the special case where all univariate marginal distributions are equal, i.e. $p_i := p$, it is possible to obtain an analytical solution for $p(t)$.

We cite from Mühlenbein (1997) the analytical solutions for the linear function OneMax$(n) = \sum_i x_i$. For completeness we give the difference equation and its solution.

Theorem 13.4. *If in the initial population all univariate marginal frequencies are identical to $p_0 > 0$, then we obtain for UMDA and OneMax: proportionate selection:*

(13.22) $$R(t) = 1 - p(t)$$

(13.23) $$p(t) = 1 - (1 - p_0)\left(1 - \tfrac{1}{n}\right)^t$$

truncation selection:

(13.24) $$R(t) \approx I_\tau \sqrt{np(t)(1-p(t))}$$

(13.25) $$p(t) \approx 0.5 \left(1 + \sin\left(\frac{I_\tau}{\sqrt{n}}t + \arcsin(2p_0 - 1)\right)\right)$$

tournament selection:

$$R(t) = np(1-p)\left(2\sum_{k=1}^{n}\sum_{j=0}^{k-1}\binom{n-1}{k-1}\binom{n}{j}p^{k+j-1}(1-p)^{2n-k-j-1}\right.$$

(13.26) $$\left. + \sum_{k=1}^{n-1}\binom{n-1}{k-1}\binom{n}{k}p^{2k-1}(1-p)^{2n-2k-1} - \sum_{j=0}^{2n-2}p^j\right)$$

$$R(t) \approx 0.564\sqrt{np(t)(1-p(t))}.$$

(13.27)

The formulas can be used to compute the number of generations until convergence (GEN_e). For truncation selection convergence is defined by $p(t) = 1$, for proportionate selection by $p(t) = 1 - \epsilon$.

Corollary 13.1. *The number of generations until convergence is given by:*

proportionate selection:

(13.28) $$\text{GEN}_e = n \cdot \ln\frac{1-p_0}{\epsilon}$$

truncation selection:

(13.29) $$\text{GEN}_e = \left(\frac{\pi}{2} - \arcsin(2p_0 - 1)\right)\frac{\sqrt{n}}{I_\tau}.$$

Truncation selection converges in $O(\sqrt{n})$ and proportionate selection in $O(n \cdot \ln(1/\epsilon))$ generations. Numerical results have shown that truncation selection converges in about $O\sqrt{n}$ to $O(n)$ generations (Mühlenbein and Mahnig, 2000) for all fitness functions optimized.

The analytical solutions almost perfectly match the results obtained from actual UMDA runs (see figure 13.1). With proportionate selection the population requires a long time to approach the optimum. In contrast, truncation selection and tournament selection lead to much faster convergence. p increases almost linearly until near the optimum. Equation (13.26) for binary tournament selection has p^{2n} as the largest exponent. This complicated equation can be approximated by equation (13.27) with surprising accuracy.

We next present numerical results for some popular fitness functions.

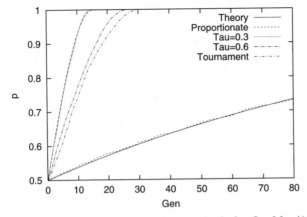

FIGURE 13.1. Comparison of selection methods for OneMax(128).

13.4 Numerical Results for UMDA

This section solves the problem put forward by Mitchell et al. (1994): to define the class of problems for which genetic algorithms are best suited, and in particular, for which they will outperform other search algorithms. We start with the *royal road* function, which was erroneously believed to lay out a "royal road" for the GA to follow to the optimal string.

13.5 Royal Road Function

The royal road function R_1 was used by Mitchell et al. (1994). It is defined as follows:

$$(13.30) \qquad R_1(l, \mathbf{x}) = \sum_{i=0}^{l-1} \prod_{j=1}^{8} x_{8i+j} \, .$$

The function is of order 8. The building block hypothesis (BBH; Holland, 1975/1992) states that "the GA works well when instances of low-order, short schemas that confer high fitness can be recombined to form instances of larger schemas that confer even higher fitness." In our terminology a schema defines a marginal distribution. Thus a first-order schema defines a univariate marginal distribution. Our analysis has shown that only the first half of the BBH is correct: first-order schemata of high fitness are recombined. Larger schemata play no role.

Table 13.1 confirms and extends the results of Mitchell et al. (1994). The extremely poor performance of SGA is mainly a result of proportionate selection. UMDA with proportionate selection (U: p) requires

TABLE 13.1

Mean Function Evaluations for Royal Road(8)
U is UMDA, F is FDA.

$1 + 1$	SGA	U: p	U: $\tau = 0.3$	U: $\tau = 0.05$	F: $\tau = 0.3$
6,334	61,334	55,586	28,000	14,264	7,634

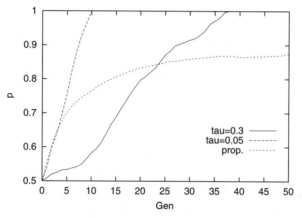

FIGURE 13.2. Convergence of royal road.

slightly fewer evaluations. With very strong selection, UMDA needs only about twice as many function evaluations as the $(1+1)$-algorithm. This algorithm performs a random bit flip and accepts a new configuration if its fitness is equal or better. This algorithm performs fairly well, as has already been shown by Mühlenbein (1991). But it performs well only if the fitness function never decreases with an increasing number of bits. An almost identical performance to that of the $(1 + 1)$-algorithm can be obtained by FDA. It uses marginal distributions of size 8 instead of univariate marginal distributions. FDA will be explained in section 14.2.

Figure 13.2 shows once again the importance of selection. Proportionate selection performs very well in the beginning, because the fitness values of all strings containing no building blocks are zero. These strings do not reproduce. But after 5 generations proportionate selection gets weaker, and truncation selection with $\tau = 0.3$ overtakes it after 23 generations. (The numerical results would be much worse for proportionate selection if we added 1 to the royal road function. In that case proportionate selection also selects many strings with no a building blocks.)

We will now explain the results by using our theory to analytically solve the equations. We have

$$\tilde{W}(\mathbf{p}) = \sum_{i=0}^{l-1} \prod_{j=1}^{8} p_{8i+j}$$

$$\frac{\partial \tilde{W}}{\partial p_k} = \prod_{\substack{j=1 \\ 8i+j \neq k}}^{7} p_{8i+j} \qquad 8i \leq k < 8i+8 \,.$$

For truncation selection we apply the response-to-selection equation. Therefore we have to compute the variance $V_l(t)$. We simplify the computation by observing that the blocks of 8 variables are independent, and therefore:

$$V_l(t) = l \cdot V(t) \,.$$

Recall that all function values are 0 except $f(1,\dots,1)$. Therefore:

$$V(t) = \sum_x p(\mathbf{x},t) f(\mathbf{x})^2 - W^2$$

$$= \prod p_i - \left(\prod p_i\right)^2 \,.$$

If we assume that $p_i = p$ for all i we obtain:

(13.31) $$V_8(t) = 8p(t)^8(1 - p(t)^8) \,.$$

We can now formulate the theorem. The equations are exact for proportionate selection. For truncation selection the concept of heritability plays a role.

Theorem 13.5. *If all univariate marginal distributions are identical to* $p(t)$ *and* $p(0) = p_0$, *then we obtain for proportionate selection:*

(13.32) $$p(t+1) - p(t) = \frac{1 - p(t)}{8}$$

(13.33) $$p(t) = 1 - (1 - p_0)(\tfrac{7}{8})^t.$$

For truncation selection with threshold τ *we get approximately*

(13.34) $$R(t) \approx b(t)I_\tau \sqrt{8p(t)^8(1 - p(t)^8)}$$

(13.35) $$p(t)^8 \approx 0.5\left(1 + \sin\left(\frac{b(t)I_\tau}{\sqrt{8}}t + \arcsin(2p_0^8 - 1)\right)\right) \,.$$

Proof. The conjectures for proportionate selection follow directly from equation (12.5). From the response-to-selection equation we obtain

$$8p(t+1)^8 - 8p(t)^8 \approx b(t)I_\tau \sqrt{8p(t)^8(1 - p(t)^8)} \,.$$

If we set $q(t) = p(t)^8$ the above equation is identical to the equation for OneMax(8). The approximate solution is given by equation (13.25). $\square$

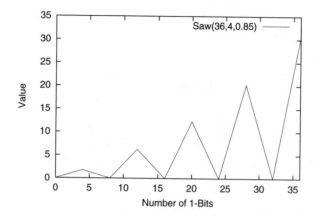

Figure 13.3. Definition of Saw$(36, 4, 0.85)$.

To apply equation (13.35) we need an estimate for the realized heritability $b(t)$. Experiments show that $b(t)$ increases approximately linearly from about 0 to 1. Thus we set $b(t) \propto t$. A numerical comparison between equation (13.35) and a simulation with a truncation threshold of 0.05 shows only 5% difference. Thus the coincidence between theory and simulation is very high.

This example shows that the response-to-selection equation can in special cases be used to compute an analytical solution for $p(t)$. The difficulty is to determine the heritability $b(t)$.

13.6 Multimodal Functions Suited for UMDA Optimization

Equation (12.5) shows that UMDA performs a gradient ascent in the landscape given by W. This helps our search for functions best suited for UMDA. We take the Saw landscape as a spectacular example. The definition of the function can be extrapolated from figure 13.3. In Saw(n, m, k), n denotes the number of bits and $2m$ the distance from one peak to the next. The highest peak is multiplied by k (with $k \leq 1$), the second highest by k^2, third by k^3, and so on. The landscape is very rugged; to get from one local optimum to another, one has to cross a deep valley.

But again the transformed landscape $W(\mathbf{p})$ is fairly smooth. An example is shown in figure 13.4. Whereas $f(\mathbf{x})$ has 5 isolated peaks, $W(\mathbf{p})$ has three plateaus, a local peak, and the global peak. We will use UMDA with truncation selection. We have not been able to derive precise analytical expressions. Figure 13.4 displays the results.

In the simulation two truncation thresholds, $\tau = 0.05$ and $\tau = 0.01$,

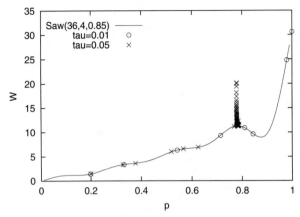

FIGURE 13.4. Results with normal and strong selection.

have been used. For $\tau = 0.05$ the probability p stops at the local maximum for $\tilde{W}(\mathbf{p})$. It is approximately $p = 0.78$. For $\tau = 0.01$ UMDA is able to converge to the optimum $p = 1$—it does so by going even downhill.

This example confirms our theory: *UMDA transforms the original fitness landscape defined by $f(\mathbf{x})$ into a fitness landscape defined by $\tilde{W}(\mathbf{p})$. This transformation smoothes the rugged fitness landscape $f(\mathbf{x})$ so that if there is a tendency toward the global optimum, UMDA may find it.*

Thus UMDA can solve difficult multimodal optimization problems. It is obvious that any search method using a single search point, like the $(1 + 1)$-algorithm, needs instead an almost exponential number of function evaluations to obtain the optimum of Saw.

13.7 Deceptive Functions

There are many optimization problems where UMDA is misleading. We demonstrate this problem with a deceptive function. We use the definition

$$(13.36) \qquad \text{Decep}(\mathbf{x}, k) := \begin{cases} k - 1 - |\mathbf{x}|_1 & 0 \le |\mathbf{x}|_1 < k \\ k & |\mathbf{x}|_1 = k. \end{cases}$$

The global maximum is isolated at $x = (1, \ldots, 1)$. A deceptive function of order n is a "needle in a haystack" problem. Such functions are far too difficult for any optimization method to optimize. We simplify the optimization problem by adding l distinct $\text{Decep}(k)$ functions to give a fitness function of size $n = lk$. This function is also deceptive. The local optimum $x = (0, \ldots, 0)$ is surrounded by high fitness values, whereas

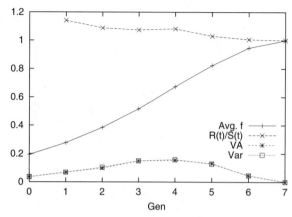

Figure 13.5. Heritability and variance for a multiplicative function (variance and VA multiplied by 10); $s = 0.1$, $n = 32$.

the global optimum is isolated.

$$(13.37) \quad \text{Decep}(n, k) = \sum_{i=1,k+1,\ldots}^{n} \text{Decep}\big((x_i, x_{i+1}, \ldots, x_{i+k-1}), k\big).$$

Our theory easily shows that at $p_i = 0.5$ the gradient points to $x_i = 0$. Thus starting at $p(0) = 0.5$ UMDA converges to the local optimum $\mathbf{x} = (0, \ldots, 0)$. This problem can be solved if higher-order marginal distributions are used. This will be discussed later in the context of the factorized distribution algorithm (FDA).

We next show how the science of breeding can be used to control UMDA.

13.8 Numerical Investigations of the Science of Breeding

The application of the science of breeding requires the computation of the average fitness $\bar{f}(t)$, the variance $V(t)$, and the additive genetic variance $\text{VA}(t)$. The first two terms are standard statistical terms. The computation of VA requires $\bar{f}_i(x_i)$ and $p_i(x_i)$. The computation of the first term poses only a few difficulties. It can be approximated by

$$(13.38) \quad \bar{f}_i(X_i = 1, t) = \sum_{x, X_i = 1} \frac{p(\mathbf{x})}{p_i(X_i = 1)} f(\mathbf{x}) \approx \frac{1}{N} \sum_{k=1}^{N} \frac{f(\zeta_i^k)}{p_i(x_i)},$$

where ζ_i^k are those $\mathbf{x}$ values in the population that contain $x_i = 1$.

Linear functions are the ideal case for the theory. The heritability $b(t)$ is 1 and the additive genetic variance is identical to the variance. We skip

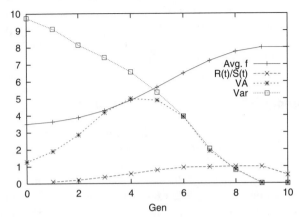

FIGURE 13.6. Heritability and variance for Decep(32, 4): Average, Var, and VA divided by 3; $\tau = 0.3$, $n = 32$.

this trivial case and start with a multiplicative fitness function $f(\mathbf{x}) = \prod_i (1 - s)^{1 - x_i}$. For a multiplicative function we also have $R(t) = S(t)$ (theorem 12.2).

Figure 13.5 confirms the theoretical results from section 11 (VA and Var are multiplied by 10 in this figure). Additive genetic variance is almost identical to the variance and the heritability is 1. The function is highly nonlinear of order n, but nevertheless it is easy to optimize. The function has also been investigated by Rattray and Shapiro (in press), but their calculations become highly complex.

An interesting case is the function Decep(32, 4). In figure 13.6 the function is optimized for 32 bits. As predicted by the theory, UMDA converges to the local optimum $\mathbf{x} = (0, \ldots, 0)$. Heritability is almost zero at the beginning, indicating that the competition between setting the genes to 0 or to 1 is undecided. UMDA decides to go to the direction of 0. If there is a high percentage of zeros in the population, then heritability increases to almost 1. In this area the fitness function is almost linear. This shows that heritability can depend strongly on the gene frequencies.

These examples demonstrate that it is worthwhile to compute the quantities used for a scientific breeding program. They indicate clearly how difficult the optimization problem is. In the breeding of livestock, heritability is normally greater than 0.2. If we optimize arbitrary fitness functions the heritability can be almost 0. But because we can easily compute 1000 generations on a computer in a few minutes, UMDA can be used for problems with very low heritability.

We have shown that UMDA can optimize difficult multimodal functions, thus explaining the success of genetic algorithms in optimization. We have also shown that UMDA can be deceived easily by simple functions called deceptive functions. These functions require more complex search distributions. This problem is investigated next.

14 Graphical Models and Optimization

The simple product distribution of UMDA cannot capture dependencies between variables. If these dependencies are necessary to find the global optimum, UMDA and simple genetic algorithms fail. We take an extreme case as example, the *"needle in a haystack" problem*. The fitness function is everywhere equal to 1, except for a single $\mathbf{x}$ where it is 10. All x_i values have to be set in the right order to obtain the optimum. Of course, there is no clever search method for this problem. But there is a continuum of increasing complexity from the simple OneMax function to the "needle in a haystack" problem. For such complex problems we need a complex search distribution. A good candidate for a search distribution for optimization is the Boltzmann distribution.

Definition 14.1. *For $\beta \geq 0$ define the* weighted Boltzmann distribution *of a function $f(\mathbf{x})$ as*

$$(14.1) \qquad p_{\beta,f}(\mathbf{x}) := \frac{p_0(\mathbf{x})e^{\beta f(\mathbf{x})}}{\sum_y p_0(\mathbf{y})e^{\beta f(\mathbf{y})}} := \frac{p_0(\mathbf{x})e^{\beta f(\mathbf{x})}}{Z_f(\beta, p_0)} ,$$

where $Z_f(\beta, p_0)$ is the partition function. To simplify the notation β and/or f can be omitted. $p_0(\mathbf{x})$ is the distribution for $\beta = 0$.

The Boltzmann distribution concentrates its search around good fitness values. Thus it is theoretically a very good candidate for a search distribution used for optimization. The problem lies in the efficient computation of the Boltzmann distribution.

In this section we will present a method for computing the Boltzmann distribution. The method is based on the factorization of the distribution. If the factorization needs only a polynomial number of parameters, then the distribution can be computed in polynomial time. The corresponding factorization theorem is important for many areas of computer science dealing with the problem of decomposition.

With a suitable annealing schedule convergence of the algorithm can easily be shown. We will derive a new annealing schedule for Boltzmann distribution algorithms. This annealing schedule makes the result of Boltzmann selection similar to the results of truncation selection.

The theory presented in this section unifies simulated annealing and population-based algorithms with the general theory of estimating distributions.

14.1 Boltzmann Selection and Convergence

The Boltzmann distribution is usually defined as $e^{-\frac{g(\mathbf{x})}{T}}/Z$. The term $g(\mathbf{x})$ is called the *energy* and $T = 1/\beta$ the *temperature*. Some properties of the weighted Boltzmann distribution are described by the following lemma.

Lemma 14.1. *Let $x_m \in \mathcal{M}$ be a global optimum of the function $f(\mathbf{x})$ and $\mathbf{x}_l$ a point with $f(\mathbf{x}_l) < f(\mathbf{x}_m)$. Then*

- *Let $g(\mathbf{x}) := f(\mathbf{x}) + c$. Then $p_{\beta,f}(\mathbf{x}) = p_{\beta,g}(\mathbf{x})$.*
- *Let $g(\mathbf{x}) := c \cdot f(\mathbf{x})$. Then $p_{\beta,g}(\mathbf{x}) = p_{c\beta,f}(\mathbf{x})$.*

The first property means that the distribution is invariant under addition of a constant. It is, however, not invariant under multiplication. We will discuss how to overcome this shortcoming in section 14.3.

Closely related to the Boltzmann distribution is Boltzmann selection. An early study about this selection method can be found in de la Maza and Tidor (1993).

Definition 14.2. *Given a distribution p and a selection parameter γ, Boltzmann selection calculates the distribution of the selected points according to*

$$(14.2) \qquad p^s(\mathbf{x}) = p(\mathbf{x})\frac{e^{\gamma f(\mathbf{x})}}{\sum_y p(\mathbf{y})e^{\gamma f(\mathbf{y})}} \, .$$

Boltzmann selection can be seen as proportionate selection applied to the fitness function $e^{\beta f(\mathbf{x})}$. We now define the BEDA (Boltzmann estimated distribution algorithm).

BEDA – Boltzmann estimated distribution algorithm

- STEP 0: $t \Leftarrow 0$. Generate N points according to the $p(\mathbf{x}, 0) = p_0(\mathbf{x})$.
- STEP 1: With a given $\Delta\beta(t) > 0$, let

$$p^s(\mathbf{x}, t) = \frac{p(\mathbf{x}, t)e^{\Delta\beta(t)f(\mathbf{x})}}{\sum_y p(\mathbf{y}, t)e^{\Delta\beta(t)f(\mathbf{y})}} \, .$$

- STEP 2: Generate N new points according to the distribution $p(\mathbf{x}, t+1) = p^s(\mathbf{x}, t)$.
- STEP 3: $t \Leftarrow t + 1$.
- STEP 4: If stopping criterion not met go to STEP 1.

BEDA is a conceptional algorithm, because the calculation of the distribution requires the computation of the sum of exponentially many terms. The following convergence theorem is easily proven.

Theorem 14.1 (Convergence). *Let $\Delta\beta(t)$ be an annealing schedule, i.e. for every t increase the inverse temperature β by $\Delta\beta(t)$. Then for BEDA the distribution at time t is given by*

$$(14.3) \qquad p(\mathbf{x}, t) = \frac{p_0(\mathbf{x}) e^{\beta(t) f(\mathbf{x})}}{Z_f(\beta(t), p_0)}$$

with the inverse temperature

$$(14.4) \qquad \beta(t) = \sum_{\tau=1}^{t} \Delta\beta(\tau).$$

Let $\mathcal{M}$ be the set of global optima. If $\beta(t) \to \infty$, then

$$(14.5) \qquad \lim_{t \to \infty} p(\mathbf{x}, t) = \begin{cases} 1/|\mathcal{M}| & x \in \mathcal{M} \\ 0 & \text{otherwise.} \end{cases}$$

Proof. Let $\mathbf{x}^m \in \mathcal{M}$ be a point with optimal fitness and $\mathbf{x} \notin \mathcal{M}$ a point with $f(\mathbf{x}) < f(\mathbf{x}^m)$. Then

$$p(\mathbf{x}, t) = \frac{p_0(\mathbf{x}) e^{\beta(t) f(\mathbf{x})}}{\sum_{\mathbf{y}} p_0(\mathbf{y}) e^{\beta(t) f(\mathbf{y})}} \leq \frac{e^{\beta(t) f(\mathbf{x})}}{|\mathcal{M}| \cdot C \cdot e^{\beta(t) f(\mathbf{x}^m)}}$$

$$\leq \frac{1}{|\mathcal{M}| \cdot C \cdot e^{\beta(t) [f(\mathbf{x}^m) - f(\mathbf{x})]}}.$$

As $\beta(t) \to \infty$, $p(\mathbf{x}, t)$ converges (exponentially quickly) to 0. Because $p(\mathbf{x}, t) = p(\mathbf{y}, t)$ for all $\mathbf{x}^m, \mathbf{y}^m \in \mathcal{M}$, the limit distribution is the uniform distribution on the set of optima. $\square$

Equation (14.5) shows only that the distribution converges to 0 for nonoptimal points. But we can also make an estimate for the rate of convergence.

Lemma 14.2. *Let $p_0(\mathbf{x})$ be the uniform distribution. Let there be a δ such that for any nonoptimal point $\mathbf{x}$ we have with $\mathbf{x}^m \in \mathcal{M}$:*

$$(14.6) \qquad f(\mathbf{x}) \leq f(\mathbf{x}^m) - \delta.$$

Then

$$(14.7) \qquad \beta \geq \frac{n \cdot \ln 2}{\delta} \qquad \Longrightarrow \qquad p_\beta(\mathcal{M}) \geq 0.5.$$

Proof. Let $|\mathcal{M}|$ be the number of optima. The number of terms in the partition function is smaller than 2^n. For $\mathbf{x}^m \in \mathcal{M}$ we have with $M := f(\mathbf{x}^m)$:

$$p_\beta(\mathbf{x}^m) = \frac{e^{\beta M}}{\sum_{\mathbf{y}} e^{\beta f(\mathbf{y})}}$$

$$\geq \frac{e^{\beta M}}{2^n \cdot e^{\beta(M-\delta)} + |\mathcal{M}| \cdot e^{\beta M}} = \frac{1}{e^{n \ln 2 - \beta\delta} + |\mathcal{M}|}$$

(14.8) $$\overset{!}{\geq} \frac{1}{2|\mathcal{M}|} .$$

So, to have $p_\beta(\mathcal{M}) \geq 1/2$, we need

(14.9) $$e^{n \ln 2 - \beta\delta} \leq 2|\mathcal{M}| \iff \beta \geq \frac{n \cdot 2 - \ln(2|\mathcal{M}|)}{\delta}$$

or as a sufficient condition (14.7). $\square$

Corollary 14.1. *For a binary fitness function with integer values, half of the generated points will have maximum fitness if $\beta \geq 0.7n$, independent of the fitness function.*

We next transform BEDA into a practical algorithm. This means the reduction of the parameters of the distribution and the computation of an adaptive schedule.

14.2   Factorization of the Distribution and the FDA

In this section we describe a method for computing a factorization of the probability, given an additive decomposition of the function:

Definition 14.3. *Let $s_1, \ldots, s_m$ be index sets, $s_i \subseteq \{1, \ldots, n\}$. Let f_{s_i} be functions depending only on the variables x_j with $j \in s_i$. These variables we denote as x_{s_i}. Then*

(14.10) $$f(\mathbf{x}) = \sum_{i=1}^{m} f_{s_i}(\mathbf{x}) = f_i(x_{s_i})$$

is an additive decomposition of the fitness function f.

We also need the following definitions.

Definition 14.4. *Given $s_1, \ldots, s_m$, we define for $i = 1, \ldots, m$ the sets d_i, b_i and c_i:*

$$(14.11) \qquad d_i := \bigcup_{j=1}^{i} s_j, \qquad b_i := s_i \setminus d_{i-1}, \qquad c_i := s_i \cap d_{i-1}.$$

We set $d_0 = \emptyset$.

In the theory of decomposable graphs, d_i are called *histories*, b_i *residuals*, and c_i *separators* (Lauritzen, 1996). Recall the following definition.

Definition 14.5. *The* conditional probability $p(\mathbf{x}|\mathbf{y})$ *is defined as*

$$(14.12) \qquad p(\mathbf{x}|\mathbf{y}) = \frac{p(\mathbf{x}, \mathbf{y})}{p(\mathbf{y})}.$$

In Mühlenbein et al. (1999), we have shown the following theorem.

Theorem 14.2 (Factorization Theorem). *Let $p(\mathbf{x})$ be a Boltzmann distribution with*

$$(14.13) \qquad p(\mathbf{x}) = \frac{e^{\beta f(\mathbf{x})}}{Z_f(\beta)}$$

and $f(\mathbf{x}) = \sum_{i=1}^{m} f_{s_i}(\mathbf{x})$ be an additive decomposition. If

$$(14.14) \qquad b_i \neq \emptyset \quad \forall i = 1, \ldots, l; \quad d_l = \tilde{X}$$

$$(14.15) \qquad \forall i \geq 2 \, \exists j < i \text{ such that } c_i \subseteq s_j$$

then

$$(14.16) \qquad p(\mathbf{x}) = \prod_{i=1}^{m} p(x_{b_i}|x_{c_i}).$$

The constraint defined by equation (14.15) is called the *running intersection property* (Lauritzen, 1996).

FDA – factorized distribution algorithm

- STEP 0: Calculate b_i and c_i from the decomposition of the function.
- STEP 1: Generate an initial population with N individuals.
- STEP 2: Select N individuals using Boltzmann selection.
- STEP 3: Estimate the conditional probabilities $p(x_{b_i}|x_{c_i}, t)$ from the selected points.
- STEP 4: Generate new points according to $p(\mathbf{x}, t + 1) = \prod_{i=1}^{m} p(x_{b_i}|x_{c_i}, t)$.
- STEP 5: If not stopping criterion reached: $t \Leftarrow t + 1$ Go To STEP 2.

With the help of the factorization theorem, we have turned the conceptional algorithm BEDA into FDA, the factorized distribution algorithm. As the factorized distribution is identical to the Boltzmann distribution, the convergence proof of BEDA also applies to FDA. There exist a number of algorithms that compute a factorization of an additive decomposed function (Lauritzen, 1996).

Not every additive decomposed function fulfills the assumption of the factorization theorem. In these cases, more sophisticated methods have to be used. But FDA can also be used with an approximate factorization. We discuss just two simple examples.

Example 14.1. *For linear functions*

$$(14.17) \qquad \text{Linear}(\mathbf{x}) = \sum_{i=1}^{n} \alpha_i x_i ,$$

we have $s_i = \{i\}$ and thus all c_i are empty. This leads to the factorization

$$(14.18) \qquad p(\mathbf{x}) = \prod_{i=1}^{n} p_i(x_i) .$$

As this is the distribution used by UMDA, FDA behaves like UMDA (and thus like a simple genetic algorithm) for linear functions.

Example 14.2. *Functions with a chainlike interaction can also be factorized:*

$$(14.19) \qquad \text{Chain}(\mathbf{x}) = \sum_{i=2}^{n} f_i(x_{i-1}, x_i) .$$

Here the factorization is

$$(14.20) \qquad p(\mathbf{x}) = p(x_1) \prod_{i=2}^{n} p(x_i | x_{i-1}) .$$

FDA can be used with any selection scheme, but convergence has been shown only for Boltzmann selection. Therefor we think that Boltzmann selection is an essential part in using the FDA. In order to obtain a practical numerical algorithm, we still have to solve two problems: to find a good annealing schedule for Boltzmann selection and to determine a reasonable sample size (population size).

We investigate these two problems next.

14.3 A New Annealing Schedule for the Boltzmann Distribution

Boltzmann selection requires an annealing schedule. Lemma 14.2 has shown how quickly we have to anneal in order to reach convergence within a given time frame. But if we anneal too quickly, the approximation of the Boltzmann can be very poor because of the sampling error.

14.3.1 Taylor Expansion of the Average Fitness

To determine an adaptive annealing schedule, we make a Taylor expansion of the average fitness of the Boltzmann distribution.

Definition 14.6. *The **average fitness** of a fitness function and a distribution is*

$$(14.21) \qquad W_f(p) = \sum_x f(\mathbf{x}) p(\mathbf{x}) \,.$$

For the Boltzmann distribution, we use the abbreviation $W_f(\beta) := W_f(p_{\beta,f})$.

Theorem 14.3. *The average fitness of the Boltzmann distribution $W_f(\beta)$ has the following expansion in β:*

$$(14.22) \qquad W_f(\tilde\beta) = W_f(\beta) + \sum_{i \geq 1} \frac{(\tilde\beta - \beta)^i}{i!} M_{i+1}^c(\beta) \,,$$

where M_i^c are the centered moments:

$$(14.23) \qquad M_i^c(\beta) := \sum_x \left[f(\mathbf{x}) - W_f(\beta) \right]^i p(\mathbf{x})$$

They can be calculated using the derivatives of the partition function:

$$(14.24) \qquad M_{i+1}^c(\beta) = \left(\frac{Z_f'(\beta)}{Z_f(\beta)} \right)^{(i)} \qquad \text{for } i \geq 1, \quad M_1^c = 0 \,.$$

Proof. The kth derivative of the partition function obeys, for $k \geq 0$:

$$(14.25) \qquad Z_f^{(k)}(\beta) = \sum_x f(\mathbf{x})^k e^{\beta f(\mathbf{x})} \,.$$

Thus the moments for $k \geq 1$ can be calculated as

$$(14.26) \qquad M_k(\beta) := \sum_x f(\mathbf{x})^k p(\mathbf{x}) = \frac{Z_f^{(k)}(\beta)}{Z_f(\beta)}$$

and thus

$$(14.27) \qquad W_f(\beta) = M_1(\beta) = Z_f'(\beta)/Z_f(\beta) \,.$$

Direct evaluation of the derivatives of W leads to complicated expressions. The proof, by induction, is rather technical. We omit it here. $\square$

Corollary 14.2. *We have approximative:*

$$(14.28) \qquad W_f(\tilde\beta) \approx W_f(\beta) + (\tilde\beta - \beta) \cdot \sigma_f^2(\beta) \,,$$

where $\sigma_f^2(\beta)$ is the variance of the distribution, defined as $\sigma_f^2(\beta) := M_2^c(\beta)$.

This approximation can also be found in Kirkpatrick et al. (1983).

Lemma 14.3. *The variance of the Boltzmann distribution obeys*

(14.29) $$f(\mathbf{x}) \neq \text{const.} \implies \sigma_f^2(\beta) > 0.$$

Proof. We have $\forall x : p_\beta(\mathbf{x}) > 0$. In order to have

(14.30) $$\sigma_f^2(\beta) = \sum_x [f(\mathbf{x}) - W_f(\beta)]^2 p_\beta(\mathbf{x}) \stackrel{!}{=} 0,$$

we must have for all x: $f(\mathbf{x}) = W_f$ in contradiction to the assumption. $\square$

Corollary 14.3. *With $f(\mathbf{x}) \neq$ const., we have*

(14.31) $$\tilde{\beta} > \beta \implies W_f(\tilde{\beta}) > W_f(\beta).$$

The corollary shows that the average fitness never decreases for Boltzmann selection. A similar result was already obtained in theorem 12.1 for proportionate selection; see also Mühlenbein and Mahnig (2000).

14.3.2 The SDS Annealing Schedule

From (14.28) we can derive an adaptive annealing schedule. The variance (and the higher moments) can be estimated from the generated points. As long as the approximation is valid, one can choose a desired increase in the average fitness and set $\beta(t+1)$ accordingly. So we can set

(14.32) $$\Delta\beta(t) := \beta(t+1) - \beta(t) = \frac{W_f^{\text{new}}(t) - W_f(\beta(t))}{\sigma_f^2(\beta(t))}.$$

From (14.28) we see that choosing $\Delta\beta$ proportional to the inverse of the variance leads in the approximation to a constant increase in the average fitness. This is much too fast, especially near the optimum. As truncation selection has proven to be a robust and efficient selection scheme, we can try to approximate the behavior of this method. For truncation selection the *response to selection $R_f(t)$* is given approximatively by equation: (13.17)

(14.33) $$R(t) := W(t+1) - W(t) \approx I_\tau b(t)\sqrt{\sigma_f^2},$$

where I_τ is the selection intensity, depending on the truncation threshold τ. Because truncation selection has been shown to be an effective selection method, we will make the Boltzmann schedule proportional to the inverse of the square root of the variance:

Definition 14.7. *The standard deviation schedule (SDS) is defined by*

(14.34) $$\Delta\beta(t) = \frac{c}{\sigma_f(\beta(t))}.$$

We already know that FDA with Boltzmann selection remains unchanged if we add a constant to the fitness function. For SDS we have additionally the following lemma.

Lemma 14.4. *For Boltzmann selection with SDS, BEDA is invariant under linear transformations of the fitness function with a positive factor.*

Proof. This lemma is true because the standard deviation scales linearly under multiplication. Let $f(\mathbf{x})$ be a fitness function; consider $\hat{f}(\mathbf{x}) = \hat{c} \cdot f(\mathbf{x})$. The claim is that if $\hat{\beta}(t) = \beta(t)/\tilde{c}$, then the distributions are the same for every t. With $t=0$, β and $\hat{\beta}$ are 0, so it is true. Now let t and $\beta=\beta(t)$ be given. From the previous iteration we know that $\hat{\beta} = \beta/\hat{c}$.

According to lemma 14.1, we have $p_{\beta,f}(\mathbf{x})=p_{\hat{\beta},\hat{f}}(\mathbf{x})$. Also, $\sigma_f^2(\beta) = \hat{c}^2 \cdot \sigma_{\hat{f}}^2(\hat{\beta})$. Hence we have $\Delta\hat{\beta}(t)=\Delta\beta(t)/\hat{c}$. $\qquad\square$

Corollary 14.4. *Let $\sigma(t)$ be the standard deviation. Then the response to selection for Boltzmann selection with the SDS is given by*

(14.35)
$$R_f(t) = \sum_{i\geq 1} \frac{c^i}{i!\,\sigma(t)^i} M_{i+1}^c$$
$$= c \cdot \sigma(t) + \frac{c^2 M_3^c}{2\,\sigma(t)^2} + \frac{c^3 M_4^c}{6\,\sigma(t)^3} + \dots .$$

Note that this annealing schedule cannot be used for simulated annealing, as the estimation of the variance of the distribution requires samples that are drawn independently and the sequence of samples generated by simulated annealing are not independent.

14.3.3 Linear Functions

For linear functions,

(14.36)
$$\text{Linear}(\mathbf{x}) = \sum_{i=1}^{n} \alpha_i x_i ,$$

the factorization of the Boltzmann distribution was calculated in equation (14.18). We can also calculate the partition function and get

(14.37)
$$Z_f(\beta) = \prod_{i=1}^{n} (1 + e^{\beta\alpha_i})$$

and

(14.38)
$$p_i(\beta) := p_\beta(X_i=1) = \frac{e^{\beta\alpha_i}}{1 + e^{\beta\alpha_i}} .$$

Because the variables are independent of each other, the variance is just the sum of the variance of the factors and we have

$$(14.39) \qquad \sigma_f^2(\beta) = \sum_{i=1}^{n} \frac{\alpha_i^2 e^{\beta \alpha_i}}{(1 + e^{\beta \alpha_i})^2} = \sum_{i=1}^{n} \alpha_i^2 p_i(\beta)\big(1 - p_i(\beta)\big)$$

and thus

$$(14.40) \qquad \beta(t+1) = \beta(t) + \frac{c}{\sqrt{\sum_i \alpha_i^2 p_i(\beta)\big(1 - p_i(\beta)\big)}}.$$

By differentiating (14.38) we get

$$\frac{dp_i(\beta)}{dt} = \frac{\alpha_i e^{\beta \alpha_i}(1 + e^{\beta \alpha_i})\beta' - e^{\beta \alpha_i}\alpha_i e^{\beta \alpha_i}\beta'}{(1 + e^{\beta \alpha_i})^2}$$

$$(14.41) \qquad = p_i(\beta)\big(1 - p_i(\beta)\big)\alpha_i \tfrac{d\beta}{dt}.$$

Therefore we obtain the differential equation

$$(14.42) \qquad \frac{dp_i(\beta)}{dt} = c \cdot \frac{p_i(\beta)\big(1 - p_i(\beta)\big)\alpha_i}{\sqrt{\sum_i \alpha_i^2 p_i(\beta)\big(1 - p_i(\beta)\big)}}.$$

Note that the solution of these differential equations remains the same if we multiply all α_i by a constant factor, as predicted.

For OneMax we have $\alpha_i = 1$. In this case all marginal frequencies are equal to p_β. We obtain the differential equation

$$(14.43) \qquad \frac{dp_\beta}{dt} = c\sqrt{p_\beta(1 - p_\beta)/n}.$$

This equation is identical to the approximate equation derived for truncation selection. The solution of this equation is given by equation (13.25).

The theory presented so far has been derived under the assumption of large (infinite) populations. We turn next to the problem of finite populations.

14.4 Finite Populations

In finite populations convergence of UMDA or FDA can be only probabilistic. Since UMDA is a simplified FDA, it is sufficient to discuss FDA. This section is extracted from Mühlenbein and Mahnig (1999b).

Definition 14.8. *Let ϵ be given. Let $P_{\text{conv}}(N)$ denote the probability that FDA with a population size of N converges to the optima. Then the critical population size is defined as*

$$(14.44) \qquad N^*(\epsilon) = \min_N P_{\text{conv}}(N) \geq 1 - \epsilon.$$

Table 14.1

Cumulative Fixation Probability for Int(16)
Truncation selection vs. Boltzmann selection with $\Delta\beta = 0.01$
and Boltzmann SDS; N denotes size of population.

t	$\tau = 0.25$ $N = 30$	$\tau = 0.5$ $N = 30$	$\tau = 0.25$ $N = 80$	$\tau = 0.5$ $N = 60$	Boltz. $N = 700$	SDS $N = 100$
1	0.0955	0.0035	0.0	0.0	0.0885	0.0
2	0.4065	0.0255	0.0025	0.0095	0.1110	0.0
3	0.5955	0.1040	0.0165	0.0205	0.1275	0.0
4	0.6880	0.2220	0.0355	0.0325	0.1375	0.002
5	0.7210	0.3270	0.0575	0.0490	0.1455	0.002
6	0.7310	0.4030	0.0695	0.0630	0.1510	0.008
7	0.7310	0.4470	0.0740	0.0715	0.1555	0.018
8	0.7310	0.4705	0.0740	0.0780	0.1565	0.030
9	0.7310	0.4840	0.0740	0.0806	0.1575	0.036
14						0.084

If FDA with a finite population does not converge to an optimum, then
at least one gene is fixed to a wrong value. The probability of fixation is
reduced if the population size is increased. We have, obviously, for FDA:

$$P_{\text{conv}}(N_1) \leq P_{\text{conv}}(N_2) \quad N_1 \leq N_2 .$$

The critical question is: How many sample points are necessary to
reasonably approximate the distribution used by FDA? A general estimate from Vapnik (1998) can be used as a guideline. One should use a
sample size that is about twenty times larger than the number of free
parameters.

We discuss the problem with a special function called Int. Int($\mathbf{x}$) gives
the integer value of the binary representation.

$$(14.45) \qquad \text{Int}(n) = \sum_{i=1}^{n} 2^{i-1} x_i .$$

The fitness distribution of this function is not normally distributed.
The function has 2^n distinct fitness values. We show the cumulative fixation probability in table 14.1 for Int(16). The fixation probability is
larger for stronger selection. For a given truncation selection the maximum fixation probability is at generation 1 for very small N. For larger
values of N the fixation probability increases until a maximum is reached
and then decreases again. This behavior has been observed for many fitness distributions.

For truncation selection with $\tau = 0.25$, we have for $N = 80$ a fixation
probability of about 0.075. A larger τ reduces the fixation probability.

But this advantage is offset by the larger number of generations required for convergence. The problem of an optimal population size for truncation selection is investigated in Mühlenbein and Mahnig (1999b). Boltzmann selection with $\Delta\beta = 0.01$ is still very strong for the fitness distribution given by Int(16). For $N = 700$ the largest fixation probability is still at the first generation. Therefore the critical population size for Boltzmann selection for $\Delta\beta = 0.01$ is very high ($N^* > 700$). In comparison, the adaptive Boltzmann schedule SDS has a total fixation probability of 0.084 for a population size of $N = 100$. This is almost as small as truncation selection.

This example shows that Boltzmann selection in finite populations depends critically on a good annealing schedule. Normally we run FDA with truncation selection. This selection method is a good compromise, but Boltzmann selection with SDS schedule is of comparable performance.

Estimates for the necessary size of the population can also be found in Harik et al. (1999), but they use a weaker performance definition. The goal is to have a certain percentage of the bits of the optimum in the final population. Furthermore their result is valid only for fitness functions that are approximately normally distributed.

The danger of fixation can be reduced further by a technique very popular in Bayesian statistics. This is discussed in the next section.

14.5 Population Size, Mutation, and Bayesian Prior

To derive the results of this section we will use a normalized representation of the distribution. This representation is called a *Bayesian network* and can be displayed as a *directed* graph. The interested reader is referred to Jordan (1999).

Theorem 14.4 (Bayesian Factorization). *Each probability can be factored into*

$$(14.46) \qquad p(\mathbf{x}) = p(x_1) \prod_{i=2}^{n} p(x_i | \mathrm{pa}_i) \,.$$

Proof. By definition of conditional probabilities we have

$$(14.47) \qquad p(\mathbf{x}) = p(x_1) \prod_{i=2}^{n} p(x_i | x_1, \ldots, x_{i-1}) \,.$$

Let $\mathrm{pa}_i \subset \{x_1, \ldots, x_{i-1}\}$. If x_i and $\{x_1, \ldots, x_{i-1}\} \setminus \mathrm{pa}_i$ are conditionally independent given pa_i, we can simplify $p(x_i | x_1, \ldots, x_{i-1}) = p(x_i | \mathrm{pa}_i)$. $\square$

The PA_i are called the *parents* of variable X_i. This factorization can be represented by a directed graph. In the context of graphical models the graph and the conditional probabilities are called a *Bayesian network* (Jordan, 1999; Frey, 1998). It is obvious that the factorization used in theorem 14.2 can be transformed easily into a Bayesian factorization.

Usually the empirical probabilities are computed by the maximum likelihood estimator. For N samples with $m \leq N$ instances of x the estimate is defined by

$$\hat{p}(\mathbf{x}) = \frac{m}{N}.$$

For $m = N$ we obtain $p(\mathbf{x}) = 1$ and for $m = 0$ we obtain $p(\mathbf{x}) = 0$. This leads to our gene fixation problem, because both values are attractors. The fixation problem is reduced if $\hat{p}(\mathbf{x})$ is restricted to an interval $0 < p_{\min} \leq \hat{p}(\mathbf{x}) \leq 1 - p_{\min} < 1$. This is exactly what results from the *Bayesian estimation*. The estimate $\hat{p}(\mathbf{x})$ is the expected value of the posterior distribution after applying Bayes formula to a prior distribution and the given data. For binary variables $\mathbf{x}$ the estimate

$$(14.48) \qquad \hat{p}(\mathbf{x}) = \frac{m + r}{N + 2r}$$

is used with $r > 0$. r is derived from a Bayesian prior, and $r = 1$ is the result of the uniform Bayesian prior. The larger r is, the more the estimate tends toward $\hat{p}(\mathbf{x}) = 0.5$. The reader interested in a derivation of this estimate in the context of Bayesian networks is referred to Jordan (1999).

The Bayesian prior can be seen as a mutation force. Wright (1970) included mutation with a recurrent symmetric mutation rate of $0 \leq \mu < 1$ into his equation as follows:

$$(14.49) \qquad \Delta p_i = p_i(t)(1 - p_i(t))\frac{\frac{\partial \tilde{W}}{\partial p_i}}{\tilde{W}} - \mu\big(p_i(t) - (1 - p_i(t))\big).$$

We will show that a similar equation is obtained if a Bayesian prior is used. We use the formula

$$p_i(t + 1) = \frac{p_i^s(t)N + r}{N + 2r}$$

where $p_i^s(t)$ is given by Wright's equation (12.5). Setting $\gamma = r/N$ we obtain

$$\Delta p_i(t) \quad = \quad p_i(t)(1 - p_i(t))\frac{\frac{\partial \tilde{W}}{\partial p_i}}{\tilde{W}} + \frac{\gamma}{1 + 2\gamma}$$

$$(14.50) \qquad\qquad - \frac{2\gamma}{1 + 2\gamma}\left(p_i(t) + p_i(t)(1 - p_i(t))\frac{\partial \tilde{W}}{\tilde{W}}\right).$$

Equations (14.49) and (14.50) are very similar if we set $\mu = \gamma/(1 + 2\gamma)$. Wright assumed that mutation occurs independent from selection, whereas in our model mutation occurs only during mating. The attractors of equation (14.50) are given by $\Delta p_i(t) = 0$. They are located in the interior of the unit cube. For each selection method and each fitness function the locations of the attractors are different. We give just one example.

Theorem 14.5. *For proportionate selection and OneMax the attractors are given by*

$$(14.51) \qquad p_i^* = \frac{1 + \gamma(n - 2)}{1 + 2\gamma(n - 1)}.$$

If we set $N = n$ and $r = 1$ we have $\gamma = 1/(n + 2)$. We obtain

$$(14.52) \qquad \lim_{t \to \infty} p(x_{\text{opt}}, t) = \prod_{i=1}^{n} p_i(t) \approx (\tfrac{2}{3})^n = 0.$$

The theorem shows that a mutation rate of $\mu = 1/n$ is too large for proportionate selection.

The analysis is more difficult for truncation selection. In this chapter we derive only an optimistic upper bound for the mutation rate. The attractors are given by an equilibrium between selection and mutation. How can we determine an appropriate value for r for our FDA application? The location should be as far as possible in the interior under the constraint that the optima are generated with high probability.

The uniform prior gives for $m = 0$ the value $\hat{p}_{\min} = 1/(N + 2)$. If N is small, then $p_{\min}$ might be so large that we generate the optima with only a very small probability. This means we perform more of a random search instead of converging to the optima. This consideration leads to a constraint: $1 - p_{\min}$ should be so large that the optima are still generated with high probability. We now heuristically derive $p_{\min}$ under the assumption that there is a unique optimum. To simplify the formulas we require that $\max \hat{p}(\mathbf{x}_{\text{opt}}) \geq e^{-1}$.

This means that the optimum string x_{opt} should be generated more than 30% at equilibrium. This is large enough to observe equilibrium and convergence. Let us first investigate the UMDA factorization $p(\mathbf{x}) = \prod p(x_i)$. For $r = 1$ the largest probability is $p_{\max} = (N + 1)/(N + 2)$. From this, we have

$$p_{\max} = 1 - \frac{1}{N + 2} = 1 - p_{\min}.$$

The largest probability to generate the optimum is given by

$$\hat{p}(\mathbf{x}_{\mathrm{opt}}) = \prod_{i=1}^{n} \left(1 - \frac{1}{N+2}\right) \approx e^{-\frac{n}{N+2}}.$$

If $N = O(n^{1-\alpha})$ with $\alpha > 0$, then $p(\mathbf{x}_{\mathrm{opt}})$ becomes arbitrarily small for large n. For $N = n$ we obtain $\hat{p}(\mathbf{x}_{\mathrm{opt}}) \approx e^{-1}$. This results in the following guideline, which is actually a lower bound of the population size.

Rule of Thumb. *For UMDA the size of the population should be at least equal to the size of the problem, if a Bayesian prior of $r = 1$ is used.*

Bayesian priors are also defined for conditional distributions. The above heuristic derivation can also be used for general Bayesian factorizations. For binary variables, the Bayesian estimator is

$$\hat{p}(x_i|\mathrm{pa}_i) = \frac{m+r}{P+2r},$$

where P is the number of occurrences of pa_i. We assume that in the best case the optimum constitutes 25% of the population. This yields $P \geq N/4$. For $r = 1$ we compute as before

$$\hat{p}(x_{\mathrm{opt}}) = \prod_{i=1}^{n} \hat{p}(x_{\mathrm{opt}_i}|\mathrm{pa}_{\mathrm{opt}_i}) = \prod_{i=1}^{n} \left(1 - \frac{1}{N/4+2}\right) \approx e^{-\frac{n}{N/4+2}}.$$

If we set $N = 4n$ we obtain $\hat{p}(x_{\mathrm{opt}}) \approx e^{-1}$. Thus we obtain a lower bound for the population size.

Rule of Thumb. *For FDA using a factorization with many conditional distributions and Bayesian prior of $r = 1$, the size of the population should be about four times the size of the problem.*

These rules of thumb have been derived heuristically and they have to be confirmed by numerical studies. Our FDA estimate is a crude lower bound. There exist more general estimates, e.g. Vapnik (1998). In order to approximate a distribution with a reasonable accuracy, he proposes to use a sample size that is about 20 times larger than the number of free parameters of the distribution. For UMDA this means $20n$, i.e. 20 times our estimate.

We demonstrate the importance of using a Bayesian prior by an example. It is a deceptive function of order 4 and problem size of $n = 32$. Our convergence theorem gives convergence of FDA with Boltzmann selection and an exact factorization. The exact factorization consists of marginal distributions of size 4. We compare in figure 14.1 FDA with SDS Boltzmann selection and truncation selection without Bayesian prior. We also show a run with SDS Boltzmann selection and Bayesian prior.

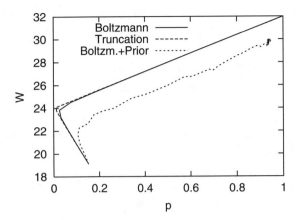

FIGURE 14.1. Average fitness $W(p)$ for FDA for Decep$(32, 4)$; population size $N = 20000$ without prior and $N = 200$ with prior $r = 1$.

The simulation was started at $p = 0.15$, i.e. near the local optimum $p = 0$. Nevertheless, FDA converges to the global optimum at $p = 1$. Note that FDA moves at first in the direction of the local optimum. At the very last moment the direction of the curve changes dramatically. SDS Boltzmann selection behaves almost identically to truncation selection with threshold $\tau = 0.35$. But both methods require a huge population size in order to converge to the optimum. In this example it is $N = 20000$. If a prior of $r = 1$ is used the population size can be reduced to $N = 200$. With this prior the curve changes direction earlier. Because of the prior, the univariate marginal probabilities never reach $p = 0$ or $p = 1$: in this example it stops at about $p = 0.975$.

To summarize the results: because FDA uses finite samples of points to estimate the conditional probabilities, convergence to the optimum depends on the size of the samples (the population size). FDA has proven to be very successful experimentally on a number of functions where standard genetic algorithms fail to find the global optimum. Mühlenbein and Mahnig (1999b) studies the scaling behavior for various test functions. The estimation of the probabilities and the generation of new points can be performed in polynomial time. Using a Bayesian prior reduces the influence of the population size. But there is a tradeoff: if no prior is used then convergence is fast, although a large population size might be needed. If a prior is used, the population size can be much smaller, but the number of generations until convergence increases. We do not have enough numerical results yet, and so we can only conjecture:

Conjecture. *FDA, with a finite population of size $N = 4n$, SDS Boltzmann selection, Bayesian prior, and a Bayesian factorization where the number of parents is restricted by k independent of n, will converge to the optimum in polynomial time with high probability.*

14.6 Constraint Optimization Problems

One advantage of FDA over genetic algorithms is that it can handle optimization problems with constraints. Mendelian recombination or crossover in genetic algorithms often creates points that violate the constraints. If the structure of the constraints and the structure of the ADF are compatible, then FDA generates only legal points.

Definition 14.9. *A constraint optimization problem is defined by*

$$(14.53) \qquad \max f(\mathbf{x}) = \sum_{i=1}^{m} f_i(\mathbf{x}_{s_i})$$

such that $C_i(\mathbf{x}_{u_i})$.

$C_i(\mathbf{x}_{u_i})$ stands for the ith constraint function. $\mathbf{x}_{s_i}, \mathbf{x}_{u_i} \subseteq X$ are sets of variables. The constraints are defined locally. Thus they can be used to test which marginal probabilities are 0. This is technically somewhat complicated, but nevertheless straightforward. For instance, if we have $C_1(x_1, x_2) = \{x_1 + x_2 \leq 1\}$, then $p(X_1 = 1, X_2 = 1) = 0$. Thus the constraints are mapped to marginal distributions: if $C_i(\mathbf{x}_{u_i})$ is violated then we set $p_i(x_{u_i}) = 0$.

We can now factorize $f(\mathbf{x})$ as before. But we can also factorize the graph defined by $C_i(x_{u_i})$. Our theory can handle both cases: the factorization of the constraints is contained in the factorization of the function, i.e. $x_{u_i} \subseteq x_{s_i}$, or the factorization of the function is contained in the factorization of the constraints, i.e. $x_{s_i} \subseteq x_{u_i}$.

Let Ω_c be the set of *feasible* solutions. Then the Boltzmann distribution on Ω_c is defined as

$$(14.54) \qquad p_{b,f,c}(\mathbf{x}) = \frac{p_0(x)e^{\beta f(\mathbf{x})}}{\sum_{y \in \Omega_c} p_0(\mathbf{y})e^{\beta f(\mathbf{y})}} .$$

Then the following convergence theorem holds.

Theorem 14.6 (Convergence). *Let (1) the initial population be feasible. Let (2) the factorization of the constraints and the factorization of the function be contained in the FDA factorization. Let (3) $\Delta\beta(t)$ be an annealing schedule. Then for FDA the distribution at time t is given by*

$$(14.55) \qquad p(\mathbf{x}, t) = \frac{p_0(\mathbf{x})e^{\beta(t)f(\mathbf{x})}}{\sum_{y \in \Omega_c} p_0(\mathbf{y})e^{\beta(t)f(y)}}$$

with the inverse temperature

$$(14.56) \qquad \beta(t) = \sum_{\tau=1}^{t} \Delta\beta(\tau) \,.$$

Let $\mathcal{M}$ be the set of global optima. If $\beta(t) \to \infty$, then

$$(14.57) \qquad \lim_{t\to\infty} p(x,t) = \begin{cases} 1/|\mathcal{M}| & x \in \mathcal{M} \\ 0 & \text{otherwise.} \end{cases}$$

Proof. The proof is almost identical to the proof of theorem 14.1. We have to show only that the factorization generates only feasible solutions, if the probabilities are computed from a set of feasible solutions. The proof is indirect. Suppose there exists an $\mathbf{x}$ that does not satisfy the kth constrain $C_k(\mathbf{x}_{u_k})$. Then

$$0 \neq p(\mathbf{x}, t+1) = \prod_{i=1}^{n} p^s(\mathbf{x}_{b_i}|\mathbf{x}_{c_i}, t) \,.$$

Thus we have $p^s(\mathbf{x}_{u_k}) \neq 0$. This means that there exists at least one individual in generation t that violates the constraint. But this contradicts assumption (1). $\qquad\square$

The factorization theorem requires an analytical description of the function. But it is also possible to determine the factorization from the sampled data points. This is described next.

15 Computing a Bayesian Network from Data

The FDA factorization is based on the decomposition of the fitness function. This has two drawbacks: first, the structure of the function has to be known. Second, for a given instance of the fitness function, the structure might not give the smallest possible factorization. In other words: Complex structures do not necessarily lead to complex dependency structures for a given instance of a fitness function. The actual dependencies are determined by the function values. This problem can be circumvented by computing the dependency structure from the data.

Computing the structure of a Bayesian network from data is called *learning*. Learning gives an answer to the question: given a population of selected points $M(t)$, what is a good Bayesian factorization fitting the data? The most difficult part of the problem is to define a quality measure also called a *scoring measure*.

A Bayesian network with more arcs fits the data better than one with less arcs. Therefore a scoring metric should give the best score to the minimal Bayesian network that fits the data. It is outside the scope of this paper to discuss this problem in more detail. The interested reader is referred to the two papers by Heckerman and Friedman et al. in Jordan (1999).

For Bayesian networks two quality measures are used most frequently—the *Bayes Dirichlet* (BDe) score and the *minimal description length* (MDL) score. We concentrate on the MDL principle. This principle is motivated by universal coding. Suppose we are given a set D of instances, which we would like to store. Naturally, we would like to conserve space and save a compressed version of D. One way of compressing the data is to find a suitable model for D that the encoder can use to produce a compact version of D. In order to be able to recover D we must also store the model used by the encoder to compress D. Thus the total description length is defined as the sum of the length of the compressed version of D and the length of the description of the model. The MDL principle postulates that the optimal model is the one that minimizes the total description length.

15.1   LFDA—Learning a Bayesian Factorization

In the context of learning Bayesian networks, the model is a network B describing a probability distribution p over the instances appearing in the data. Several authors have approximately computed the MDL score. Let $M = |D|$ denote the size of the data set. Then MDL is approximately given by

$$(15.1) \quad \mathrm{MDL}(B, D) = -\log_2(P(B)) + M \cdot H(B, D) + \tfrac{1}{2}\mathrm{PA} \cdot \log_2(M)$$

where $P(B)$ denotes the prior probability of network B and $\mathrm{PA} = \sum_i 2^{|\mathrm{pa}_i|}$ gives the total number of probabilities to compute. $H(B, D)$ is defined by

$$(15.2) \qquad H(B, D) = -\sum_{i=1}^{n} \sum_{\mathrm{pa}_i} \sum_{x_i} \frac{m(x_i, \mathrm{pa}_i)}{M} \log_2 \frac{m(x_i, \mathrm{pa}_i)}{m(\mathrm{pa}_i)} ,$$

where $m(x_i, \mathrm{pa}_i)$ denotes the number of occurrences of x_i given configuration pa_i and $m(\mathrm{pa}_i) = \sum_{x_i} m(x_i, \mathrm{pa}_i)$. If $\mathrm{pa}_i = \emptyset$, then $m(x_i, \emptyset)$ is set to the number of occurrences of x_i in D.

The formula has an interpretation that can be easily understood. If no prior information is available, $P(B)$ is identical for all possible networks. For minimizing, this term can be left out. $0.5\,\mathrm{PA} \cdot \log_2(M)$ is the length required to code the parameter of the model with precision $1/\mathrm{M}$. Normally one would need $\mathrm{PA} \cdot \log_2(M)$ bits to encode the parameters. However, the central limit theorem says that these frequencies are roughly normally distributed with a variance of $M^{-1/2}$. Hence the higher

$0.5 \log_2(M)$ bits are not very useful and can be left out. $-M \cdot H(B, D)$ has two interpretations. First, it is identical to the logarithm of the maximum likelihood $(\log_2(L(B|D)))$. Thus we arrive at the following principle:

Choose the model that maximizes $\log_2(L(B|D)) - \frac{1}{2}\mathrm{PA} \cdot \log_2(M)$.

The second interpretation arises from the observation that $H(B, D)$ is the conditional entropy of the network structure B, defined by PA_i, and the data D. The above principle is appealing, because it has no parameter to be tuned. But the formula has been derived under many simplifications. In practice, one needs more control about the quality vs. complexity tradeoff. Therefore we use a weight factor α. Our measure is defined by BIC:

(15.3) $$\mathrm{BIC}(B, D, \alpha) = -M \cdot H(B, D) - \alpha \mathrm{PA} \cdot \log_2(M).$$

This measure with $\alpha = 0.5$ has been first derived by Schwarz (1978) as *Bayesian information criterion*. Therefore we abbreviate our measure as $\mathrm{BIC}(\alpha)$.

To compute a network B^* that maximizes BIC requires a search through the space of all Bayesian networks. Such a search is more expensive than a search for the optima of the function. Therefore we use the following greedy algorithm. k_{max} is the maximum number of incoming edges allowed.

$$\mathbf{BN}(\alpha, \mathbf{k}_{\mathrm{max}})$$

- STEP 0: Start with an arc-less network.
- STEP 1: Add the arc (x_i, x_j) which gives the maximum increase of $\mathrm{BIC}(\alpha)$ if $|\mathrm{PA}_j| \leq k_{\mathrm{max}}$ and adding the arc does not introduce a cycle.
- STEP 2: Stop if no arc is found.

Whether an arc would introduce a cycle can be checked easily by maintaining for each node a list of parents and ancestors, i.e. parents of parents etc. Then $(x_i \to x_j)$ introduces a cycle if x_j is ancestor of x_i.

The BOA algorithm of Pelikan (Pelikan et al., 2000) uses the BDe score. This measure has as a drawback that it is more sensitive to coincidental correlations implied by the data than the MDL measure. As a consequence, the BDe measure prefers network structures with more arcs over simpler networks (Bouckaert, 1994). The BIC measure with $\alpha = 1$ has also been proposed by Harik (1999). But Harik allows only factorizations without conditional distributions. This distribution is correct only for separable functions.

Table 15.1

Numerical Results for Different Algorithms, LFDA with $BN(\alpha, 8)$

Function	n	α	N	τ	Succ.%	SDev
OneMax	30	UMDA	30	0.3	75	4.3
	30	0.25	100	0.3	2	1.4
	30	0.50	100	0.3	38	4.9
	30	0.75	100	0.3	80	4.0
	30	0.25	200	0.3	71	4.5
Saw $(32, 2, 0.5)$	32	UMDA	50	0.5	71	4.5
	32	UMDA	200	0.5	100	0.0
	32	0.25	200	0.5	41	2.2
	32	0.50	200	0.5	83	1.7
	32	0.75	200	0.5	96	0.9
	32	0.25	400	0.5	84	3.7
Decep-4	32	UMDA	800	0.3	0	0.0
	32	FDA	100	0.3	81	3.9
	32	0.25	800	0.3	92	2.7
	32	0.50	800	0.3	72	4.5
	32	0.75	800	0.3	12	3.2

Given the BIC score we have several options to extend FDA to LFDA, which learns a factorization. Given limitations of space, we can show results only of an algorithm that computes a Bayesian network at each generation using algorithm $BN(0.5, k_{max})$. FDA and LFDA should behave fairly similarly, if LFDA computes factorizations that are probabilistically very similar to the FDA factorization. FDA uses the same factorization for all generations, whereas at each step LFDA computes a new factorization that depends on the given data M.

We have applied LFDA to many problems (Mühlenbein and Mahnig, 1999b). The results are encouraging. Here we discuss only the functions introduced in section 13.4. Recall that UMDA finds the optimum of the multimodal function Saw. UMDA uses univariate marginal distributions only. Therefore its Bayesian network has no arcs.

Table 15.1 summarizes the results. For LFDA we used three values of α, namely $\alpha = 0.25, 0.5, 0.75$. The smaller α, the less penalty for the size of the structure. Let us discuss the results in more detail. $\alpha = 0.25$ gives by far the best results when a network with many arcs is required. This is the case for Decep -4. Here a Bayesian network with three parents is optimal. $\alpha = 0.25$ performs poorly on problems where a network with no arcs defines a good search distribution. For the linear function OneMax $BIC(0.25)$ has a success rate of only 2%. The success rate can be improved if a larger population size N is used, for the following reason. BIC(0.25) allows denser networks; but if a small population is used, spurious correlations may arise. These correlations have a negative impact on the search distribution. The problem can be solved by using a larger population. Increasing the value from $N = 100$ to $N = 200$ increases the success rate from 2% to 71% for OneMax.

For Saw a Bayesian network with no arcs is able to generate the optimum. An exact factorization requires a factor with n parameters. We used the heuristic BN with $k_{max} = 8$. Therefore the exact factorization cannot be found. In all these cases $\alpha = 0.75$ gives the best results. BIC(0.75) enforces smaller networks. But BIC(0.75) performs very poorly on Decep $- 4$. Taking all results together, BIC(0.5) gives promising results. These numerical results support the theoretical estimate.

The numerical result indicates that control of the weight factor α can substantially reduce the amount of computation. For Bayesian networks we have not yet experimented with control strategies. We have studied the problem extensively in the context of neural networks (Zhang et al., 1997).

UMDA is most efficient at optimizing the functions OneMax and Saw. FDA is efficient if the exact factorization requires a small number of parents in the Bayesian graph ($k \leq 5$). LFDA also finds the optimum most of the time. From the functions considered it has the greatest difficulty with the function Saw. The performance of LFDA can be improved substantially, if for each fitness function a suitable value of α is chosen. Recall that a small value of α leads to more complex Bayesian factorizations. The BIC score uses $\alpha = 0.5$, a good compromise. But $\alpha = 0.75$ results in a much better performance for the functions OneMax and Saw, whereas $\alpha = 0.25$ yields the best results for the function Decep$(36, 4)$. These results are explained next.

15.2 Optimization, Dependencies, and Search Distributions

We have proven in section 14.1 convergence of FDA with Boltzmann selection to the set of global maxima. If the Boltzmann distribution can be factorized, the computational complexity for one generation is bounded by $O(n \cdot N \cdot 2^k)$. k denotes the maximum number of parents. A factorization can be determined if the fitness function is decomposed. It can also be obtained from the data sampled. Unfortunately, for many interesting applications k is very large. If the fitness function is decomposed additively on a 2-D grid of size n, then k scales like $O(\sqrt{n})$. It is easy to show that k even scales like $O(n)$ for the function Saw.

But we have demonstrated that the simple search distribution used by UMDA guides the search to the optimum of Saw. The reason is that Saw has the following tendency: the more bits on, the higher the fitness value.

Therefore an exact Boltzmann factorization is not needed for optimization. The problem of finding a good approximation of the Boltzmann distribution that generates the optima with high probability cannot be solved theoretically. Therefore we propose the following heuristic:

Multi-Factorization LFDA. *Use different values of α in order to obtain factorizations of various complexity. In a standard setting, use $\alpha = 0.25$, 0.5, and 0.75. Generate new search points using the different factorizations for a certain percentage of the population.*

16 The System Dynamics Approach to Optimization

So far we have transformed genetic algorithms that use a population of strings and probabilistic recombination of strings into algorithms that use probability distributions to generate new strings. We have derived Wright's equation and used it to analyze the behavior of UMDA. We have shown that UMDA converges to local attractors of the average fitness. These attractors are local optima of the fitness function.

We can go even one step further: We can use the difference equations directly, without generating a population of strings at all. This approach seems surprising at first, but it has been used in mathematics a number of times. The approach is called called the *systems dynamics approach to optimization*. We discuss just a few examples that are related to our previous algorithms.

16.1 The Replicator Equation

In this section we investigate the relation between Wright's equation and a popular equation called the *replicator equation*. Replicator dynamics is a standard model in evolutionary biology used to describe the dynamics of growth and decay of a number of species under selection. Let $S = \{1, 2, \ldots, s\}$ be a set of species and p_i the frequency of species i in a fixed population of size N. Then the replicator equation is defined on a simplex $S^s = \{p : \sum p_i = 1, 0 \le p_i \le 1\}$:

$$(16.1) \qquad \frac{dp_i}{dt} = p_i(t) \left(f_i(\mathbf{p}) - \sum_{i=1}^{s} p_i(t) f_i(\mathbf{p}) \right),$$

where f_i gives the fitness of species i in relation to the others. The replicator equation is discussed in detail in Hofbauer and Sigmund (1998). For the replicator equation a maximum principle can be shown.

Theorem 16.1. *If there exists a potential V with $\partial V / \partial p_i = f_i(\mathbf{p})$, then $dV/dt \ge 0$, i.e. the potential V increases using the replicator dynamics.*

If we want to apply the replicator equation to a binary optimization problem of size n, we have to set $s = 2^n$. Thus the number of species is exponential in the size of the problem. The replicator equation can be used only for small size problems.

Voigt (1989) had the idea to generalize the replicator equation by introducing continuous variables $0 \leq p_i(x_k) \leq 1$ with $\sum_k p_i(x_k) = 1$. Thus $p_i(x_k)$ can be interpreted as univariate probabilities. Voigt (1989) proposed the following discrete equation.

Definition 16.1. *The* discrete diversified replicator equation (DDRP) *is given by*

$$(16.2) \quad p_i(x_k)(t+1) - p_i(x_k)(t) = p_i(x_k)(t) \frac{f_{ik}(\mathbf{p}) - \sum_{x_k} p_i(x_k) f_{ik}(\mathbf{p})}{\sum_{x_k} p_i(x_k) f_{ik}(\mathbf{p})}.$$

The name discrete diversified replicator equation was not a good choice, as the DDRP is more similar to Wright's equation than to the replicator equation. This is the content of the next theorem.

Theorem 16.2. *If the average fitness $W(\mathbf{p})$ is used as potential, then Wright's equation and the discrete diversified replicator equation are identical.*

Proof. The average fitness is defined as

$$W(\mathbf{p}) = V(\mathbf{p}) = \sum_x a_x \prod_{i=1}^{n} p_i(x_i).$$

We compute the derivatives

$$\frac{\partial V(\mathbf{p})}{\partial p_i(1)} = \sum_{x|x_i=1} a_x \prod_{j \neq i}^{n} p_j(x_j)$$

$$\frac{\partial V(\mathbf{p})}{\partial p_i(0)} = \sum_{x|x_i=0} a_x \prod_{j \neq i}^{n} p_j(x_j).$$

Then, obviously:

$$p_i(1) \frac{\partial V}{\partial p_i(1)} + p_i(1) \frac{\partial V}{\partial p_i(1)} = V(\mathbf{p}).$$

The conjecture now follows from the proof of Wright's equation. $\quad\square$

We recently discovered that Baum and Eagon (1967) have proven a discrete maximum principle for certain instances of the DDRP.

Theorem 16.3 (Baum-Eagon). *Let $V(\mathbf{p})$ be a polynomial with non-negative coefficients homogeneous of degree d in its variables $p_i(x_j)$ with $p_i(x_j) \geq 0$ and $\sum_{x_j} p_i(x_j) = 1$. Let $\mathbf{p}(t+1)$ be the point given by*

$$(16.3) \qquad p_i(x_j, t+1) = \frac{p_i(x_j, t) \frac{\partial V}{\partial p_i(x_j)}}{\sum_{x_k} p_i(x_k) \frac{\partial V}{\partial p_i(x_k)}} .$$

The derivatives are taken at $\mathbf{p}(t)$. Then $V(\mathbf{p}(t+1)) > V(\mathbf{p}(t))$ unless $\mathbf{p}(t+1) = \mathbf{p}(t)$.

Equation (16.3) is exactly the DDRP with a potential V. Thus the DDRP could be called the Baum-Eagon equation. From the above theorem the discrete maximum principle for Wright's equation follows by setting $V = W$ and $d = n$. Thus the potential is the average fitness, which is homogeneous of degree n.

16.2 Boltzmann Selection and the Replicator Equation

For FDA with Boltzmann selection we have a closed solution for the probability $p(\mathbf{x}, t)$. It is given by

$$(16.4) \qquad p_{\beta, p_0}(\mathbf{x}, t) = \frac{p_0(\mathbf{x}) e^{\beta f(\mathbf{x})}}{\sum_y p_0(\mathbf{y}) e^{\beta f(\mathbf{y})}} .$$

If we differentiate this equation we obtain after some computation:

$$(16.5) \qquad \frac{dp_{\beta, p_0}(\mathbf{x}, t)}{dt} = \frac{d\beta}{dt} p_{\beta, p_0}(\mathbf{x}, t) \left(f(\mathbf{x}) - \sum_y p_{\beta, p_0}(\mathbf{y}, t) f(y) \right) .$$

For $\beta' = 1$ we obtain a special case of the replicator equation (16.1). We have only to set $f(\mathbf{p}) = f_i$.

Theorem 16.4. *The dynamics of Boltzmann selection with $\Delta\beta(t) = 1$ is given by the replicator equation.*

From the convergence theorem 14.1 we know that the global optima are the only stable attractors of the replicator equation. Thus the replicator equation is an ideal starting point for a system dynamics approach to optimization discussed in section 16. Unfortunately, the replicator equation consists of 2^n different equations for a problem of size n.

Thus we are led to the same problem encountered when analyzing the Boltzmann distribution: We have to factorize the probability $p(\mathbf{x})$ if we want to use the equation numerically.

Example 16.1. *Linear function $f(\mathbf{x}) = \sum_i^n \alpha_i x_i$. In this case the UMDA factorization is valid $p(\mathbf{x}) = \prod_{i=1}^n p_i(x_i)$. By summation we ob-*

tain from equation (16.5), *after some manipulation:*

$$(16.6) \qquad \frac{dp_i}{dt} = \frac{d\beta}{dt} p_i (1 - p_i) \alpha_i \,.$$

For $d\beta/dt = 1$ this is just Wright's equation without the denominator $\tilde{W}$.

If we extend this equation we obtain another proposal for the systems dynamics approach to optimization:

$$(16.7) \qquad \frac{dp_i}{dt} = \frac{d\beta}{dt} p_i (1 - p_i) \frac{\partial \tilde{W}}{\partial p_i} \,.$$

This leads to the difference equation:

$$(16.8) \qquad \Delta p_i = \Delta \beta p_i (1 - p_i) \frac{\partial \tilde{W}}{\partial p_i} \,.$$

We just recently derived this equation, and so we have not yet used it for numerical experiments.

16.3 Some System Dynamics Equations for Optimization

Theorem 16.3 shows that both Wright's equation and the DDRP maximize some potential. This means that both equations can be used for maximization. But there is a problem: both equations are deterministic. For difficult optimization problems, there exists a large number of attractors, each with a corresponding attractor region. If the iteration starts at a point within the attractor region, it will converge to the corresponding attractor at the boundary. But if the iteration starts at points that lie at the boundary of two or more attractors, i.e. on the separatrix, the iteration will be confined to the separatrix. The deterministic system cannot decide on one of the attractors.

UMDA with a finite population does not have a sharp boundary between attractor regions. We model this behavior by introducing randomness. The new value $p_i(x_j, t + 1)$ is randomly chosen from the interval

$$[(1 - c)p_i'(x_j, t + 1), (1 + c)p_i'(x_j, t + 1)] \,,$$

where $p_i'(x_j, t + 1)$ is determined by the deterministic equation. c is a small number. For $c = 0$ we obtain the deterministic equation. In order to use the difference equation optimally, we do not allow the boundary values $p_i = 0$ or $p_i = 1$, but use instead $p_i = p_{\min}$ and $p_i = 1 - p_{\min}$.

A second extension concerns the determination of the solution. All dynamic equations presented use variables, which can be interpreted as probabilities. Thus instead of waiting that the dynamic system converges to some boundary point, we terminate the iteration at a suitable time and generate a set of solutions. Thus, given the values for $p_i(x_j)$, we generate points x according to the UMDA distribution $p(\mathbf{x}) = \prod_{i=1}^{n} p_i(x_i)$.

We can now formulate a family of optimization algorithms, based on difference equations (DIFFOPT).

DIFFOPT

- STEP 0: Set $t \Leftarrow 0$ and $p_i(x_j, 0) = 0.5$. Input $p_{\min}$.
- STEP 1: Compute $p_i'(x_j, t+1)$ according to a dynamic difference equation. If $p_i'(x_j, t+1) < p_{\min}$ then $p_i'(x_j, t+1) = p_{\min}$. If $p_i'(x_j, t+1) > 1 - p_{\min}$ then $p_i'(x_j, t+1) = 1 - p_{\min}$
- STEP 2: Compute randomly $p_i(x_j, t+1)$ in the interval $(1 - c)p_i'(x_j, t+1), (1 + c)p_i'(x_j, t+1)$. Set $t \Leftarrow t+1$
- STEP 3: If termination criteria are not met, go to STEP 1.
- STEP 4: Generate N solutions according to $p(\mathbf{x}, t) = \prod_{i=1}^{n} p_i(x_i, t)$ and compute $\max f(\mathbf{x})$ and $\operatorname{argmax} f(\mathbf{x})$.

DIFFOPT is not restricted to Wright's equation or to DDRP. We propose a third one. Its rationale is as follows: from the analysis of UMDA we know that Wright's equation models proportionate selection. But this method converges very slowly when approaching the boundary. We have not been able to derive dynamic equations for truncation selection. Therefore we experimented with a number of faster versions of Wright's equation and finally chose the following difference equation.

Definition 16.2. *F-Wright(α) (Fast Wright) is defined by the following difference equation:*

$$(16.9) \quad p_i(x_i, t+1) = p_i(x_i, t) + \operatorname{sign}(\Delta) \cdot \exp\left(\alpha \ln|\Delta|\right)$$

$$(16.10) \quad \Delta = p_i(x_i, t) \frac{\frac{\partial \tilde{W}}{\partial p_i(x_i)} - \sum_{y_i \in \bar{\Lambda}_i} p_i(y_i, t) \frac{\partial \tilde{W}}{\partial p_i(y_i)}}{\tilde{W}(\mathbf{p})}.$$

If a value outside the interval $[p_{\min}, 1 - p_{\min}]$ is generated, we just set the value to the corresponding boundary value of the interval. For $\alpha = 1$ we obtain Wright's equation. We usually set $\alpha = 0.5$. The reason for this choice is that we wanted a difference equation that resembles as much as possible *truncation selection*. If we take the fitness function OneMax, we obtain for F-Wright(0.5) the difference equation:

$$(16.11) \quad p(t+1) - p(t) = \frac{\sqrt{p(t)(1 - p(t))}}{np(t)} = \frac{\sqrt{1 - p(t)}}{n}.$$

This equation is similar to the approximate equation we have computed for UMDA with truncation selection: only the multiplication by p is missing. This means that F-Wright normally will converge faster than UMDA with truncation selection.

We next evaluate the three difference equations with optimization problems.

16.4   Optimization of Binary Functions

The DDRP opens the possibility of using an arbitrary potential. If the potential is not a representation of the average fitness, Wright's equation and DDRP are different. We demonstrate this with a simple example, a quadratic potential.

Example 16.2. $V(\mathbf{p}) = \sum_{ij} a_{ij} p_i(1) p_j(0) + c.$ c *is chosen such that* $V(\mathbf{p}) > 0.$ *We assume* $a_{ii} = 0.$

We obtain

$$\frac{\partial V}{\partial p_i(1)} = \sum_j a_{ij} p_j(0)$$

$$\frac{\partial V}{\partial p_i(0)} = \sum_j a_{ji} p_j(1)$$

$$V_i(\mathbf{p}) = p_i(1) \frac{\partial V}{\partial p_i(1)} + p_i(0) \frac{\partial V}{\partial p_i(0)}.$$

Obviously $\sum_i p_i(1) \sum_j a_{ij} p_j(0) = \sum_i p_i(0) \sum_j a_{ji} p_j(1)$. Therefore we get the following proposition.

Proposition. $V(\mathbf{p}) = \frac{1}{2} \sum_i V_i(\mathbf{p})$ *if* c *is suitably chosen.*

The DDRP is given by

$$\Delta p_i(1) = p_i(1) \frac{\sum_{j \neq i} a_{ij} p_j(0) - V_i}{V_i + c_i}.$$

c_i has to be chosen such that $V_i(\mathbf{p}) + c_i > 0$. If we eliminate $p_i(0) = 1 - p_i(1)$ and abbreviate $p_i := p_i(1)$ we obtain

$$(16.12) \qquad \Delta p_i = p_i(1 - p_i) \frac{\sum_{j \neq i} a_{ij}(1 - p_j) - \sum_{j \neq i} a_{ji} p_j}{V_i + c_i}.$$

We now determine Wright's equation for the same problem. This means we have to find a fitness function, which will give $V(\mathbf{p}) = \tilde{W}(\mathbf{p})$.

Example 16.3. $f(\mathbf{x}) = \sum_{ij} a_{ij} x_i(1 - x_j) + c.$ c *is chosen such that* $f(\mathbf{x}) > 0.$

We compute $\tilde{W}(\mathbf{p})$ using our lemma

$$(16.13) \qquad \tilde{W}(\mathbf{p}) = \sum_{ij} a_{ij} p_i(1 - p_j) + c.$$

Obviously $\tilde{W}(\mathbf{p}) = V(\mathbf{p})$. Wright's equation is given by

(16.14) $$\Delta p_i = p_i(1 - p_i)\frac{\sum_{j\neq i} a_{ij}(1 - p_j) - \sum_{j\neq i} a_{ji}p_j}{\tilde{W}(\mathbf{p})}.$$

We now compare the two difference equations. We assume that $c = c_i = 0$ and obtain

$$\Delta p_i = p_i(1 - p_i)\frac{\sum_{j\neq i} a_{ij}(1 - p_j) - \sum_{j\neq i} a_{ji}p_j}{\tilde{W}(\mathbf{p})}$$

$$\Delta p_i = p_i(1 - p_i)\frac{\sum_{j\neq i} a_{ij}(1 - p_j) - \sum_{j\neq i} a_{ji}p_j}{p_i \sum_j a_{ij}(1 - p_j) + (1 - p_i)\sum_j a_{ji}p_j}.$$

The two equations differ in the denominator only. The denominator of DDRP is normally smaller than the denominator of Wright's equation, and thus DDRP will converge faster. We compare three different examples.

Problem 1. $a_{i,i+1} = 1, a_{i,i-1} = 1$. All other values are set to 0.

The two global optima of this problem are $1, 0, 1, 0, \ldots$ and $0, 1, 0, 1, \ldots$ with a fitness value of $n - 1$. The fitness function is symmetric. $f(\mathbf{x})$ and $f(\bar{\mathbf{x}})$ have the same fitness value where $\bar{\mathbf{x}}$ is the string with all bits inverted. We have an unstable attractor at $p_i = 0.5$.

Problem 2. $a_{i,i+1} = 1, a_{i,i-1} = 2, a_{n-1,n-2} = 3$. All other values are set to 0.

Here the matrix a is not symmetric. The value $a_{n-1,n-2} = 3$ deceives the system to set $x_{n-1} = 1$. But the optimal solution is $x_{\max} = (0, 1, 0, 1, \ldots)$ with $x_{n-1} = 0$ for n even. The optimum fitness value is $1.5n - 1$.

Problem 3. $a_{i,j} = 1, \quad j < i$. All other values are set to 0.

Here the maximum is $x_{\max} = (0, 0, \ldots, 0, 1, \ldots, 1, 1)$, i.e. the first half of the bits are 0, the second half of the bits are 1. For $n = 30$ the optimal value is 225.

Table 16.1 displays the numerical results. In problem 1 with $n = 30$ the optimum is found at least once by all three methods. On the average one bit is wrong. This behavior can be understood because of the parallel search and the symmetry of the problem. For $n = 60$ we have 3 bits wrong on the average. In problem 2 bit $n - 1$ is always set to 1 (because $a_{n-1,n-3} = 3$). Therefore the optimum is missed, which has a 0 at this place. The same behavior is observed for $n = 60$. The optimum is missed by one point. A large difference in the performance can be seen in problem 3. Here the results for the more local DDRP are really poor. DDRP is not able to set the bits correct in the area where

TABLE 16.1

Numerical Results (Average over 10 runs)
The number in brackets give the number of times S
a global optimum has been found.

Algorithm	Prob.	n	Iter.	Maximum (S)
Wright	1	30	250	28.2 (2)
DDRP	1	30	70	27.8 (1)
F-Wright(0.5)	1	30	20	27.6 (1)
Wright	1	60	500	55.6 (0)
DDRP	1	60	140	55.6 (0)
F-Wright(0.5)	1	60	20	54.5 (0)
Wright	2	30	60	43.0 (0)
DDRP	2	30	70	43.1 (1)
F-Wright(0.5)	2	30	20	43.0 (0)
Wright	2	60	500	88.0 (0)
DDRP	2	60	50	87.7 (0)
F-Wright(0.5)	2	60	20	88.0 (0)
Wright	3	30	250	225.0 (10)
DDRP	3	30	250	204.4 (00)
F-Wright(0.5)	3	30	20	225.0 (10)

TABLE 16.2

Numerical Results for UMDA with
Proportionate Selection (p) and Truncation Selection (tr) and
a Genetic Algorithm with Uniform Crossover (uc).

Algorithm	Prob.	n	N	Iter.	Maximum (S)
UMDA p.	1	30	300	230	27.2 (4)
UMDA tr.	1	30	300	90	26.9 (2)
GA uc	1	30	300	100	27.4 (1)
UMDA p.	1	60	600	400	53.0 (0)
UMDA tr.	1	60	600	150	53.3 (0)
GA uc	1	60	600	150	55.3 (0)
UMDA p.	3	30	300	200	225.0 (10)
UMDA tr.	3	30	300	10	225.0 (10)
GA uc	3	30	300	30	225.0 (10)

all 1 meets all 0. This problem is the simplest for Wright's equation and F-Wright.

All three examples taken together show that F-Wright(0.5) is the fastest and most efficient algorithm.

Table 16.2 shows the numerical results for a genetic algorithm GA and UMDA. The results of UMDA with proportionate selection and Wright's

Table 17.1

Three Classes of Evolutionary Algorithms

Algorithm	Selection	Reproduction
Genetic Algorithm	microscopic	microscopic
UMDA	microscopic	macroscopic
System Dynamics	macroscopic	macroscopic

equation are fairly similar. The results for problem 2 are omitted because they are similar to those for problem 1. Note that no algorithm is able to locate the global optimum for problem 1 with size $n = 60$. For this problem FDA has to be used.

17 Three Royal Roads to Optimization

In this section we will classify the different approaches presented. Population search methods are based on two components at least: selection and reproduction with variation. In our research we have transformed genetic algorithms to a family of algorithms using search distributions instead of recombination/mutation of strings. The simplest algorithm of this family is the univariate marginal distribution algorithm UMDA.

Wright's equation describes the behavior of UMDA using an infinite population and proportionate selection. The equation shows that UMDA does *not* primarily optimize the *fitness function* $f(\mathbf{x})$, but the *average fitness* of the population $W(\mathbf{p})$, which depends on the continuous marginal frequencies $p_i(x_i)$. Thus the important landscape for population search is *not* the landscape defined by the fitness function $f(\mathbf{x})$, but, rather the landscape defined by $W(\mathbf{p})$.

The two components of population-based search methods—selection and reproduction with variation—can work on a microscopic (individual) or a macroscopic (population) level. The level can be different for selection and reproduction. It is possible to classify the various approaches according to the level at which the components work. Table 17.1 shows three classes of evolutionary algorithms, each with a representative member.

A genetic algorithm uses a population of individuals. Selection and recombination are performed by manipulating individual strings. UMDA uses marginal distributions to create individuals. These are macroscopic variables. Selection is performed on a population of individuals, as with genetic algorithms. In the system dynamics approach, selection is modeled by a specific dynamic difference equation for macroscopic variables.

We believe that a fourth class—macroscopic selection and microscopic reproduction—makes no sense.

Each of the approaches has its specific pros and cons. Genetic algorithms are very flexible, but the standard recombination operator has limited capabilities. UMDA can use any kind of selection method that is used by a genetic algorithm. UMDA can also be extended to an algorithm that uses a more complex factorization of the distribution, namely the factorized distribution algorithm FDA. Selection is very difficult to model on a macroscopic level. Wright's equations are valid only for proportionate selection. Other selection schemes lead to very complicated system dynamics equations.

Thus for proportionate selection and gene pool recombination all methods behave similarly. But each of the methods allows extensions that cannot be modeled with an approach using a different level.

Especially interesting mathematically is the extension of UMDA to FDA with an adaptive Boltzmann annealing schedule. For this algorithm convergence for a large class of discrete optimization problems has been shown.

18 Conclusion and Outlook

This chapter describes a complete mathematical analysis of evolutionary methods for optimization. The optimization problem is defined by a fitness function with a given set of variables. Part of the theory consists of an adaptation of classical population genetics and the science of breeding to optimization problems. The theory is extended to general population-based search methods by introducing search distributions instead of performing string recombination. This theory also can be used for continuous variables, a mixture of continuous and discrete variables as well as constraint optimization problems. The theory combines *learning* and *optimization* into a common framework based on *graphical models*.

We have presented three approaches to optimization. We believe that the optimization methods based on search distributions (UMDA, FDA, LFDA) have the greatest optimization power. The dynamic equations derived for UMDA with proportionate selection are fairly simple. For UMDA with truncation or tournament selection and FDA with conditional marginal distributions, the dynamic equations can become very complicated. FDA with Boltzmann selection SDS is an extension of simulated annealing to a population of points. It shares with simulated annealing the convergence property, but convergence is much faster.

Ultimately our theory leads to a synthesis problem: finding a good factorization for a search distribution defined by a finite sample. This is a central problem in probability theory. One approach to this problem uses Bayesian networks. For Bayesian networks, researchers have developed numerically efficient algorithms. Our LFDA algorithm computes a Bayesian network by minimizing the Bayesian information criterion.

The computational effort of both FDA and LFDA is substantially higher than that of UMDA. Thus UMDA should be the first algorithm tried in a practical problem. Next the multi-factorization LFDA should be applied.

Our theory is defined for optimization problems that are defined by quantitative variables. The optimization problem can be defined by a cost function or a complex process to be simulated. The theory is not applicable directly if either the optimization problem is qualitatively defined or the *problem solving method is nonnumeric*. A popular example of a nonnumeric problem solving method is *genetic programming*. In genetic programming we try to find a program that optimizes the problem, not an optimal solution. Understanding these kinds of problem-solving methods will be a challenge for the next decade. We are convinced that the theory presented here can be extended to design and analyze those methods.

References

Asoh, H. and Mühlenbein, H. (1994a). Estimating the heritability by decomposing the genetic variance. In Davidor, Y., Schwefel, H.-P., and Männer, R. (eds.), *Parallel Problem Solving from Nature* (pp. 98–107). Lecture Notes in Computer Science 866. Berlin: Springer-Verlag.

Asoh, H. and Mühlenbein, H. (1994b). On the mean convergence time of evolutionary algorithms without selection and mutation. In Davidor, Y., Schwefel, H.-P., and Männer, R. (eds.), *Parallel Problem Solving from Nature* (pp. 88–97). Lecture Notes in Computer Science 866. Berlin: Springer-Verlag.

Ballard, D. (1997). *An Introduction to Natural Computation.* Cambridge, MA: MIT Press.

Baum, L. and Eagon, J. (1967). An inequality with applications to statistical estimation for probabilistic functions of markov processes and to a model for ecology. *Bull. Am. Math. Soc.* 73:360–363.

Bouckaert, R. (1994). Properties of bayesian network learning algorithms. In de Mantaras, R. L. and Poole, D. (eds.), *Proc. Tenth Conference on Uncertainty in Artificial Intelligence* (pp. 102–109). San Francisco: Morgan Kaufmann.

Christiansen, F. and Feldman, M. (1998). Algorithms, genetics, and populations: The schemata theorem revisited. *Complexity* 3:57–64.

de la Maza, M. and Tidor, B. (1993). An analysis of selection procedures with particular attention paid to proportional and boltzmann selection. In Forrest, S. (ed.), *Proc. of the Fifth Int. Conf. on Genetic Algorithms* (pp. 124–131). San Mateo, CA: Morgan Kaufmann.

Falconer, D. S. (1981). *Introduction to Quantitative Genetics*. London: Longman.

Freedman, D., R.Pisani, Purves, R., and Adhikkari, A. (1991). *Statistics*, second edition. New York: W. W. Norton.

Frey, B. (1998). *Graphical Models for Machine Learning and Digital Communication*. Cambrigde, MA: MIT Press.

Geiringer, H. (1944). On the probability theory of linkage in mendelian heredity. *Annals of Math. Stat.* 15:25–57.

Goldberg, D. (1989). *Genetic Algorithms in Search, Optimization, and Machine Learning*. Reading: Addison-Wesley.

Goldberg, D. and Deb, K. (1991). A comparative analysis of selection schemes used in genetic algorithms. In Rawlins, G. (ed.), *Foundations of Genetic Algorithms* (pp. 69–93). San Mateo, CA: Morgan-Kaufmann.

Harik, G. (1999). Linkage learning via probabilistic modeling in the ecga. Technical Report IlliGal 99010, University of Illinois, Urbana-Champaign.

Harik, G., Cantu-Paz, E., Goldberg, D., and Miller, B. (1999). The gambler's ruin problem, genetic algorithms, and the sizing of populations. *Evolutionary Computation* 7:231–255.

Hofbauer, J. and Sigmund, K. (1998). *Evolutionary Games and Population Dynamics*. Cambridge: Cambridge University Press.

Holland, J. (1975/1992). *Adaptation in Natural and Artificial Systems*. Ann Arbor, MI: Univ. of Michigan Press.

Jordan, M. (1999). *Learning in Graphical Models*. Cambridge, MA: MIT Press.

Kirkpatrick, S., Gelatt, C., and Vecchi, M. (1983). Optimization by simulated annealing. *Science* 220:671–680.

Lauritzen, S. L. (1996). *Graphical Models*. Oxford: Clarendon Press.

Mitchell, M., Holland, J., and Forrest, S. (1994). When will a genetic algorithm outperform hill climbing? *Advances in Neural Information Processing Systems* 6:51–58.

Mühlenbein, H. (1991). Evolution in time and space—The parallel genetic algorithm. In Rawlins, G. (ed.), *Foundations of Genetic Algorithms* (pp. 316–337). San Mateo, CA: Morgan-Kaufmann.

Mühlenbein, H. (1997). The equation for the response to selection and its use for prediction. *Evolutionary Computation* 5(3):303–346.

Mühlenbein, H. and Mahnig, T. (1999a). Convergence theory and applications of the factorized distribution algorithm. *Journal of Computing and Information Technology* 7:19–32.

Mühlenbein, H. and Mahnig, T. (1999b). FDA—A scalable evolutionary algorithm for the optimization of additively decomposed functions. *Evolutionary Computation* 7(4):353–376.

Mühlenbein, H. and Mahnig, T. (2000). Evolutionary algorithms: From recombination to search distributions. In Kallel, L., Naudts, B., and Rogers, A. (eds.), *Theoretical Aspects of Evolutionary Computing* (pp. 137–176). Natural Computing series. Berlin: Springer Verlag.

Mühlenbein, H., Mahnig, T., and Ochoa, A. R. (1999). Schemata, distributions and graphical models in evolutionary optimization. *Journal of Heuristics* 5:215–247.

Mühlenbein, H. and Schlierkamp-Voosen, D. (1994). The science of breeding and its application to the breeder genetic algorithm. *Evolutionary Computation* 1:335–360.

Mühlenbein, H. and Voigt, H.-M. (1996). Gene pool recombination in genetic algorithms. In Kelly, J. and Osman, I. (eds.), *Metaheuristics: Theory and Applications* (pp. 53–62). Norwell: Kluwer Academic Publishers.

Nagylaki, T. (1992). *Introduction to Theoretical Population Genetics*. Berlin: Springer.

Pelikan, M., Goldberg, D., and Cantu-Paz, E. (2000). Linkage problem, distribution estimation, and Bayesian networks. *Evolutionary Computation* 8: 311–341.

Prügel-Bennet, A. and Shapiro, J. (1997). An analysis of a genetic algorithm for simple random ising systems. *Physica D* 104:75–114.

Rao, C. (1973). *Linear Statisticcal Inference and Its Application*. New York: Wiley.

Rattray, L. M. and Shapiro, J. (in press). Cumulant Dynamics of a Population under Multiplicative Selection, Mutation and Drift. *Theoretical Population Biology*.

Schwarz, G. (1978). Estimating the dimension of a model. *Annals of Statistics* 7:461–464.

Vapnik, V. (1998). *Statistical Learning Theory*. New York: Wiley.

Voigt, H.-M. (1989). *Evolution and Optimization*. Berlin: Akademie-Verlag.

Vose, M. (1999). *The Simple Genetic Algorithm: Foundations and Theory*. Cambridge: MIT Press.

Wright, S. (1970). Random drift and the shifting balance theory of evolution. In Kojima, K. (ed.), *Mathematical Topics in Population Genetics* (pp. 1–31). Berlin: Springer Verlag.

Zhang, B.-T., Ohm, P., and Mühlenbein, H. (1997). Evolutionary induction of sparse neural trees. *Evolutionary Computation* 5:213–236.

IV

Distributed and Active Learning

RWC Theoretical Foundation NEC Laboratory

Naoki Abe, Kenji Yamanishi, Atsuyohsi Nakamura,
Hiroshi Mamitsuka, Jun'ichi Takeuchi, and Hang Li

Our research goal in the five-year period of the RWI project has been to develop theoretical foundations of adaptive intelligent systems that function satisfactorily in real-world environments. By a real-world environment we mean one in which realistic limitations and restrictions apply on various computational resources, such as computational time and space. Through our experience with the methodology of learning probabilistic knowledge representations, which we used in the first half of the Real World Computing project, we have learned that overcoming the computational complexity issue requires a different approach. The approach we have chosen is to enhance the intelligent agent with distributed information sources and active learning functions. With this in mind, we have developed theories of distributed and active learning.

Owing to space limitations, we will be able to touch on only a fraction of the activities that we have been engaged in. We chose the following three topics that are particularly characteristic of our distributed and active learning approach:

1. Cooperative learning by agents that have distributed information sources.

2. Learning by an agent that has access to a set of learning agents, each with its own specialty.

3. On-line active learning in which the goal is to maximize the total pay-off.

Foundations of Real-World Intelligence.
Yoshinori Uesaka et al. (eds.).
Copyright © 2001, CSLI Publications.

For the first of these topics, we will describe the theory of distributed cooperative Bayesian learning strategies. For the second topic, we will exhibit the theoretical analysis of new learning methods for decision lists of specialists. For the last topic, we will introduce an on-line active learning problem called the lob-pass problem and analyze a number of learning methods for this problem.

19 Distributed Cooperative Bayesian Learning[†]
KENJI YAMANISHI

19.1 Introduction

19.1.1 Problem Statement

Consider a situation in which each example is generated according to an unknown parametric probability density function, which we call the *target density*. We are concerned with the problem of determining the target density, or equivalently, estimating the parameters specifying the target density, using a *distributed learning system*. A distributed learning system consists of a number of agent learners (for short, agents) and the population learner (for short, the p-learner). Each agent independently observes a sequence of examples and outputs an estimate of the parameter specifying the target density or statistics of the examples. The p-learner doesn't have direct access to the random examples, but only to a set of outputs of the agents. The p-learner combines the outputs of the agents in order to obtain a significantly better estimate of the parameter for the target density.

The main purpose of designing a distributed learning system is to use its parallelism to accelerate the learning process, compared to that of the nondistributed system. Here the nondistributed learning system is a system that receives all examples given to the agents and outputs an estimate of the parameter for the target density. Distributed learning systems can also handle the type of situation where there is sufficient communication bandwidth for the agents to send their outputs to the p-learner, but not enough time or bandwidth for the p-learner itself to receive all the examples themselves.

We measure the performance of a distributed learning system in terms of the *average logarithmic loss* it incurs when predicting the probability density of some unknown example. The average is taken to account for the data generation and the randomness that the system may induce.

The goal is to design a distributed learning system whose average logarithmic loss is as small as possible and whose p-learner eventually can predict future data approximately as well as the *nondistributed Bayesian learning strategy* (NDB), which can observe all examples at once and attains the lowest average logarithmic loss.

We propose two models of distributed learning, the *plain model* and the *hierarchical model*, of which we describe only the first owing to space limitations. The plain model deals with the case where each agent observes a data sequence generated according to an identical target density, and the parameter value specifying the target density is generated randomly according to a fixed prior density. The output of the p-learner is an estimate of the parameter for the target density, which is itself an output of the distributed learning system in this model.

In this model we propose specific types of distributed learning systems and analyze their performance for particular classes of probability distributions (e.g. Gaussian distributions, Poisson distributions, multidimensional discrete distributions) and prior densities.

19.1.2 Previous Work

The framework of distributed learning that we propose here is inspired by Kearns and Seung's seminal model of *population learning* (Kearns and Seung, 1993); (see also Nakamura, Abe, and Takeuchi, 1994). Our framework is similar to theirs in that each agent independently observes a data sequence and the p-learner has access only to the outputs of the agents. The differences between our framework and Kearns and Seung's are as follows.

Kearns and Seung's model may be characterized by the following features:

1. The target to be learned is a deterministic rule taking values in $\{0,1\}$.

2. The prediction loss is measured in terms of the 0–1 loss, or equivalently, the discrete loss.

3. Each agent uses a *deterministic version* of the Gibbs algorithm; i.e. a deterministic hypothesis is chosen randomly according to the uniform distribution from the set of hypotheses consistent with examples.

4. The p-learner uses the maximum likelihood learning strategy.

5. The performance of a distributed learning system is evaluated within the PAC (probably approximately correct) learning model.

6. There is no feedback of information from the p-learner to agents.

In contrast, our model may be characterized by the following features:

1'. The target to be learned is a probability density or a probability mass function. It is assumed that prior densities of the parameter specifying the target density exist in several levels and form a hierarchical structure.

2'. The prediction loss is measured in terms of the average logarithmic loss.

3'. Each agent uses a *probabilistic version* of the Gibbs algorithm; i.e. a parameter value of a hypothesis is chosen randomly according to the Bayes posterior distribution from the whole parameter space.

4'. The p-learner uses a simple algebraic operation or the Gibbs algorithm.

5'. The performance of a distributed learning system is evaluated in terms of the *additional loss*, defined as the difference between its average logarithmic loss and the average Bayes risk for NDB (the nondistributed Bayesian learning strategy).

6'. There is feedback of information from the p-learner to agents (in the hierarchical model).

In summary, our framework may be considered a *probabilistic version of Kearns and Seung's*, and also includes an extension of theirs to the case where there is a hierarchical parameter structure and a feedback loop between each agent and the p-learner.

This work also is technically related to *hierarchical Bayesian inference* (Berger, 1990) and the *Markov chain Monte Carlo* (MCMC) method (Hastings, 1970; Geman and Geman, 1984; Tanner and Wong, 1987; Gelfand and Smith, 1990; Rosenthal, 1993).

We apply MCMC to the iterative learning process induced by the feedback of information from the p-learner to agents in the hierarchical model. MCMC mainly has been applied to efficient approximations of analytically intractable Bayesian inference (Tanner and Wong, 1987; Gelfand and Smith, 1990; Rosenthal, 1993; Yamanishi, 1996). Our work suggests a new application of MCMC to the design of distributed learning systems.

19.2 Plain Model

19.2.1 Model

Let s be a positive integer. A *distributed learning system* $\mathcal{S}$ consists of s *agent learners* (for short, *agents*) and a single *population learner* (for short, a *p-learner*). We call the number s the *population size*.

Let $\mathcal{D}$ be a measurable space. Let $\mathcal{C} = \{p(D|\theta) : \theta \in \Theta \subset \mathbf{R}^k\}$ be a given class of probability density functions over $\mathcal{D}$ specified by a k-dimensional real-valued parameter θ, belonging to a parameter space

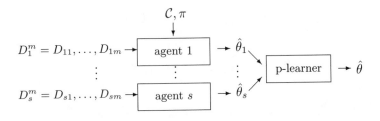

$$\mathcal{C}, \pi$$

$$D_1^m = D_{11}, \ldots, D_{1m} \rightarrow \boxed{\text{agent 1}} \rightarrow \hat{\theta}_1$$

$$\vdots$$

$$D_s^m = D_{s1}, \ldots, D_{sm} \rightarrow \boxed{\text{agent } s} \rightarrow \hat{\theta}_s$$

$$\boxed{\text{p-learner}} \rightarrow \hat{\theta}$$

FIGURE 19.1. Distributed learning system of type 1: plain model.

Θ. (*Note:* Throughout the paper we use the terminology "a probability density function" or simply "a probability density" assuming that $\mathcal{D}$ is continuous, but it should be replaced with a "probability mass function" when $\mathcal{D}$ is a discrete space.) We call $\mathcal{C}$ the *hypothesis class*. We now make the following assumption about the data generation:

Assumption 19.1.

1. *Each agent independently observes a sequence of examples, each of which is generated independently according to an identical* target *probability density function (for short, a* target density*)* $p(D|\theta)$, *belonging to* $\mathcal{C}$.

2. *The value of the parameter* θ *specifying the target density is unknown and is generated according to a known prior probability density function* $\pi(\theta)$ *(for short, a* prior density*) over* Θ.

We call the model of learning in which assumption 19.1 is satisfied the *plain model*.

Consider two types of distributed learning systems, *type 1* and *type 2*, respectively. In a *distributed learning system* $\mathcal{S}$ *of type 1*, in the plain model, agents and the p-learner perform as follows. Let a positive integer m be given. For each $i \ (= 1, \ldots, s)$, the ith agent takes as input a sequence $D_i^m = D_{i1} \cdots D_{im}$ of m examples, $\mathcal{C}$, and π, then outputs an estimate of θ. Letting $\hat{\theta}_i$ be the output of the ith agent, the p-learner takes $\hat{\theta}_1, \ldots, \hat{\theta}_s$ as input, then outputs an estimate $\hat{\theta}$ as a function of $\hat{\theta}_1, \ldots, \hat{\theta}_s$, which is itself an output of $\mathcal{S}$. Note that the p-learner does not have direct access to the random examples, $\mathcal{C}$, or π, but only to a set of outputs of the agents. (See figure 19.1.)

In a *distributed learning system* $\mathcal{S}$ *of type 2* in the plain model agents and the p-learner perform as follows. Letting ϕ be a given function $\phi : \mathcal{D}^m \rightarrow \mathbf{R}^d$ for some positive integer d, for each $i \ (= 1, \ldots, s)$, the ith agent takes a sequence $D_i^m = D_{i1} \cdots D_{im}$ as input, then outputs $\phi(D_i^m)$.

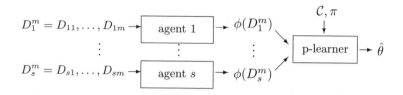

FIGURE 19.2. Distributed learning system of type 2: plain model.

The p-learner takes $\phi(D_1^m), \ldots, \phi(D_s^m), \mathcal{C}$, and π as input, then outputs an estimate $\hat{\theta}$, which is itself an output of $\mathcal{S}$. (See figure 19.2.)

The difference between the two types is that in type 1, the agents take the most intelligent action and the p-learner just combines the outputs of the agents without knowing $\mathcal{C}$ or π, whereas in type 2, the agents send statistics to the p-learner and the p-learner takes the most intelligent action, knowing $\mathcal{C}$ and π. This difference arose from the situations. Type 1 handles the situation where each agent is computationally powerful enough to learn θ from the training examples (specifically, to make a random number generation in order to run the Gibbs algorithm), while the p-learner is less powerful. The p-learner in type 1 might be thought of as a nonexpert general manager who makes decisions on the basis of his subordinates' reports only. On the other hand, type 2 handles the situation where each agent is not computationally powerful enough to learn θ from examples, while the p-learner is powerful enough.

Furthermore, type 1 allows us to design algorithms for agents and the p-learner independently, which means we can exchange their algorithms for those of other agents and p-learners independently, in order to make the distributed learning system stronger.

Type 2 sends a larger amount of information from each agent to the p-learner than does type 1 when the dimension of ϕ is larger than that of θ. Hence type 1 might be more applicable than type 2 for cases where there is insufficient bandwidth between each agent and the p-learner.

Remark. Although for the sake of analytical simplicity we assume that the sample size m is uniform over all agents, the model can be immediately extended into a general case where the sample size is not uniform.

Let $D^{sm} = D_1^m \cdots D_s^m$ be the *training sequence*. For a distributed learning system $\mathcal{S}$, let $q(\theta|D^{sm})$ be the probability density according to which the output $\hat{\theta}$ of the p-learner is generated. Then we can think of a mixture density $\int p(D|\theta)q(\theta|D^{sm})d\theta$ as an average probability density of D

induced by D^{sm} for $\mathcal{S}$. We measure the performance of $\mathcal{S}$ in terms of its *average logarithmic loss* $L(\mathcal{S})$ for predicting the probability density of an unseen example using the average probability density for $\mathcal{S}$, where $L(\mathcal{S})$ is defined by

$$L(\mathcal{S}) \stackrel{\text{def}}{=} E_\theta E_{D^{sm}|\theta} E_{D|\theta} \left[-\ln \int p(D|\theta) q(\theta|D^{sm}) d\theta \right],$$

where E_θ, $E_{D^{sm}|\theta}$, and $E_{D|\theta}$ denote the expectations taken with respect to $\pi(\theta), p(D^{sm}|\theta)$, and $p(D|\theta)$, respectively, and ln denotes the natural logarithm. Note that the range of $L(\mathcal{S})$ is $(-\infty, \infty)$.

Let $p^*(\theta|D^{sm})$ be the *Bayes posterior density* over Θ from D^{sm} defined as:

$$p^*(\theta|D^{sm}) = \frac{\pi(\theta) \prod_{i=1}^s \prod_{j=1}^m p(D_{ij}|\theta)}{\int \pi(\theta) \prod_{i=1}^s \prod_{j=1}^m p(D_{ij}|\theta) d\theta}.$$

We define the *average Bayes risk* L^* for the sample size sm by

$$L^* \stackrel{\text{def}}{=} E_\theta E_{D^{sm}|\theta} E_{D|\theta} \left[-\ln \int p(D|\theta) p^*(\theta|D^{sm}) d\theta \right],$$

which is obtained by substituting $q(\theta|D^{sm}) = p^*(\theta|D^{sm})$ in the formula of $L(\mathcal{S})$. We define the *nondistributed Bayesian learning strategy* (in the plain model), which we abbreviate NDB, as a strategy that takes as input D^{sm} at once (not in parallel), and then chooses an estimate $\hat{\theta}$ randomly according to $p^*(\theta|D^{sm})$ and outputs it. We can think of L^* as the average logarithmic loss for NDB for the sample size sm. Below we show a general relationship between $L(\mathcal{S})$ and L^*.

Lemma 19.2. *For a distributed learning system $\mathcal{S}$ (both type 1 and type 2), let $q(\theta|D^{sm})$ be the probability density according to which the output $\hat{\theta}$ of the p-learner in $\mathcal{S}$ is generated, and let*

$$m^*(D|D^{sm}) \stackrel{\text{def}}{=} \int p(D|\theta) p^*(\theta|D^{sm}) d\theta,$$

$$m_{\mathcal{S}}(D|D^{sm}) \stackrel{\text{def}}{=} \int p(D|\theta) q(\theta|D^{sm}) d\theta,$$

$$D(m^* \parallel m_{\mathcal{S}}) \stackrel{\text{def}}{=} \int m^*(D|D^{sm}) \ln \frac{m^*(D|D^{sm})}{m_{\mathcal{S}}(D|D^{sm})} dD,$$

where $m^*(D|D^{sm})$ is the average probability density function of D induced by the training sequence D^{sm} for NDB, $m_{\mathcal{S}}(D|D^{sm})$ is that induced for the distributed learning system $\mathcal{S}$, and $D(m^* \parallel m_{\mathcal{S}})$ is the Kullback-Leibler divergence between m^* and $m_{\mathcal{S}}$ for fixed D^{sm}. Then for any distributed learning system $\mathcal{S}$, the following equation holds:

(19.1) $$L(\mathcal{S}) = L^* + E_{D^{sm}} [D(m^* \parallel m_{\mathcal{S}})],$$

where $E_{D^{sm}}$ denotes the expectation taken with respect to $p(D^{sm}) = \int \pi(\theta)p(D^{sm}|\theta)d\theta$.

Proof of Lemma 19.2. Observe first that for any random variable f independent of θ,

$$E_\theta E_{D^{sm}|\theta} E_{D|\theta}[f]$$

$$= \int d\theta \pi(\theta) \int dD^{sm} p(D^{sm}|\theta) \int dD p(D|\theta) f$$

$$= \int dD^{sm} \int dD \int d\theta p(D^{sm}) p(D|\theta) \left(\frac{\pi(\theta)p(D^{sm}|\theta)}{p(D^{sm})} \right) f$$

$$= \int dD^{sm} p(D^{sm}) \int dD \int d\theta p(D|\theta) p^*(\theta|D^{sm}) f$$

$$= E_{D^{sm}} E_{D|D^{sm}}[f],$$

where $E_{D|D^{sm}}$ and $E_{D^{sm}}$ denote the expectations taken with respect to $m^*(D|D^{sm}) = \int p(D|\theta)p^*(\theta|D^{sm})d\theta$ and $p(D^{sm}) = \int \pi(\theta)p(D^{sm}|\theta)d\theta$, respectively. Since m^* and $m_\mathcal{S}$ are both independent of θ by definition, the above relation immediately yields

$$
\begin{aligned}
L(\mathcal{S}) &= E_\theta E_{D^{sm}|\theta} E_{D|\theta}[-\ln m^*(D|D^{sm})] \\
&\quad + E_\theta E_{D^{sm}|\theta} E_{D|\theta} \left[\ln \frac{m^*(D|D^{sm})}{m_\mathcal{S}(D|D^{sm})} \right] \\
&= L^* + E_\theta E_{D^{sm}|\theta} E_{D|\theta} \left[\ln \frac{m^*(D|D^{sm})}{m_\mathcal{S}(D|D^{sm})} \right] \\
&= L^* + E_{D^{sm}} E_{D|D^{sm}} \left[\ln \frac{m^*(D|D^{sm})}{m_\mathcal{S}(D|D^{sm})} \right] \\
&= L^* + E_{D^{sm}}[D(m^*\|m_\mathcal{S})].
\end{aligned}
$$

This completes the proof of lemma 19.2. $\qquad\square$

Since $D(m^* \| m_\mathcal{S}) \geq 0$ holds in general, we immediately see from (19.1) that

$$L(\mathcal{S}) \geq L^*,$$

where the equality holds if and only if

$$(19.2) \qquad q(\theta|D^{sm}) = p^*(\theta|D^{sm}),$$

for every θ and D^{sm}. A distributed learning system that realizes (19.2) is *ideal* in the sense that it can attain the same average logarithmic loss as NDB. However, (19.2) doesn't hold for most distributed learning systems with s (≥ 2) agents. Then the effectiveness of a distributed learning system is measured in terms of how much its average logarithmic loss deviates from L^*. Hence we may measure the performance of a distributed learning system $\mathcal{S}$ in terms of $L(\mathcal{S}) - L^*$, which we call the *additional average logarithmic loss* (for short, the *additional loss*) for $\mathcal{S}$. We wish to design a distributed learning system such that the additional loss is as small as possible, while attaining a significant acceleration of learning over NDB.

Remark. Let L^{**} be the average logarithmic loss associated with the target density $p(D|\theta)$, i.e. $L^{**} \overset{\text{def}}{=} E_\theta E_{D^{sm}|\theta} E_{D|\theta}[-\ln p(D|\theta)]$. Then the Bayes risk for NDB is not smaller than L^{**}, i.e. $L^* \geq L^{**}$. However, only the strategy that knows θ can attain L^{**}. Note that NDB achieves the least average logarithmic loss over all learning strategies that are *given no information in advance about the parameter θ for the target density other than the prior density π*.

19.2.2 Algorithms

The performance of a distributed learning system depends on what types of algorithms are used for the agents and the p-learner. We first introduce a specific form of distributed learning systems of type 1.

Definition 19.3. *We define the* distributed cooperative Bayesian learning strategy of type 1 *(in the plain model), which we abbreviate as* DCB1, *as the distributed learning system of type 1 satisfying the following:*

1. Each agent employs the Gibbs algorithm, *i.e. the ith agent takes as input $D_i^m = D_{i1} \cdots D_{im}, \mathcal{C}$, and π, and then outputs the parameter value $\hat{\theta}_i$ chosen randomly according to the Bayes posterior density $p(\theta|D_i^m)$, which is calculated as*

$$p(\theta|D_i^m) = \frac{\pi(\theta) \prod_{j=1}^m p(D_{ij}|\theta)}{\int \pi(\theta') \prod_{j=1}^m p(D_{ij}|\theta')d\theta'} \quad (i = 1, \ldots, s).$$

2. The p-learner receives $\hat{\theta}_1, \ldots, \hat{\theta}_s$ as input, and then outputs the parameter value of the following form:

$$(19.3) \qquad\qquad f(\hat{\theta}_1, \ldots, \hat{\theta}_s),$$

where f is a given function from Θ^s to Θ, which does not depend on any D^{sm}.

Remarks. 1. In designing DCB1, we assume that each agent is computationally powerful enough to make random samplings according to a given probability distribution. On the other hand, the p-learner is required to perform only a simple algebraic operation (19.3), which should be designed to be as simple as possible in order to make the computational complexity as small as possible for the p-learner. As will be seen in examples 19.4 and 19.5, this paper specifically considers the case where f in (19.3) is the *arithmetic mean operation*.

2. As will be seen in example 19.4 (Gaussian distributions) and example 19.5 (Poisson distributions), there exist some cases where the times required by the agent and the p-learner to run the Gibbs algorithm are linear in the sample size m and the population size s, respectively. For such cases the computation time for each agent is $O(m)$, while that for NDB is $\Omega(sm)$. Further assume that the computation time for the p-learner in DCB1 is $O(s)$ (this assumption is satisfied for the case where f in (19.3) is the arithmetic mean operation). Then the overall computational time for DCB1 is $O(s+m)$. For the total sample size $\ell = sm$, the overall computation time for DCB1 is $O(\sqrt{\ell})$ if we set $s = \Theta(\sqrt{\ell})$ and $m = \Theta(\sqrt{\ell})$ (i.e. s and m are set to be of the same order so that $(s + \ell/s)$ is smallest). Then we say that *DCB1 achieves an acceleration in computation time from* $\Omega(\ell)$ *for NDB to* $O(\sqrt{\ell})$.

Example 19.4. Let $\mathcal{D} = \mathbf{R}$ and

$$\mathcal{C} = \{N(\theta, \sigma^2 : D) : \ \theta \in (-\infty, \infty), \ \sigma \text{ is known }\}.$$

Here $N(\theta, \sigma^2 : D)$ denotes the Gaussian distribution with mean θ and variance σ^2: $(1/\sqrt{2\pi}\sigma) \exp(-(D-\theta)^2/2\sigma^2)$. (*Note:* We may write $N(\theta, \sigma^2)$ instead of $N(\theta, \sigma^2 : D)$ when D is trivial given the context.) Let the prior density of θ be $N(\theta_0, \sigma_0^2 : \theta)$ where $\theta_0 \in (-\infty, \infty)$ and $0 < \sigma_0 < \infty$ are known. Then the ith agent outputs $\hat{\theta}_i$ chosen randomly according to the following probability density:

$$
\begin{aligned}
\hat{\theta}_i \ &\sim \ p(\theta | D_i^m) \\
(19.4) \quad &= \ N\left(\frac{\sigma_0^2 \sum_{j=1}^{m} D_{ij} + \sigma^2 \theta_0}{m\sigma_0^2 + \sigma^2}, \ \frac{\sigma^2 \sigma_0^2}{m\sigma_0^2 + \sigma^2}\right) \quad (i = 1, \ldots, s).
\end{aligned}
$$

Here $p(\theta | D_i^m)$ is derived easily by noting that the joint density of θ and D_i^m is proportional to $\exp(-(\theta - \theta_0)^2 / 2\sigma_0^2) \exp(-\sum_{j=1}^{m}(D_{ij} - \theta)^2 / 2\sigma^2)$.

Let the p-learner use the arithmetic mean operation as f in (19.3), i.e. the p-learner outputs $\hat{\theta}$ calculated as

$$(19.5) \qquad\qquad \hat{\theta} = \frac{1}{s} \sum_{i=1}^{s} \hat{\theta}_i;$$

then $\hat{\theta}$ is generated according to the following probability density:

$$
\begin{aligned}
\hat{\theta} \ &\sim \ q(\theta | D^{sm}) \\
&= \ N\left(\frac{\sigma_0^2 (\sum_{i=1}^{s} \sum_{j=1}^{m} D_{ij}) + s\sigma^2 \theta_0}{s(m\sigma_0^2 + \sigma^2)}, \ \frac{\sigma^2 \sigma_0^2}{s(m\sigma_0^2 + \sigma^2)}\right),
\end{aligned}
$$

which can be verified by transforming the random variables $(\theta_1, \ldots, \theta_s)$

with joint density $\prod_{i=1}^{m} p(\theta_i | D_i^m)$ into $(\hat{\theta}, \xi_1, \ldots, \xi_{s-1})$ where

$$\hat{\theta} = (1/s) \sum_{i=1}^{s} \theta_i,$$

$$\xi_1 = (\theta_1 - \theta_2)/\sqrt{2},$$

$$\xi_2 = (\theta_1 + \theta_2 - \theta_3)/\sqrt{6},$$

$$\ldots,$$

$$\xi_{s-1} = (\theta_1 + \theta_2 + \cdots + \theta_{s-1} - (s-1)\theta_s)/\sqrt{s(s-1)}$$

and examining the joint density of $\hat{\theta}, \xi_1, \ldots, \xi_{s-1}$. (*Note:* $\hat{\theta}, \xi_1, \ldots, \xi_{s-1}$ are independent.)

On the other hand, by noting that the joint density of θ and D^{sm} is proportional to $\exp(-(\theta - \theta_0)^2/2\sigma_0^2) \exp(-\sum_{i=1}^{s} \sum_{j=1}^{m} (D_{ij} - \theta)^2/2\sigma^2)$, we can verify that the Bayes posterior density $p^*(\theta | D^{sm})$ is given by

$$p^*(\theta | D^{sm}) = N \left(\frac{\sigma_0^2 (\sum_{i=1}^{s} \sum_{j=1}^{m} D_{ij}) + \sigma^2 \theta_0}{sm\sigma_0^2 + \sigma^2}, \frac{\sigma^2 \sigma_0^2}{sm\sigma_0^2 + \sigma^2} \right).$$

(19.6)

In this case $q(\theta | D^{sm})$ and $p^*(\theta | D^{sm})$ differ from each other when $s \geq 2$ and $\sigma_0 < \infty$. We bound the additional loss induced by this difference subsequently. It is straightforward to extend the above analysis to the case where θ is multidimensional.

Notice again that the running time required by the ith agent to compute $\hat{\theta}_i$ with density (19.4) and that required by NDB to compute $\hat{\theta}$ with density (19.6) are both linear in the sample size, since the computation time required for a random sampling according to a Gaussian distribution specified by a given parameter value is $O(1)$ in s and m, supposing that a program for a random number generation according to a Gaussian distribution is given to all the agents. There is an efficient algorithm for generating random numbers according to a given Gaussian distribution (see chapter 4 in Knuth, 1981).

Example 19.5. Let $\mathcal{D} = \mathbf{Z}^+ \cup \{0\}$ and let $\mathcal{C} = \{e^{-\theta}\theta^D/D! : \theta > 0\}$ be a class of Poisson distributions. Let the prior distribution of θ be the Gamma distribution with density $G(\alpha, \beta) = \theta^{\alpha-1}e^{-\theta/\beta}/\beta^\alpha\Gamma(\alpha)$, where $\alpha > 0$ and $\beta > 0$ are given, and Γ denotes the Gamma function defined as $\Gamma(x) = \int_0^\infty e^{-t}t^{x-1}dt$ $(x > 0)$. Then each agent outputs $\hat{\theta}_i$ chosen randomly according to the following probability density:

$$\hat{\theta}_i \sim p(\theta|D_i^m)$$

$$(19.7) \qquad = G\left(\alpha + \sum_{j=1}^{m} D_{ij}, \left(m + \frac{1}{\beta}\right)^{-1}\right) \qquad (i = 1, \ldots, s).$$

Let the p-learner output $\hat{\theta}$ using the arithmetic mean operation as in (19.5). Then the probability density of $\hat{\theta}$ is given by

$$\hat{\theta} \sim q(\theta|D^{sm})$$

$$= G\left(s\alpha + \sum_{i=1}^{s}\sum_{j=1}^{m} D_{ij}, \left(sm + \frac{s}{\beta}\right)^{-1}\right),$$

which can be verified by transforming the random variables $(\theta_1, \ldots, \theta_s)$ with joint density $\prod_{i=1}^{m} p(\theta_i|D_i^m)$ into $(\hat{\theta}, \xi_1, \ldots, \xi_{s-1})$, where

$$\hat{\theta} = (1/s)\sum_{i=1}^{s} \theta_i, \xi_1 = \theta_2/\theta_1, \ldots, \xi_{s-1} = \theta_s/\theta_1$$

and examining the joint density of $\hat{\theta}, \xi_1, \ldots, \xi_{s-1}$.

On the other hand, the Bayes posterior density $p^*(\theta|D^{sm})$ is given by

$$(19.8) \qquad p^*(\theta|D^{sm}) = G\left(\alpha + \sum_{i=1}^{s}\sum_{j=1}^{m} D_{ij}, \left(sm + \frac{1}{\beta}\right)^{-1}\right).$$

Here the derivations of $p(\theta|D_i^m)$ and $p^*(\theta|D^{sm})$ are performed similarly to those for example 19.4.

In this case $q(\theta|D^{sm})$ and $p^*(\theta|D^{sm})$ differ from each other when $s \neq 1$. Notice again that the running time required by the ith agent to compute $\hat{\theta}_i$ with density (19.7) and that required by NDB to compute $\hat{\theta}$ with density (19.8) are both linear in the sample size, since the computation time required for a random sampling according to a fixed Gamma distribution is $O(1)$, supposing that a program for a random number generation according to a Gamma distribution is given to all the agents. There is also an efficient algorithm for generating random numbers according to a given Gamma distribution (again see chapter 4 in Knuth, 1981).

Next we consider the design of distributed learning systems of type 2 for the case where the p-learner is allowed to take as input $\mathcal{C}$ and π as well as $\hat{\theta}_1, \ldots, \hat{\theta}_s$, while each agent employs a simple algebraic operation.

We say that $\mathcal{C} = \{p(D|\theta) : \theta \in \Theta\}$ belongs to the *exponential family* if and only if for some positive integer d, for some scalar-valued functions

$g, h, \kappa_l,$ and ψ_l $(l = 1, \ldots, d)$, any probability density $p(D|\theta)$ in $\mathcal{C}$ is decomposed as

$$p(D|\theta) = g(\theta)h(D)\exp\left(-\sum_{l=1}^{d}\kappa_l(\theta)\psi_l(D)\right).$$

Assuming that the data generation is independent, we see that for any given $D^\ell = D_1 \cdots D_\ell$, the joint density of D^ℓ is given by

$$p(D^\ell|\theta) = (g(\theta))^\ell \left(\prod_{j=1}^{\ell} h(D_j)\right)\exp\left(-\sum_{l=1}^{d}\kappa_l(\theta)\sum_{j=1}^{\ell}\psi_l(D_j)\right),$$

where a d-dimensional statistic:

$$\phi(D^\ell) = \left(\sum_{j=1}^{\ell}\psi_1(D_j), \ldots, \sum_{j=1}^{\ell}\psi_d(D_j)\right)$$

is called a *sufficient statistic* for θ (from D^ℓ). The following definition gives a general form of the distributed cooperative Bayesian learning strategy of type 2 for classes belonging to the exponential family.

Definition 19.6. *Suppose that $\mathcal{C} = \{p(D|\theta) : \theta \in \Theta\}$ belongs to the exponential family and that for some positive integer d, for some scalar-valued functions $g, h, \kappa_l,$ and ψ_l $(l = 1, \ldots, d)$, each probability density $p(D|\theta)$ in $\mathcal{C}$ is decomposed as*

$$p(D|\theta) = g(\theta)h(D)\exp\left(-\sum_{l=1}^{d}\kappa_l(\theta)\psi_l(D)\right).$$

We define the distributed cooperative Bayesian learning strategy of type 2 *(in the plain model), which we abbreviate as DCB2, as the distributed learning system of type 2 satisfying the following:*

1. The ith agent takes as input a sequence $D_i^m = D_{i1} \cdots D_{im}$ of examples, then outputs a d-dimensional vector:

$$\phi(D_i^m) = (\phi^{(1)}(D_i^m), \ldots, \phi^{(d)}(D_i^m))$$

$$(19.9) \qquad = \left(\sum_{j=1}^{m}\psi_1(D_{ij}), \ldots, \sum_{j=1}^{m}\psi_d(D_{ij})\right).$$

2. The p-learner receives as input $\phi(D_1^m), \ldots, \phi(D_s^m), \mathcal{C},$ and π, then outputs the parameter value $\hat{\theta}$ chosen randomly according to

$p(\theta|\phi(D_1^m), \ldots, \phi(D_s^m))$ *calculated as follows:*

$$p(\theta|\phi(D_1^m), \ldots, \phi(D_s^m))$$

(19.10)
$$= \frac{\pi(\theta)(g(\theta))^{sm} \exp(-\sum_{l=1}^{d} \kappa_l(\theta)x_l)}{\int \pi(\theta)(g(\theta))^{sm} \exp(-\sum_{l=1}^{d} \kappa_l(\theta)x_l)d\theta},$$

where

$$x_l = \sum_{i=1}^{s} \phi^{(l)}(D_i^m) \quad (l = 1, \ldots, d).$$

Remark. In designing DCB2, it is assumed that the p-learner is computationally powerful enough to make random samplings according to a given probability distribution. On the other hand, each agent is required to perform only a computationally simple algebraic operation, $\phi(D_i^m)$.

Example 19.7. For $\mathcal{C}$ and π in example 19.4, we see that $\mathcal{C}$ belongs to the exponential family with $d = 1$ and $\psi_1(D) = D$. We may design DCB2 in which $\phi(D_i^m)$ as in (19.9) and $p(\theta|\phi(D_1^m), \ldots, \phi(D_s^m))$ as in (19.10) are given by

(19.11)
$$\phi(D_i^m) = \sum_{j=1}^{m} D_{ij}$$

and

$$p(\theta|\phi(D_1^m), \ldots, \phi(D_s^m))$$

(19.12)
$$= N\left(\frac{sm\sigma_0^2 x + \sigma^2\theta_0}{sm\sigma_0^2 + \sigma^2}, \frac{\sigma^2\sigma_0^2}{sm\sigma_0^2 + \sigma^2}\right),$$

where $x = \sum_{i=1}^{s} \phi(D_i^m)$. Note that $p(\theta|\phi(D_1^m), \ldots, \phi(D_s^m))$ matches $p^*(\theta|D^{sm})$ as in (19.6).

The computation time required for a random sampling according to a Gaussian distribution specified by a fixed parameter value is $O(1)$ in s and m. Thus, assuming the p-learner has a program for a random number generation according to a Gaussian distribution, the running time required for the ith agent to compute (19.11) is $O(m)$ and that required for the p-learner to compute $\hat{\theta}$ with density (19.12) is $O(s)$.

Example 19.8. Let $\mathcal{D} = \mathbf{R}$ and $\mathcal{C} = \{N(\mu, \theta^2 : D) : \theta \in (0, \infty), \mu$ is known$\}$. We see that $\mathcal{C}$ belongs to the exponential family with $d = 2$. Let the prior distribution of θ be the inverse Gamma distribution with density $IG(\alpha, \beta) = (\beta^\alpha e^{-\beta/\theta})/(\Gamma(\alpha)\theta^{\alpha+1})$ where α and β are given positive constants. We may design DCB2 in which $\phi(D_i^m)$ as in (19.9) and $p(\theta|\phi(D_1^m), \ldots, \phi(D_s^m))$ as in (19.10) are calculated as

$$\phi(D_i^m) = (\phi^{(1)}(D_i^m), \phi^{(2)}(D_i^m))$$

(19.13)
$$= \left(\sum_{j=1}^{m} D_{ij}, \sum_{j=1}^{m} D_{ij}^2 - \frac{1}{m}\left(\sum_{j=1}^{m} D_{ij}\right)^2 \right),$$

$$p(\theta|\phi(D_1^m), \ldots, \phi(D_s^m))$$

(19.14)
$$= \mathrm{IG}\left(sm + \alpha, \ \frac{1}{2}\left(sm\left(\frac{x}{sm} - \mu\right)^2 + y + 2\beta \right) \right),$$

where $x = \sum_{i=1}^{s} \phi^{(1)}(D_i^m)$ and $y = \sum_{i=1}^{s} \phi^{(2)}(D_i^m)$.

Again, the computation time required for a random sampling according to a fixed inverse Gamma distribution is $O(1)$ in s and m; thus, assuming the p-learner has a program for a random number generation according to an inverse Gamma distribution, the running time for the ith agent to compute (19.13) is $O(m)$ and that for the p-learner to compute $\hat{\theta}$ with density (19.14) is $O(s)$. There is in fact an efficient algorithm for generating random numbers according to a given inverse Gamma distribution (see chapter 4 in Knuth, 1981).

Example 19.9. For C and π in example 19.5, we see that C belongs to the exponential family with $d = 1$. We may design DCB2 in which $\phi(D_i^m)$ as in (19.9) and $p(\theta|\phi(D_1^m), \ldots, \phi(D_s^m))$ as in (19.10) are given by

(19.15)
$$\phi(D_i^m) = \sum_{j=1}^{m} D_{ij}$$

and

(19.16)
$$p(\theta|\phi(D_1^m), \ldots, \phi(D_s^m)) = G\left(\alpha + x, (sm + 1/\beta)^{-1} \right),$$

where $x = \sum_{i=1}^{s} \phi(D_i^m)$.

The computation time required for a random sampling according to a fixed Gamma distribution is $O(1)$ in s and m; thus, assuming the p-learner has a program for random number generation according to a Gamma distribution, the running time for the ith agent to compute (19.15) is $O(m)$ and that for the p-learner to compute $\hat{\theta}$ with density (19.16) is $O(s)$.

Example 19.10. Let $\mathcal{D} = \{0, 1, \ldots, k\}$ and $C = \{p(l|\theta) = \theta_l \ (l = 0, 1, \ldots, k) : \theta = (\theta_0, \theta_1, \ldots, \theta_k) \in [0, 1]^k, \sum_{l=0}^{k} \theta_l = 1\}$, which is the class of k-dimensional discrete distributions. We see that C belongs to the exponential family with $d = k$. Let the prior distribution of θ be the Dirichlet distribution with density $D(\alpha_0, \ldots, \alpha_k) = (\Gamma(\alpha_0 + \cdots + \alpha_k)/\Gamma(\alpha_0) \cdots \Gamma(\alpha_k))\theta_0^{\alpha_0-1} \cdots \theta_k^{\alpha_k-1}$ where $\alpha_0, \ldots, \alpha_k$ are given positive constants. We may design DCB2 in which $\phi(D_i^m)$ as in (19.9) and $p(\theta|\phi(D_1^m), \ldots, \phi(D_s^m))$ as in (19.10) are calculated as

$$
\begin{aligned}
\phi(D_i^m) &= (\phi^{(1)}(D_i^m), \ldots, \phi^{(k)}(D_i^m)) \\
(19.17) \qquad &= (m_i(1), \ldots, m_i(k)),
\end{aligned}
$$

$$(19.18) \qquad p(\theta|\phi(D_1^m), \ldots, \phi(D_s^m)) = D(\alpha_0 + x_0, \ldots, \alpha_k + x_k),$$

where $m_i(l)$ is the number of occurrences of $D = l$ in D_i^m, $x_l = \sum_{i=1}^s \phi^{(l)}(D_i^m)$ $(i = 1, \ldots, s, \ l = 1, \ldots, k)$, and $x_0 = sm - \sum_{l=1}^k x_l$.

The running time for the ith agent to compute (19.17) is $O(km)$ and that for the p-learner to compute $\hat{\theta}$ with density (19.18) is $O(ks)$, since the computation time required for a random sampling according to a fixed Dirichlet distribution is $O(1)$ in s and m, assuming the p-learner has a program for a random number generation according to a Dirichlet distribution. There is in fact an efficient algorithm for generating random numbers according to a given Dirichlet distribution (see chapter 4 in Knuth, 1981).

19.2.3 Analysis

This section first gives analyses of DCB1 for the particular classes introduced in the previous section. Theorem 19.11 provides an upper bound on the additional loss for DCB1 in example 19.4.

Theorem 19.11. *For the class of Gaussian distributions with a constant variance as in example 19.4, for sufficiently large $\ell = sm$, the additional loss for DCB1 is given as follows:*

$$(19.19) \qquad L(\text{DCB1}) - L^* = \frac{\sigma^2 \sigma_0^2}{2(m\sigma_0^2 + \sigma^2)^2} \left(\frac{s-1}{s}\right)^2 (1 + o(1)),$$

where $o(1)$ tends to zero as $\ell = sm$ approaches infinity.

Corollary 19.12. *For the total sample size $\ell = sm$, setting $s = \Theta(\sqrt{\ell})$, the additional loss for DCB1 in example 19.4 can be made $O(1/\ell)$ while DCB1 achieves an acceleration in computation time from $\Omega(\ell)$ for NDB to $O(\sqrt{\ell})$.*

Remarks. 1. When $\ell = sm$ is fixed, substituting $m = \ell/s$ into (19.19), we see that the main term of the additional loss for DCB1 is $\Theta(s^2)$, which is an increasing function of s. When m is fixed, we see that as s increases, the main term of the additional loss for DCB1 approaches $\sigma^2 \sigma_0^2 / 2(m\sigma_0^2 + \sigma^2)^2$, which can be thought of as an inevitable loss due to the parallelism.

2. As seen from (19.19), for any $\varepsilon > 0$, if we set $m = \Theta(1/\sqrt{\varepsilon})$ and $s = \Theta(1/\sqrt{\varepsilon})$, then the additional loss for DCB1 can be held at ε, while DCB1 achieves an acceleration in computation time from $\Omega(1/\varepsilon)$ for NDB to $O(1/\sqrt{\varepsilon})$.

3. Consider the case where π is the *uniform prior* for θ, which can be thought of as the Gaussian prior $N(\theta_0, \sigma_0^2)$ with $\sigma_0 = \infty$. This prior density makes $q(\theta|D^{sm})$ coincide completely with $p^*(\theta|D^{sm})$. Thus setting $s = \Theta(\sqrt{\ell})$, DCB1 using the uniform prior attains the same average logarithmic loss as NDB, while DCB1 achieves an acceleration in computation time from $\Omega(\ell)$ for NDB to $O(\sqrt{\ell})$.

Proof of Theorem 19.11. We start with a lemma concerning the Kullback-Leibler divergence between two Gaussian distributions.

Lemma 19.13. *For $p = N(\mu_1, \sigma_1^2)$ and $q = N(\mu_2, \sigma_2^2)$, the Kullback-Leibler divergence $D(p\|q)$ is given by*

$$D(p\|q) = \ln \frac{\sigma_2}{\sigma_1} + \frac{1}{2\sigma_2^2}\left(\sigma_1^2 + (\mu_1 - \mu_2)^2\right) - \frac{1}{2}.$$

(The proof of lemma 19.13 is omitted.)

Note that for $p(D|\theta) = N(\theta, \sigma_1^2 : D)$ and $\pi(\theta) = N(\mu, \sigma_2^2 : \theta)$ for constants μ, σ_1 and σ_2, the mixture density $m(D) = \int p(D|\theta)\pi(\theta)d\theta$ is proportional to $\int \exp(-(D-\theta)^2/2\sigma_1^2)\exp(-(\theta-\mu)^2/2\sigma_2^2)d\theta$, which is also proven to be proportional to $\exp(-(D-\mu)^2/2(\sigma_1^2 + \sigma_2^2))$. This implies that $m(D) = N(\mu, \sigma_1^2 + \sigma_2^2 : D)$. Applying this fact in the cases of $\pi(\theta) = q(\theta|D^{sm})$ and $\pi(\theta) = p^*(\theta|D^{sm})$ obtained in example 19.4, we see that $m^*(D|D^{sm})$ and $m_S(D|D^{sm})$ are calculated as follows:

$$m^*(D|D^{sm}) = N\left(\frac{\sigma_0^2 \sum_{i,j} D_{ij} + \sigma^2\theta_0}{sm\sigma_0^2 + \sigma^2}, \sigma^2 + \frac{\sigma^2\sigma_0^2}{sm\sigma_0^2 + \sigma^2}\right),$$

$$m_S(D|D^{sm}) = N\left(\frac{\sigma_0^2 \sum_{i,j} D_{ij} + s\sigma^2\theta_0}{s(m\sigma_0^2 + \sigma^2)}, \sigma^2 + \frac{\sigma^2\sigma_0^2}{s(m\sigma_0^2 + \sigma^2)}\right).$$

Using lemma 19.13 we see that $D(m^*\|m_S)$ is expanded as follows:

$$D(m^* \| m_S)$$
$$= \frac{1}{2}\ln \frac{\sigma^2 + \sigma^2\sigma_0^2/s(m\sigma_0^2 + \sigma^2)}{\sigma^2 + \sigma^2\sigma_0^2/(sm\sigma_0^2 + \sigma^2)} + \frac{\sigma^2 + \sigma^2\sigma_0^2/(sm\sigma_0^2 + \sigma^2)}{2(\sigma^2 + \sigma^2\sigma_0^2/s(m\sigma_0^2 + \sigma^2))}$$

$$\text{(19.20)} \qquad + \frac{\sigma^4\sigma_0^4\left(\sum_{i,j} D_{ij} - sm\theta_0\right)^2 \left(\frac{s-1}{s}\right)^2}{2\left(\sigma^2 + \frac{\sigma^2\sigma_0^2}{s(m\sigma_0^2+\sigma^2)}\right)(m\sigma_0^2 + \sigma^2)^2(sm\sigma_0^2 + \sigma^2)^2} - \frac{1}{2}.$$

Letting $x = 1/(sm + s(\sigma^2/\sigma_0^2)) = O(1/sm)$ and $y = 1/(sm + (\sigma^2/\sigma_0^2)) = O(1/sm)$, the sum of the first and second terms in the right-hand side of (19.20) is evaluated for sufficiently large $\ell = sm$ as follows:

$$\frac{1}{2} \ln \frac{1+x}{1+y} + \frac{1+y}{2(1+x)}$$

$$= \frac{1}{2} \left(x - \frac{x^2}{2} - y + y^2 - O(1/(sm)^3) \right)$$

$$+ \frac{1}{2}(1+y)\left(1 - x + x^2 + O(1/(sm)^3)\right)$$

$$= \frac{1}{2} + \frac{1}{4}\left(\frac{s-1}{s}\right)^2 \frac{\sigma^4 \sigma_0^4}{(sm\sigma_0^2 + \sigma^2)^2(m\sigma^2 + \sigma^2)^2} + O\left(1/(sm)^3\right).$$

The third term in the right-hand side of (19.20) is $\sigma^2/(2(m\sigma_0^2 + \sigma^2)^2)$ $((s-1)/s)^2((1/sm)\sum_{i,j} D_{ij} - \theta_0)^2(1 + o(1))$. Hence we have

$$D(m^* \parallel m_\mathcal{S})$$

$$= \frac{\sigma^2}{2(m\sigma_0^2 + \sigma^2)^2}\left(\frac{s-1}{s}\right)^2\left(\frac{1}{sm}\sum_{i,j}D_{ij} - \theta_0\right)^2(1 + o(1)),$$

(19.21)

where $o(1)$ approaches zero uniformly with respect to D^{sm} as $\ell = sm$ approaches infinity. Notice here that it can be proven immediately that

$$(19.22) \qquad E_{D^{sm}}\left[\left(\frac{1}{sm}\sum_{i,j}D_{ij} - \theta_0\right)^2\right] = \sigma_0^2 + \frac{\sigma^2}{sm}.$$

Taking an expectation of (19.21) with respect to D^{sm} and then applying (19.22) yield

$$E_{D^{sm}}\left[D(m^* \parallel m_\mathcal{S})\right] = \frac{\sigma^2\sigma_0^2}{2(m\sigma_0^2 + \sigma^2)^2}\left(\frac{s-1}{s}\right)^2(1 + o(1)).$$

Combining this fact with lemma 19.2 yields (19.19). This completes the proof of theorem 19.11. $\qquad\square$

The next theorem provides an upper bound on the additional loss for DCB1 in example 19.5.

Theorem 19.14. *For the class of Poisson distributions as in example 19.5, for sufficiently large $\ell = sm$, the additional loss for DCB1 is upper-bounded as follows:*

$$(19.23) \qquad L(\text{DCB1}) - L^* \leq \frac{2\alpha}{m}\left(\frac{s-1}{s}\right)(1 + o(1)),$$

where $o(1)$ approaches zero as $\ell = sm$ approaches infinity.

Corollary 19.15. *For the total sample size $\ell = sm$, setting $s = \Theta(\sqrt{\ell})$, the additional loss for DCB1 in example 19.5 can be made $O(1/\sqrt{\ell})$ while DCB1 achieves an acceleration in computation time from $\Omega(\ell)$ for NDB to $O(\sqrt{\ell})$.*

Remarks. 1. As seen from (19.23), the main term of the additional loss for DCB1 is $\Theta(s)$ for fixed $\ell = sm$, which is an increasing function of s. Further, we see that as s increases *for fixed m*, the main term of the right-hand side of (19.23) approaches $2\alpha/m$, which can be thought of as an inevitable loss due to the parallelism.

2. As seen from (19.23), for any $\varepsilon > 0$, if we set $m = \Theta(1/\varepsilon)$ and $s = \Theta(1/\varepsilon)$, then the additional loss for DCB1 can be held at ε, while DCB1 achieves an acceleration in computation time from $\Omega(1/\varepsilon^2)$ for NDB to $O(1/\varepsilon)$.

Proof of Theorem 19.14. Note that for $p(D|\theta) = e^{-\theta}\theta^D/D!$ and $\pi(\theta) = G(\alpha, \beta)$ for constants $\alpha, \beta > 0$, the mixture density $m(D) = \int p(D|\theta)\pi(\theta)d\theta$ is $(1 + 1/\beta)^{(\alpha+D)}\Gamma(\alpha + D)/(D!\Gamma(\alpha))$. Applying this fact to the cases of $\pi(\theta) = q(\theta|D^{sm})$ and $\pi(\theta) = p^*(\theta|D^{sm})$ obtained in example 19.5 and writing $\sum_{i,j} D_{i,j}$ as τ for the sake of notational simplicity, we calculate $m^*(D|D^{sm})$ and $m_S(D|D^{sm})$ as follows:

$$m^*(D|D^{sm}) = \frac{(sm + 1/\beta)^{\alpha+\tau}\Gamma(\alpha + D + \tau)}{(1 + sm + 1/\beta)^{D+\alpha+\tau}D!\Gamma(\alpha + \tau)},$$

$$m_S(D|D^{sm}) = \frac{(sm + s/\beta)^{s\alpha+\tau}\Gamma(s\alpha + D + \tau)}{(1 + sm + s/\beta)^{D+s\alpha+\tau}D!\Gamma(s\alpha + \tau)}.$$

Using these formulas we immediately obtain

$$\ln \frac{m^*(D|D^{sm})}{m_S(D|D^{sm})}$$

$$
\begin{aligned}
(19.24) \quad =& \ (D + s\alpha + \tau)\ln(1 + sm + s/\beta) \\
&- (D + \alpha + \tau)\ln(1 + sm + 1/\beta) \\
&+ (\alpha + \tau)\ln(sm + 1/\beta) - (s\alpha + \tau)\ln(sm + s/\beta) \\
&+ \ln \frac{\Gamma(\alpha + D + \tau)\Gamma(s\alpha + \tau)}{\Gamma(s\alpha + D + \tau)\Gamma(\alpha + \tau)}
\end{aligned}
$$

$$(19.25) \quad = \ D\ln \frac{1 + sm + s/\beta}{1 + sm + 1/\beta}$$

$$(19.26) \quad + s\alpha \ln \frac{1 + sm + s/\beta}{sm + s/\beta} + \alpha \ln \frac{sm + 1/\beta}{1 + sm + 1/\beta}$$

$$(19.27) \quad + \tau \ln \frac{(1 + sm + s/\beta)(sm + 1/\beta)}{(sm + s/\beta)(1 + sm + 1/\beta)} +$$

$$(19.28) \qquad + \ln \frac{\Gamma(\alpha + D + \tau)\Gamma(s\alpha + \tau)}{\Gamma(s\alpha + D + \tau)\Gamma(\alpha + \tau)}.$$

As for the expectation of D, we have

$$E_{D^{sm}} E_{D|D^{sm}}[D] = E_{D^{sm}} \left[\sum_D D \int p(D|\theta)p^*(\theta|D^{sm})d\theta \right]$$

$$(19.29) \qquad = E_{D^{sm}} \left[\int \theta p^*(\theta|D^{sm})d\theta \right]$$

$$(19.30) \qquad = E_{D^{sm}} \left[\left(\alpha + \sum_{i,j} D_{i,j} \right)(sm + 1/\beta)^{-1} \right]$$

$$(19.31) \qquad = \alpha(1 + \beta sm)(sm + 1/\beta)^{-1}$$

$$(19.32) \qquad = \alpha\beta(1 + o(1)),$$

where $o(1)$ approaches zero as $\ell = sm$ approaches infinity. In deriving (19.29) we used the fact that the mean of the Poisson distribution with density $e^{-\theta}\theta^D/D!$ is θ. In deriving (19.30) and (19.31) we used the fact that the mean of the Gamma distribution with density $G(\alpha, \beta)$ is $\alpha\beta$. Thus taking expectations of (19.25) with respect to D and D^{sm} and then substituting (19.32) into the expected form of (19.25) yields

$$E_{D^{sm}} E_{D|D^{sm}} \left[D \ln \frac{1 + sm + s/\beta}{1 + sm + 1/\beta} \right]$$

$$(19.33) \qquad = \frac{\alpha}{m} \left(\frac{s-1}{s} \right)(1 + o(1)),$$

where $\ln((1 + sm + s/\beta)/(1 + sm + 1/\beta)) = (s - 1)(1 + o(1))/\beta sm$.

As for (19.26), we have

$$s\alpha \ln \frac{1 + sm + s/\beta}{sm + s/\beta} + \alpha \ln \frac{sm + 1/\beta}{1 + sm + 1/\beta}$$

$$(19.34) \qquad = \frac{\alpha}{m} \left(\frac{s-1}{s} \right)(1 + o(1)).$$

Further, notice that neither (19.27) nor (19.27) is larger than zero when $s \geq 1$. Thus taking a sum of (19.33) and (19.34), we see that the expected value of $\ln(m^*(D|D^{sm})/m_S(D|D^{sm}))$ is upper-bounded by $(2\alpha(s - 1)/sm)(1 + o(1))$. Hence we obtain (19.23) using lemma 19.2. This completes the proof of theorem 19.14. □

Next we give an analysis of DCB2 for general classes belonging to the exponential family.

Theorem 19.16. *Suppose that $C = \{p(D|\theta) : \theta \in \Theta\}$ belongs to the exponential family and that for some positive integer d, for some scalar-*

valued functions g, h, κ_l, *and* ψ_l ($l = 1, \ldots, d$), *each density* $p(D|\theta)$ *in* $\mathcal{C}$ *is decomposed as* $p(D|\theta) = g(\theta)h(D)\exp\left(-\sum_{l=1}^{d}\kappa_l(\theta)\psi_l(D)\right)$. *Suppose that the computation time for a random sampling of* θ *according to (19.10) is* $O(ds)$. *Then for the total sample size* $\ell = sm$, *the additional loss for DCB2 with* $s = \Theta(\sqrt{\ell})$ *can be reduced to zero while DCB2 achieves an acceleration in computation time from* $\Omega(\ell)$ *for NDB to* $O(d\sqrt{\ell})$.

Corollary 19.17. *For each of examples 19.7, 19.8, and 19.9, for the total sample size* $\ell = sm$, *the additional loss for DCB2 with* $s = \Theta(\sqrt{\ell})$ *can be reduced to zero while DCB2 achieves an acceleration in computation time from* $\Omega(\ell)$ *for NDB to* $O(\sqrt{\ell})$. *For the class of* k-*dimensional discrete distributions as in example 19.10, the additional loss for DCB2 with* $s = \Theta(\sqrt{\ell})$ *can be reduced to zero, while DCB2 achieves an acceleration in computation time from* $\Omega(\ell)$ *for NDB to* $O(k\sqrt{\ell})$.

Proof of Theorem 19.16. For $\mathcal{C}$ satisfying the assumption as in theorem 19.16, the Bayes posterior density of θ for NDB is given by

$$
\begin{aligned}
p^*(\theta|D^{sm}) &= \frac{\pi(\theta)\prod_{i=1}^{s}\prod_{j=1}^{m}p(D_{ij}|\theta)}{\int \pi(\theta)\prod_{i=1}^{s}\prod_{j=1}^{m}p(D_{ij}|\theta)d\theta} \\
&= \frac{\pi(\theta)(g(\theta))^{sm}\exp(-\sum_{l=1}^{d}\kappa_l(\theta)\sum_{i=1}^{s}\psi_l(D_i^m)))}{\int \pi(\theta)(g(\theta))^{sm}\exp(-\sum_{l=1}^{d}\kappa_l(\theta)\sum_{i=1}^{s}\psi_l(D_i^m))d\theta},
\end{aligned}
$$

which coincides with $p(\theta|\phi(D_1^m), \ldots, \phi(D_s^m))$ as in (19.10). Hence the average logarithmic loss for DCB2 coincides with that for NDB.

Since the running time for each agent to compute (19.9) is $O(dm)$ and that for the p-learner to compute $\hat{\theta}$ chosen randomly according to (19.10) is $O(ds)$ under the assumption as in theorem 19.16, the total computation time for DCB2 is $O(d(m+s)) = O(d\sqrt{\ell})$ letting $s = \Theta(\sqrt{\ell})$, while that for NDB is $\Omega(\ell)$. This completes the proof of theorem 19.16. □

20 Learning Specialist Decision Lists[†]
Atsuyoshi Nakamura

In this paper, we propose an evaluation criterion for on-line learning algorithms with *specialists* in terms of the best *specialist decision list* and present and analyze the performance of algorithms with respect to the

[†]Copyright © 1999, ACM. Reprinted, with permission, from *Proceedings of the 12th Annual Conference on Computational Learning Theory* (pp. 215–225), 1999. This is a slightly revised version.

proposed criterion. The on-line learning model with specialists was first proposed and studied by Blum (1995). In this model, learning proceeds in a sequence of trials. At each trial, a learning algorithm receives predictions from a group of specialists, some of whom may not be *awake*, i.e. may abstain from predicting, makes a prediction based on these, and then receives an outcome. The key issue in designing an algorithm in this model is therefore how to combine the specialists' predictions in an intelligent manner.

This learning model can be thought of as a variant of the on-line learning model with *experts*, in which every expert is assumed to make some prediction at every trial. We call this model the *insomniac* model. For certain practical situations, the specialist model is more applicable than the original expert model. A case in point is the problem of "collaborative filtering" (Resnick et al., 1994), in which an algorithm predicts the preference of a user over various contents, based on other users' preferences for and evaluations of them, available via a network or otherwise. This model has been applied and proven effective in other domains as well, such as the calendar scheduling domain (Blum, 1995) and text categorization (Cohen and Singer, 1996).

On the theoretical side, Freund et al. (1997) showed how to transform on-line algorithms in the expert model with multiplicative weight updates to algorithms in the specialist model and how to derive corresponding bounds on their prediction performance. In their work, however, they evaluate the prediction performance of an algorithm by comparing it to the performance of the best *mixture* of the specialists. Here we evaluate an algorithm's performance by comparing it to the performance of the best *prioritization* over the specialists.

A prioritization of the specialists can be formalized as a predictor that always makes that prediction made with the highest priority by the awake specialist. This can be represented as a list of specialists ordered by their priorities, which we call a *specialist decision list* (SDL). Note that SDLs cannot be represented by mixtures of specialists in general.

We can now state the proposed performance criterion more precisely. We measure the performance of an on-line algorithm in this model by the cumulative loss it suffers on the worst-case sequence of trials, *expressed as a function of the cumulative loss suffered by the best SDL on that sequence*.

Using our criterion, we analyze the predictive performance of an algorithm S-Loss-Update, which is closely related to SBayes (Freund et al., 1997) and two of its modifications. S-Loss-Update is a specialist version of Loss-Update (Haussler, Kivinen, and Warmuth, 1998; Herbster and Warmuth, 1998) and can also be thought of as an unnormalized version of SBayes, generalized for general loss functions. The two modifications we propose, SWML and S-Fixed-Share-Update, are designed not to make any of the weights too small to improve the worst case performance of S-Loss-Update. More precisely, SWML, which is a specialist version of Littlestone's algorithm WML (Littlestone and Warmuth, 1994), does not update weights that are smaller than γA, where A is the average of all the weights of awake specialists and γ is a parameter $(0 < \gamma < 1/2)$. S-Fixed-Share-Update, which is a specialist version of Fixed-Share-Update (Herbster and Warmuth, 1998), lets each awake specialist share a portion of its weight with the other awake specialists.

In our theoretical worst-case analysis, both SWML and S-Fixed-Share-Update have better loss bounds than S-Loss-Update. In particular, we showed that, for any sequence of sets of awake specialists, specialist predictions, and outcomes, the losses of SWML and S-Fixed-Share-Update are upper bounded by $O(N(L_S + u \ln N))$ and $O(N(L_S + u \ln N + l))$, respectively, while S-Loss-Update suffers a loss of at least $\Omega((N - u)^u L_S)$, where S is the best SDL on that sequence, u is the *used length* of S (that is, used in that sequence), L_S is the loss suffered by S, N is the number of specialists, and l is the number of trials.

To evaluate the range of applicability of our worst-case analysis, we conducted some experiments with artificial data. The results of our experiments indicate that the two modifications, SWML and S-Fixed-Share-Update, outperform S-Loss-Update not only when outcomes are generated by an SDL but also when good performing specialists sometimes suffer big losses.

20.1 Preliminaries

We consider the on-line learning model with specialists as defined in (Freund et al., 1997), which we will review briefly below. We assume that there are N specialists, indexed by $1, \ldots, N$. In this model, learning proceeds in a sequence of trials $t = 1, \ldots, l$. In each trial t, each specialist i makes a prediction $x_{t,i} \in [0, 1]$ or abstains from predicting. We say that a specialist is *awake* when it makes a prediction and that it is *asleep* otherwise. Let $E_t \subseteq \{1, \ldots, N\}$ denote the set of awake specialists in trial t. We assume that $E_t \neq \emptyset$ for all t. Based on predictions $x_{t,i}$ made by specialist i in E_t, a learning algorithm A produces a prediction $\hat{y}_t \in [0, 1]$ and then receives the outcome $y_t \in [0, 1]$. We consider a *loss* function $L : [0, 1] \times [0, 1] \to [0, \infty)$ that measures how far a prediction is from an outcome. In trial t, algorithm A suffers loss $L(y_t, \hat{y}_t)$ and each awake specialist i suffers loss $L(y_t, x_{t,i})$. The goal of an on-line algorithm is to suffer the least loss as possible accumulatively in the worst case. Here, the worst case is when an adversary selects the set of awake specialists

E_t, the prediction value $x_{t,i}$ of each awake specialist i, and outcome y_t for each trial t.

A *specialist decision list* (SDL) is a list of specialists ordered by priority. Let $S = (s_1, \ldots, s_N)$ be an SDL. Then S represents the following predictor: at each trial t, S predicts with prediction x_{t,s_i} of the first specialist s_i in S that are awake ($i \in E_t$). We let $T(S, i)$ denote the set of trials t at which S predicts with x_{t,s_i}, that is, $T(S, i) = \{t : s_1, \ldots, s_{i-1} \notin E_t, s_i \in E_t\}$. For a sequence of sets of awake specialists $E_1, \ldots, E_l$, we define the *used length* of S as the largest index i such that $T(S, i) \neq \emptyset$. By $L_{S,i}$, we denote the loss that S suffers at trials in $T(S, i)$. The cumulative loss L_S of S can then be defined as $\sum_{i=1}^{u} L_{S,i}$, where u is the used length of S for sequence $E_1, \ldots, E_l$.

In our model, the performance of an on-line algorithm is evaluated in terms of the loss it suffers on the worst-case sequence of trials as compared to the loss suffered by the *best* SDL on that sequence. We make this precise in the following definition.

Definition 20.1. *An on-line learning algorithm A has a loss bound $F(L_S, u)$ if for every sequence of sets of awake specialists, specialist predictions, and outcomes, and for every SDL S, the total loss suffered by A on that sequence does not exceed $F(L_S, u)$, where u is the used length of S for that sequence.*

In this paper, we restrict our attention to prediction functions that make their predictions at any trial t based solely on weights $w_{t,i} \geq 0$ and on predictions $x_{t,i} \in [0, 1]$ of the specialists that are awake ($i \in E_t$). Let $\mathbf{v}_{t,E_t}$ denote the normalized weight vector at trial t, which is composed of $w_{t,i}/\sum_{j \in E_t} w_{t,j}$ for all $i \in E_t$. Let $\mathbf{x}_{t,E_t}$ denote a vector composed of awake specialist predictions $x_{t,i}$ at trial t. A prediction function is thus a function from $(\mathbf{v}_{t,E_t}, \mathbf{x}_{t,E_t})$ to predictions, and we generally use 'pred' to denote such a function.

We deal uniformly with both the binary and continuous cases. In the binary case, we assume that all the predictions made by specialists and prediction algorithms as well as the actual outcomes are either 0 or 1. In this case, we use the binary loss function L_{bin} as defined below:

$$L_{\mathrm{bin}}(y, \hat{y}) = \begin{cases} 0 & \text{if } \hat{y} = y \\ 1 & \text{otherwise.} \end{cases}$$

We also make use of the weighted majority prediction function $\mathrm{pred}_{\mathrm{wmaj}}$ as defined below:

$$\mathrm{pred}_{\mathrm{wmaj}}(\mathbf{v}, \mathbf{x}) = \arg \max_{a \in \{0,1\}} \sum_{x_i = a} v_i.$$

When an algorithm predicts with $\hat{y}$, the real outcome is y, and $L_{\text{bin}}(y, \hat{y})$ $= 1$, then we say that the algorithm *made a mistake*. Thus, in this case, the cumulative loss suffered by an algorithm coincides with the number of mistakes it makes.

In the continuous case, we assume that all predictions made by specialists and learning algorithms and all outcomes are values in $[0, 1]$. We consider four loss functions: the square, the relative entropy, the hellinger, and the absolute loss:

$$L_{\text{sq}}(y, \hat{y}) = (y - \hat{y})^2,$$

$$L_{\text{ent}}(y, \hat{y}) = y \ln \frac{y}{\hat{y}} + (1 - y) \ln \frac{1 - y}{1 - \hat{y}},$$

$$L_{\text{hel}}(y, \hat{y}) = \frac{1}{2} \left(\left(\sqrt{1 - y} - \sqrt{1 - \hat{y}} \right)^2 + \left(\sqrt{y} - \sqrt{\hat{y}} \right)^2 \right),$$

$$L_{\text{abs}}(y, \hat{y}) = |y - \hat{y}|.$$

We consider the following two prediction functions: for $\mathbf{v}, \mathbf{x} \in [0, 1]^n$,

$$\text{pred}_{\text{wmean}}(\mathbf{v}, \mathbf{x}) = \sum_{i=1}^{n} v_i x_i \quad \text{and}$$

$$\text{pred}_{\text{Vovk}}(\mathbf{v}, \mathbf{x}) = \frac{L_0^{-1}(\Delta(0)) + L_1^{-1}(\Delta(1))}{2},$$

where $\Delta(y) = -\frac{1}{\eta} \ln \sum_{i=1}^{n} v_i e^{-\eta L(y, x_i)}$, and $L_0^{-1}(z)$ and $L_1^{-1}(z)$ are the inverses of $L_0(x) \triangleq L(0, x)$ and $L_1(x) \triangleq L(1, x)$, respectively.

The on-line algorithms considered in this paper make use of a prediction function and a loss function, and thus are in effect "parameterized" by the choice of the exact prediction and loss function employed.

Note that Z^+ denotes the set of natural numbers throughout this paper.

20.2 Algorithm S-Loss-Update

In this section, we prove a lower bound on the worst-case cumulative loss suffered by algorithm S-Loss-Update. Algorithm Loss-Update (Haussler, Kivinen, and Warmuth, 1998; Herbster and Warmuth, 1998), which is an insomniac version of S-Loss-Update, is a popular algorithm that has one weight for each expert and multiplies the weight by $e^{-\eta L}$ when the expert suffers a loss L, where η is a learning rate parameter. Algorithm S-Loss-Update (figure 20.1) is derived from Loss-Update, modified to predict only from awake specialists' predictions and update only their weights. Note that S-Loss-Update with normalization coincides with SBayes (Freund et al., 1997) when the relative entropy loss is used.

With respect to our proposed criterion, S-Loss-Update does not per-

Algorithm S-Loss-Update

Parameter: $0 < \eta$
Initialize: $w_{1,i} = 1$ for all $i = 1, \ldots, N$.

At each trial t, execute following three steps:

1. Let $v_{t,i} = w_{t,i}/W_{t,E_t}$ for all $i \in E_t$, where $W_{t,E_t} = \sum_{i \in E_t} w_{t,i}$.
   Predict with $\hat{y}_t = \mathrm{pred}(\mathbf{v}_{t,E_t}, \mathbf{x}_{t,E_t})$.
2. Observe outcome y_t.
3. Update the weights as follows:
   If $i \in E_t$, then $w_{t+1,i} = w_{t,i} e^{-\eta L(y_t, x_{t,i})}$.
   Otherwise, $w_{t+1,i} = w_{t,i}$.

Algorithm SWML

Parameter: $0 \leq \gamma < 1/2$
Initialize: $w_{1,i} = 1$ for all $i = 1, \ldots, N$.

At each trial t, execute following three steps:

1. Let $F_t = \{i \in E_t : w_{t,i} > \left(\gamma \sum_{i \in E_t} w_{t,i}\right)/|E_t|\}$. Let $v_{t,i} = w_{t,i}/W_{t,F_t}$
   for all $i \in F_t$, where $W_{t,F_t} = \sum_{i \in F_t} w_{t,i}$. Predict with
   $\hat{y}_t = \mathrm{pred}(\mathbf{v}_{t,F_t}, \mathbf{x}_{t,F_t})$.
2. Observe outcome y_t.
3. Update the weights as follows:
   If $i \in F_t$, then $w_{t+1,i} = w_{t,i} e^{-\eta L(y_t, x_{t,i})}$.
   Otherwise, $w_{t+1,i} = w_{t,i}$.

FIGURE 20.1. Description of algorithms S-Loss-Update and SWML.

form well because it can suffer a loss[1] of $\Omega((N - u)^u L_S)$, where N is the number of specialists, S is any SDL, L_S is the loss of S, and u is the used length of S.

The following definition is useful to prove a lower bound on an algorithm's loss. Note that in the definition, only those losses suffered in the special case where $\mathbf{x} \in \{0,1\}^n$ are considered, but we use this definition even in the continuous case.

Definition 20.2. *For any pair of a loss function L and a prediction function* pred, (L, pred), R *is a lower bound on the loss when majority*

---

[1]The proof of this lower bound only applies to the "unnormalized" version of S-Loss-Update. A lower bound for the normalized case is left as an open problem.

errs *(or the* ME-loss *for short) if they satisfy the following condition:*

For all $n \in Z^+$, *all* $\mathbf{x} \in \{0,1\}^n$, *and all weight vectors* $\mathbf{v} \in [0,1]^n$ *of total weight* 1,

$$\sum_{x_i=1} v_i > \sum_{x_i=0} v_i \Rightarrow L(0, \mathrm{pred}(\mathbf{v},\mathbf{x})) \geq R.$$

Proposition 20.3. *For any loss function* L, *if a function* $L_0(x) \stackrel{\triangle}{=} L(0,x)$ *is monotone increasing,* $L(0,1/2)$ *is a lower bound on the ME-loss for the pair* $(L, \mathrm{pred}_{\mathrm{wmean}})$.

Proof. This proposition follows trivially from the definition since, when $\sum_{x_i=1} v_i > \sum_{x_i=0} v_i$, $\mathrm{pred}_{\mathrm{wmean}}(\mathbf{v},\mathbf{x}) = \sum_{x_i=1} v_i > 1/2$ and function L_0 is monotone increasing. □

Proposition 20.4. *Let* $L_a(x) \stackrel{\triangle}{=} L(a,x)$ *for* $a = 0,1$. *If* L_0 *is a monotone increasing function and* $L_0(x) = L_1(1-x)$ *for all* $x \in [0,1]$, $L(0,1/2)$ *is a lower bound on the ME-loss for the pair* $(L, \mathrm{pred}_{\mathrm{Vovk}})$.

Proof. Let $z_0 = L_0^{-1}(\Delta(0))$ and $z_1 = L_1^{-1}(\Delta(1))$. When $\sum_{x_i=1} v_i > \sum_{x_i=0} v_i$,

$$\begin{aligned}
\Delta(1) &= -\frac{1}{\eta} \ln\left(\sum_{x_i=0} v_i e^{-\eta L(1,0)} + \sum_{x_i=1} v_i e^{-\eta L(1,1)} \right) \\
&\leq -\frac{1}{\eta} \ln\left(\sum_{x_i=0} v_i e^{-\eta L(0,0)} + \sum_{x_i=1} v_i e^{-\eta L(0,1)} \right) \\
&= \Delta(0)
\end{aligned}$$

because $L(1,1) = L(0,0) \leq L(0,1) = L(1,0)$ by the assumption that $L_0(x) = L_1(1-x)$. Thus

$$L(0, 1-z_1) = L(1, z_1) = \Delta(1) \leq \Delta(0) = L(0, z_0).$$

Since L_0 is monotone increasing, $1-z_1 \leq z_0$. Therefore, $\mathrm{pred}_{\mathrm{Vovk}}(\mathbf{v},\mathbf{x}) = (z_0 + z_1)/2 \geq 1/2$. Then $L(0, \mathrm{pred}_{\mathrm{Vovk}}(\mathbf{v},\mathbf{x}))$ is greater than $L(0,1/2)$, because L_0 is monotone increasing. □

Example 20.5. For the pair $(L_{\mathrm{bin}}, \mathrm{pred}_{\mathrm{wmaj}})$, it follows from their definition that 1 is a lower bound on the ME-loss.

Since L_0 is monotone increasing for all four loss functions L_{sq}, L_{ent}, L_{hel}, and L_{abs}, $L(0,1/2)$ is a lower bound on the ME-loss for a pair consisting of any one of these loss functions and $\mathrm{pred}_{\mathrm{wmean}}$ by proposition 20.3.

Since L_0 is monotone increasing and $L_0(x) = L_1(1-x)$ for all four loss functions L_{sq}, L_{ent}, L_{hel}, and L_{abs}, $L(0,1/2)$ is a lower bound on the ME-loss for a pair of any one of these loss functions and $\mathrm{pred}_{\mathrm{Vovk}}$ by proposition 20.4.

Note that $L_{sq}(0, 1/2) = 1/4$, $L_{ent}(0, 1/2) = \ln 2$, $L_{hel}(0, 1/2) = 1 - 1/\sqrt{2}$, $L_{abs}(0, 1/2) = 1/2$.

Theorem 20.6. *For any loss function L and any prediction function pred, let R be a lower bound on the ME-loss. Assume that $L(0, 1) < \infty$. For any SDL $S = (s_1, \ldots, s_N)$, any integer u and any nonnegative reals $I_1, \ldots, I_u$, there exists a sequence of sets of awake specialists, specialist predictions, and outcomes such that the used length of S is u, $L_{S,i} \geq I_i$ for $i = 1, \ldots, u$ and algorithm S-Loss-Update suffers a loss of at least $(R/L(0, 1)) \sum_{i=1}^{u} (N - u)^{u-i+1} L_{S,i}$.*

Proof. We exhibit an adversary strategy that forces algorithm S-Loss-Update to suffer a loss of at least $(R/L(0, 1)) \sum_{i=1}^{u} (N - u)^{u-i+1} L_{S,i}$.

The strategy consists of u stages. In the nth stage, the adversary takes the following strategy. Assume that the weight of s_n is $e^{-\eta p_n}$ and all the weights of specialists in $\{1, \ldots, N\} - \{s_1, \ldots, s_n\}$ are $e^{-\eta q_n}$, and that $p_n \geq q_n$ holds for each n. In the first $d_{n,0}$ trials, the adversary sets only s_n to be awake and forces the algorithm to suffer a loss of at least I_n. Let

$$(20.1) \qquad b_n = p_n - q_n + I_n.$$

In the next $d_{n,1} \overset{\triangle}{=} \lceil b_n/L(0, 1) \rceil$ trials, the adversary makes s_n and s_{n+1} predict with 0 and 1, respectively, and the other specialists abstain from predicting. In all of these trials, the adversary rules that the prediction of s_n is correct. After these trials, for $i = 1, \ldots, N - (n + 1)$ and $j = 1, \ldots, d_{n,1}$, in the $(d_{n,0} + d_{n,1}i + j)$th trial of the nth stage, the adversary makes s_n predict with 0 and makes s_{n+1} and s_{n+i+1} predict with 1, and all the other specialists abstain from predicting. In all of these trials again, the adversary rules that the prediction of s_n is correct. Notice that the nth stage consists of $d_{n,0} + (N-n)d_{n,1}$ trials, and the cumulative loss of algorithm S-Loss-Update is at least $I_n + (R/L(0, 1))(N-n)b_n$ because the algorithm suffer a loss of at least R in each of the last $(N - n)d_{n,1}$ trials of the nth stage. We denote this lower bound of the loss in the nth stage by m_n, that is,

$$(20.2) \qquad m_n = I_n + (R/L(0, 1))(N - n)b_n.$$

After the nth stage, the weight of s_{n+1} is $e^{-\eta(q_n + (N-n)d_{n,1}L(0,1))}$ and the weights of the specialists in $\{1, \ldots, N\} - \{s_1, \ldots, s_{n+1}\}$ are $e^{-\eta(q_n + d_{n,1}L(0,1))}$. Therefore,

$$(20.3) \qquad \begin{aligned} p_{n+1} &= q_n + (N - n)d_{n,1}L(0, 1) \quad \text{and} \\ q_{n+1} &= q_n + d_{n,1}L(0, 1). \end{aligned}$$

By (20.1) and (20.3), we obtain that

$$b_n = (N - n)d_{n-1,1}L(0,1) + I_n \geq (N - n)b_{n-1} + I_n.$$

Thus it follows that

$$b_n \geq b_1 \prod_{j=2}^{n}(N - j) + \sum_{i=2}^{n} I_i \prod_{j=i+1}^{n}(N - j).$$

Since $p_1 = q_1 = 0$, b_1 is equal to I_1. Therefore,

$$(20.4) \qquad\qquad b_n \geq \sum_{i=1}^{n} I_i \prod_{j=i+1}^{n}(N - j).$$

By (20.2) and (20.4),

$$\sum_{n=1}^{u} m_n \;\geq\; m_u$$

$$\geq\; (R/L(0,1))(N - u)\sum_{i=1}^{u} I_i \prod_{j=i+1}^{u}(N - j)$$

$$\geq\; (R/L(0,1))\sum_{i=1}^{u}(N - u)^{u-i+1}I_i.$$

Thus, by using this strategy, the adversary forces algorithm S-Loss-Update to suffer a loss of at least $(R/L(0,1))\sum_{i=1}^{u}(N - u)^{u-i+1}I_i$ and $L_S^i \geq I_i$ for $i = 1, \ldots, u$. $\qquad\square$

Remark 20.7 Since $L_{\mathrm{ent}}(0,1) = \infty$, we cannot apply theorem 20.6 on L_{ent}. It is possible, however, to generalize the theorem so that it becomes applicable.

Consider the following generalization of the definition of "lower bound on the ME-loss" by introducing a parameter $0 \leq a < 1/2$: For all $n \in Z^+$, all $\mathbf{x} \in \{a, 1 - a\}^n$, and all weight vectors $\mathbf{v} \in [0,1]^n$ of total weight 1,

$$\sum_{x_i=1-a} v_i > \sum_{x_i=a} v_i \Rightarrow L(a, \mathrm{pred}(\mathbf{v}, \mathbf{x})) \geq R_a.$$

Then, for any $0 \leq a < 1/2$, $L(a, 1/2)$ is a lower bound on the ME-loss for a pair consisting of any one of the four loss functions L_{sq}, L_{ent}, L_{hel}, and L_{abs} and any one of the two prediction functions $\mathrm{pred}_{\mathrm{wmean}}$ and $\mathrm{pred}_{\mathrm{Vovk}}$. The lower bound of theorem 20.6 can be generalized to be $(R_a/L(a, 1-a))\sum_{i=1}^{u}(N - u)^{u-i+1}L_{S,i}$, which is meaningful even for L_{ent}. $\qquad\square$

By the adversary strategy in the proof of theorem 20.6, the adversary can select a sequence of sets of awake specialists, specialist predictions, and outcomes such that $L_{S,i} = 0$ for all $i = 2, \ldots, u$ when $I_2 = \cdots = I_u = 0$. Thus the following corollary holds.

Corollary 20.8. *For any loss function L and any prediction function pred, let R be a lower bound on the ME-loss. Assume that $L(0,1) < \infty$. For any SDL S of used length u, there exists a sequence of sets of awake specialists, specialist predictions, and outcomes such that algorithm S-Loss-Update suffers a loss of at least $(R/L(0,1))(N - u)^u L_S$, where N is the number of specialists.*

20.3 Algorithm SWML

20.3.1 Analysis

In this section, we prove an upper bound on the worst-case cumulative loss of algorithm SWML. Algorithm SWML (figure 20.1) is derived from S-Loss-Update, modified to not make any weights too small. More precisely, SWML does not update weights that are smaller than γA, where A is the average of all the weights of awake specialists and γ is a parameter $(0 < \gamma < 1/2)$. The insomniac version of SWML was proposed by Littlestone and Warmuth (1994) to make their weighted majority algorithm WM robust against temporal changes of the best expert.

Our result shows that the modification (not to update small weights) helps to improve the worst-case loss bound significantly.

In the binary case, we can consider a simpler version SCML that uses counters instead of weights. By applying SCML to on-line learning of decision lists, we can obtain a noise tolerant algorithm. (See subsection 4.2 in Nakamura, 1999.)

Definition 20.9. *A pair of a loss function L and a prediction function pred, (L, pred), has the* better-than-worst *property if*

$$L(y, \text{pred}(\mathbf{v}, \mathbf{x})) \leq \max_{i \in \{1, \ldots, n\}} L(y, x_i),$$

for all $n \in Z^+$, all $(\mathbf{x}, y) \in [0,1]^n \times [0,1]$, and all weight vectors $\mathbf{v} \in [0,1]^n$ of total weight 1.

Proposition 20.10. *If a loss function L has the property that for any fixed $y \in [0,1]$ the function L_y defined as $L_y(x) \overset{\triangle}{=} L(y,x)$ is convex, then the pair $(L, \text{pred}_{\text{wmean}})$ has the better-than-worst property.*

Proof. By Jensen's inequality,

$$L\left(y, \sum_{i=1}^{n} v_i x_i\right) \leq \sum_{i=1}^{n} v_i L(y, x_i) \leq \max_{i \in \{1, \ldots, n\}} L(y, x_i).$$

$\square$

Proposition 20.11. *If a loss function L has the property that for any fixed $y \in [0,1]$ the function L_y defined as $L_y(x) \stackrel{\triangle}{=} L(y,x)$ is monotone decreasing for $x \in [0,y]$ and monotone increasing for $x \in [y,1]$, then the pair $(L, \mathrm{pred}_{\mathrm{Vovk}})$ has the better-than-worst property.*

Proof. Assume that L_y for any fixed $y \in [0,1]$ is monotone decreasing for $x \in [0,y]$ and monotone increasing for $x \in [y,1]$. Then L_0 is an increasing function and L_1 is a decreasing function. Let $z_0 = L_0^{-1}(\Delta(0))$ and $z_1 = L_1^{-1}(\Delta(1))$. By definition,

$$e^{-\eta L(0,z_0)} = \sum_{i=1}^{n} v_i e^{-\eta L(0,x_i)} \quad \text{and}$$

$$e^{-\eta L(1,z_1)} = \sum_{i=1}^{n} v_i e^{-\eta L(1,x_i)}.$$

Since

$$e^{-\eta L(0,\max_{i \in \{1,\ldots,n\}} x_i)} \leq \sum_{i=1}^{n} v_i e^{-\eta L(0,x_i)}$$

$$\leq e^{-\eta L(0,\min_{i \in \{1,\ldots,n\}} x_i)} \quad \text{and}$$

$$e^{-\eta L(1,\min_{i \in \{1,\ldots,n\}} x_i)} \leq \sum_{i=1}^{n} v_i e^{-\eta L(1,x_i)}$$

$$\leq e^{-\eta L(1,\max_{i \in \{1,\ldots,n\}} x_i)},$$

both z_0 and z_1 are between $\min_{i \in \{1,\ldots,n\}} x_i$ and $\max_{i \in \{1,\ldots,n\}} x_i$. Thus

$$\min_{i \in \{1,\ldots,n\}} x_i \leq \mathrm{pred}_{\mathrm{Vovk}}(\mathbf{v},\mathbf{x}) = \frac{z_0 + z_1}{2} \leq \max_{i \in \{1,\ldots,n\}} x_i.$$

Therefore, by the assumption on L_y, and when $\mathrm{pred}_{\mathrm{Vovk}}(\mathbf{v},\mathbf{x}) \in [\min_{i \in \{1,\ldots,n\}} x_i, y]$, we have

$$L(y, \mathrm{pred}_{\mathrm{Vovk}}(\mathbf{v},\mathbf{x})) \leq L(y, \min_{i \in \{1,\ldots,n\}} x_i),$$

and when $\mathrm{pred}_{\mathrm{Vovk}}(\mathbf{v},\mathbf{x}) \in [y, \max_{i \in \{1,\ldots,n\}} x_i]$, we have

$$L\big(y, \mathrm{pred}_{\mathrm{Vovk}}(\mathbf{v},\mathbf{x})\big) \leq L\big(y, \max_{i \in \{1,\ldots,n\}} x_i\big).$$

$\square$

Example 20.12. The pair $(L_{\mathrm{bin}}, \mathrm{pred}_{\mathrm{wmaj}})$ has the better-than-worst property, because whenever the majority vote prediction is wrong there exists a wrong specialist prediction.

Four loss functions, $L_{\mathrm{sq}}(y,x)$, $L_{\mathrm{ent}}(y,x)$, $L_{\mathrm{hel}}(y,x)$, $L_{\mathrm{abs}}(y,x)$, are convex functions of x for any fixed y, so a pair consisting of any one of these loss functions and $\text{pred}_{\text{wmean}}$ has the better-than-worst property by proposition 20.10.

For any fixed y, four loss functions, $L_{\text{sq}}(y,x)$, $L_{\text{ent}}(y,x)$, $L_{\text{hel}}(y,x)$, $L_{\text{abs}}(y,x)$, are functions of x that are monotone decreasing for $x \in [0,y]$ and monotone increasing for $x \in [y,1]$, so any one of these functions paired with $\text{pred}_{\text{Vovk}}$ has the better-than-worst property by proposition 20.11.

Lemma 20.13. *Assume that $L(y,x) \leq L(0,1)$ for all (x,y). For any sequence of sets of awake specialists, their predictions, and outcomes, for every SDL $S = (s_1, \ldots, s_N)$ of used length u on that sequence and for each specialist s of SWML, its weight $w_{l+1,s}$ satisfies*

$$(20.5) \qquad w_{l+1,s} \geq e^{-\eta(L_S + u(-\frac{1}{\eta}\ln\frac{\gamma}{N} + L(0,1)))}$$

where N is the number of specialists and l is the length of the sequence. In particular, for the weight w_{l+1,s_i} of specialist s_i for $i = 1, \ldots, u$, we have

$$(20.6) \qquad w_{l+1,s_i} \geq e^{-\eta(\sum_{j=1}^{i} L_{S,j} + (i-1)(-\frac{1}{\eta}\ln\frac{\gamma}{N} + L(0,1)))}.$$

Proof. First, we prove inequality (20.6). We proceed by induction on i. When $i = 1$, inequality (20.6) holds trivially because w_{t,s_1} is changed only when $t \in T(S,1)$ and s_1 suffers a total loss of at most $L_{S,1}$ at trials in $T(S,1)$. Assume that inequality (20.6) holds when $i \leq k$. We prove that

$$w_{l+1,s_{k+1}} \geq e^{-\eta(\sum_{j=1}^{k+1} L_{S,j} + k(-\frac{1}{\eta}\ln\frac{\gamma}{N} + L(0,1)))}.$$

Note that this inequality implies that the total loss suffered by s_{k+1}, when its weight is changed, i.e. for $t \in T_{s_{k+1}} = \{t : s_{k+1} \in F_t\}$, is at most $\sum_{j=1}^{k+1} L_{S,j} + k(-\frac{1}{\eta}\ln\frac{\gamma}{N} + L(0,1))$, where F_t is as defined in the description of SWML (figure 20.1). When $t \in T_{s_{k+1}} - T(S,k+1)$, there is a specialist s_i in $E_t \cap \{s_1, \ldots, s_k\}$, so by the inductive assumption,

$$w_{t,s_{k+1}} > \frac{\gamma}{N} e^{-\eta(\sum_{j=1}^{k} L_{S,j} + (k-1)(-\frac{1}{\eta}\ln\frac{\gamma}{N} + L(0,1)))}$$

$$= e^{-\eta(\sum_{j=1}^{k} L_{S,j} - \frac{k}{\eta}\ln\frac{\gamma}{N} + (k-1)L(0,1))}$$

Let $t_0 = \max(T_{s_{k+1}} - T(S,k+1))$. The above inequality implies that the total loss suffered by s_{k+1} when $t \in T_{s_{k+1}} - T(S,k+1) - \{t_0\}$ is at most $\sum_{j=1}^{k} L_{S,j} - \frac{k}{\eta}\ln\frac{\gamma}{N} + (k-1)L(0,1)$. Since specialist s_{k+1} suffers a loss of at most $L(0,1)$ in trial t_0, the total loss suffered by s_{k+1} when $t \in T_{s_{k+1}} - T(S,k+1)$ is at most $\sum_{j=1}^{k} L_{S,j} + k(-\frac{1}{\eta}\ln\frac{\gamma}{N} + L(0,1))$. Since the total loss suffered by s_{k+1} at trials $t \in T(S,k+1)$ is $L_{S,k+1}$, the total loss suffered by s_{k+1} is at most $\sum_{j=1}^{k+1} L_{S,j} + k(-\frac{1}{\eta}\ln\frac{\gamma}{N} + L(0,1))$.

Next we prove inequality (20.5). If $s \in \{s_1, \ldots, s_u\}$, inequality (20.6) implies inequality (20.5), so we assume that $s \notin \{s_1, \ldots, s_u\}$. When $t \in T_s = \{t : s \in F_t\}$, there is a specialist s_i in $E_t \cap \{s_1, \ldots, s_u\}$, so by inequality (20.6):

$$
\begin{aligned}
w_{t,s} &> \frac{\gamma}{N} e^{-\eta(L_s + (u-1)(-\frac{1}{\eta}\ln\frac{\gamma}{N} + L(0,1)))} \\
&= e^{-\eta(L_s - \frac{u}{\eta}\ln\frac{\gamma}{N} + (u-1)L(0,1))}
\end{aligned}
$$

Given that the loss suffered by s in trial $\max T_s$ is at most $L(0,1)$, the total loss suffered by s is at most $L_s + u(-\frac{1}{\eta}\ln\frac{\gamma}{N} + L(0,1))$. $\quad\square$

Theorem 20.14. *Assume that a pair consisting of a loss function L and a prediction function* pred *has the better-than-worst property and $L(y,x) \leq L(0,1)$ for all (x,y). Then for any sequence of sets of awake specialists, their predictions, and outcomes, and for every SDL S of used length u on that sequence, the total loss suffered by SWML is at most $\sum_{i=1}^{u}(N-i+1)L_{S,i} + \frac{1}{2}u(2N-u-1)(-\frac{1}{\eta}\ln\frac{\gamma}{N} + L(0,1)) \leq N(L_S + u(-\frac{1}{\eta}\ln\frac{\gamma}{N} + L(0,1)))$, where N is the number of specialists.*

Proof. First, by the better-than-worst property, for all $t = 1, \ldots, l$,

$$
L(y_t, \text{pred}(\mathbf{v}_{t,F_t}, \mathbf{x}_{t,F_t})) \leq \sum_{i \in F_t} L(y_t, x_{t,i}).
$$

Thus

$$
\sum_{t=1}^{l} L(y_t, \text{pred}(\mathbf{v}_{t,F_t}, \mathbf{x}_{t,F_t})) \leq \sum_{i \in \{1, \ldots, N\}} \sum_{t \in T_i} L(y_t, x_{t,i}),
$$

where $T_i = \{t : i \in F_t\}$. Since $w_{l+1,i} = e^{-\eta \sum_{t \in T_i} L(y_t, x_{t,i})}$,

$$
\sum_{t=1}^{l} L(y_t, \text{pred}(\mathbf{v}_{t,F_t}, \mathbf{x}_{t,F_t})) \leq \sum_{i \in \{1, \ldots, N\}} -\frac{1}{\eta} \ln w_{l+1,i}
$$

By lemma 20.13,

$$
\begin{aligned}
\sum_{t=1}^{l} &L(y_t, \text{pred}(\mathbf{v}_{t,F_t}, \mathbf{x}_{t,F_t})) \\
&\leq \sum_{i=1}^{u} \left(\sum_{j=1}^{i} L_{S,j} + (i-1)(-\frac{1}{\eta}\ln\frac{\gamma}{N} + L(0,1)) \right) \\
&\quad + (N-u)\left(L_S + u(-\frac{1}{\eta}\ln\frac{\gamma}{N} + L(0,1)) \right) =
\end{aligned}
$$

Algorithm S-Fixed-Share-Update

Initialize: $w_{1,i} = z_{1,i} = 1$ for all $i = 1, \ldots, N$.

Do the following four steps in trial t:

1. Let $v_{t,i} = w_{t,i}/W_{t,E_t}$ for all $i \in E_t$, where $W_{t,E_t} = \sum_{i \in E_t} w_{t,i}$. Predict with $\hat{y}_t = \text{pred}(\mathbf{v}_{t,E_t}, \mathbf{x}_{t,E_t})$.
2. Observe outcome y_t.
3. Update the intermediate weights as follows:
   If $i \in E_t$, then $z_{t+1,i} = w_{t,i}e^{-\eta L(y_t, x_{t,i})}$.
   Otherwise, $z_{t+1,i} = w_{t,i}$.
4. Update the weights as follows:
   If $i \in E_t$, then
   $$w_{t+1,i} = (1 - \alpha)z_{t+1,i} + \sum_{j \in E_t} \frac{\alpha}{|E_t|} z_{t+1,j}.$$
   Otherwise, $w_{t+1,i} = z_{t+1,i}$.

FIGURE 20.2. Description of algorithm S-Fixed-Share-Update.

$$= \sum_{i=1}^{u}(N - i + 1)L_{S,i}$$

$$+ \frac{1}{2}u(2N - u - 1)\left(-\frac{1}{\eta}\ln\frac{\gamma}{N} + L(0,1)\right)$$

$$\leq N\left(L_S + u\left(-\frac{1}{\eta}\ln\frac{\gamma}{N} + L(0,1)\right)\right).$$

$\square$

20.4 Algorithm S-Fixed-Share-Update

In this section, we consider another modification of S-Loss-Update and prove an upper bound on its loss. In order not to make any weights too small, algorithm S-Fixed-Share-Update (figure 20.2) makes each awake specialist share a portion α of its weight with the other specialists. The insomniac version of this algorithm is proposed by Herbster and Warmth (1998) to make Loss-Update robust against temporal changes of the best expert.

We obtain an upper bound similar to the bound obtained for SWML in the previous section.

Definition 20.15. (Herbster and Warmuth, 1998; Haussler et al., 1998) *A loss function L and prediction function 'pred' are (c, η)-realizable for*

TABLE 20.1

η Values for Known $(1/\eta, \eta)$-realizable Pairs

	pred$_{\text{wmean}}$	pred$_{\text{Vovk}}$
L_{sq}	$1/2$	2
L_{ent}	1	1
L_{hel}	1	$\sqrt{2}$

the constants c and η if

$$L(y, \text{pred}(\mathbf{v}, \mathbf{x})) \leq -c \ln \sum_{i=1}^{n} v_i e^{-\eta L(y, x_i)},$$

for all $n \in Z^+$, all $(\mathbf{x}, y) \in [0,1]^n \times [0,1]$, and all weight vectors $\mathbf{v} \in [0,1]^n$ of total weight 1.

The η values for known $(1/\eta, \eta)$-realizable pairs of loss and prediction function (Herbster and Warmuth, 1998) are shown in table 20.1.

Lemma 20.16. *Let L and* pred *be $(1/\eta, \eta)$-realizable. Then for any trial t, algorithm S-Fixed-Share-Update has at least one specialist $i \in E_t$ such that*

$$w_{t+1,i} \leq w_{t,i} e^{-\eta L(y_t, \text{pred}(\mathbf{v}_{t,E_t}, \mathbf{x}_{t,E_t}))}.$$

Proof. By definition of $(1/\eta, \eta)$-realizable and the fact that $\sum_{i \in E_t} z_{t,i} = \sum_{i \in E_t} w_{t+1,i}$, we have

$$L(y_t, \text{pred}(\mathbf{v}_{t,E_t}, \mathbf{x}_{t,E_t})) \leq -\frac{1}{\eta} \ln \frac{\sum_{i \in E_t} w_{t+1,i}}{\sum_{i \in E_t} w_{t,i}}.$$

Thus

$$(20.7) \qquad e^{-\eta L(y_t, \text{pred}(\mathbf{v}_{t,E_t}, \mathbf{x}_{t,E_t}))} \geq \frac{\sum_{i \in E_t} w_{t+1,i}}{\sum_{i \in E_t} w_{t,i}}.$$

By assuming that no specialist $i \in E_t$ satisfies

$$w_{t+1,i} \leq w_{t,i} e^{-\eta L(y_t, \text{pred}(\mathbf{v}_{t,E_t}, \mathbf{x}_{t,E_t}))},$$

we know that

$$e^{-\eta L(y_t, \text{pred}(\mathbf{v}_{t,E_t}, \mathbf{x}_{t,E_t}))} < \frac{\sum_{i \in E_t} w_{t+1,i}}{\sum_{i \in E_t} w_{t,i}},$$

which contradicts inequality (20.7). $\qquad \square$

Lemma 20.17. *For any sequence of sets of awake specialists, specialist predictions, and outcomes, for every SDL $S = (s_1, \ldots, s_N)$ of used length u on that sequence, and for each specialist s of S-Fixed-Share-Update,* *its weight $w_{l+1,s}$ satisfies*

(20.8) $$w_{l+1,s} \geq \left(\frac{\alpha}{N}\right)^u (1-\alpha)^l e^{-\eta L_S},$$

where N is the number of specialists and l is the length of the sequence. In particular, for $i = 1, \ldots, u$, the weight w_{l+1,s_i} of specialist s_i satisfies

(20.9) $$w_{l+1,s_i} \geq \left(\frac{\alpha}{N}\right)^{i-1} (1-\alpha)^{\sum_{j=1}^{i} |T(S,j)|} e^{-\eta \sum_{j=1}^{i} L_{S,j}}.$$

Proof. Inequality (20.8) and inequality (20.9) hold trivially for the initial weights, so we assume $l \geq 1$. First, we prove inequality (20.9). Here, we prove the following inequality:

$$\min\{w_{t+1,s_i}, z_{t,s_i}\}$$
$$\geq \left(\frac{\alpha}{N}\right)^{i-1} (1-\alpha)^{\sum_{j=1}^{i} |T(S,j)|} e^{-\eta \sum_{j=1}^{i} L_{S,j}}$$

(20.10) for all $i = 1, \ldots, u$ and all $t = 1, \ldots, l$.

To prove inequality (20.10) we make use of the fact that

$$\min\{w_{t+1,s_i}, z_{t,s_1}\} \geq w_{t,s_i}(1-\alpha)e^{-\eta L(y_t, x_{t,s_i})}$$

(20.11) for all $i = 1, \ldots, u$ and all $t = 1, \ldots, l$.

Inequality (20.11) is trivial given the update in step 3 and step 4 of S-Fixed-Share-Update.

We use induction on i. Consider the case where $i = 1$. Since weights w_{t+1,s_1} and z_{t+1,s_1} are changed only at trial t for $t \in T(S, 1)$, the following inequality holds for all $t = 1, \ldots, l$ by inequality (20.11).

$$\min\{w_{t+1,s_1}, z_{t+1,s_1}\}$$
$$\geq w_{1,s_1}(1-\alpha)^{|T(S,1)|} \prod_{t \in T(S,1)} e^{-\eta L(y_t, x_{t,s_1})}$$
$$= (1-\alpha)^{|T(S,1)|} e^{-\eta \sum_{t \in T(S,1)} L(y_t, x_{t,s_1})}$$
$$= (1-\alpha)^{|T(S,1)|} e^{-\eta L_{S,1}}.$$

Thus inequality (20.10) holds when $i = 1$.

Assume that inequality (20.10) holds for $i \leq k$. We prove that inequality (20.10) also holds for $i = k + 1$. Let $T_{s_{k+1}} = \{t : s_{k+1} \in E_t\}$. Trivially, $T(S, k+1) \subseteq T_{s_{k+1}}$. Since weights $w_{t+1,s_{k+1}}$ and $z_{t+1,s_{k+1}}$ are changed only at trial t for $t \in T_{s_{k+1}}$, we consider only when $t \in T_{s_{k+1}}$. Let $T(t) = \{t' \leq t : t' \in T_{s_{k+1}} - T(S, k+1)\}$. If $T(t) = \emptyset$,

$$\min\{w_{t+1,s_{k+1}}, z_{t+1,s_{k+1}}\}$$
$$\geq w_{1,s_{k+1}}(1-\alpha)^{|T(S,k+1)|} \prod_{t \in T(S,k+1)} e^{-\eta L(y_t, x_{t,s_{k+1}})}$$
$$= (1-\alpha)^{|T(S,k+1)|} e^{-\eta L_{S,k+1}}$$

holds by inequality (20.11). Thus inequality (20.10) holds for $i = k + 1$ in this case. If $T(t) \neq \emptyset$, let $t_0 = \max T(t)$. Let i_0 be an index of a specialist such that $i_0 \leq k$ and $t_0 \in T(S, i_0)$. By the update in step 4 of S-Fixed-Share-Update, $w_{t_0+1, s_{k+1}} \geq \frac{\alpha}{N} z_{t_0+1, s_{i_0}}$. By inequality (20.11), for all $t \in \{1, \ldots, l\}$, the following inequality holds:

$$\min\{w_{t+1, s_{k+1}}, z_{t+1, s_{k+1}}\}$$

$$\geq \quad w_{t_0+1, s_{k+1}} (1 - \alpha)^{|T(S, k+1)|} \prod_{t \in T(S, k+1)} e^{-\eta L(y_t, x_{t, s_{k+1}})}$$

$$(20.12) \quad \geq \quad \frac{\alpha}{N} z_{t_0+1, s_{i_0}} (1 - \alpha)^{|T(S, k+1)|} e^{-\eta L_{S, k+1}}.$$

By the assumption that inequality (20.10) holds for $i \leq k$,

$$z_{t_0+1, s_{i_0}} \quad \geq \quad \left(\frac{\alpha}{N}\right)^{i_0 - 1} (1 - \alpha)^{\sum_{j=1}^{i_0} |T(S, j)|} e^{-\eta \sum_{j=1}^{i_0} L_{S, j}}$$

$$(20.13) \quad \geq \quad \left(\frac{\alpha}{N}\right)^{k-1} (1 - \alpha)^{\sum_{j=1}^{k} |T(S, j)|} e^{-\eta \sum_{j=1}^{k} L_{S, j}}.$$

Inequality (20.12) and inequality (20.13) imply:

$$\min\{w_{t+1, s_{k+1}}, z_{t+1, s_{k+1}}\}$$

$$\geq \quad \left(\frac{\alpha}{N}\right)^{(k+1)-1} (1 - \alpha)^{\sum_{j=1}^{k+1} |T(S, j)|} e^{-\eta \sum_{j=1}^{k+1} L_{S, j}}$$

$$\text{for all } t = 1, \ldots, l.$$

Thus inequality (20.10) holds for $i = k + 1$.

Next we prove inequality (20.8). When $s = s_i$ for $i \leq u$, inequality (20.9) implies inequality (20.8). Thus we consider only the case when $s = s_i$ for $i > u$. Let $t_0 = \max T_s$ and let i_0 be an index of a specialist such that $i_0 \leq u$ and $t_0 \in T(S, i_0)$. Then $w_{l+1, s} = w_{t_0+1, s} \geq \frac{\alpha}{N} z_{t_0+1, s_{i_0}}$. Thus, by inequality (20.10),

$$w_{l+1, s} \quad \geq \quad \frac{\alpha}{N} \cdot \left(\frac{\alpha}{N}\right)^{i_0 - 1} (1 - \alpha)^{\sum_{j=1}^{i_0} |T(S, j)|} e^{-\eta \sum_{j=1}^{i_0} L_{S, j}}$$

$$(20.14) \quad \geq \quad \left(\frac{\alpha}{N}\right)^{u} (1 - \alpha)^{l} e^{-\eta L_S}.$$

$$\square$$

Theorem 20.18. *Let (L, pred) be (c, η)-realizable. For any sequence of sets of awake specialists, their predictions, and outcomes, and for every SDL S of used length u on that sequence, the cumulative loss suffered by S-Fixed-Share-Update is at most $\sum_{i=1}^{u} (N - i + 1) L_{S, i} - \frac{1}{2\eta}(2N - u - 1) u \ln \frac{\alpha}{N} - \frac{1}{\eta} \sum_{i=1}^{u} (N - i + 1)|T(S, i)| \ln(1 - \alpha) \leq \frac{N}{\eta}(\eta L_S - u \ln \frac{\alpha}{N} - l \ln(1 - \alpha))$, where N is the number of specialists and l is the length of the sequence.*

Proof. By lemma 20.16,

$$\prod_{t=1}^{l} e^{-\eta L(y_t, \text{pred}(\mathbf{v}_{t,E_t}, \mathbf{x}_{t,E_t}))} \geq \prod_{i \in \{1,\ldots,N\}} w_{l+1,i}.$$

Thus

$$(20.15) \qquad \sum_{t=1}^{l} L(y_t, \text{pred}(\mathbf{v}_{t,E_t}, \mathbf{x}_{t,E_t})) \leq -\frac{1}{\eta} \ln \prod_{i \in \{1,\ldots,N\}} w_{l+1,i}.$$

By lemma 20.17,

$$\prod_{i \in \{1,\ldots,N\}} w_{l+1,i}$$

$$\geq e^{-\eta \sum_{i=1}^{u}(N-i+1)L_{S,i}} \cdot \left(\frac{\alpha}{N}\right)^{\frac{1}{2}(2N-u-1)u}$$

$$(20.16) \qquad \cdot (1-\alpha)^{\sum_{i=1}^{u}(N-i+1)|T(S,i)|}.$$

By inequality (20.15) and inequality (20.16), we have

$$\sum_{t=1}^{l} L(y_t, \text{pred}(\mathbf{v}_{t,E_t}, \mathbf{x}_{t,E_t}))$$

$$\leq \sum_{i=1}^{u}(N-i+1)L_{S,i} - \frac{1}{2\eta}(2N-u-1)u \ln \frac{\alpha}{N}$$

$$- \frac{1}{\eta}\sum_{i=1}^{u}(N-i+1)|T(S,i)| \ln(1-\alpha)$$

$$\leq \frac{N}{\eta}\left(\eta L_S - u \ln \frac{\alpha}{N} - l \ln(1-\alpha)\right).$$

$$\square$$

21 The Lob-Pass Problem[†]

JUN'ICHI TAKEUCHI, NAOKI ABE, AND SHUN'ICHI AMARI

We consider an on-line, one-sided model of tennis play, in which the only actions that a player can take are a "pass" (passing shot) and a "lob," and the goal of the player is to win as many points as possible. For simplicity, we assume that with each shot the player either wins or loses a point. We model the opponent by two probabilistic functions, $f_L(r)$ and $f_P(r)$, which determine the probability that a lob (and a pass, respectively) played by the player will win, as a function of the proportion of lobs in the past trials. We call these probabilistic functions *rate probabilistic functions*. In particular, we assume that these are linear (probabilistic) functions $f_L(r) = a_1 r + b_1$ and $f_P(r) = a_2 r + b_2$, satisfying $a_1 < 0$, $a_2 > 0$, $0 \le f_L(r), f_P(r) \le 1$, and for some $r_m \in [0, 1]$, $f_L(r_m) = f_P(r_m)$, where r denotes the proportion of lobs in the past trials. (Figure 21.1 exhibits an example lob-pass game.) We assume that the form of these functions is known to the player, but *not* the specific coefficients. We also assume that the player is not told in advance how many trials there will be in total. Within this model, we ask how many trials out of t trials in total the best player can expect to win. Specifically, we quantify the performance of a playing strategy by measuring the expected *regret*[2] of the player where the regret is defined to be how many fewer trials it expects to win as compared to the *ideal* player. Here the ideal player is one that knows the rate probabilistic functions exactly and uses an optimal playing strategy for those specific functions.

This model can be thought of as an instance of a more general on-line learning model in which the goal of an agent is to choose its actions so as to maximize the number of successes, while learning about its reacting environment through those very actions. This particular way of modeling the environment (and modeling tennis play in particular) in terms of two linear probabilistic functions was considered by Herrnstein (1990) in the context of behavioral psychology. Simple though it may seem, the model is applicable in a wide range of natural phenomena, such as animals' choices in feeding and consumers' choices in economic consumptions. He observed that if we assume that the player employs a *random* strategy, namely one that plays a lob with probability (bias) r and a pass with probability $1 - r$ at each trial, then the asymptotically optimal strategy is easily characterized. First the instantaneous success rate of a random strategy with bias r, written $w(r)$, is given as follows.

$$(21.1) \qquad w(r) = r f_L(\hat{r}) + (1 - r) f_P(\hat{r}),$$

where $\hat{r}$ denotes the proportion of lobs in the past trials. In the asymptotics when the rate $\hat{r}$ of lobs in the past trials approaches r, $w(r)$ becomes a quadratic function in r (see figure 21.1) and hence the optimal bias r^* is obtained by maximizing that quadratic function. We call such a quadratic function the *stationary* winning rate, since it is obtained whenever $r = \hat{r}$ holds. We refer to the strategy that always plays lobs

---

[2]The notion of *regret* has been used to evaluate the performance of an on-line learning algorithm, for example, in Helmbold, Littlestone, and Long, 1992.

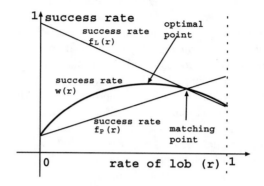

FIGURE 21.1. A lob-pass problem.

with probaiblity r^* as *the optimal stationary random strategy*, since it asymptotically attains the maximum winning rate among all stationary random strategies.

Our model is related to several existing on-line learning models (e.g., Littlestone, 1988), especially the "apple tasting model" (Helmbold, Littlestone, and Long, 1992), but it can be most naturally viewed as an extension of the classic "bandit problem" (Berry and Fristedt, 1985), modified to handle Herrnstein's formulation of success probabilities in terms of linear rate probabilistic functions. The bandit problem is the problem of choosing one of two "arms" (of the bandit) at each trial, each of which has a constant but unknown probability of success, and the goal of the agent is to choose its actions so as to maximize the number of successes in a given number of trials. The bandit problem would in fact be a special case of our model if we allowed the slopes a_1 and a_2 to be zero, but this is explicitly prohibited in our model. It is a singular point of our model that the problem of parameter optimization (of the lob rate) reduces to that of model selection (between lob and pass). The conditions stated earlier, i.e. $a_1 < 0$, $a_2 > 0$ and $f_L(r_m) = f_P(r_m)$ for some r_m, ensure that the stationary winning rate $w(r)$ is a quadratic function that attains its maximum at some point in $[0, 1]$. The learning algorithms and their analysis in our model make use of this fact and hence differ significantly from those for the bandit problem.

Within this model, we obtain a variety of results. As it appears to be difficult to obtain good upper bounds for the general case, we give several upper bounds for restrictions and assumptions of varying degrees. The most important restriction is that the rate probabilistic functions have "matching shoulders," i.e. $f_L(0) = f_P(1)$ or equivalently $b_1 = a_2 + b_2$

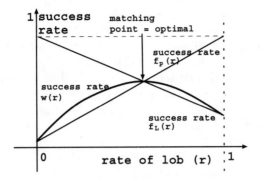

FIGURE 21.2. A lob-pass problem with matching shoulders.

TABLE 21.1

Upper Bounds on Expected Regret

Additional condition	Expected cumulative regret	Expected regret per trial
(iii)	$O(\log t)$	$O(t^{-1})$
(i), (ii)	$O(\sqrt{t})$	$O(t^{-1/2})$
(i)	$O(t^{3/5})$	$O(t^{-2/5})$
(ii)	$O(t^{2/3})$	$O(t^{-1/3})$
none	$O(t^{5/7})$	$O(t^{-2/7})$

holds (see figure 21.2). We assume this condition for *all* cases considered in this paper;[3] other additional restrictions we consider are optional. These are: (i) the sum of (the absolute values of) the slopes is bounded below by some positive constant $(a_2 - a_1 \geq a > 0)$; (ii) the optimal rate r^*, at which $w(r)$ is maximized, is bounded away from 0 and 1 $(0 < r_1 \leq r^* \leq r_2 < 1)$; and (iii) the sum of (the absolute values of) the slopes is bounded below by $1/4\delta^2 + \xi$ and r^* satisfies $\delta \leq r^* \leq 1 - \delta$, where δ is a constant not less than $1/2\sqrt{2}$ and ξ is any positive constant. Depending on which of these additional restrictions are assumed, we obtain different upper bounds on the expected regret, as shown in table 21.1.

The algorithm (named "Arthur") we use to prove the last four of these bounds is an incremental, hill-climbing type algorithm that optimizes the lob rate and is designed to overcome the trade-off between winning and

---

[3]We can prove that without the matching shoulders condition, obtaining a non-trivial regret bound for the general case would require doing better than the best stationary (random) strategy (cf. lemma 5 in Takeuchi, Abe, and Amari, 2000).

learning of the rate probabilistic functions. At any point in its execution, we can imagine that Arthur is *at* its current rate (of lobs to the total number of trials), and it *travels* to different rates by playing lobs or passes appropriately. At each iteration it tries to estimate the optimal lob rate by moving within an interval from its current rate, which is large enough to get information but small enough that traveling there does not cause too many losses. We can show in each case that the expected position, i.e. the current lob rate, approaches the optimal rate at an appropriate rate and the expected regret incurred in the process is also appropriately bounded.

The algorithm (named "Chris") we use to prove the first bound (i.e. under condition (iii)) is a randomized algorithm based on the technique of *stochastic approximation* (Wasan, 1969) and works roughly as follows. At each iteration, it plays a lob with probability $p + \delta$ (or a pass with probability $1 - p - \delta$) and plays a lob with probability $p - \delta$ (or a pass with probability $1 - p + \delta$). If it wins with the former play and loses with the latter, then it increases p by a small amount, and if it loses with the former play and wins with the latter, then it decreases p by a small amount. Otherwise it leaves p unchanged. It then plays lobs and passes accordingly to adjust its current lob rate so that it (approximately) equals p. Iterating this process forces p to converge to the optimal lob rate.

Part of the difficulty in obtaining good upper bounds on the expected regret in the general case is the fact that the total number of trials t is not given to the player in advance.[4] When the total number of trials t is given to the player in advance, we can obtain better upper bounds with fewer restrictions, also assuming the matching shoulders condition. The algorithm (named "Bjorn") used to show these bounds works in two phases (the learning phase and the winning phase), and it decides when to go into the winning phase as a function of t given as input. First, given that the sum of the slopes $a_2 - a_1$ is bounded from below by some positive constant, we can obtain an upper bound of order $O(\sqrt{t})$. In the general case with no restriction on the sum of the slopes, we can obtain an upper bound of order $O(t^{1/2+\epsilon})$ for any $\epsilon > 0$. Note that the $O(\log t)$ bound proven for the unknown-t case with condition (iii) clearly holds in the known-t case.

---

[4]In usual on-line models of learning functions, "a doubling technique" can be employed essentially to reduce the model with an unknown t to the model with a known t. Here this is not the case because the *rate* is dependent on all of the past trials, and thus the problem does not easily divide up into subsequences.

21.1 Preliminaries

21.1.1 Notation and Definitions

In this subsection, we give notation and definitions necessary for subsequent discussions. The lob-pass playing machine is a (possibly randomized) Turing machine equipped with a probabilistic oracle. The playing machine can "query" the oracle with an "action," which is either "L" or "P," and the oracle responds to it probabilistically with either 0 or 1, according to two regression functions, f_L and f_P. Here f_L and f_P each define the probability of 1 as a function of the proportion of L's in the past trials. (We call such functions *rate probabilistic functions*.) We call a pair of a query and the reinforcement for it "a trial." Let F be any class of pairs of rate probabilistic functions. The lob-pass game for F proceeds as follows. First the oracle picks an arbitrary pair of rate probabilistic functions (f_L, f_P) (or (f_1, f_0)) belonging to F. At any (ith) trial, the playing machine, say A, queries the oracle with an action of its choice $\lambda_i \in \{0, 1\}$ ($\lambda_i = 1, 0$ stand respectively for L and P) and the oracle responds to λ_i with $\rho_i \in \{0, 1\}$ according to (f_L, f_P). That is, $\rho_i = 1$ with probability $f_{\lambda_i}(r_i)$ and $\rho_i = 0$ with probability $1 - f_{\lambda_i}(r_i)$, where r_i is the proportion of Ls in the past queries made by A.

Within this context, we define the *expected number of successes* of a playing machine A for (f_L, f_P) in t trials, written $E(A(f_L, f_P), t)$, to be $E(\sum_{i=1}^{t} \rho_i)$, where the expectation is taken over any coin-flips that A may use during the protocol up to the tth trial, and the randomization used by the oracle to determine the reinforcement from f_L and f_P. We say that the *expected regret* of a player A for (f_L, f_P), written $R(A(f_L, f_P), t)$, has an upper bound $G(t)$, if for an arbitrary playing machine B that may "know" f_L and f_P, $E(B(f_L, f_P), t) - E(A(f_L, f_P), t) \leq G(t)$. We then say that the *expected regret* of a player A on the lob-pass problem for F has an upper bound $G(t)$, if for an arbitrary member (f_L, f_P) of F, $G(t)$ is an upper bound on the expected regret of A for (f_L, f_P). When this holds for some playing machine A, we say that the expected regret for F is upper bounded by $G(t)$ and write $R(F) \leq G(t)$. We also say that $R(F)$ has an upper bound *of order* $G(t)$ and write $R(F) = O(G(t))$, if for some constant c, $c \cdot G(t)$ is an upper bound for $R(F)$. We say that the *expected regret* of a player A for (f_L, f_P) has a *lower bound* of order $G(t)$, if for some playing machine B that may "know" f_L and f_P, $E(B(f_L, f_P), t) - E(A(f_L, f_P), t) = \Omega(G(t))$. Finally, we say that the *expected regret* of a player A on the lob-pass problem for F has a lower bound of order $G(t)$, if there is some member (f_L, f_P) of F such that the expected regret of A for (f_L, f_P) has a lower bound of order $G(t)$. When this holds for an arbitrary player A, we say that the expected regret for F has a lower bound of order $G(t)$ and write $R(F) = \Omega(G(t))$.

We also consider the performance of an arbitrary *lob-pass sequence*. We let λ^t denote the sequence $\lambda_1 \lambda_2 \cdots \lambda_t$ and $E(\lambda^t(f_L, f_P))$ the expected number of successes in λ^t, when the outcomes are dictated by (f_L, f_P). We also use $E_{t_0}^{t_1}(\lambda^t(f_L, f_P))$ to denote the expected number of successes in λ^t between the t_0th and t_1st trials.

As mentioned in the introduction, we also consider an alternative model in which the total number of trials t is given to the player prior to the start of each protocol. We call this alternative model the *known-t model* and the original model the *unknown-t model*. Although we have just defined the lob-pass problem in general for any class of rate probabilistic functions, in this paper we consider only rate probabilistic functions of the form $ar + b$. We let LINEAR denote the class of pairs of all well-defined rate probabilistic functions of this form, such that one is decreasing and the other increasing, and they cross each other. Formally, LINEAR $= \{(f_L(r) = a_1 r + b_1, f_P(r) = a_2 r + b_2) : 0 \le f_L(r) \le 1, 0 \le f_P(r) \le 1, a_1 < 0, a_2 > 0,$ and for some $r_m \in [0, 1], f_L(r_m) = f_P(r_m)\}$. As noted in introduction, when the rate probabilistic functions are linear, the *stationary winning rate* $w(r)$ or the asymptotic success probability of a random strategy that always plays a lob with probability r is given by $w(r) = r f_L(r) + (1-r) f_P(r) = r(a_1 r + b_1) + (1-r)(a_2 r + b_2)$. We let r^* denote the point at which $w(r)$ is maximized and is given explicitly by $r^* = -(b_1 - b_2 + a_2)/2(a_1 - a_2)$. For the linear rate probabilistic functions, the matching shoulders (MS) condition mentioned earlier is stated explicitly as $b_1 = b_2 + a_2$. Note that, for the linear case, the MS condition holds if and only if $f_L(r^*) = f_P(r^*)$. To specify subclasses of LINEAR meeting a set of restrictions, we explicitly write out those restrictions in parentheses. For example, LINEAR$(a_2 - a_1 \ge 1, b_1 = b_2 + a_2)$ denotes the subclass of LINEAR in which both $a_2 - a_1 \ge 1$ and $b_1 = b_2 + a_2$, the MS condition hold. As shorthand, we also let LINEAR$(a_2 - a_1 \ge 1,$ MS$)$ denote the same class. Finally, we write "log" for the natural logarithm and will in general use angular brackets $\langle x \rangle$ to denote the expectation of a random variable x, omitting what the expectation is with respect to whenever it is clear from the context.

21.1.2 Basic Lemmas

In this subsection, we establish some lemmas that serve as the common basis for the subsequent analyses. First, we prove lemma 21.1 under the MS condition. The reason we assume the MS condition throughout this paper is that this condition allows us to prove this key lemma providing an upper bound on the performance (expected number of successes) of an ideal player. This lemma is apparently crucial for showing another lemma (lemma 21.4), which relates the cumulative regret of a player to the sequence of its lob-rates; it appears difficult to do so without it (see lemma 5 in Takeuchi, Abe, and Amari, 2000).

Lemma 21.1. *For an arbitrary playing machine A and for any (f_L, f_P) $\in$ LINEAR(MS), if we let a denote the sum of the absolute values of the slopes, $a = a_2 - a_1$, r_i the rate of lobs used by A up to the ith trial, and r^* the rate at which $w(r)$ attains maximum, then A's expected number of successes up to the tth trial, $E(A(f_L, f_P), t)$, is bounded as follows.*

$$E(A(f_L, f_P), t) \leq w(r^*)t + a(1 + (\log t)/2).$$

This lemma is proved using two sublemmas, stated as lemmas below, as they will be used again in a later section. We first introduce some notation that will be used throughout the proof. First note that $r_i = \sum_{j=1}^{i} \lambda_j / i$. Now define $y_i = \lambda_i - r^*$ and $\sigma_i = r_i - r^* = \sum_{j=1}^{i} y_j / i$. We assume for simplicity that $r_0 = r^*$, which is equivalent to assuming $w_1 = w(r^*)$, where we let in general w_i denote the (instantaneous) winning rate at the ith trial.

Lemma 21.2. *For an arbitrary lob-pass game, which does not necessarily satisfy the MS condition, the following equality holds for all $i \geq 1$.*

$$
\begin{aligned}
w_i \quad = \quad & w(r^*) - a(r_{i-1} - r^*)(\lambda_i - r^*) \\
(21.2) \quad & + (f_L(r^*) - f_P(r^*))(\lambda_i - r_{i-1}).
\end{aligned}
$$

When the MS condition is satisfied,

$$(21.3) \qquad w_i = w(r^*) - a(r_{i-1} - r^*)(\lambda_i - r^*)$$

holds.

Proof. We can write w_i as follows.

$$
\begin{aligned}
w_i \quad = \quad & f_L(r_{i-1})\lambda_i + f_P(r_{i-1})(1 - \lambda_i) \\
= \quad & (a_1\sigma_{i-1} + f_L(r^*))(r^* + y_i) + (a_2\sigma_{i-1} + f_P(r^*))(1 - r^* - y_i) \\
= \quad & w(r^*) + (a_1 r^* + a_2(1 - r^*))\sigma_{i-1} + (f_L(r^*) - f_P(r^*))y_i \\
& - (a_2 - a_1)\sigma_{i-1} y_i.
\end{aligned}
$$

Noting that $(a_1 - a_2)r^* = -(b_1 - b_2 + a_2)/2$ holds by definition of r^*, we have

$$
\begin{aligned}
a_1 r^* + a_2(1 - r^*) \quad = \quad & a_2 - (b_1 - b_2 + a_2)/2 \\
= \quad & -(b_1 - b_2 - a_2)/2 \\
= \quad & (b_1 - b_2 + a_2)/2 - (b_1 - b_2) \\
= \quad & -(a_1 - a_2)r^* - (b_1 - b_2) \\
= \quad & -(f_L(r^*) - f_P(r^*)).
\end{aligned}
$$

The above two equalities yield (21.2). Notice that the second term of (21.2) equals zero when the MS condition holds. Hence we have (21.3). □

Lemma 21.3. *For an arbitrary lob-pass sequence* λ^i *and for any* $(f_L, f_P) \in \text{LINEAR(MS)}$, *if we define* a, r_i, *and* r^* *as in lemma 21.1, then the expected number of successes in* λ^t *from the* t_0th *to* tth *trials* $(t_0 \geq 2)$, *written* $E_{t_0}^t(\lambda^t(f_L, f_P))$, *can be written as follows.*

$$E_{t_0}^t(\lambda^t(f_L, f_P))$$

$$= w(r^*)(t - t_0 + 1) + \frac{a}{2}\left(\sum_{i=t_0}^{t} \frac{(\lambda_i - r^*)^2}{i - 1} + (t_0 - 1)(r_{t_0-1} - r^*)^2\right)$$

$$(21.4) \quad -\frac{a}{2}\left(\sum_{i=t_0}^{t} \frac{i(r_i - r^*)^2}{i - 1} + t(r_t - r^*)^2\right).$$

Proof. From lemma 21.2, we have $w_i = w(r^*) - a\sigma_{i-1}y_i$. So it suffices to evaluate $\sum_{i=1}^{t} \sigma_{i-1}y_i$. From the definition of σ_i and y_i, we have $y_i = i\sigma_i - (i-1)\sigma_{i-1}$, and thus $i\sigma_i = y_i + (i-1)\sigma_{i-1}$. Therefore $i^2\sigma_i^2 = y_i^2 + (i-1)^2\sigma_{i-1}^2 + 2(i-1)y_i\sigma_{i-1}$ holds. Hence we have

$$(21.5) \quad y_i\sigma_{i-1} = \frac{1}{2(i-1)}(i^2\sigma_i^2 - (i-1)^2\sigma_{i-1}^2 - y_i^2)$$

for $i \geq 1$. What we must evaluate is therefore

$$(21.6) \quad \sum_{i=t_0}^{t} y_i\sigma_{i-1} = -\frac{1}{2}\sum_{i=t_0}^{t} \frac{y_i^2}{i - 1} + \frac{1}{2}\sum_{i=t_0}^{t} \frac{i^2\sigma_i^2 - (i-1)^2\sigma_{i-1}^2}{i - 1}.$$

Applying the general identity $\sum_{i=t_0}^{t} a_i(b_{i+1} - b_i) = (a_{t+1}b_{t+1} - a_{t_0}b_{t_0}) - \sum_{i=t_0}^{t}(a_{i+1} - a_i)b_{i+1}$ on $T_i = (i^2\sigma_i^2 - (i-1)^2\sigma_{i-1}^2)/(i-1)$ with $a_i = 1/(i-1)$ and $b_i = (i-1)^2\sigma_{i-1}^2$, we get $\sum_{i=t_0}^{t} T_i = t\sigma_t^2 - (t_0 - 1)\sigma_{t_0-1}^2 + \sum_{i=t_0}^{t} i\sigma_i^2/(i-1)$. Hence we obtain the following by substituting the above expression into (21.6).

$$\sum_{i=t_0}^{t} y_i\sigma_{i-1}$$

$$(21.7) \quad = -\frac{1}{2}\left(\sum_{i=t_0}^{t} \frac{y_i^2}{i - 1} + (t_0 - 1)\sigma_{t_0-1}^2\right) + \frac{1}{2}\left(\sum_{i=t_0}^{t} \frac{i\sigma_i^2}{i - 1} + t\sigma_t^2\right).$$

This yields the claim of the lemma. □

Proof of Lemma 21.1 (Given Lemma 21.3). From lemma 21.3, $E_2^t(\lambda^t(f_L, f_P))$ is upper bounded as follows.

$$E_2^t(\lambda^t(f_L, f_P)) \leq w(r^*)(t-1) + \frac{a}{2}\Big(\sum_{i=2}^{t} \frac{(\lambda_i - r^*)^2}{i-1} + (r_1 - r^*)^2\Big)$$

$$\leq w(r^*)(t-1) + \frac{a}{2}\Big(\sum_{i=2}^{t} \frac{1}{i-1} + 1\Big)$$

$$\leq w(r^*)(t-1) + \frac{a}{2}(2 + \log(t-1)).$$

Noting that $w_1 = w(r^*)$, we have $E_1^t(\lambda^t(f_L, f_P)) \leq w(r^*)t + a(2 + \log(t-1))/2$, yielding the statement of the lemma. $\square$

Finally, from lemma 21.1 and lemma 21.3, the following lemma follows.

Lemma 21.4. *For an arbitrary playing machine A and for any (f_L, f_P) $\in$ LINEAR(MS), if we define a, r_i, and r^* as in lemma 21.1, then the expected regret of A up to the tth trial, $R(A(f_L, f_P), t)$, is bounded as follows.*

$$R(A(f_L, f_P), t) \leq a\Big(1 + \frac{\log t + t\langle(r_t - r^*)^2\rangle}{2} + \sum_{i=1}^{t}\langle(r_i - r^*)^2\rangle\Big).$$

Proof. From lemma 21.3, $E_2^t(\lambda^t(f_L, f_P))$ is lower bounded as

$$E_2^t(\lambda^t(f_L, f_P)) \geq w(r^*)(t-1) - \frac{a}{2}\Big(\sum_{i=2}^{t} \frac{i(r_i - r^*)^2}{i-1} + t(r_t - r^*)^2\Big)$$

$$\geq w(r^*)(t-1) - \frac{a}{2}\Big(\sum_{i=2}^{t} 2(r_i - r^*)^2 + t(r_t - r^*)^2\Big).$$

Noting that $w_1 = w(r^*)$, we have $E_1^t(\lambda^t(f_L, f_P)) \geq w(r^*)t - a\big(\sum_{i=2}^{t}(r_i - r^*)^2 + t(r_t - r^*)^2/2\big)$. Hence, by lemma 21.1, for an ideal machine I for (f_L, f_P), we have

$$E(I(f_L, f_P), t) - E_1^t(\lambda^t(f_L, f_P))$$

$$\leq a\Big(1 + (\log t)/2 + \sum_{i=2}^{t}(r_i - r^*)^2 + t(r_t - r^*)^2/2\Big).$$

Taking the expectation over all λ^t that may be output by A, we obtain the lemma. $\square$

As lemma 21.4 relates the deviation of the lob rate from r^* and the cumulative regret, it motivates us to design a playing machine whose lob rates approach r^* quickly. It also establishes that, *under the MS condition*, it suffices to evaluate the convergence speed of lob rates to

r^* in order to analyze the performance of a lob-pass machine. Below we present two lemmas that will be useful for this purpose. Lemma 21.5 is usually known as Hoeffding's inequality (Pollard, 1984) and is used to obtain a bound on the estimation accuracy for the probability of an event. Lemma 21.6 can be used to obtain a bound on the expectation of a random variable, given an exponential bound on the probability that it exceeds a certain threshold (ϵ).

Lemma 21.5 (Hoeffding). *Let X_i's ($1 \leq i \leq N$) be independent random variables with 0 mean and a bounded range, i.e. $|X_i| \leq M$. Then $\Pr\{|\sum_{i=1}^{N} X_i/N| \geq \varepsilon\} \leq 2\exp(-2\varepsilon^2 N/M^2)$ holds.*

Lemma 21.6. *For any nonnegative integrable function f over $[0,\infty)$, for any $a \geq 0$ and $A > 0$ and $B > 0$, if $\forall \varepsilon \geq a$, $\int_{\varepsilon}^{\infty} f(x)dx \leq A\exp(-B\varepsilon)$, then $\int_{a}^{\infty} xf(x)dx \leq A/B$.*

Proof. Let $G(\varepsilon) = A\exp(-B\varepsilon) - \int_{\varepsilon}^{\infty} f(x)dx$. Differentiating both sides with respect to ε, we have $f(\varepsilon) = G'(\varepsilon) + AB\exp(-B\varepsilon)$. Hence we have $\int_{a}^{\infty} xf(x)dx = \int_{a}^{\infty} xG'(x)dx + \int_{a}^{\infty} xAB\exp(-Bx)dx$. The first term of this last expression can be shown to be nonpositive: $\int_{a}^{\infty} xG'(x)dx = [xG(x)]_{a}^{\infty} - \int_{a}^{\infty} G(x)dx = -aG(a) - \int_{a}^{\infty} G(x)dx \leq 0$, where we used the fact that $0 \leq G(x) \leq A\exp(-Bx)$. Similarly, the second term can be bounded from above as: $\int_{a}^{\infty} xAB\exp(-Bx)dx \leq \int_{0}^{\infty} xAB\exp(-Bx)dx = -[Ax\exp(-Bx)]_{0}^{\infty} + \int_{0}^{\infty} A\exp(-Bx)dx = A/B$, completing the proof. □

21.2 Upper Bounds on the Expected Regret

Here we state the upper bounds we obtained for the lob-pass problem under various assumptions. In the statements below, we let MS denote the matching shoulders condition, i.e. $b_1 = a_2 + b_2$, and BO the condition that the optimal rate r^* satisfies $r_1 \leq r^* \leq r_2$ for some constants r_1 and r_2 such that $0 < r_1 < r_2 < 1$.

Theorem 21.7. *In the unknown-t model, each of the following upper bounds holds, where $\tilde{a}$ is any unknown constant satisfying $0 < \tilde{a} \leq 2$ and b is any constant satisfying $0 \leq b \leq 1$.*

1. $R(\text{LINEAR}(a_2 - a_1 \geq \tilde{a}, \text{BO}, \text{MS})) = O(t^{1/2})$.
2. $R(\text{LINEAR}(a_2 - a_1 \geq \tilde{a}, \text{MS})) = O(t^{3/5})$.
3. $R(\text{LINEAR}(\text{BO}, \text{MS})) = O(t^{2/3})$.
4. $R(\text{LINEAR}(\text{MS})) = O(t^{5/7})$.

Theorem 21.8. *Let δ and ξ be constants satisfying $1/2 \geq \delta > 1/2\sqrt{2}$ and $0 < \xi \leq 2 - 1/4\delta^2$. Then the following holds in the unknown-t model.*

$$R(\text{LINEAR}(a_2 - a_1 \geq \frac{1}{4\delta^2} + \xi, \delta \leq r^* \leq 1 - \delta, \text{MS})) = O(\log t).$$

Theorem 21.9. *In the known-t model, each of the following holds, where* $\tilde{a}$ *is any unknown constant satisfying* $0 < \tilde{a} \leq 2$.

1. $R(\text{LINEAR}(a_2 - a_1 \geq \tilde{a}, \text{MS})) = O(t^{1/2})$.
2. $\forall \epsilon > 0, R(\text{LINEAR}(\text{MS})) = O(t^{1/2+\epsilon})$.

In the above theorem statements, the constants δ, ξ and r_1, r_2 of BO are "known" constants, in the sense that they are used by the lob-pass machines exhibited to prove these bounds. In contrast, $\tilde{a}$ is an "unknown" constant, namely one that the lob-pass machine need not know.

21.2.1 Lob-Pass Machine Arthur

The upper bounds in theorem 21.7 are all attained by a lob-pass playing machine we call "Arthur," exhibited in figures 21.3, 21.4, and 21.5. Here *Play* is a procedure/function, such that when it is called with L as in $\text{Play}(L)$ (with P as in $\text{Play}(P)$), the machine plays a lob (a pass), returns the reinforcement it obtains (1 if the play results in a win and 0 if the play results in a loss), and updates the relevant parameters accordingly.

We roughly illustrate the behavior of Arthur below. We can imagine that Arthur is located at r when his current total lob rate is r. Arthur performs a kind of search for the approximate maximum of the (quadratic) stationary winning rate function $w(r)$ by moving around in the dimension of r. The search proceeds in stages: in the ith stage Arthur sets $M = 10C^i$, plays $2M$ shots (lobs and passes), moves within a *testing interval*, $\Delta = M^{-\beta}$, and estimates the maximum point of $w(r)$. Arthur does so by testing the success rates of lobs and passes, $f_L(r)$ and $f_P(r)$ at the current lob rate r, and another lob rate $r' = r \pm \Delta$. Here note that when the lob rate becomes close to 0 or 1, it becomes harder to test the success rate for lobs or passes, respectively. So we restrict the algorithm's lob rates to never go below $\Lambda = C_0 M^{-\gamma}$ or exceed $1 - \Lambda = 1 - C_0 M^{-\gamma}$. As the stages proceed, the estimates of f_L and f_P become more accurate and Δ and Λ become smaller. Naturally, a smaller value of Δ (or Λ) makes the estimation of $w(r)$ harder, but a larger value can force Arthur to play at lob rates that are far from the optimal, resulting in the so-called exploration–exploitation trade-off. How to set the parameters β and γ intelligently, therefore, is a key to the design of Arthur. We actually use several versions of Arthur in the proof of theorem 21.7. We indicate these different versions of Arthur by subscripts, as in Arthur$_1$,..., Arthur$_4$, where Arthur$_x$ denotes the version of Arthur used to prove the xth bound in theorem 21.7. The four versions of Arthur set the values β, γ, and C_0 differently, as shown in table 21.2.

Playing Machine Arthur(C, β, γ, C_0)

/* Uses subroutines Move (figure 21.4) and Test (figure 21.5) */
1. /* Initialization of global variables */
   $r := 0$, $T := 0$, $M := 10$, $K := 0$, $dr := 0$
   $\#L := 0$, $\#P := 0$, $p := 1/2$,
   $WL1 := 0, WP1 := 0, WL2 := 0, WP2 := 0$
2. /* Try to move to p playing M times */
   Move(p, M), $T := T + M$, $r := \#L/(\#L + \#P)$
3. /* Move and test winning rates at two points */
   $\Delta := M^{-\beta}$, $\Lambda := C_0 M^{-\gamma}$
   $K := \lfloor (M - 10M^{1-\beta})/2 \rfloor$, $S := M - 2K$
   If $r > 0.5$ Then $E := -1$ Else $E := 1$
   Test$(r, K, WL1, WP1)$, $T := T + K$
   Move$(r + E\Delta, S)$, $T := T + S$, $r := r + E\Delta$
   Test$(r, K, WL2, WP2)$, $T := T + K$
   $dr := \dfrac{E\Delta(WL2 - WP2)}{-(WL2 - WL1) + (WP2 - WP1)}$
4. /* Calculate next target point*/
   $p := r + dr$
   If $p < \Lambda$, then $p := \Lambda$
   If $p > 1 - \Lambda$, then $p := 1 - \Lambda$
5. /* update M*/
   $M := CM$, Goto 2.

FIGURE 21.3. The playing machine Arthur.

TABLE 21.2

Arthur's Parameters, where $C_M = \max\{r_1, 1 - r_2\}$

Version	Bound	Restrictions in addition to MS	β	γ	C_0
Arthur$_1$	Thm 21.7, 1	$a_2 - a_1 \geq \tilde{a}$, $r_1 \leq r^* \leq r_2$	1/4	0.0	C_M
Arthur$_2$	Thm 21.7, 2	$a_2 - a_1 \geq \tilde{a}$	1/5	1/5	1.0
Arthur$_3$	Thm 21.7, 3	$r_1 \leq r^* \leq r_2$	1/6	0.0	C_M
Arthur$_4$	Thm 21.7, 4	None	1/7	1/7	1.0

Note in table 22.2 that C_0 is determined by the range of r^* given in BO; thus Arthur needs to know the constants r_1 and r_2. A first parameter C is any sufficiently large constant (to be specified later), but here we assume that at least $C \geq 4$ holds.

In the sequel, let M_i, Δ_i, Λ_i and E_i respectively denote the values

Subroutine Move(p, M)

/* Tries to move to p playing at most M times */
1. $I := 0$

   If $p > \frac{\#L}{\#L + \#P}$

       Repeat until $p < \frac{\#L}{\#L + \#P}$ or $I \geq M$

       Play(L), $\#L := \#L + 1, I := I + 1$

       End Repeat

   Else

       Repeat until $p > \frac{\#L}{\#L + \#P}$ or $I \geq M$

       Play(P), $\#P := \#P + 1, I := I + 1$

       End Repeat
2. If $I \geq M$ Then Return
3. /* If it reaches p before M trials it stalls there */

   If $\frac{\#L}{\#L + \#P} < p$

       Play(L), $\#L := \#L + 1, I := I + 1$

   Else

       Play(P), $\#P := \#P + 1, I := I + 1$
4. If $I \geq M$ Then Return Else Goto 3

FIGURE 21.4. Subroutine Move.

Subroutine Test(r, K, W_L, W_P)

/* Test the winning rates at current point r */
/* W_L and W_P are called by name */
1. $I := 0, \#W_L := 0, \#W_P := 0, \#LC := 0, \#PC := 0$
2. If $r < \frac{\#L}{\#L + \#P}$

       $\#W_L := \#W_L +$ Play(L)

       $\#LC := \#LC + 1, \#L := \#L + 1$

   Else

       $\#W_P := \#W_P +$ Play(P)

       $\#PC := \#PC + 1, \#P := \#P + 1$

   $I := I + 1$
3. If $I < K$ Goto 2.
4. $W_L := \frac{\#W_L}{\#LC}, W_P := \frac{\#W_P}{\#PC}$
5. Return

FIGURE 21.5. Subroutine Test.

of M, Δ, Λ, and E after Block 3 is executed in the ith iteration of Arthur. Let p_i denote the value of p before Block 2 is executed in the ith iteration, and r_i denote the value of r after Block 2 is executed in the ith iteration.

Note that M_i is of the same order as the total number of trials up to the ith iteration, as it is multiplied by a constant at each iteration.

We begin by noting that $\langle (p_{i+1} - r^*)^2 \rangle$ can be bounded from above as follows.

Lemma 21.10. *Let a^* denote $a_2 - a_1$. Let r^*, p_{i+1}, M_i, Λ_i and Δ_i be as defined earlier. Then, for some constant K independent of a^*, $\langle (p_{i+1} - r^*)^2 \rangle \leq K/a^{*2} M_i \Lambda_i \Delta_i^2$ holds.*

The proof can be found in Takeuchi, Abe, and Amari (2000).

From this lemma, we see that by appropriately choosing the values of M_i, Λ_i and Δ_i, the desired bound on $\langle (p_{i+1} - r^*)^2 \rangle$ for each of the four cases can be obtained.

Next, we need to show that Arthur's lob rate r_i can be made sufficiently close to his estimate p_i of r^*, i.e. we need to bound $\langle (r_{i+1} - r^*)^2 \rangle$ from above. To this end, the following two lemmas prove useful.

Lemma 21.11. $\langle (r_{i+1} - r^*)^2 \rangle \leq \langle (p_{i+1} - r^*)^2 \rangle + \Pi_i^2 + D \langle (r_i - r^*)^2 \rangle / C^2$ *holds for all large enough i, where $\Pi_i \equiv \max\{\Lambda_i - r*, \Lambda_i - (1 - r^*), 0\}$ and D is a constant less than $5^2 \cdot 13^2 / 2^4$.*

The proof can be found in Takeuchi, Abe, and Amari (2000).

Lemma 21.12. *Let $A \geq 0$, $B \geq 0$, $0 < a, b, c < 1$ and suppose that $c < \min\{a, b\}$ holds. If a series of positive reals $\{x_i\}$ $(i = 1, 2, \ldots)$ satisfies $x_{i+1} \leq Aa^i + Bb^i + cx_i$, then $\forall i \geq 2$ $x_{i+1} \leq k_1 \cdot Aa^i + k_2 \cdot Bb^i + x_1 \cdot c^i$ holds, where k_1 and k_2 are positive reals determined by a, b, and c.*

Proof of Lemma 21.12. It is easily verified by induction that the recurrence relation in the statement of the lemma implies

$$x_{i+1} \leq \frac{Aa(a^i - c^i)}{a - c} + \frac{Bb(b^i - c^i)}{b - c} + c^i x_1.$$

If we now let $k_1 = a/(a - c)$ and $k_2 = b/(b - c)$, we obtain the claim of the lemma. $\square$

Now we are ready to prove theorem 21.7. (We prove just part 4 owing to space limitations and refer the reader to Takeuchi, Abe, and Amari (2000). for the other proofs.)

Proof of Theorem 21.7, Part 4. Let d_i denote $\langle (r_i - r^*)^2 \rangle$ and K equal D/C^2. (D is the constant in lemma 21.11.) Recall that $\beta = \gamma = 1/7$ and $C_0 = 1$ in Arthur$_4$ and thus $\Delta_i = \Lambda_i = \kappa C^{-i/7}$ (where κ is some constant.) Moreover, we have $\sup_{r*} \Pi_i = \sup_{r*} \max\{\Lambda_i - r^*, \Lambda_i - (1 -$

$r^*), 0\} = \Lambda_i$ for LINEAR(MS). Hence, from lemmas 21.11 and 21.10, we have $d_{i+1} \leq A_1 C^{-4i/7}/a^{*2} + A_2 C^{-2i/7} + K d_i$, where we let in general A_i ($i = 1, 2, \dots$) denote a constant that is independent of a^*. If we choose C to be sufficiently large, then $K < C^{-4/7}$ holds. Then, by lemma 21.12, we have $d_{i+1} \leq A_3 C^{-4i/7}/a^{*2} + A_4 C^{-2i/7} + K^i d_1$. Since $d_1 \leq 1$, C can be chosen to make K small enough that $d_{i+1} \leq A_5 C^{-4i/7}/a^{*2} + A_4 C^{-2i/7}$ holds. Since $d_{i+1} \leq 1$ holds, $a^* d_{i+1} \leq \min\{A_5 C^{-4i/7}/a^* + A_4 a^* C^{-2i/7}, a^*\}$, and thus $a^* d_{i+1} \leq \min\{2 \cdot \max\{A_5 C^{-4i/7}/a^*, A_4 a^* C^{-2i/7}\}, a^*\}$ holds. Assuming $2A_4 \geq 1$ without loss of generality, this yields $a^* d_{i+1} \leq 2 \min\{\max\{A_5 C^{-4i/7}/a^*, A_4 a^* C^{-2i/7}\}, A_4 a^*\}$. Now, if $A_5 C^{-4i/7}/a^* \leq A_4 a^* C^{-2i/7}$ holds, then the right-hand side of the above inequality equals $2 \min\{A_4 a^* C^{-2i/7}, A_4 a^*\} = 2A_4 a^* C^{-2i/7}$. If on the other hand $A_5 C^{-4i/7}/a^* \geq A_4 a^* C^{-2i/7}$ holds, then the right-hand side equals $2 \min\{A_5 C^{-4i/7}/a^*, A_4 a^*\}$, which attains the maximum value of $2(A_5 A_4 C^{-4i/7})^{1/2}$ when $a^* = (A_5 C^{-4i/7}/A_4)^{1/2}$. In both cases, we have $a^* d_{i+1} = O(C^{-2i/7})$.

Hence, from lemma 21.4, we obtain the following upper bound on the expected cumulative regret of Arthur. (Below we let $i^* = \lceil \log_C t \rceil$.)

$$R(A(f_L, f_P), t) \leq \sum_{i=1}^{i^*} (M_i \cdot O(C^{-2i/7})) + \log t$$

$$= \sum_{i=1}^{i^*} O(C^{5i/7}) + \log t = O(C^{5i^*/7}) + \log t.$$

Since $t > M_{i^*} = C^{i^*-1} M_1$, we have $R(A(f_L, f_P), t) = O(t^{5/7}) + \log t = O(t^{5/7})$. $\qquad\square$

21.2.2   Lob-Pass Algorithm Bjorn

In the "known-t" model, where the knowledge of the total number of trials is available to the player in advance, a simpler playing strategy having basically two phases—the learning phase and the winning phase—can be used. We use this type of playing algorithms, referred to collectively as "Bjorn," to prove the bounds in theorem 21.9. Here we exhibit the proof for part 1 only. (See Takeuchi, Abe, and Amari, 2000 for the proof of part 2.)

Proof of Theorem 21.9, Part 1. We prove $O(\sqrt{t})$ bound on the expected regret for the version of Bjorn exhibited in figure 21.6 for the subclass LINEAR($a_2 - a_1 \geq \tilde{a}$, MS). Less formally, this version of Bjorn (i) uses the first $\sqrt{t}$ trials to estimate the optimal lob rate by estimating the winning rates of lobs and passes at two distinct points (the learning phase), (ii) moves to the estimated optimal rate (the moving phase), and (iii) stays there until the end (the winning phase). Note that since Bjorn

Algorithm Bjorn(T)

1. /* Initialization of global variable */
   $N := 0$, $M := \sqrt{T}$
2. /* Move and test winning rates at $\frac{1}{2}$ and $\frac{1}{3}$. */
   Move($\frac{1}{2}, \frac{M}{6}$), Test($\frac{1}{2}, \frac{M}{3}, W1, W2$)
   Move($\frac{1}{3}, \frac{M}{6}$), Test($\frac{1}{3}, \frac{M}{3}, W3, W4$)
   $N := N + M$
3. /* Calculate sum of estimated slopes */
   $A1 := 6(W3 - W1)$, $A2 := 6(W4 - W2)$, $A := A2 - A1$
4. /* Calculate estimate for the optimal rate r^* */
   $B1 := W1 - \frac{A1}{2}$, $B2 := W2 - \frac{A2}{2}$, $\hat{r} := \frac{A2 + B1 - B2}{2(A2 - A1)}$
5. /* Move to the optimal rate and stay there */
   Move($r^*, T - N$), Return

FIGURE 21.6. Lob-pass algorithm Bjorn (version 1).

estimates the optimal lob rate $\hat{r}$ in a manner similar to Arthur (namely by estimating the success rates of lobs and passes at two distinct lob rates), we can show that for some constant K independent of a^* (the sum of the absolute values of the slopes),

$$(21.8) \qquad \langle (\hat{r} - r^*)^2 \rangle \leq \frac{K}{a^{*2}\sqrt{t}},$$

by an argument similar to the proof of lemma 21.10.

We now bound the expected regret of Bjorn, considering the three phases one by one. First note that by virtue of lemma 21.1 it suffices to compare the expected number of successes to $w(r^*)t$. Let us say that (i) goes from the first to the sth trials, (ii) from the $s + 1$st to the s'th, and (iii) from the $s' + 1$st to the tth.

First, since the learning phase (i) consists of $s = \sqrt{t}$ trials, it follows for any lob-pass sequence λ^t that

$$(21.9) \qquad E_1^s(\lambda^t(f_L, f_P)) \geq w(r^*) \cdot s - \sqrt{t}.$$

For the moving phase (ii), there are three cases to consider, depending on the ordering between r_s, r^*, and $\hat{r}$.

Case 1. ($r_s \leq \hat{r} \leq r^*$ or $r^* \leq \hat{r} \leq r_s$). In this case, since Bjorn tries to move from r_s to $\hat{r}$, he is always moving *toward* r^*. Moving toward r^* at the ith trial means formally that $\lambda_i = 1$ if $r_{i-1} < r^*$ and $\lambda_i = 0$ if $r_{i-1} > r^*$. Thus, by lemma 21.2, Bjorn's instantaneous winning rate w_i is greater than $w(r^*)$ in the moving phase. Therefore, for any lob-pass sequence λ^t belonging to case 1, we have

$$(21.10) \qquad E_{s+1}^{s'}(\lambda^t(f_L, f_P)) \geq w(r^*)(s' - s).$$

Case 2. ($\hat{r} \leq r_s \leq r^*$ or $\hat{r} \leq r_s \leq r^*$). In this case, from lemma 21.3 we have the following lower bound on the number of successes for any λ^t belonging to case 2.

$$E_{s+1}^{s'}(\lambda^t(f_L, f_P))$$

$$\geq \; w(r^*)(s' - s) - \frac{a^*}{2} \Big(\sum_{i=s+1}^{s'} \frac{i(r_i - r^*)^2}{i - 1} + s'(r_s - r^*)^2 \Big)$$

$$\geq \; w(r^*)(s' - s) - \frac{a^*}{2} \Big(\sum_{i=s+1}^{s'} \frac{i(\hat{r} - r^*)^2}{i - 1} + s'(\hat{r} - r^*)^2 \Big)$$

$$(21.11) \quad \geq \; w(r^*)(s' - s) - \frac{a^*}{2} 3s'(\hat{r} - r^*)^2.$$

Case 3. ($\hat{r} \leq r^* \leq r_s$ or $r_s \leq r^* \leq \hat{r}$). In this case, suppose that the player's lob rate reaches (or exceeds) r^* after the s''th trial for the first time. Then for the first half (until s''th trial), we can show by an argument similar to case 1 that

$$(21.12) \qquad E_{s+1}^{s''}(\lambda^t(f_L, f_P)) \geq w(r^*)(s'' - s),$$

for all λ^t belonging to case 3. For the second half (from s''th trial on), we again invoke lemma 21.3 to show that

$$(21.13) \qquad E_{s''+1}^{s'}(\lambda^t(f_L, f_P)) \geq w(r^*)(s' - s'') - \frac{a^*}{2} 3s'(\hat{r} - r^*)^2.$$

So combining (21.10), (21.11), (21.12), and (21.13), it holds in all three cases that

$$(21.14) \qquad E_{s+1}^{s'}(\lambda^t(f_L, f_P)) \geq w(r^*)(s' - s) - \frac{a^*}{2} 3t(\hat{r} - r^*)^2.$$

Finally, during the winning phase, Bjorn maintains its lob rate at $\hat{r}$ within $O(1/t)$ error. Thus again it follows from lemma 21.3 that for any lob-pass sequence λ^t we have

$$E_{s'+1}^{t}(\lambda^t(f_L, f_P))$$

$$\geq \; w(r^*)(t - s') - \frac{a^*}{2} \Big(\sum_{i=s'+1}^{t} \frac{i(\hat{r} - r^*)^2}{i - 1}$$

$$+ s'(\hat{r} - r^*)^2 - t \cdot O\Big(\frac{1}{t^2}\Big) \Big)$$

$$(21.15) \quad \geq \; w(r^*)(t - s') - \frac{a^*}{2} 3t(\hat{r} - r^*)^2 - O\Big(\frac{1}{t}\Big).$$

Finally, taking the expectations of (21.9), (21.14), and (21.15) over λ^t probabilistically output by Bjorn, we get the following bound on the expected number of successes.

$$
\begin{aligned}
E(\text{Bjorn}(f_L, f_P), t) & \\
\geq\ & \langle E_1^s(\lambda^t(f_L, f_P)) + E_{s+1}^{s'}(\lambda^t(f_L, f_P)) \\
& + E_{s'+1}^t(\lambda^t(f_L, f_P)) \rangle \\
\geq\ & w(r^*)s - \sqrt{t} + \Big\langle w(r^*)(s' - s) \\
& - \frac{a^*}{2} 3t(\hat{r} - r^*)^2 + w(r^*)(t - s') \\
& - \frac{a^*}{2} 3t(\hat{r} - r^*)^2 \Big\rangle - O\Big(\frac{1}{t}\Big) \\
=\ & w(r^*)t - \sqrt{t} - \frac{a^*}{2} 6t\langle(\hat{r} - r^*)^2\rangle - O\Big(\frac{1}{t}\Big)
\end{aligned}
$$

$$
(21.16) \qquad \geq\ w(r^*)t - \Big(1 + \frac{3K}{a^*}\Big)\sqrt{t} - O\Big(\frac{1}{t}\Big) \qquad \text{by (21.8).}
$$

Finally, by lemma 21.1, the expected regret of Bjorn is bounded above as follows.

$$
\begin{aligned}
R(\text{Bjorn}(f_L, f_P), t) &= \max_A E(A(f_L, f_P), t) - E(\text{Bjorn}(f_L, f_P), t) \\
&\leq \Big(w(r^*)t + a^*(1 + (\log t)/2)\Big) \\
&\quad - \Big(w(r^*)t - \Big(1 + \frac{3K}{a^*}\Big)\sqrt{t} - O\Big(\frac{1}{t}\Big)\Big) \\
&= O\Big(\sqrt{t} + \log t + \frac{1}{t}\Big) \\
(21.17) \qquad\qquad &= O(\sqrt{t}).
\end{aligned}
$$

□

21.2.3 Lob-Pass Machine Chris

The lob-pass machines described so far are deterministic machines. Here we consider a randomized machine called "Chris" (figure 21.7). Chris has access to a probabilistic oracle "COIN," which receives a real number $x \in [0, 1]$ as input and outputs 1 with probability x, and 0 with probability $1 - x$. The following lemma on the performance of Chris serves to prove the upper bound of theorem 21.8.

Lemma 21.13. *In the unknown-t model, for any δ satisfying $1/2 \geq \delta > 1/2\sqrt{2}$ and any $\xi \in (0, 2 - 1/4\delta^2]$, the following upper bound on the expected regret holds for Chris, for some appropriate values of the input*

Machine Chris(δ, θ, M)

1. /* Initialization of global variables */
   $r := 0.5$, $\Delta = \delta$, $p := 0.5$, $q = 0.5$
   $T := 0$, $\#L := 0$, $\#P := 0$, $Z^+ := 0$, $Z^- := 0$, $Y := 0$, $G := 0$, $GR := 0$
2. /* Try to move to p playing M times */
   Move(p, M), $r := \frac{\#L}{\#L + \#P}$
3. /* Try playing at two lob rates */
   If COIN$(r + \Delta) = 1$
   $\quad Z^+ := \text{Play}(L)$, $\#L := \#L + 1$
   Else
   $\quad Z^+ := \text{Play}(P)$, $\#P := \#P + 1$
   If COIN$(r - \Delta) = 1$
   $\quad Z^- := \text{Play}(L)$, $\#L := \#L + 1$
   Else
   $\quad Z^- := \text{Play}(P)$, $\#P := \#P + 1$
   $T := \#L + \#P$
4. /* Calculate next target point */
   $q := r + \frac{Z1 - Z0}{\theta \Delta T}$,
   If $q < \Delta$, then $q := \Delta$,
   If $q > 1 - \Delta$, then $q := 1 - \Delta$,
   $G := q * (\#L + \#P + M)$, $\gamma := G - \lfloor G \rfloor$
   $GR := \text{COIN}(\gamma) + \lfloor G \rfloor$, $p := \frac{GR}{(\#L + \#P + M)}$
   Goto 2.

FIGURE 21.7. The lob-pass machine Chris.

parameters M and θ.

$$R\Big(\text{Chris}, \text{LINEAR}\big(a_2 - a_1 \geq \frac{1}{4\delta^2} + \xi, \delta \leq r^* \leq 1 - \delta, \text{MS}\big)\Big)$$
$$= O(\log t).$$

This lemma can be proved using a theorem from the theory of stochastic approximation (Wasan, 1969). Stochastic approximation is a methodology of approximating the maximum (or any other point of interest) of a regression function. In particular, we make use of the Kiefer-Wolfowitz method in designing Chris.

Below we describe intuitively how Chris works. Assume that Chris is currently in the nth iteration and the lob rate equals r_n. First, Chris plays a lob with probability $r_n + \delta$ (or a pass with probability $1 - r_n - \delta$). Let Z^+ denote the random variable representing the result of this trial.

Then she plays a lob with probability $r_n - \delta$ (or a pass with probability $1 - r_n + \delta$). Let Z^- denote the result of the second trial. There are four possible values that can be assumed by (Z^+, Z^-): $(1, 1)$, $(0, 0)$, $(1, 0)$ and $(0, 1)$. Based on the value of (Z^+, Z^-), Chris makes a decision of whether to increase her lob rate p or decrease it. More specifically, she sets $p_{n+1} := r_n + (Z^+ - Z^-)/(\theta \delta T)$, where θ and δ are constants described in the lemma and T equals t, the number of trials up to that point. Chris then moves to the lob rate p_{n+1} and then goes into the next $(n + \text{1st})$ iteration.

It can be shown that for this strategy $\langle (r_n - r^*)^2 \rangle = O(1/n)$ holds for the subclass specified in the lemma, and hence the expected cumulative regret is $O(\log t)$.

Lemma 21.13 is proved via a series of sublemmas, lemma 21.14 through lemma 21.16 below.

Lemma 21.14. *Let p_n and r_n denote, respectively, the values of p and r at the end of Block 2 of Chris, in the nth iteration. Then, provided that $\theta M \geq 1/\delta^2 + \theta/\delta$ holds, $p_n = r_n$ holds for sufficiently large n.*

See Takeuchi, Abe, and Amari (2000) for the proof.

Note that p_n is the goal lob rate that Chris wishes to attain at the nth iteration and r_n is the rate she actually attains. Depending on the value of p_n and the number of plays Chris can use in the nth iteration in trying to get to p_n, it may or may not be possible to set r_n exactly (or approximately) equal to r_n. The above lemma says that under the condition that $\theta M \geq 1/\delta^2 + \theta/\delta$ holds, this can be achieved. This will be necessary for proving the following lemma.

Lemma 21.15. *Assume $r^* \in [\delta, 1 - \delta]$ and $\delta > 1/2\sqrt{2}$ and $0 < \xi < 2 - 1/4\delta^2$, and let $x_n = r_n - r^*$. Then there exists $K > 1$, θ, and M, such that the following holds for any (f_L, f_P) satisfying $|a_1| + |a_2| \geq 1/4\delta^2 + \xi$.*

$$\langle x_{n+1}^2 \rangle \leq \left(1 - \frac{K}{n-1}\right) \langle x_n^2 \rangle + O\left(\frac{1}{n^2}\right).$$

Proof of Lemma 21.15. Assume that $\theta M \geq 1/\delta^2 + \theta/\delta$.

If we let y_n denote the value of $p - r$ at the end of Block 4 in the nth iteration, then $x_{n+1} = x_n + y_n$ holds from lemma 21.14. Thus we have

$$(21.18) \qquad \langle x_{n+1}^2 \rangle = \langle x_n^2 \rangle + 2\langle x_n y_n \rangle + \langle y_n^2 \rangle$$

Since $|y_n| = O(1/n)$, we have $\langle y_n^2 \rangle = O(1/n^2)$. Next, using the identity $\langle x_n y_n \rangle = E(x_n y_n) = E(x_n E(y_n | x_n))$, we evaluate $\langle x_n y_n \rangle$. Since $p_{n+1} = (\text{COIN}(\gamma) + \lfloor G \rfloor)/(T + M)$, it follows that $E(p_{n+1} | q_{n+1}, x_n) = (\gamma + \lfloor G \rfloor)/(T + M) = G/(T + M) = q_{n+1}$, where q_{n+1} denotes the value of q

at the end of Block 4 of Chris in the $n + 1$st iteration. Hence we have

(21.19) $$E(y_n|x_n) = E(p_{n+1} - r_n|x_n) = E(q_{n+1} - r_n|x_n).$$

Thus it suffices to evaluate the expectation of $q_{n+1} - r_n$. First we consider the case that $r_n + (Z^+ - Z^-)/\theta\delta T \in [\delta, 1-\delta]$ holds. In this case, we have $q_{n+1} = r_n + (Z^+ - Z^-)/\theta\delta T$ and hence $q_{n+1} - r_n = (Z^+ - Z^-)/\theta\delta T$.

Since Z^+ is a random variable standing for the win/loss when playing a lob with probability $r_n + \delta$, we have

(21.20) $$\langle Z^+ \rangle = (r_n + \delta)f_L(r_n) + (1 - r_n - \delta)f_P(r_n).$$

Next, if we write $r_n + \eta_n$ ($\eta_n = O(1/n)$) for the lob rate after the third line of Block 3 in the nth iteration, we have

$$\begin{aligned} \langle Z^- \rangle &= (r_n - \delta)f_L(r_n + \eta_n) + (1 - r_n + \delta)f_P(r_n + \eta_n) \\ (21.21) \qquad &= (r_n - \delta)f_L(r_n) + (1 - r_n + \delta)f_P(r_n) + k\eta_n, \end{aligned}$$

where k is some constant. Hence, from (21.20) and (21.21), it follows that

$$\begin{aligned} \langle Z^+ - Z^- \rangle &= 2\delta(f_L(r_n) - f_P(r_n)) + O\left(\frac{1}{n}\right) \\ &= -2\delta(a_2 - a_1)(r_n - r^*) + O\left(\frac{1}{n}\right) \\ &= -2\delta(a_2 - a_1)x_n + O\left(\frac{1}{n}\right). \end{aligned}$$

Since $q_{n+1} - r_n = (Z^+ - Z^-)/\theta\delta T$, it follows that $E(q_{n+1} - r_n|x_n) = -2(a_2-a_1)x_n/\theta T + O(1/n^2)$. Hence from (21.19), $\langle x_n y_n \rangle = -2(a_2-a_1) \cdot \langle x_n^2 \rangle/\theta T + O(1/n^2)$ follows. Thus it now follows from (21.18) that

(21.22) $$\langle x_{n+1}^2 \rangle = \left(1 - \frac{4(a_2 - a_1)}{\theta T}\right)\langle x_n^2 \rangle + O\left(\frac{1}{n^2}\right).$$

So far we have considered the case that $r_n + (Z^+ - Z^-)/\theta\delta T \in [\delta, 1 - \delta]$ holds, but since in the general case we have $|q_{n+1} - r^*| \le |r_n + (Z^+ - Z^-)/\theta\delta T - r^*|$ from the condition $r^* \in [\delta, 1 - \delta]$, we know that in either case (21.22) holds. That is, we have in general

$$\langle x_{n+1}^2 \rangle \le \left(1 - \frac{4(a_2 - a_1)}{\theta(2 + M)(n - 1)}\right)\langle x_n^2 \rangle + O\left(\frac{1}{n^2}\right).$$

We now show that θ and M can be chosen so that both $4(a_2 - a_1)/\theta(2 + M) > 1$ and $\theta M \ge 1/\delta^2 + \theta/\delta$ are satisfied. First note that these two inequalities are equivalent to the following: $4(a_2 - a_1) > \theta(2 + M) > 1/\delta^2 + \theta/\delta + 2\theta$. Furthermore, since we have $a_2 - a_1 \ge 1/4\delta^2 + \xi$, it suffices to show $1/\delta^2 + 4\xi > \theta(2 + M) > 1/\delta^2 + \theta/\delta + 2\theta$. Since $\delta \ge 1/2\sqrt{2}$, by choosing θ to be sufficiently small, the last expression can be made smaller than $1/\delta^2 + 4\xi$. Having done this, we can then choose

M so that the above inequalities are satisfied. Now assume that θ and M have been chosen in the above manner. That is, we assume that $4(a_2 - a_1)/\theta(2 + M) > 1$ holds, in addition to $\theta M \geq 1/\delta^2 + \theta/\delta$. Then, for some $K > 1$, it holds that $\langle x_{n+1}^2 \rangle \leq (1 - K/(n - 1))\langle x_n^2 \rangle + O(1/n^2)$, which completes the proof. □

Lemma 21.16 (Wasan). *Let $c > p > 0$, $c' > 0$. Then for arbitrary $n \geq n_0$, if $b_{n+1} \leq (1 - c/n)b_n + c'n^{-(p+1)}$, then $b_n \leq c'n^{-p}/(c - p) + O(n^{-(p+1)} + n^{-c})$ holds.*

Proof of Lemma 21.13. Applying lemma 21.16, which is due to Wasan (lemma 2 in Wasan, 1969), to the inequality of lemma 21.15 by letting $b_n = \langle x_n^2 \rangle$ yields $\langle x_n^2 \rangle = \langle (r_n - r^*)^2 \rangle = O(1/n)$. □

21.3 Concluding Remarks

We have proposed a new variant of the on-line learning model and analyzed the lob-pass problem within this general framework. Our analyses are for the parametric case, i.e. the target probabilistic rate functions are assumed to belong to a given target class.

References

Abe, N. and Takeuchi, J. (1993). The "Lob-Pass" problem and an on-line learning model of rational choice. *Proceedings of the Sixth Annual ACM Workshop on Computational Learning Theory* (pp. 422–428).

Amari, S. and Murata, N. (1993). Statistical theory of learning curves under entropic loss criterion. *Neural Computation* 5:40–153.

Berger, J. O. (1985). *Statistical Decision Theory and Bayesian Analysis*. New York: Springer-Verlag.

Berry, D. and Fristedt, F. (1985). *Bandit Problems*. Chapman and Hall.

Blum, A. (1995). Empirical support for winnow and weighted-majority based algorithms: results on a calendar scheduling domain. In *Proceedings of the 12th International Conference on Machine Learning* (pp. 64–72).

Clarke, B. S. and Barron, A. R. (1990). Information-theoretic asymptotics of Bayes methods. *IEEE Trans. Inform. Theory* IT-36:453–471.

Cohen, W. and Singer, Y. (1996). Context-sensitive learning methods for test categorization. In *SIGIR '96* (pp. 307–315).

Freund, Y., Schapire, R., Singer, Y., and Warmuth, M. (1997). Using and combining predictors that specialize. In *Proceedings of the Twenty-Ninth Annual ACM Symposium on the Theory of Computing* (pp. 334–343).

Gelfand, A. E. and Smith, A. F. M. (1990). Sampling-based approach to calculating marginal densities. *J. Am. Statist. Assoc.* 85:398–409.

Geman, S. and Geman, D. (1984). Stochastic relaxation, Gibbs distributions, and the Bayes restoration of images. *IEEE Trans. on Pattern Analysis and Machine Intelligence* PAMI-6:721–741.

Hastings, W. K. (1970). Monte Carlo sampling method using Markov chains and their applications. *Biometrika* 57:97–109.

Haussler, D., Kivinen, J., and Warmuth, M. (1998). Sequential prediction of individual sequences under general loss functions. *IEEE Transactions on Information Theory* 44(5):1906–1925.

Haussler, D., Kivinen, J., and Warmuth, M. (1995). Tight worst-case loss bounds for predicting with expert advice. *Computational Learning Theory: Second European Conference, EuroCOLT'95* (pp. 69–83). Springer.

Helmbold, D., Littlestone, N., and Long, P. (1992). Apple tasting and nearly one-sided learning. *Proceedings of the 33rd Symposium on the Foundations of Comp. Sci.* (pp. 493–502).

Herbster, M. and Warmuth, M. (1998). Tracking the best expert. *Machine Learning* 32:151–178.

Herrnstein, R. (1990). Rational choice theory. *American Psychologist* 45(3): 356–367.

Hiraoka, K. and Amari, S. (1998). Strategy under the unknown stochastic environment: The nonparametric Lob-Pass problem. *Algorithmica* 22:138–156.

Kearns, M. and Seung, H. S. (1993). Learning from a population of hypotheses. *Proceedings of the Sixth Annual ACM Conference of Computational Learning Theory* (pp. 101–110). ACM Press.

Kilian, J., Lang, K. and Pearlmutter, B. (1994). Playing the matching-shoulders Lob-Pass game with logarithmic regret. *Proceedings of the Seventh Annual ACM Workshop on Computational Learning Theory* (pp. 159–164).

Knuth, D. E. (1981). *The Art of Computer Programming vol. 2: Seminumerical Algorithms*, 2nd ed. Reading MA: Addison-Wesley.

Littlestone, N. (1988). Learning quickly when irrelevant attributes abound: A new linear-threshold learning algorithm. *Machine Learning* 2:285–318.

Littlestone, N. and Warmuth, M. (1994). The weighted majority algorithm. *Information and Computation* 108:212–261.

Nakamura, A. (1999). Learning specialist decision lists. *Proc. of the 12th Annual Conference on Computational Learning Theory* (pp. 215–225).

Nakamura, A., Abe, N., and Takeuchi, J. (1994). Efficient distribution-free population learning of simple concepts. *ALT'96 Algorithmic Learning Theory* (pp. 500–515). Springer.

Nummelin, E. (1984). *General irreducible Markov chains and non-negative operators*. Cambridge: Cambridge University Press.

Pollard, D. (1984). *Convergence of stochastic processes*. Springer Verlag.

Resnick, P., Iacovou, N., Suchak, M., Bergstom, P., and Riedl, J. (1994). GroupLens: An open architecture for collaborative filtering of netnews. *Proc. of CSCW* (pp. 175–186).

Rissanen, J. (1987). Stochastic complexity. *J. Roy. Statis. Soc. B.* 49(3):223–239, 252–265.

Rosenthal, J. (1993). Rates of convergence for Gibbs sampling for variance component models. Technical report no. 9322, Dept. of Statistics, Univ. of Toronto.

Simon, H. (1995). Learning decision lists and trees with equivalence-queries. *Proceedings of the 2nd European Conference on Computational Learning Theory* (pp. 322–336).

Sinclair, A. (1993). *Algorithms for Random Generation & Counting: A Markov Chain Approach*. Birkhauser.

Takeuchi, J. Abe, N., and Amari, S. (2000). The Lob-Pass problem. *Journal of Computer and System Sciences* 61(3):523–557.

Tanner, M. A. and Wong, H. W. (1987). The calculation of posterior distributions by data augmentation. *Jr. American Statist. Assoc.* 82:528–550.

Vovk, V. G. (1990). Aggregating strategies. *Proceedings of the Third Annual Workshop on Computational Learning Theory* (pp. 371–386). Morgan Kaufmann.

Wasan, M. (1969). *Stochastic Approximation*. Cambridge: Cambridge University Press.

Yamanishi, K. (1996). A randomized approximation of the MDL for stochastic models with hidden variables. *Proceedings of the Ninth Annual Conference on Computational Learning Theory* (pp. 99–109). ACM Press.

Yamanishi, K. (1997). Distributed cooperative Bayesian learning strategies. *Proceedings of the Tenth Annual Conference on Computational Learning Theory* (pp. 250–262). ACM Press.

Yamanishi, K. (1998). A decision-theoretic extension of stochastic complexity and its approximation to learning. *IEEE Trans. Information Theory* 44(4):1424–1439.

Yamanishi, K. (1998). Minimax relative loss analysis for sequential prediction algorithms using parametric hypotheses. *Proceedings of the Eleventh Annual Conference on Computational Learning Theory* (pp. 32–43). ACM Press.

V

Computing with Large Random Patterns

RWC Theoretical Foundation SICS Laboratory
Swedish Institute of Computer Science

PENTTI KANERVA, GUNNAR SJÖDIN, JAN KRISTOFERSON,
ROLAND KARLSSON, BJÖRN LEVIN, ANDERS HOLST, JUSSI KARLGREN,
AND MAGNUS SAHLGREN

In this chapter we discuss a style of computing that differs from traditional numeric and symbolic computing and is suited for modeling neural networks. We focus on one aspect of "neurocomputing," namely, computing with large random patterns, or high-dimensional random vectors, and ask what kind of computing they perform and whether they can help us understand how the brain processes information and how the mind works.

The human mind remains a deep mystery to science. The issues are far-ranging, from philosophy to biology to engineering to everything human. It is not even obvious how is is possible to understand the mind scientifically, because understanding is itself a product of the mind—it presupposes a mind. However, we will not dwell here on the philosophical issues but simply assume that mind is a proper object of scientific investigation when understood in terms of the workings of the brain. More generally, the human mind is to be understood in terms of a nervous system that controls the body and is controlled by it, in an environment that includes many others of its kind, because that is the setting in which the mind has come into existence. We are therefore interested in

Foundations of Real-World Intelligence.
Yoshinori Uesaka et al. (eds.).

mechanisms that produce lifelike behavior, and we associate mind with the internal states of those mechanisms. Although the mechanisms are material, the task is to understand them in the abstract, i.e. in terms of their states.

The study of machines with states is part of the science of computing. The abstract model of traditional computing is the Turing Machine, consisting of a finite automaton with unlimited tape—the tape is a kind of working memory. A Turing Machine is defined completely by the initial contents of its tape together with a state-transition table that gives the output symbol, tape motion, and the next state as a function of the current state and input symbol.

The most compelling result of the Turing Machine concerns universality. It is not difficult to describe a Universal Turing Machine, i.e. one that can perform the function of any other Turing Machine. This involves encoding the state-transition table of one machine onto the tape of the other, the universal machine. The computer term for this is "emulation." Just about any computer can be made into a universal emulator, one that can emulate any other computer.

Some unfortunate conclusions have been drawn from this universality of computers: first that the brain cannot be more than a Universal Turing Machine; then that it too can be emulated by the universal emulator; and finally that our computers can do anything that a brain can. What this line of reasoning overlooks is that the brain must work in real time, whereas a Turing Machine needs only to accomplish its computations in a finite time. Therefore the Turing Machine is too abstract a model for brain's computing; it hardly helps us understand information precessing by the nervous system.

To highlight the essential abstractness of the Turing Machine, note that its definition is not at all concerned with the construction of the machine. It matters only that there be distinct states and symbols, and orderly state transitions based on them. In computing practice as well as in nervous systems, however, the actual mechanisms are crucial, for they constrain what can be done in a given time. Therefore, in trying to understand brains in computing terms, we are deeply concerned with their construction and must look at them with the eye of a computer engineer.

Construction, too, can be addressed at many levels. Most concrete is material construction. With brains this falls in the domain of neuroscience, and with computers in the domains of materials science and electronics. However, if the goal is to build computers with brainlike powers, the primary task is to understand the computing principles involved, which means understanding brains in terms of mathematical models that allow the principles to be studied and tested.

When we describe a task for a computer, it is done in terms of functions, variables, and values. In the computer these are realized by *circuits*, and there are different kinds of circuits for different functions. Although the circuits are built of more basic electronic components, a computer-design engineer is concerned primarily with the circuits and only secondarily with the components. In other words, circuits are the lowest level for describing what a computer does, i.e. describing in computationally meaningful terms the computing task being performed. This suggests that brains, too, should be viewed at the circuit level in interpreting what they do, and that the meaningful states are the states of the circuits. Individual neurons make up the circuits, but in themselves they have very little meaning for understanding the mind.

The term neural circuit can be understood in several ways. Here we mean a circuit made of many essentially similar components, either neurons or mini-circuits, that operate in parallel and provide input to other circuits over large numbers of axons. Another common use of the term "neural circuit" describes situations like this: Excitatory neuron of type A is connected to neurons of type B and C that inhibit each other, and C also inhibits A. For us, this would be a component of a circuit, essential for its working but meaningless otherwise, and hence we call it a "mini-circuit."

Circuits in the brain are large; they are composed of thousands or millions of neurons. Their construction follows a general plan—certain kinds of neurons make certain kinds of connections—but no two brains are alike in their details. The simplest mathematical model of the brain's architecture maps a component of a circuit to a component of a high-dimensional vector, or of a large pattern, so that the entire pattern–vector represents the state of the circuit. Information representation of this kind is called *population coding* in neuroscience and *distributed representation* in cognitive science (connectionism) and in artificial neural nets. Note also that the terms "large pattern," "high-dimensional vector," and "point of a high-dimensional space" all mean the same thing. The size of the pattern is the same as the dimensionality of the space.

The states and symbols of a Turing Machine are defined as sets without further structure, so that two states (or symbols) are either the same or different, with nothing in between. All the "know-how" is in the state-transition table (and the initial tape). Similarly for pointers, with which traditional data structures and symbolic expressions are built: any two pointers are either the same or different—there are no degrees of similarity or difference—and all the structure is encoded by chaining pointers. When the machine's states are represented by points of a high-dimensional space, however, a new possibility emerges: the computation can take advantage of the *algebraic* and *metric* properties of the space. It is this fact that makes computing with large patterns interesting and worthy of investigation and holds promise for explaining the computational powers of the brain—for making brains understandable to us.

In this chapter we use very simple spaces, starting with the binary, to illustrate the principal ideas of computing with large random patterns. Section 22 describes the binary spatter code and its use for modeling analogy. The powerful idea here is that of mapping between structures, and it relies on the algebra of the space. However, the simplest spaces have flaws that can be avoided in spaces with richer structure. Dense binary codes (with 0s and 1s equally likely) have a scaling problem that is avoided with *sparse* codes. which are explained and explored mathematically in sections 23–24. An item memory or "clean-up" memory is an essential part of any computing architecture based on large random patterns. Section 25 describes its efficient simulation on a conventional computer. The last section takes on challenges presented by language. First, sparse random vectors are used to capture meanings of words from text, and finally the ultimate challenge for brainlike computing is outlined, namely, dealing with the remarkable flexibility with which we use language.

Research into distributed representation spans several decades and is considerable. The ideas most germane to the ones presented here are Hinton's (1990) reduced representation, Smolensky's (1990) tensor-product variable binding, Pollack's (1990) recursive auto-associative memory (RAAM), Plate's (1994) holographic reduced representation (HRR), and Rachkovskij and Kussul's (2001) context-dependent thinning.

22 Analogy as a Basis of Computation
Pentti Kanerva

Analogy is a defining process of the human mind (Hofstadter, 1985; Gentner, Holyoak, and Kokinov, 2001). In this section we contrast the workings of the mind with traditional computing, particularly in dealing with analogy and language, and argue for the need for a new kind of computing that could support humanlike artificial intelligence. We then suggest that such computing can be performed with large random patterns (or high-dimensional random vectors; the words "pattern" and "vector" will be used synonymously) and describe operations on such patterns. We are led to a class of models foreseen by Hinton (1990) and pioneered by Plate (1994), called *holographic reduced representation*

(HRR). The ideas are illustrated with the simplest of such models, the binary *spatter code* (Kanerva, 1996), and several examples are worked out to show their relevance to analogy.

The human mind is unlike any computer or program we know. It is not literal, and when meaning is taken literally, the result can be funny or total nonsense. That's the humor of puns. This must mean that the human mind, although capable of being literal, is fundamentally figurative, or symbolical or analogical. How else could we judge a literal interpretation of a sentence as being at once both accurate and wrong?

The development of the human mind—our growing grasp of things—is largely the result of analogical perceiving and thinking. Some things are meaningful to us at birth or require no learning; they are mostly things necessary for survival. The rest we learn through experience. Some learning is associative, as when we learn cause and effect, and such learning prevails throughout the animal kingdom.

To follow an example, or imitate, is an advanced form of learning and is common in at least mammals and birds. It involves a basic form of analogy: The learner identifies with a role model—perceives itself as the other, makes an analogical connection or mapping between itself and the other.

Full-fledged analogy is central to human intelligence. We relate the unfamiliar to the familiar, and we see the new in terms of the old. This is most evident in language, which is thoroughly metaphorical. New and unfamiliar things are expressed and explained in familiar terms that are themselves understood not literally but figuratively. It is possible that full-fledged analogy and human language need each other, and our faculties for them may have coevolved.

Analogy is such an integral part of us that we hardly notice it or pay it its proper dues—until we try to program a computer to act in human ways, that is. AI has puzzled over the programming of humanlike behavior for nearly half a century. At first it was thought that programming computers to understand language—to translate, and the like—was just around the corner, waiting only for computers to get powerful enough. Now computers are powerful, many things have been tried and much has been learned, but the puzzle remains and we don't seem to have an idea of how to solve it. Apparently we must rethink computing and put figurative meaning and analogy at its center; we must find computing mechanisms that make these notions natural. This can be construed as designing a new kind of computer, a "cognitive computer," that is a better model of the brain than are present-day computers.

22.1 The Computer as a Brain and the Brain as a Computer

Equating computers with brains is itself an example of analogical thinking. Early computers were dubbed "electronic brains," computers have memory, and we even say that a program knows, wants, or believes so and so. Such anthropomorphizing seems natural to us and it serves a purpose. It brings a technological mystery within the realm of the familiar; we already have an idea of what the brain does, even if we don't know just how it does it, and speaking analogically expresses this.

We also talk of the brain as a computer. The appeal of doing so is that whereas the mechanisms of the brain are hidden, those of the computer are available to us; through them we might understand the brain's mechanisms. This is the principle behind Turing's imitation game in which a human interrogator tries to decide which of two respondents is human and which is a machine imitating a human. Accordingly, if we can build a machine that behaves in the same way as a natural system does, we have understood the natural system.

Analogies not only help our thinking but also channel and limit it. The computer analogy of the brain or of the mind has certainly done so, in that modeling in cognitive science and AI has been dominated by programs written for the computer, while philosophical and qualitative approaches have been looked on with suspicion.

Many things are modeled successfully on computers, such as weather, traffic flow, strength of materials and structures, industrial processes, and so forth. There are pitfalls, however, when the thing being modeled—the brain—is itself some kind of a computer. The danger is that our models begin to look like the computers they run on or the programming languages they are written in. For example, we talk of human short-term or working memory and think of the computer's active registers, or we talk of human long-term memory and think of the computer's permanent storage (RAM or disk), or we talk of the grammar of a language and think of a tree-structure or a set of rewriting rules programmed in Lisp. Of course these are analogical counterparts, but there is a danger of taking them too literally. Human memory works very differently than does computer memory, and the brain is not a Lisp machine nor the mind a logic program. Some analogical comparisons have not been at all useful in understanding how the mind works. Equating the brain with the computer's hardware and the mind with its software is an example. Finally, there is a worse danger of failing to notice what is missing in our models of the mind because it is missing or invisible in computers. To safeguard against this, we must treat the subject qualitatively: Our models may behave as we claim, but we must also ask, is that how people behave? Is that, for example, how they use language? (See sec. 26 "From Words to Understanding.")

22.2 Artificial Neural Nets as Biologically Motivated Models of Computing

The computer's and brain's architectures are very different, and it is possible that the differences account for the difficulty of programming computers to be more lifelike and less literal-minded. This has motivated the study of alternative computing architectures called (artificial) neural nets (ANN), or parallel distributed processing (PDP), or connectionist architectures. We study these alternatives hoping that an architecture more similar to the brain's should produce behavior more similar to the brain's, which is a valid analogical argument. Unfortunately it does not tell us what in the architecture matters and what is incidental, and unfortunately meaning in our neural nets is hardly more figurative than in traditional computers.

However, neural-net research has made a valuable contribution by focusing on representation. Computer theoreticians and engineers know, for example, that the representation of numbers has a major effect on circuit design. A representation that works well for addition works reasonably well also for multiplication, whereas a representation that allows very fast multiplication is useless for addition. Thus a representation is a compromise that favors some operations and hinders others.

Information in computers is stored locally, that is, in data records composed of fields. Local representation—one unit per concept—is common also in artificial neural nets. The alternative is to distribute information from many sources over shared units. This is more brainlike, at least superficially, and it has been studied and has long been used with neural nets. Distributed representation appears to be fundamental to the brain's operation, and therefore a cognitive computer should be based on it. This means we must find out how to encode information into, and how to operate with, distributed representations.

Neural-net research has shown that distributed representations are robust and support some forms of generalization: representations (patterns) that are similar on the surface—close according to some metric—are treated similarly, for example as belonging to the same or similar classes. Distributed representations are also suitable for learning from examples. This type of learning takes place by statistical averaging or clustering of representations (self-organizing). It is not very creative but it can be subtle and lifelike, which makes it cognitively interesting. It can produce behavior that looks like rule-following although the system has no explicit rules, as Rumelhart and McClelland (1986) demonstrated with the learning of the past tense of English verbs. This is a significant discovery, in that it demonstrates a principle that apparently governs the working of the mind in general and thus should govern the working of a cognitive computer. What we see and describe as rule-following is an emergent phenomenon that reflects an underlying mechanism; however, the rules need not produce the behavior even if they do accurately describe it.

22.3   Description vs. Explanation

The distinction between the description and explanation of behavior is so central that I will highlight it with an example. Consider heredity. Long before the genetic mechanisms of heredity were known, people knew about dominant and recessive traits and had figured out the basic laws of inheritance. For example, a plant species may come in three varieties, with white, pink, or red flowers, and cross-pollinating the white with the red always produces pink flowers. The specific rule is that all of the first generation is pink, and when pink-flowered plans are crossed with each other, one-fourth of the offspring is white, one-fourth red, and half pink. So we can say that the inheritance follows this rule. But no mechanism in the reproductive system keeps counting offspring to make sure that the proportions come out right, as if to say: "I have made so and so many white flowers, so it's time to make the same number of red flowers." It is not the rule that makes the proportions come out in a certain way; rather, the proportions are an outward reflection of the mechanism that passes traits from one generation to the next. It is significant, however, that long before chromosomes or genes or RNA and DNA were discovered, people speculated correctly about a hereditary mechanism that would produce offspring in those proportions. Clearly, the laws provided a useful description of the behavior, and accurate description can lead to discovery and explanation.

The situation is similar with regard to language and to mental functions at large. For example, we attribute the patterns of a language to its grammar and we devise sets of rules by which the grammar works. However, it is not the grammar that generates sentences in us when we speak or write. The regularities captured in the grammar are an outward expression of our underlying mechanisms for language—the grammar is an emergent phenomenon. This distinction is easily lost when we produce language output with computers, for there we actually use the grammar to generate sentences, and we work hard to develop a comprehensive grammar for a language. And when we think of the computer as a model of the brain and use computers to model mental functions, we tacitly assume that the brain uses grammatical rules to generate language. Formal logic as a model of thinking can be criticized on similar grounds: It may describe rational thought but it does not explain rational thought. If taken in the right spirit, however, a proper description of thinking and language can help us discover the underlying mechanisms.

22.4 The Brain as a Computer for Modeling the World, and Our Model of the Brain's Computing

It is useful to think of the brain as a computer if we make the analogy between the two sufficiently abstract. But what in computers should we look at? Executing a sequence of programmed instructions for manipulating pieces of data stored in memory seems like an overly specified model of how the brain or the mind works. A more useful analogy is made at the level of computers as state machines, the states being realized as configurations of matter, or patterns in some physical medium. Mental states and subjective experience then correspond to—or are caused by—physical states so that when a physical state repeats, the corresponding subjective experience repeats. Thus the patterns that define the states are the objective counterpart of subjective experience. Our senses are the primary source of the patterns, and our built-in faculties for pleasure and pain give primary meaning to some of them. Brains are wired for rich feedback, and when the feedback works in such a way that an experience created by the senses—i.e. a succession of states—can later be created internally, we have the basis for learning. With learning, rich networks of meaningful states can be built.

The evolutionary function of this "computer" is to make the world predictable: The brain models the world as the world is presented to it by our senses. We are immersed in data received through multiple senses, and the sensory data defines our world, except that the real world cannot be fully sensed by any individual. Therefore, from the individual's point of view the world is *open-ended*.

Peripheral processing of sensory data is highly specialized data reduction refined by millions of years of evolution. Even with the reduction, the amount of data that we process further is huge compared to what we usually give our computer programs, and it is more like raw input than meaningful information or interpreted symbols. For example, our eyes do not pass letters and words on to the brain; rather, they pass patterns that the brain can interpret as letters and words.

Much of our sensory data is about the external environment, but an important part is internal. This internal component tells of our welfare, and its meaning is built in by evolution. We know at birth that pain is painful and should be avoided.

In addition to sensors, we interact with the environment with motors that allow us to move and to affect the environment. The brain generates activity patterns in the motor neurons, and thus, computationally, the connection to the environment is in terms of activity *patters* over very large arrays of sensory and motor neurons. The function of the brain is to convert sensory patterns into motor patterns that promote the individual's welfare, which the brain measures by the internal sensory patterns with built-in meanings. This, then, is the computational setting for the development of human intelligence.

22.5 Pattern Space of Representations

Modeling the brain's computations in minute detail is neither possible nor necessary, because no two brains are identical. Instead, a model should capture some fundamental principle and allow it to be tested. The modeling itself is abstract, but when it corresponds to plausible neural mechanisms it can lead to an understanding of real brains and to the ability to build practical systems that employ the brain's processing principles.

The representation of information used in the model—that is, the entities or items with which the model computes—must reflect the brain's structures and mechanisms for collecting, combining, and transforming sensory data. This is overlooked in traditional AI, where the data structures are not correlated with brainlike mechanisms, and it has even been claimed that such correlating is wholly unnecessary (Fodor and Pylyshyn, 1988). In contrast, low-level representation—the physical configurations that carry the information—plays a central role in our modeling. It is governed by two ideas.

1. The representation is *uniform*: All things are represented by points of the same mathematical space, be they objects, properties, relations, functions, roles, fillers, composed structures, mappings of structures, and so on.

2. *Meaning* is internal and it *follows form*: Points close by in the representation space mean similar things—semantics cannot be separated from syntax.

This contrasts with traditional numeric and symbolic computing, which is mostly syntactic and takes meaning as supplied from the outside (the exception is some robots, where we are beginning to see examples of a system's own internal meaning).

A vector space is a particularly simple mathematical model that can satisfy the above two conditions, provided that its dimensionality N is high enough, say, several to ten thousands. Real vectors have been used for this kind of modeling by Plate (1994) and by Gayler and Wales

(1998); complex vectors have been used by Plate (1994) as well. The high dimensionality is more important than the nature of the dimensions, so that good modeling is possible even with binary dimensions (Kanerva, 1996; Rachkovskij and Kussul, 2001). Since the information capacity of one such binary vector is roughly equivalent to a page of text, every step of a computation can be thought of as turning a page.

We think of the system as attending to one N-dimensional pattern (N-vector) at a time and call it the system's attentional *focus* (Kanerva, 1988). The focus combines information from all the senses and for all the motors. Obviously it is possible to represent one thing very precisely in the focus, or to represent many things at once, each of them less precisely.

In traditional computing, a computer word or a database record is divided into fields that represent the parts of a whole that should be considered simultaneously and that make up a higher-level unit or concept. For example, a person could be identified by five attributes, name, sex, age, height, and marital status, so that the record would have these five fields. However, such fields are hard to justify in a brainlike computer, and therefore we make do without fields altogether. Instead, we combine N-vectors for the attributes into a single N-vector for their combination. This results in *distributed representation*, also called *holographic* or *holistic*. Operations on N-vectors for composing, decomposing, and mapping of representations are discussed next.

22.5.1 Operations and Their Algebra

We will write N-vectors (N-component patterns) in boldface letters and scalar quantities in italics. Thus v_n is the nth component of the N-vector $\mathbf{v}$. For matrixes we use bold uppercase Greek letters (e.g. $\mathbf{\Gamma}$). Specific examples of operations are given for binary vectors.

Computers have built-in operations (machine instructions) for combining and transforming data: for adding, subtracting, multiplying, and dividing two numbers, and for negating and shifting bits of a binary word, bitwise Boolean AND, OR, and XOR of two binary words, testing for a 0, and a few others. Similar operations are needed for computing with large patterns (with N-vectors). The following ones have been used for representing structure and for mapping of representations:

Unary Operations. A single pattern is transformed by scalar multiplication ($\mathbf{v} = k\mathbf{x}$, i.e. $v_n = kx_n$) without losing information, and it is transformed more generally by matrix multiplication ($\mathbf{v} = \mathbf{\Gamma}\mathbf{x}$) with or without information loss, depending on the matrix $\mathbf{\Gamma}$. By "without information loss" we mean that the operation is invertible.

Unary operations on binary patterns include complementing and permuting of coordinates ($\mathbf{v} = \neg\mathbf{x}$ and $\mathbf{v} = \Pi\mathbf{x}$ where Π is a permutation matrix) without loss of information, and more generally multiplying with a matrix followed by thresholding ($\mathbf{v} = \langle\Gamma\mathbf{x}\rangle$), with loss of information.

Binary Operations. Two patterns are combined by coordinate-wise addition ($\mathbf{v} = \mathbf{x} + \mathbf{y}$) without loss of information, coordinate-wise multiplication ($v_n = x_n y_n$) with possible information loss, and more generally by compressing their outer-product matrix $\mathbf{x}\mathbf{y}^\mathsf{T}$ into an N-vector (notated with $\mathbf{v} = \mathbf{x} * \mathbf{y}$) with information loss.

The commonly used operations on binary patterns are coordinate-wise AND, OR, and Exclusive-OR ($\mathbf{v} = \mathbf{x} \wedge \mathbf{y}$, $\mathbf{v} = \mathbf{x} \vee \mathbf{y}$, and $\mathbf{v} = \mathbf{x} \otimes \mathbf{y}$), the first two of which lose information.

Ternary and Higher Operations. Three or more patterns are combined by coordinate-wise addition, possibly followed by scaling,

$$\mathbf{v} = \langle\mathbf{x} + \mathbf{y} + \cdots + \mathbf{z}\rangle$$

with information loss. This same notation also is used for the thresholded sum of binary patterns.

The algebraic properties of these operations govern composition and decomposition. *Distributivity* is important and it will be demonstrated below.

Typical of some operations is that they lose information, so that computing with them gives approximate results and iterated computing diverges. To counter the tendency to diverge, clean-up is required. We can think of it as being done by an *item memory* or a *clean-up memory* that stores all valid patterns—ones that the system knows—and retrieves the best-matching known pattern when cued with an approximate one, or retrieves nothing if the best match is no better than what results from random chance. The clean-up is reliable only if the dimensionality is in the thousands, which is the reason for requiring that the patterns be truly high-dimensional.

22.5.2 Composition and Decomposition, or Synthesis and Analysis

The following examples are based on traditional symbol processing, using roles and fillers, or variables and values, to compose information. Since it is most unlikely that the brain's computing would be organized in such a categorical fashion, we are merely demonstrating the power of these operations to combine syntax and semantics, or form and meaning, in a uniform representation. Our conjecture is that such combining is necessary if a system is to give its own internal meaning to things sensed about the environment.

We will demonstrate composition and decomposition with the very simplest of patterns—namely, patterns with binary components (binary vectors). If the variables x, y, z have values a, b, c, respectively, their conjunction

$$(x = a) \;\&\; (y = b) \;\&\; (z = c)$$

can be encoded as follows. First, the three variables and the three values are represented by independent random 10,000-bit vectors $\mathbf{x}, \mathbf{y}, \mathbf{z}, \mathbf{a}, \mathbf{b}, \mathbf{c}$, with independent and identically distributed components that are 1s with probability $1/2$ (the vectors are *dense*). The conjunction can then be encoded by the 10,000-bit vector sum

$$\mathbf{s} = \mathbf{x} \otimes \mathbf{a} + \mathbf{y} \otimes \mathbf{b} + \mathbf{z} \otimes \mathbf{c}$$

thresholded at 1.5: $\mathbf{v} = \langle \mathbf{s} \rangle$. This shows two levels of composition. One operation (XOR) is used to associate or *bind* each variable to a value, and another operation (normalized sum) is used to *merge* the three bound pairs into a single vector. Merging has also been called "super(im)posing," "bundling," and "chunking."

The following algebraic properties allow a composed pattern to be analyzed or decoded into its constituents:

1. binding is invertible (at least approximately) and the inverse is called the "unbinding" operator;

2. binding and unbinding distribute over merging (at least approximately);

3. the binding of two patterns produces a pattern that is *dissimilar* to both; and

4. the merging of patterns produces a pattern that is *similar* to the merged patterns.

The XOR is its own inverse so that given the bound pair $\mathbf{u} = \mathbf{x} \otimes \mathbf{a}$, XORing it with either yields the other; for example, $\mathbf{x} \otimes \mathbf{u} = \mathbf{x} \otimes (\mathbf{x} \otimes \mathbf{a})$ $= (\mathbf{x} \otimes \mathbf{x}) \otimes \mathbf{a} = \mathbf{a}$ finds the pattern to which $\mathbf{x}$ is bound in $\mathbf{v}$ (it finds the value of x in $\mathbf{u}$).

Decoding the composed pattern $\mathbf{v} = \langle \mathbf{x} \otimes \mathbf{a} + \mathbf{y} \otimes \mathbf{b} + \mathbf{z} \otimes \mathbf{c} \rangle$ relies on distributivity. For example, to find the value of x, we XOR $\mathbf{v}$ with $\mathbf{x}$ and get

$$\begin{aligned}
\mathbf{a}' &= \mathbf{x} \otimes \mathbf{v} \\
&= \mathbf{x} \otimes \langle \mathbf{x} \otimes \mathbf{a} + \mathbf{y} \otimes \mathbf{b} + \mathbf{z} \otimes \mathbf{c} \rangle \\
\text{(22.1)} \qquad &= \langle \mathbf{x} \otimes \mathbf{x} \otimes \mathbf{a} + \mathbf{x} \otimes \mathbf{y} \otimes \mathbf{b} + \mathbf{x} \otimes \mathbf{z} \otimes \mathbf{c} \rangle
\end{aligned}$$

because XOR distributes over the thresholded sum of an odd number k of Boolean variables threshold at $k/2$ (Kanerva, 1996). This reduces to

$$\mathbf{a}' = \langle \mathbf{a} + \mathbf{x} \otimes \mathbf{y} \otimes \mathbf{b} + \mathbf{x} \otimes \mathbf{z} \otimes \mathbf{c} \rangle,$$

which is similar to $\mathbf{a}$ (see item 4 above); it is also similar to $\mathbf{x} \otimes \mathbf{y} \otimes \mathbf{b}$ and to $\mathbf{x} \otimes \mathbf{z} \otimes \mathbf{c}$, but they are not stored in the item memory and thus act as random noise.

22.5.3 Holistic Mapping

Mappings between composed patterns can be done in a like manner. We will demonstrate it with a mapping vector $\mathbf{M}$ that performs multiple substitutions at once, i.e. that substitutes the values d, e, f for a, b, c, respectively: $a \rightarrow d$, $b \rightarrow e$, and $c \rightarrow f$. It is given by

$$\mathbf{M} = \langle \mathbf{a} \otimes \mathbf{d} + \mathbf{b} \otimes \mathbf{e} + \mathbf{c} \otimes \mathbf{f} \rangle,$$

and it maps the pattern $\mathbf{v}$ as follows:

$$\mathbf{v} \otimes \mathbf{M} = \mathbf{w}' \approx \mathbf{w},$$

where $\mathbf{w} = \langle \mathbf{x} \otimes \mathbf{d} + \mathbf{y} \otimes \mathbf{e} + \mathbf{z} \otimes \mathbf{f} \rangle$ represents

$$(x = d) \,\&\, (y = e) \,\&\, (z = f),$$

which is the result of the three substitutions. The derivation is an exercise in distributivity and is similar to (22.1) above:

$$
\begin{aligned}
\mathbf{v} \otimes \mathbf{M} &= \langle \mathbf{x} \otimes \mathbf{a} + \mathbf{y} \otimes \mathbf{b} + \mathbf{z} \otimes \mathbf{c} \rangle \otimes \langle \mathbf{a} \otimes \mathbf{d} + \mathbf{b} \otimes \mathbf{e} + \mathbf{c} \otimes \mathbf{f} \rangle \\
&= \langle \mathbf{x} \otimes \mathbf{a} \otimes \langle \mathbf{a} \otimes \mathbf{d} + \mathbf{b} \otimes \mathbf{e} + \mathbf{c} \otimes \mathbf{f} \rangle \\
&\quad + \mathbf{y} \otimes \mathbf{b} \otimes \langle \mathbf{a} \otimes \mathbf{d} + \mathbf{b} \otimes \mathbf{e} + \mathbf{c} \otimes \mathbf{f} \rangle \\
&\quad + \mathbf{z} \otimes \mathbf{c} \otimes \langle \mathbf{a} \otimes \mathbf{d} + \mathbf{b} \otimes \mathbf{e} + \mathbf{c} \otimes \mathbf{f} \rangle \rangle \\
&= \langle \langle \mathbf{x} \otimes \mathbf{a} \otimes \mathbf{a} \otimes \mathbf{d} + \mathbf{x} \otimes \mathbf{a} \otimes \mathbf{b} \otimes \mathbf{e} + \mathbf{x} \otimes \mathbf{a} \otimes \mathbf{c} \otimes \mathbf{f} \rangle \\
&\quad + \langle \mathbf{y} \otimes \mathbf{b} \otimes \mathbf{a} \otimes \mathbf{d} + \mathbf{y} \otimes \mathbf{b} \otimes \mathbf{b} \otimes \mathbf{e} + \mathbf{y} \otimes \mathbf{b} \otimes \mathbf{c} \otimes \mathbf{f} \rangle \\
&\quad + \langle \mathbf{z} \otimes \mathbf{c} \otimes \mathbf{a} \otimes \mathbf{d} + \mathbf{z} \otimes \mathbf{c} \otimes \mathbf{b} \otimes \mathbf{e} + \mathbf{z} \otimes \mathbf{c} \otimes \mathbf{c} \otimes \mathbf{f} \rangle \rangle \\
&= \langle \langle \mathbf{x} \otimes \mathbf{d} + \mathbf{x} \otimes \mathbf{a} \otimes \mathbf{b} \otimes \mathbf{e} + \mathbf{x} \otimes \mathbf{a} \otimes \mathbf{c} \otimes \mathbf{f} \rangle \\
&\quad + \langle \mathbf{y} \otimes \mathbf{b} \otimes \mathbf{a} \otimes \mathbf{d} + \mathbf{y} \otimes \mathbf{e} + \mathbf{y} \otimes \mathbf{b} \otimes \mathbf{c} \otimes \mathbf{f} \rangle \\
&\quad + \langle \mathbf{z} \otimes \mathbf{c} \otimes \mathbf{a} \otimes \mathbf{d} + \mathbf{z} \otimes \mathbf{c} \otimes \mathbf{b} \otimes \mathbf{e} + \mathbf{z} \otimes \mathbf{f} \rangle \rangle \\
&= \langle \langle \mathbf{x} \otimes \mathbf{d} + \text{noise}_1 + \text{noise}_2 \rangle \\
&\quad + \langle \text{noise}_3 + \mathbf{y} \otimes \mathbf{e} + \text{noise}_4 \rangle \\
&\quad + \langle \text{noise}_5 + \text{noise}_6 + \mathbf{z} \otimes \mathbf{f} \rangle \rangle \\
&= \mathbf{w}' \\
&\approx \langle \mathbf{x} \otimes \mathbf{d} + \mathbf{y} \otimes \mathbf{e} + \mathbf{z} \otimes \mathbf{f} \rangle \\
&= \mathbf{w}.
\end{aligned}
$$

(22.2)

The pattern $\mathbf{w}'$ is approximately correct; it is close enough for identifying $\mathbf{w}$ in the clean-up memory. The exact result is obtained by mapping (XORing) $\mathbf{v}$ with $\mathbf{M}_1 = \mathbf{v} \otimes \mathbf{w}$, so that $\mathbf{M}_1 \approx \mathbf{M}$. Notice that the mapping $\mathbf{M}$ performs the three substitutions simultaneously in any context, not just when the variables x, y, z are involved, and that a specific *example* of the three substitutions, such as $\mathbf{v} \to \mathbf{w}$, yields an approximate mapping $\mathbf{M}_1$ that also performs the substitutions in any context.

22.6 Simple Analogical Retrieval

Holistic mapping is a remarkable operation that has no obvious counterpart in traditional symbol processing. It is suggestive of analogy and could therefore be a mechanism for higher intelligence. The following example deals with figurative meaning and analogy. See also Eliasmith and Thagard (2001).

Let $\mathbf{F}$ be a pattern representing France: that its capital is Paris, its geographic location is Western Europe, and its monetary unit is the franc. Denote the patterns for capital, Paris, geographic location, Western Europe, money, and franc by $\mathbf{ca}$, $\mathbf{Pa}$, $\mathbf{ge}$, $\mathbf{We}$, $\mathbf{mo}$, and $\mathbf{fr}$. France is then represented by the pattern

$$\mathbf{F} = \langle \mathbf{ca} \otimes \mathbf{Pa} + \mathbf{ge} \otimes \mathbf{We} + \mathbf{mo} \otimes \mathbf{fr} \rangle.$$

Probing $\mathbf{F}$ for "the Paris of France" is done by mapping (XORing) it with $\mathbf{Pa}$. The derivation is analogous to (22.1) and it yields

$$\mathbf{F} \otimes \mathbf{Pa} = \langle \mathbf{ca} + \mathbf{ge} \otimes \mathbf{We} \otimes \mathbf{Pa} + \mathbf{mo} \otimes \mathbf{fr} \otimes \mathbf{Pa} \rangle$$

and is approximately equal to $\mathbf{ca}$:

$$\mathbf{F} \otimes \mathbf{a} \approx \mathbf{ca}.$$

Thus XORing with $\mathbf{Pa}$ has mapped $\mathbf{F}$ approximately into $\mathbf{ca}$, meaning that Paris is France's capital. Here the meaning of Paris is literal.

Much more than that can be done in a single mapping operation. Let $\mathbf{S}$ be a pattern for Sweden with capital Stockholm ($\mathbf{St}$), located in Scandinavia ($\mathbf{Sc}$), and with monetary unit krona ($\mathbf{kr}$). This information about Sweden is then represented by the pattern

$$\mathbf{S} = \langle \mathbf{ca} \otimes \mathbf{St} + \mathbf{ge} \otimes \mathbf{Sc} + \mathbf{mo} \otimes \mathbf{kr} \rangle.$$

We can now ask "What is the Paris of Sweden?" If we take the question literally and do the mapping $\mathbf{S} \otimes \mathbf{Pa}$, as above, we get nothing recognizable, so we must take Paris in a more general, figurative sense. "The Paris of France" produced a recognizable result above (i.e. approximately $\mathbf{ca}$, meaning capital), so we can use it: we can map $\mathbf{S}$ with $\mathbf{F} \otimes \mathbf{Pa}$ and get $\mathbf{S} \otimes \mathbf{F} \otimes \mathbf{Pa}$, which is recognizable as the pattern for Stockholm:

$$\mathbf{S} \otimes \mathbf{F} \otimes \mathbf{Pa} \approx \mathbf{St}.$$

The derivation is similar to (22.1). The significant thing in $\mathbf{S} \otimes \mathbf{F} \otimes \mathbf{Pa}$ is that $\mathbf{S} \otimes \mathbf{F}$ can be thought of as a *binding of two composed patterns of equal status* (Sweden and France), rather than a binding of a variable to a value, and it can also be thought of as a holistic mapping $\mathbf{M}_1$ (see sec. 22.5.3) between France and Sweden, capable of answering analogical questions of the kind "What is the Paris of Sweden?" and "What is the krona of France?"

Finally, the case of multiple substitutions as discussed in section 22.5.3 on "Holistic Mapping": What will happen to the pattern for France if we substitute Stockholm for Paris, Scandinavia for Western Europe, and krona for franc, all at once, and how is the substitution done? We create a mapping vector $\mathbf{M}$ by binding the corresponding items to each other and by merging the results:

$$\mathbf{M} = \langle \mathbf{Pa} \otimes \mathbf{St} + \mathbf{We} \otimes \mathbf{Sc} + \mathbf{fr} \otimes \mathbf{kr} \rangle.$$

Mapping the pattern for France with $\mathbf{M}$ is an example of (22.2) and yields

$$\mathbf{F} \otimes \mathbf{M} \approx \langle \mathbf{ca} \otimes \mathbf{St} + \mathbf{ge} \otimes \mathbf{Sc} + \mathbf{mo} \otimes \mathbf{kr} \rangle = \mathbf{S},$$

so that a single mapping operation composed of *multiple substitutions* changes the pattern for France to an approximate pattern for Sweden, recognizable by the clean-up memory.

22.7 Learning from Examples

We have just seen an example of a mapping vector ($\mathbf{M}$) that performs several substitutions at once. It is composed of individual substitutions (each substitution appears as a bound pair, which are then merged), and the mapping is between things that share structure (same roles, different objects). We will now do the reverse: We map between structures that share objects (same objects in two different relations). The mappings are constructed from examples, so that this demonstrates analogical inference. It is an example in miniature of the more ambitious Copycat program of Hofstadter (1984) and Mitchell (1993).

We will look at two relations, one of which implies the other: "If x is the mother of y, then x is the parent of y," represented symbolically by $m(x, y) \rightarrow p(x, y)$. We take a specific example $m(A, B)$ of the mother-of relation and compare it to the corresponding parent-of relation $p(A, B)$, to get a mapping M_1 between the two. We then use this mapping on another pair (U, V) for which the mother-of relation holds, to see whether M_1 maps $m(U, V)$ into the corresponding parent-of relation $p(U, V)$.

We encode "A is the mother of B," or $m(A, B)$, with the random N-vector $\mathbf{mAB} = \langle \mathbf{m} + \mathbf{m}_1 \otimes \mathbf{A} + \mathbf{m}_2 \otimes \mathbf{B} \rangle$, where $\mathbf{m}$ encodes (names) the relation and $\mathbf{m}_1$ and $\mathbf{m}_2$ encode its two roles. Similarly, we encode "A is the parent of B," or $p(A, B)$, with $\mathbf{pAB} = \langle \mathbf{p} + \mathbf{p}_1 \otimes \mathbf{A} + \mathbf{p}_2 \otimes \mathbf{B} \rangle$. Then

(22.3) $$\mathbf{M}_1 = \mathbf{M}_{AB} = \mathbf{mAB} \otimes \mathbf{pAB}$$

maps a specific instance of the mother-of relation into the corresponding instance of the parent-of relation, because $\mathbf{mAB} \otimes \mathbf{M}_1 = \mathbf{mAB} \otimes \mathbf{M}_{AB}$ $= \mathbf{mAB} \otimes (\mathbf{mAB} \otimes \mathbf{pAB}) = \mathbf{pAB}$.

The mapping $\mathbf{M}_{AB}$ is based on one example; so we must ask, is it possible to generalize based on only one example? When the mapping is applied to another instance $m(U, V)$ of the mother-of relation, which is encoded by $\mathbf{mUV} = \langle \mathbf{m} + \mathbf{m}_1 \otimes \mathbf{U} + \mathbf{m}_2 \otimes \mathbf{V} \rangle$, we get the pattern $\mathbf{W}$:

$$\mathbf{W} = \mathbf{mUV} \otimes \mathbf{M}_{AB}.$$

Does $\mathbf{W}$ resemble $\mathbf{pUV}$?

We will measure the similarity of patterns by their correlation ρ (i.e. by normalized covariance; $-1 \leq \rho \leq 1$). The correlations reported here are exact: They are mathematical mean values or expectations (the means are over complete sets of composed patterns—complete in the sense that they include all possible bit combinations of their component patterns, so that if the composed patterns involve a total of b "base" vectors, all patterns will be 2^b bits).

If we start with randomly selected (base) vectors $\mathbf{m}$, $\mathbf{m}_1$, $\mathbf{m}_2$, $\mathbf{p}$, $\mathbf{p}_1$, $\mathbf{p}_2$, $\mathbf{A}$, $\mathbf{B}, \ldots, \mathbf{U}$, $\mathbf{V}$ that are pairwise uncorrelated ($\rho = 0$), we observe first that $\mathbf{mAB}$ and $\mathbf{pAB}$ are uncorrelated but that $\mathbf{mAB}$ and $\mathbf{mUV}$ are correlated because they both include $\mathbf{m}$ in their composition; in fact, $\rho(\mathbf{mAB}, \mathbf{mUV}) = 0.25$ and, similarly, $\rho(\mathbf{pAB}, \mathbf{pUV}) = 0.25$. When $\mathbf{W}$ is compared to $\mathbf{pUV}$ and to other vectors, there is a tie for the best match: $\rho(\mathbf{W}, \mathbf{pUV}) = \rho(\mathbf{W}, \mathbf{pAB}) = 0.25$. All other correlations with $\mathbf{W}$ are lower: with the related (reversed) parent-of relations $\mathbf{pBA}$ and $\mathbf{pVU}$ it is 0.125, with an unrelated parent-of relation $\mathbf{pXY}$ it is 0.0625, and with $\mathbf{A}$, $\mathbf{B}, \ldots, \mathbf{U}$, $\mathbf{V}$, $\mathbf{mAB}$, and $\mathbf{mUV}$ it is 0. So based on only one example, $m(A, B) \to p(A, B)$, it cannot be decided whether $m(U, V)$ should be mapped to the original "answer" $p(A, B)$ or should generalize to $p(U, V)$.

Let us now look at generalization from three examples of the mother-of implying the parent-of relation: What is $m(U, V)$ mapped to by $\mathbf{M}_3$ that is based on $m(A, B) \to p(A, B)$, $m(B, C) \to p(B, C)$, and $m(C, D) \to p(C, D)$? This time we will use a mapping vector $\mathbf{M}_3$ that is the sum of three binary vectors,

$$\mathbf{M}_3 = \mathbf{M}_{AB} + \mathbf{M}_{BC} + \mathbf{M}_{CD},$$

where $\mathbf{M}_{AB}$ is as above and $\mathbf{M}_{BC}$ and $\mathbf{M}_{CD}$ are defined similarly. Since $\mathbf{M}_3$ itself is not binary, mapping $\mathbf{mAB}$ or $\mathbf{mUV}$ with $\mathbf{M}_3$ cannot be done with an XOR. However, we can use an equivalent system in which binary patterns are bipolar, by replacing 0s and 1s with 1s and -1s, and bitwise XOR $\otimes$ with coordinate-wise multiplication $\times$. Then the mapping can be done with multiplication, the patterns can be compared with correlation, and the results obtained with $\mathbf{M}_1$ still hold. Notice that now $\mathbf{M}_{AB} = \mathbf{mAB} \times \mathbf{pAB}$, for example (cf. eqn. (22.3)).

Mapping with $\mathbf{M}_3$ gives the following results. To check whether it works at all, consider $\mathbf{W}_{AB} = \mathbf{mAB} \times \mathbf{M}_3$. It is most similar to $\mathbf{pAB}$ ($\rho = 0.71$), as expected, because $\mathbf{M}_3$ contains $\mathbf{M}_{AB}$. Its other significant correlations are with $\mathbf{mAB}$ (0.41) and with $\mathbf{pUV}$ and $\mathbf{pVU}$ (0.18). Thus the mapping $\mathbf{M}_3$ strongly supports $m(A, B) \to p(A, B)$. It also unambiguously supports the generalization $m(U, V) \to p(U, V)$, as seen by comparing $\mathbf{W}_{UV} = \mathbf{mUV} \times \mathbf{M}_3$ with $\mathbf{pUV}$. The correlation is $\rho(\mathbf{W}_{UV}, \mathbf{pUV}) = 0.35$; the other significant correlations of $\mathbf{W}_{UV}$ are with $\mathbf{pAB}$ and $\mathbf{pVU}$ (0.18) and with $\mathbf{pBA}$ (0.15) because they all include the pattern $\mathbf{p}$ (parent-of).

To track the trend further, we look at generalization from five examples, $m(A, B) \to p(A, B), m(B, C) \to p(B, C), \ldots, m(E, F) \to p(E, F)$, giving the mapping vector

$$\mathbf{M}_5 = \mathbf{M}_{AB} + \mathbf{M}_{BC} + \mathbf{M}_{CD} + \mathbf{M}_{DE} + \mathbf{M}_{EF}.$$

Applying it to $\mathbf{mAB}$ yields $\rho(\mathbf{mAB} \times \mathbf{M}_5, \mathbf{pAB}) = 0.63$ (the other correlations are lower, as they were for $\mathbf{M}_3$), and applying it to $\mathbf{mUV}$ yields $\rho(\mathbf{mUV} \times \mathbf{M}_5, \mathbf{pUV}) = 0.40$ (again the other correlations are lower).

When the individual mappings $\mathbf{M}_{XY}$ are analyzed, each is seen to contain the three *kernel vectors* $\mathbf{m} \times \mathbf{p}$, $\mathbf{m}_1 \times \mathbf{p}_1$, and $\mathbf{m}_2 \times \mathbf{p}_2$, plus other vectors that act as noise and average out as more and more of the mappings $\mathbf{M}_{XY}$ are added together. The analysis is analogous to (22.2) and yields:

$$\begin{aligned} \mathbf{M}_{XY} &= \mathbf{mXY} \times \mathbf{pXY} \\ &= \langle \mathbf{m} + \mathbf{m}_1 \times \mathbf{X} + \mathbf{m}_2 \times \mathbf{Y} \rangle \times \langle \mathbf{p} + \mathbf{p}_1 \times \mathbf{X} + \mathbf{p}_2 \times \mathbf{Y} \rangle \\ &= \langle \langle \mathbf{m} \times \mathbf{p} + \text{noise}_0 \rangle + \langle \mathbf{m}_1 \times \mathbf{p}_1 + \text{noise}_1 \rangle \\ &\quad + \langle \mathbf{m}_2 \times \mathbf{p}_2 + \text{noise}_2 \rangle \rangle. \end{aligned}$$

The three kernel vectors are responsible for the generalization, and from them we can construct a *kernel mapping* from mother-of relation to the parent-of relation:

$$\mathbf{M}^* = \mathbf{m} \times \mathbf{p} + \mathbf{m}_1 \times \mathbf{p}_1 + \mathbf{m}_2 \times \mathbf{p}_2.$$

When it is used to map $\mathbf{mUV}$, we get a maximum correlation with $\mathbf{pUV}$, as expected, i.e. $\rho(\mathbf{mUV} \times \mathbf{M}^*, \mathbf{pUV}) = 0.43$; correlations with other parent-of relations are $\rho(\mathbf{mUV} \times \mathbf{M}^*, \mathbf{pXY}) = 0.14$ ($\mathbf{X} \neq \mathbf{U}$, $\mathbf{Y} \neq \mathbf{V}$) and 0 with everything else.

The results are summarized in figure 22.1, which relates the amount of data to the strength of inference and generalization. The data are examples or instances of the mother-of relation implying the parent-of relation, $m(x, y) \rightarrow p(x, y)$, and the task is to map either an old (fig. 22.1a) or a new (fig. 22.1b) instance of mother-of into parent-of. The data are taken into account by encoding them into the mapping vector $\mathbf{M}_k$.

Figure 22.1a shows the effect of new data on old examples. Adding examples into the mapping makes it less specific, and consequently the correlation for old inferences (i.e. with $\mathbf{pAB}$) decreases, but it decreases also for all incorrect alternatives. Figure 22.1b shows the effect of data on generalization. When the mapping is based on only one example, generalization is inconclusive ($\mathbf{mUV} \times \mathbf{M}_1$ is equally close to $\mathbf{pAB}$ and $\mathbf{pUV}$), but when it is based on three examples, generalization is clear, as $\mathbf{M}_3$ maps $\mathbf{mUV}$ much more closely to $\mathbf{pUV}$ than to any of the others. Finally, the kernel mapping $\mathbf{M}^*$ represents a very large number of examples, a limit as the number of examples approaches infinity, at which point the correct inference is the clear winner.

22.8 Toward a New Model of Computing

Analogical mapping between two information structures was first modeled with the methods of traditional symbolic processing (e.g. Gentner, 1983), and analogy appears to be fundamentally symbolical (Gentner and Markman, 1993). The simplest form of holographic reduced representation, the binary spatter code, has been used here to demonstrate it in a setting more appropriate for neural nets. Similar demonstrations have been made by Chalmers (1990) and others (e.g. Boden and Niklasson, 1995) using Pollack's (1990) RAAM, and by Plate (1994) using real-vector HRR. The lesson from such demonstrations is that certain kinds of representations and operations on them make it possible to perform symbolic tasks with distributed representations suitable for neural nets. Furthermore, when patterns are used as if they were symbols (Gayler and Wales, 1998), we do not need to configure different neural nets for different data structures. A general-purpose net that operates with such patterns is thus somewhat like a general-purpose computer that runs programs for a variety of tasks.

Our two examples use a traditional symbolic setting with roles and fillers, an operation for binding the two, and another operation for combining bound pairs (and singular identifiers) into representations for new, higher-level compound entities such as relations. The point, however, is not to develop a neural-net Lisp machine but to see what additional properties a system based on distributed representation might have, and whether they might lead to a new model of computing and to improved modeling of high-level mental functions.

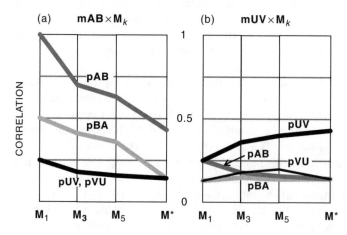

FIGURE 22.1. Leaning from example: The mappings M_k map the mother-of relation to the parent-of relation. They are computed from k specific instances or examples of **mXY** being mapped to **pXY**. Each map M_k includes the instance "**mAB** maps to **pAB**" and excludes the instance "**mUV** maps to **pUV**." The mappings are tested by mapping an "old" instance **mAB** (a) and a "new" instance **mUV** (b) of mother-of to the corresponding parent-of. The graphs show the closeness of the mapped result (its correlation ρ) to different alternatives for parent-of. The mapping M^* is a kernel map that corresponds to an infinite number of examples. Graph b shows good generalization (**mUV** is mapped closest to **pUV**) and discrimination (it is mapped much further from, e.g. **pAB**) based on only three examples (M_3). The thickness of the heavy lines corresponds to slightly more than ± 1 standard deviation around the expected correlation ρ when $N = 10,000$.

The binding and merging operators that are used to encode traditional data structures can also be used to encode mappings between structures, such as the kernel map between two relations. Furthermore, individual instances or examples of the mapping **M** are encoded with the binding operator—by binding corresponding instances of the two relations—and several such examples can be merged into an estimate of the kernel map by simply adding them together or averaging.

That the averaging of vectors for structured entities is meaningful is a consequence of the kind of representation used. It has no counterpart in traditional symbolic representation and is, in fact, one of the most exciting and tantalizing aspects of distributed representation. Another is the "holistic" mapping of structures with mapping vectors such as **M**. This type of mapping suggests the possibility of learning structured representations from examples without using explicitly encoded roles and fillers or relying on high-level rules. This would be somewhat like how humans learn. For example, children can learn to use language grammatically without explicit instruction in grammar rules, just as they pick up the sound patterns of their local dialect without being told about vowel shifts and so on. To model this kind of learning, we would still use the binding and merging operators and possibly one or two additional operators, but instead of binding the objects of a new instance to abstract roles, as was done in the examples of this section, we would bind them to the objects of an old instance—an example, or prototype—so that the example, rather than an abstract frame consisting of roles, would serve as the template. Averaging over many such examples could then produce representations from which the abstract notions of role and filler and other high-level concepts could be inferred. In essence, some traditions of AI and computational linguistics would be overturned. Instead of basing our systems on abstract structures such as grammars, we would base them on examples and would discover grammars in the representations that the system produces by virtue of its mechanisms. The rules of grammar would then reflect underlying mental mechanisms the way that the rules of heredity reflect underlying genetic mechanisms; and it is just the underlying mechanisms that interest us and that we want to understand.

Correlations obtained with HRRs tend to be low. Even the highest correlation for generalization in this section is only 0.43 and it corresponds to the kernel map (fig. 22.1b); we usually have to distinguish between two quite low correlations, such as 0.3 and 0.25. Such fine discrimination is impossible if the patterns have only a few components, but when they have several thousand, even small correlations and small differences in them are statistically significant. This explains the need for very high-dimensional patterns. For example, with $N = 10,000$, correlations have a standard deviation no greater than ±0.01, so that the difference between 0.3 and 0.25 is highly significant (more than 5 standard deviations). These statistics suggest that $N = 10,000$ allows very large systems to work reliably and that $N = 100,000$ would usually be unnecessarily large. Both high-dimensionality and randomness are essential properties of the representation, and they are what make it rather brainlike. What is appealing about large random patterns is that they have rich and subtle mathematical properties, and they lend themselves to parallel computing.

For a computer to work like the human mind, it must be extremely flexible in its use of symbols. It cannot stumble over the multiplicity of meanings that a word can have; rather, it must be able to benefit from that multiplicity. The human mind conquers the unknown by making analogies to that which is known; it understands the new in terms of the old. In so doing it creates ambiguity or, rather, it creates rich networks of mental connections and becomes robust. That is the exact opposite of how we view ambiguity in traditional computing. Our challenge then is to find the right kinds of representations, ones that allow meaningful new "symbols" to be created by simple operations on existing patterns. This is the prime motive for the study of distributed representations based on large random patterns.

23 The Sparchunk Code: A Method to Build Higher-level Structures in a Sparsely Encoded SDM[†]
GUNNAR SJÖDIN

23.1 Encoding Higher-Level Concepts

Traditionally, structured information has been represented in the form of records with fields. However, the architecture of the brain suggests that it uses distributed representations: to exaggerate somewhat, "everything" is stored "everywhere." This is the approach of Plate's (1994) holographic reduced representation (HRR) for real or complex vectors and Kanerva's (1996) spatter code for *dense* binary vectors, i.e. for vectors with approximately as many 0s as 1s. The task in these approaches is to build robust representations of higher-level concepts out of lower-level ones and then to be able to analyze the composite higher-level representation by taking it apart again into its constituents.

By abuse of language, we will in the following use "concept" to mean "representation of concept." Concepts are to be thought of as vectors with binary, real, or complex values. Suppose for instance that X_1, X_2, X_3 are three concepts, all vectors of the same length, and we want to merge them into a higher-level concept Y, also a vector of the same length. This is done with different techniques for HRR and the spatter code by forming a new vector in a robust way from the X_is. The HRR uses averaging of vectors and the spatter code uses bitwise summing followed by thresholding to yield a mean vector. Robustness here means that if we change the parts, X_i, a little the Y vector will also change just a little. The process of overlaying concepts like this will in the following be called *chunking*.

The analysis, i.e. decoding or breaking a composite concept down into its constituents, is divided into two stages. First we *probe* the compound concept to get approximations of its parts. After that we need to *clean up* these approximations to get exact copies of the constituents. For the probing the HRR uses a correlation operator (Plate, 1994), whereas the spatter code makes use of the XOR operator (Kanerva, 1996).

In this paper we are interested in binary representations, specifically in their use together with Kanerva's (1988) sparse distributed memory model (SDM). It turns out that the spatter code cannot be cleaned up using the SDM model. The problem with the clean-up arises in the following way: The $\mathbf{Y}$ probed for, e.g. $\mathbf{X}_1$, could be viewed as a noisy copy of $\mathbf{X}_1$. The relative Hamming distance will in this case be 0.25. This means that they are close in Hamming space. However, they are not close enough for us to use the probed $\mathbf{Y}$ as an address approximation of $\mathbf{X}_1$ given to an SDM memory to retrieve from this memory what we have stored in $\mathbf{X}_1$, in this case $\mathbf{X}_1$ itself.

To remedy this problem we turn our attention to *sparse codes*. A sparse pattern, used as an address to SDM, may be considered a small subset of a set equal in size to the address length. In this interpretation an occurrence of a 1 indicates membership in the small subset. We will define a chunking operation for sparse codes via *thinning, translation*, and *ORing*. This is what we will call the *sparchunk code*. Chunking two sparse subsets in this way gives a subset of the same size as the constituents and with an overlap with each of these of roughly half the size of the subsets. The probing is done with translation.

A main point of this paper is that we will be able to use a variant of the SDM model, the Jaeckel (1989b) hyperplane design, to do the clean-up for the sparchunk code. In demonstrating the feasibility of this we will also show that the *load* of the memory defined as the proportion between the number of stored patterns and the number of storage vectors can be allowed to approach infinity as the memory grows. There is no contradiction in this with information theory. The reason is that a sparseness of codes implies that the entropy of a code is low; the information given by each holder of a 0 or a 1 is very low so that the information-theoretic content supplied by the memory in a reading operation is much lower than in the case of dense codes.

23.2 The SDM Model

The Kanerva sparse distributed memory (SDM) is a memory with a set of M storage locations of U-dimensional vectors of integers. The memory is addressed within a binary address space of dimension N, where $M \ll 2^N$. For relevant literature on SDM see Jaeckel (1989a,

1989b), Kanerva (1988, 1992, 1993), Kristoferson (1995), and Sjödin (1995, 1996). When a U-dimensional binary vector $\mathbf{W}$ is stored *at* an address $\mathbf{X}$ a mechanism activates a small subset of the M locations and $\mathbf{W}$ is added by vector addition to the contents of these after first transforming 0s to -1s.

There is an interpretation of SDM as a model of the cerebellum (Kanerva, 1992). In this interpretation the storage locations correspond to the granule cells, the address is delivered to the memory via the mossy fibers, and the datum length U corresponds to the number of Purkinje cells.

In the original SDM model every location is associated with a fixed binary address chosen at random, and those locations whose associated addresses are at a sufficiently small Hamming distance from $\mathbf{X}$ are activated.

In the Jaeckel (1989a) selected-coordinate model, each location is associated with a *mask* of K selected coordinates, i.e. a set of indices between 1 and N. In the interpretation of SDM as a model for cerebellum K corresponds to the number of mossy-fiber synapses of a granule cell. Each of the selected coordinates is assigned either 0 or 1. If, for a given location, the assigned values in this mask coincide with the values of the corresponding bits of $\mathbf{X}$, the location is activated. In general an activation mechanism should have the *robustness* property: two addresses at small Hamming distances from each other should activate roughly the same set of locations.

When we later read the memory at an address $\mathbf{Y}$ close to $\mathbf{X}$, the same activation mechanism is used as when storing. In the original SDM model the sum of the activated locations is thresholded at 0 for each position in the datum; i.e. if a value is smaller than 0 it is transformed to 0 and otherwise to 1. This reading procedure can be improved considerably (Sjödin, 1995, 1996).

23.3 Nonscaling for a Constant Error Probability ε

Let $T+1$ be the number of stored data vectors (i.e. the size of the training set). The sum obtained at output position u when reading can be expressed as $S^{(u)} = L_0 B_0^{(u)} + \sum_1^T L_t B_t^{(u)}$ (Kanerva, 1993; Kristoferson, 1995). Here L_0 is the number of storage locations activated both when storing the vector $(B_0^{(u)})_{1 \leq u \leq U}$ at $\mathbf{X}$ and later when trying to recover it by reading at an address $\mathbf{Y}$ close to $\mathbf{X}$, and L_t is the number of locations activated both by $\mathbf{Y}$ and the storage operation of the vector $(B_t^{(u)})_{1 \leq u \leq U}$. We will consider one position at a time and then suppress the position indicator u. Denote the load of the memory, $\frac{T}{M}$, by τ. Throughout we will use the activation probability $p = (2\tau M^2)^{-\frac{1}{3}}$, known to be the best for reading at a correct address (Kanerva, 1993; Kristoferson, 1995). Using other activation probabilities does not change anything in principle in this paper.

We say that we have a probability of error (in the address) equal to ε if for each address coordinate the probability of $\mathbf{X}$ and $\mathbf{Y}$ having different bit values in this coordinate is ε. It is furthermore required that these errors occur independently of each other.

The usual SDM model (Kanerva, 1993) does not scale with a constant probability of error ε: if we let M and T increase while ε remains constant, the probability of error in the read word B_0 will increase and actually approach $\frac{1}{2}$ for each position. In other words, the result will be just noise. This is true for both the basic model and the Jaeckel model.

Let us consider the Jaeckel model with mask lengths K. Consider a location activated by $\mathbf{X}$. To be activated also by $\mathbf{Y}$ each coordinate belonging to the mask must remain unchanged. The probability for each coordinate to remain correct is $1-\varepsilon$. Thus the probability of the location to be activated by $\mathbf{Y}$ is $(1-\varepsilon)^K$, so that the expected number of locations activated by both $\mathbf{X}$ and $\mathbf{Y}$ is

$$E(L_0) = (1 - \varepsilon)^K \times (\text{number of locations activated by } \mathbf{X}).$$

This may also be expressed by saying that the signal in $S^{(u)}$ is reduced by a factor $(1 - \varepsilon)^K$. Since the noise from other storage operations is roughly the same for $\mathbf{X}$ and $\mathbf{Y}$ we conclude that

$$(23.1) \qquad \rho(\varepsilon, \tau) \quad \approx \quad (1 - \varepsilon)^K \rho(0, \tau),$$

where $\rho(\varepsilon, \tau)$ is the signal-to-noise ratio for error probability ε and load τ. Now, let M increase and keep τ constant. Then, as is easily seen (Kanerva, 1993), $\rho(0, \tau)$ will converge to $\frac{1}{\sqrt{\tau}}$, and hence, since

$$p \;=\; 2^{-K} \;=\; (2\tau M^2)^{-\frac{1}{3}},$$

equation (23.1) reduces to 0.

Consider using the SDM as a clean-up memory for chunked dense codes. Let it have the size of the cerebellum, $M = 10^{10}$, and let $\tau = 0.1$. Then we get $K = 22$. Suppose that $\mathbf{Y}$ is the result of chunking $\mathbf{X}$ with two other patterns. Then $\varepsilon = 0.25$ and

$$(1 - \varepsilon)^K = 0.75^{22} \approx \frac{1}{560},$$

so that the expected number of activated locations containing the information, i.e. those activated not only by $\mathbf{Y}$ but also by $\mathbf{X}$, is

$$\frac{1}{560} \cdot 2^{-K} M \;=\; \frac{1}{560} \cdot 2^{-22} \cdot 10^{10} \;\approx\; 4,$$

out of an expected number of totally 2384 activated locations.

We also get

$$\rho(0.25, 0.1) \approx 0.0056.$$

Thus the result will be just noise, which means that the the clean-up cannot be done in this way.

23.4 Sparse Coding

To remedy the above problem we keep K small (e.g. 3–6, as in the cerebellum) and fixed with growing M. To avoid activating too many locations, we use sparse coding, i.e. allow only addresses with a small number $a \ll N$ of 1s. We let a location be activated by the presence of 1s in the selected coordinates associated with the location. The model we then get is in fact exactly Jaeckel's (1989b) hyperplane design. The probability that an arbitrarily chosen address will activate a given location and that a randomly chosen location will be activated by a given address is

$$p = \frac{\binom{N-K}{a-K}}{\binom{N}{a}} = \frac{\binom{a}{K}}{\binom{N}{K}} = \frac{a}{N} \cdot \frac{a-1}{N-1} \cdot \ldots \cdot \frac{a-K+1}{N-K+1}$$

$$\approx \left(\frac{a}{N}\right)^K.$$

From now on we will fix K at 3. Thus the proportion $\alpha = \frac{a}{N}$ of 1s is determined by $\alpha = p^{\frac{1}{3}}$.

23.5 The Sparchunk Code

Because of the nonscaling with constant ε, the ordinary Jaeckel model and the basic Hamming-distance model of SDM are unsuitable as a clean-up memory for the (dense) spatter code in Kanerva (1996). Here we discuss another version of sparse encoding of higher-level concepts, the sparchunk code, in which

- we only use one, noncommutative and nonassociative, binary operation;
- we construct sequences rather than sets; and
- all constituents, in particular variable names, of a compound word can be found. This can be done without prior knowledge of the structure of the compound word or of the names of the occurring variables.

In the following, we consider a sparse address $\mathbf{X}$ to be a subset of the integers between 0 and $N-1$ (inclusive), corresponding to the indices where $\mathbf{X}$ has 1s. Let the desired size of an address be a. Construct a *thinning* mechanism $\mathbf{X} \to \mathbf{X}'$, where $\mathbf{X}'$ has b elements. The size b is chosen such that if $\mathbf{X}$ and $\mathbf{Y}$ are unrelated the expected size of $\mathbf{X}' \cup \mathbf{Y}'$ is a, i.e.

$$\left(1 - \frac{b}{N}\right)^2 = 1 - \frac{a}{N},$$

which gives

(23.2)
$$b = \frac{a}{1 + \sqrt{1 - \frac{a}{N}}},$$

so that $b \approx \frac{a}{2}$ for small $\frac{a}{N}$, i.e. for a sparse address. Of course b has to be approximated to a natural number. For $\mathbf{X} = (x_0, \ldots, x_{N-1})$, let $\chi_r(\mathbf{X}) = (x_{-r}, \ldots, x_{N-1-r})$, where the indices of the variables are calculated mod N. Now define the *chunking* operation $*$ as

$$\mathbf{X} * \mathbf{Y} = \chi_1(\mathbf{X}') \cup \chi_2(\mathbf{Y}').$$

Note that $\chi_{-1}(\mathbf{X} * \mathbf{Y})$ is close to $\mathbf{X}$ but not to $\mathbf{Y}$, whereas $\chi_{-2}(\mathbf{X} * \mathbf{Y})$ is close to $\mathbf{Y}$ but not to $\mathbf{X}$. In fact, the proportional overlap between $\mathbf{X}$ and $\mathbf{X} * \mathbf{Y}$ is at least $\frac{b}{a} > \frac{1}{2}$. Multiple chunking will be replaced by

$$\mathbf{X}_1 * (\mathbf{X}_2 * (\mathbf{X}_3 * (\ldots * \mathbf{X}_n)) \ldots).$$

We can now build arbitrary recursive structures like

$$f_0(f_1(a_1, \ldots, a_{n_1}), \ldots, f_m(a_1, \ldots, a_{n_m})),$$

where the f_is are the first items in the chunked words. The chunking operator is robust provided that the thinning operator is; i.e. if $\mathbf{X}_1 \approx \mathbf{Y}_1$ and $\mathbf{X}_2 \approx \mathbf{Y}_2$ then $\mathbf{X}_1 * \mathbf{X}_2 \approx \mathbf{Y}_1 * \mathbf{Y}_2$.

There are many variations on this theme. The thinning mechanism could be used after the union operation. There are some drawbacks and some advantages with doing so. The thinning mechanism can be defined in a host of ways but it must remain deterministic and robust. One way of defining it is as follows. Let the desired number of 1s in $\mathbf{X}'$ be c, where $c = b$ in the situation above and $c = a$ if we do the thinning after the ORing. Let $f : \{0,1\}^N \to R$, where almost any function will do. Now define $\mathbf{X}'$ as

$$
\begin{aligned}
\mathbf{X}'(i) \;=\; &1 \quad \text{if } x_i = 1 \text{ and } f(\chi_i(\mathbf{X})) \text{ is among} \\
&\text{the } c \text{ largest } f(\chi_j(\mathbf{X}))\text{s among those } j \\
&\text{for which } x_j = 1. \text{ If there is a problem} \\
&\text{with ties, this is resolved, e.g. by letting} \\
&\text{low indices have priority.} \\
\mathbf{X}'(i) \;=\; &0 \quad \text{otherwise.}
\end{aligned}
$$

Note that

$$\chi_r(\mathbf{X})' = \chi_r(\mathbf{X}'),$$

which makes this method suitable also for the case when thinning is done after the ORing. As a simple example of how this works consider the following. Let $N = 10$ and $a = 3$ and let

$$f(x_0, \ldots, x_9) = \sum_{i=0}^{9} x_i \cdot i^2$$

$$\mathbf{X} = 0100100100$$

$$\mathbf{Y} = 1001010000.$$

Consider the case where thinning is done before ORing. The formula for b gives 1.63, which is approximated to 2. Thus $c = b = 2$. We get

$$f(\chi_1(\mathbf{X}')) = 2^2 + 5^2 + 8^2 = 93$$
$$f(\chi_4(\mathbf{X}')) = 1^2 + 5^2 + 8^2 = 90$$
$$f(\chi_7(\mathbf{X}')) = 1^2 + 4^2 + 8^2 = 81$$

and

$$f(\chi_0(\mathbf{Y}')) = 0^2 + 3^2 + 5^2 = 34$$
$$f(\chi_3(\mathbf{Y}')) = 3^2 + 6^2 + 8^2 = 109$$
$$f(\chi_5(\mathbf{Y}')) = 0^2 + 5^2 + 8^2 = 89$$

and hence

$$\mathbf{X}' = 0100100000$$

$$\mathbf{Y}' = 0001010000,$$

so that

$$\chi_1(\mathbf{X}') = 0010010000$$
$$\chi_2(\mathbf{Y}') = 0000010100$$

and

$$\mathbf{X} * \mathbf{Y} = 0010010100.$$

23.6 Clean-up of the Sparchunk Code

The problem we face is to retrieve, or "clean up," $\mathbf{X}_1$ and $\mathbf{X}_2$ from $\mathbf{X}_1 * \mathbf{X}_2$. Let the proportional overlap between the address $\mathbf{X}$ and the address $\mathbf{Y}$ be $\delta \geq \delta_0 > 0$, where δ_0 is known. In the clean-up case we have at least the overlap given by (23.2), i.e. $\delta_0 \geq \frac{1}{2}$. We will use the memory described in section 23.4 auto-associatively, i.e. $U = N$, to store the addresses $\mathbf{X}_1, \mathbf{X}_2, \ldots$ themselves. These are patterns that the system "knows about" and is expected to recall. In reading the memory, the sums L_0, L_t, and B_t are distributed as $\text{Bin}(M, \delta^3 p)$, $\text{Bin}(M, p^2)$, and $\text{Bin}(1, \alpha)$, respectively. B_0 is the value we want as the result of our reading. Let us use the threshold $A = \frac{\delta_0^3}{2} pM + p^2 MT\alpha$ for deciding whether to read a 0 or a 1. Note that $E(L_0) = \delta^3 pM \geq \delta_0^3 pM$. This threshold makes the probability of error about the same for the two cases if $\delta \approx \delta_0$.

Admittedly, the straightforward application of chunking results in clusters. There are methods to handle this problem, which we do not have the space to discuss in this paper. Thus we will assume that the stored addresses are stochastically independent.

The following theorem shows that, in contrast with the dense model, the sparse model can retrieve data with arbitrarily good exactness if we let the size of the memory grow. This is so even if we let the load to approach infinity. In the case where the load is constant ($t = 0$), the theorem says that if we let U approach infinity faster than $M^{\frac{2}{9}}$ then the retrieval becomes arbitrarily exact. Its precise formulation is given as a "convergence in probability" result, when the size of the memory grows.

Theorem 23.1. *Let* $0 \leq t < \frac{1}{4}$ *and let* $\lim_{M \to \infty} U M^{-\frac{2+t}{9}} = \infty$. *Then, for* $\tau \sim M^t$ *and a positive* ε,

$$\lim_{M \to \infty} P(\text{number of errors} > \varepsilon a) = 0.$$

The proof is given in the appendix below. Note that the methods used in Sjödin (1996) require U to be at least $\approx M^{\frac{1}{3}}$ and that in the cerebellum $U \approx M^{\frac{2}{3}}$. The above theorem directly implies that we may let $\tau \to \infty$ with M and still reach convergence in probability. In fact, τ may be allowed to grow as a positive power of M.

23.7 Summary

We have demonstrated how to form representations of higher-level composite concepts from lower-level sparse ones, keeping the same sparseness in the composite pattern. Used as patterns for the sparse SDM model (the Jaeckel hyperplane design) we get a system where this model can be used as a clean-up memory, i.e. used for finding the constituent parts of a composite pattern. With increasing memory the clean-up can be made arbitrarily exact.

23.8 Appendix

This appendix gives a proof of theorem 23.1. In order not to get too involved in technical details, the proof is given for the case where τ is constant. The general proof is analogous. First we need some general results.

23.8.1 Large Deviations

From the Tchebycheff inequality we get lemma 1 (see Durrett, 1995, p. 38).

Lemma 1. *Let S_n be any sequence of random variables, and let b_n be any sequence such that $\lim_{n\to\infty} \frac{b_n^2}{\sigma^2(S_n)} = \infty$. Then*

$$\lim_{n\to\infty} P\left(|S_n - E(S_n)| > b_n\right) = 0.$$

Lemma 2. *Let X have distribution $\mathrm{Bin}(n,p)$. Then, for any $c \geq 0$,*

$$(23.3) \qquad P\left(|X - np| > c\right) \leq 2e^{-\frac{2c^2}{n}}, \quad 0 \leq p \leq 1$$

$$(23.4) \qquad P\left(|X - np| > c\right) \leq 2e^{-\frac{c^2}{4np}}, \quad \frac{c}{n} \leq p \leq \frac{1}{4}.$$

Proof. Let $c = nb$. We may assume that $X = \sum_1^n X_i$, where the X_is are independent with distribution $\mathrm{Bin}(1,p)$. The usual Tchebycheff inequality trick in large deviation theory yields

$$P(X - np \leq -nb) \leq e^{-ng(b)}$$

where

$$g(b) = \max\left(b\zeta - \log E(e^{-\zeta(X_1-p)})\right)$$

$$= (p-b)\log\frac{p-b}{p} + (q+b)\log\frac{q+b}{q}.$$

We have

$$g(0) = g'(0) = 0$$

$$g''(b) = \frac{1}{(p-b)(q+b)}$$

$$g^{(3)}(b) \leq 0 \text{ for } b \leq \frac{p-q}{2}.$$

Thus $g''(b) \geq 4$, $g''(b) \geq \frac{1}{pq}$ if $p \geq q$, and $g''(b) \geq \frac{1}{2q}$ if $q \leq \frac{1}{4}$ and $b \leq q$. Integrating these inequalities twice and dualizing with respect to p and q gives us equations (23.3) and (23.4). $\qquad\square$

23.8.2 Proof of the Theorem in the Special Case Where τ is Constant

In reading from memory, let

$$Z^{(u)} = S^{(u)} - \theta$$

$$= L_0 B_0^{(u)} + \sum_1^T L_t B_t^{(u)} - p^2 MT\alpha - \frac{\delta_0^3 pM}{2}.$$

Note that L_0 and L_t are the same for all positions u, whereas the

$B_t^{(u)}$s are independent Bin$(1, \alpha)$-distributed variables. L_0 is Bin$(M, \delta^3 p)$-distributed and the L_ts are Bin(M, p^2)-distributed. We will suppress the position-index u. Let

$$
\begin{array}{llll}
L_t' &=& L_t & \text{if } L_t \leq 1 \\
L_t'' &=& 1 & \text{if } L_t = 2 \text{ and} \quad 0 \text{ otherwise} \\
\tilde{L}_t &=& L_t & \text{if } L_t \geq 3 \text{ and} \quad 0 \text{ otherwise}
\end{array}
$$

so that $L_t = L_t' + 2L_t'' + \tilde{L}_t$. Here L_t' is distributed as Bin$(1, Mp^2(1 - p^2)^{M-1})$ and L_t'' as Bin$(1, \binom{M}{2} p^4 (1 - p^2)^{M-2})$. The L_0 and L_ts are independent for different ts and hence so are the L_t's, L_t''s, and $\tilde{L}_t$s. Rewrite Z as follows

$$
\begin{aligned}
Z &= \sum_1^T L_t'(B_t - \alpha) + 2 \sum_1^T L_t''(B_t - \alpha) \\
&\quad + \sum_1^T \tilde{L}_t (B_t - \alpha) + \left(\sum_1^T L_t - p^2 M T \right) \alpha \\
&\quad + L_0 B_0 - \frac{\delta_0^3 p M}{2}.
\end{aligned}
$$

Let

$$
\begin{aligned}
\mathcal{A} &= \left\{ L_0 \geq \tfrac{3}{4} \delta_0^3 p M \right\} \\
&\quad \cap \left\{ \left| \sum_1^T L_t - p^2 M T \right| \alpha \leq \tfrac{1}{16} \delta_0^3 p M \right\} \\
&\quad \cap \left\{ \sum_1^T \tilde{L}_t \leq \tfrac{1}{16} \delta_0^3 p M \right\} \\
&\quad \cap \left\{ \left| \sum_1^T L_t' - p^2 M T \right| \leq \tfrac{1}{2} p^2 M T \right\} \\
&\quad \cap \left\{ \left| \sum_1^T L_t'' - \frac{1}{2} p^4 M^2 T \right| \leq \tfrac{1}{4} p^4 M^2 T \right\}.
\end{aligned}
$$

Let $\mathcal{A}'$ be the logical complement of $\mathcal{A}$. Using lemma 1, it is straightforward to show that

$$
\lim_{M \to \infty} P(\mathcal{A}') = 0.
$$

It remains to show that

$$
\lim_{M \to \infty} P(\text{number of errors} > \varepsilon a | \mathcal{A}) = 0.
$$

It is sufficient to show that $P(\text{number of errors} > \varepsilon a)$ conditioned on a setup of L_0, L_ts satisfying $\mathcal{A}$ converges to 0 uniformly in these L_0, L_ts. Thus assume that we have such a setup with fixed L_0 and L_ts. Then $\sum_1^T L_t' B_t$ is $\mathrm{Bin}(\sum_1^T L_t', \alpha)$–distributed and similarly for $\sum_1^T L_t'' B_t$. Furthermore,

$$\sum_1^T L_t'(B_t^{(u)} - \alpha) + 2\sum_1^T L_t''(B_t^{(u)} - \alpha)$$

are independent for different indices u. Regardless of whether the correct value B_0 is 0 or 1, an error can occur only if

$$Z = \sum_1^T L_t'(B_t - \alpha) + 2\sum_1^T L_t''(B_t - \alpha) \geq \frac{\delta_0^3}{8} pM.$$

The now-independent error probabilities in each position satisfy

$$P(\text{error}) \leq P\left(\left|\sum_1^T L_t'(B_t - \alpha)\right| > \frac{1}{16} pM\right)$$

$$+ P\left(\left|\sum_1^T L_t''(B_t - \alpha)\right| > \frac{1}{32} pM\right).$$

Hence, using (23.4) and (23.3) in lemma 2, we can find suitable positive constants C and D such that

$$P(\text{error}) \leq e^{-CM^{\frac{2}{9}}} + e^{-DM^{\frac{1}{3}}} \leq \frac{\varepsilon}{2}\alpha$$

for M large since $\alpha \sim M^{-\frac{2}{9}}$. So now the errors in different positions are distributed independently as $\mathrm{Bin}(1, \tilde{p}_u)$, where $\tilde{p}_u < \frac{\varepsilon\alpha}{2}$. Let X be $\mathrm{Bin}(U, \frac{\varepsilon\alpha}{2})$–distributed. By (23.4) in lemma 2,

$$P(\text{number of errors} > \varepsilon a) \leq P\left(X - \frac{\varepsilon\alpha}{2} > \frac{\varepsilon\alpha}{2}\right)$$

$$\leq e^{-\frac{\varepsilon\alpha U}{8}} \to 0$$

if $\alpha U \to \infty$, i.e. if $M^{-\frac{2}{9}} U \to \infty$. $\qquad\square$

Comment. We have implicitly assumed that the L_ts are i.i.d. binomially distributed. This is approximately true for memories with a long address length N and is assumed implicitly elsewhere in the literature. It has been indirectly verified by simulations (Manevitz and Nati, University of Haifa, personal communication).

24 Some Results on Activation and Scaling of Sparse Distributed Memory[†]

JAN KRISTOFERSON

In computing with large patterns, some operations produce approximate items that need to be "cleaned up" (i.e. identified with their exact counterparts). This is done with a clean-up memory that stores all valid vectors known to the system and retrieves the best-matching vector when activated by a noisy vector. Kanerva's sparse distributed memory (SDM) is a natural candidate for such a clean-up memory. Let us consider an SDM of Jaeckel's (1989a) selected-coordinates design. We first give a brief explanation of the concept.

An *address* is a binary string (vector) of 1s and 0s. A *datum* is a binary string (vector) of 1s and −1s. Let N be the length (dimension) of the addresses and U the length (dimension) of the data. A *hard location* is a place in the memory where data are stored. The *content* of a hard location is a U-dimensional vector of integers. The coordinates of the content vectors are called *positions*. In conventional neural-net terms, hard locations are hidden units, their input weights define the position, and their output weights define the contents. A hard location is given by a *mask* (a subset of K coordinates out of the N coordinates in the address strings) and there is one bit for each coordinate in the mask, so in total there are $\binom{N}{K}2^K$ possible hard locations. An address $\mathbf{X}$ *activates* a hard location h if all bits in $\mathbf{X}$ lying in h's mask match the corresponding bits in h. *Storing a datum at the address* $\mathbf{X}$ means adding (as a vector) the datum to the contents of all hard locations activated by $\mathbf{X}$. *Reading at the address* $\mathbf{X}$ means calculating by some method, from the contents of the hard locations activated by $\mathbf{X}$, a datum to be read at $\mathbf{X}$. Here we consider just the standard reading method: We sum the contents and choose, for each position, the reading 1 if the sum is ≥ 0, and −1 if the sum is < 0. Let M be the number of hard locations, and $p = 2^{-K}$ the *probability of activation*.[1]

24.1 Different Activation Probabilities for Writing and Reading?

There has been some debate in the literature whether it would be helpful to use different activation probabilities p and r for writing and reading in

---

[†]Copyright ©1998 IEEE. Reprinted, with permission, from A. P. Braga and T. B. Ludermir (eds.), *SBRN '98: Proceedings Vth Brazilian Symposium on Neural Networks* (Belo Horizonte, Brazil, December 1998), vol. 1, pp. 157–160. Los Alamitos, Calif.: IEEE Computer Society Press. This is a slightly revised version.

[1]The probability that a randomly chosen hard location is activated by a randomly chosen address.

the memory, respectively. In particular, it has been suggested by Kanerva (1993) that it might be reasonable to take $r > p$ in the situation where many noisy copies of each datum are written at noisy addresses.

Let us fix a model for this situation. Let us say that a binary vector **A** is ϵ-*disturbed* from another binary vector **B** if, for every bit in **A** independently, the probability of this bit being different from the corresponding bit in **B** is equal to ϵ. To begin with, assume $r \geq p$ and consider the following stochastic model.

(a) Choose randomly (and independently) the "ideal" addresses $\mathbf{X}_t$, $0 \leq t \leq T$.

(b) Choose **Y** and $\mathbf{X}_{t,k}$, $0 \leq t \leq T, 1 \leq k \leq n$ independently, with **Y** ϵ-disturbed from $\mathbf{X}_0$ and $\mathbf{X}_{t,k}$ η-disturbed from $\mathbf{X}_t$.

(c) Choose the M hard locations randomly, where each hard location is given by a mask with K bits. The writing activation is as usual, with probability $p = 2^{-K}$. For the reading activation a submask of the given (writing) mask with $L \leq K$ bits is chosen randomly for each hard location, giving the activation probability $r = 2^{-L} \geq p$.

As usual, we consider the signal-to-noise ratio ρ (see below) for a single content position. For this position, we take the following steps.

(d) Choose randomly the "ideal" datum bits B_t, $1 \leq t \leq T$. It is assumed that the B_ts are independent and also independent of all activation figures, i.e. stochastic variables ($L_{t,k,h}$ below) determined by which hard locations are activated by which addresses. The bit B_0 to be retrieved from the memory is assumed to be 1.

(e) Choose $B_{t,k}$, $0 \leq t \leq T, 1 \leq k \leq n$ randomly and independently, with $B_{t,k}$ β-disturbed from B_t. The $B_{t,k}$s will then also be independent of all activation figures. $B_{t,k}$ is written at $\mathbf{X}_{t,k}$,[2] $0 \leq t \leq T, 1 \leq k \leq n$.

Consider the stochastic variables $L_{t,k,h}$ defined thus: $L_{t,k,h} = 1$ if hard location h is activated by both **Y** and $\mathbf{X}_{t,k}$,[3] and $= 0$ otherwise. The sum read at the considered position is then

$$(24.1) \qquad Z = \sum_{t=0}^{T} \sum_{k=1}^{n} \sum_{h=1}^{M} L_{t,k,h} B_{t,k}.$$

Granted that Z is approximately normally distributed (this assumption will be discussed below), the probability of getting the wrong reading at the given position is approximately $\Phi(-\rho)$, where Φ is the standard normal distribution function and $\rho = \frac{E(Z)}{\sigma(Z)}$ (the signal-to-noise

---

[2]with activation probability p.

[3]with activation probabilities r and p, respectively.

ratio). We find (Kristoferson, 1997) that

$$(24.2) \qquad \rho^2 \approx f(p,r) = \frac{\text{num}}{\text{denom}}$$

where

$$\begin{aligned}
\text{num} &= nMpr^\gamma(1-2\beta)^2 \\
\text{denom} &= 1 + (n-1)(1-2\beta)^2 p^\lambda r^{\kappa-\lambda-\gamma} \\
&\quad + [M - 1 + (1-2\beta)^2(1-n-M)]pr^\gamma \\
&\quad + Tr^{1-\gamma}[1 + (n-1)(1-2\beta)^2 p^\lambda \\
&\quad + (M - 1 + (1-2\beta)^2(n-1)(M-1))pr],
\end{aligned}$$

where $\lambda = -\log_2[(1-\eta)^2 + \eta^2]$, $\kappa = -\log_2[(1-\epsilon)(1-\eta)^2 + \epsilon\eta^2]$ and $\gamma = -\log_2[(1-\epsilon)(1-\eta) + \epsilon\eta]$.

Now fix any value of r between 0 and 1. Then $f(p,r)$ is a function of p, where $0 < p \le r$. If we divide num and denom by p, we get a constant numerator and a denominator of the form $ap^{-1} + bp^{\lambda-1} + c$, where a, b, c are constants, a and b positive. Since $(1-\eta)^2 + \eta^2 \ge \frac{1}{2}$, we have $\lambda \le 1$, and hence this denominator is a decreasing function of p.

Thus, assuming $0 < p \le r$, we find that $p = r$ when $f(p,r)$ is maximal. Let us now consider the case where $0 < r \le p$. Then $K \le L$, and the writing masks are submasks of the reading masks. Then (see Kristoferson, 1997) we get equation (24.2) with num $= nMp^\gamma r(1-2\beta)^2$ and denom $= 1 + (n-1)(1-2\beta)^2 p^{\kappa-\gamma} + [M-1+(1-2\beta)^2(1-n-M)]p^\gamma r + Tp^{1-\gamma}[1 + (n-1)(1-2\beta)^2 p^\lambda + (M-1+(1-2\beta)^2(n-1)(M-1))pr]$.

Now fix any value of p between 0 and 1. Then $f(p,r)$ is a function of r, where $0 < r \le p$. If we divide num and denom by r, we get a constant numerator and a denominator of the form $ar^{-1} + b$, where a is a positive constant and b a constant.

Thus, assuming $0 < r \le p$, we find again that $p = r$ when $f(p,r)$ is maximal. To sum up: Approximately nothing is gained by allowing different probabilities of activation for writing and reading, and so in the rest of this paper we will use just one probability of activation $p = 2^{-K}$. Note that we have considered only Jaeckel's design of SDM and not, for instance, Kanerva's original design. However, the calculations are much more involved for the latter and, given experience with the different designs, it would be surprising if the result were not the same in all cases. Besides, Jaeckel's design, or the sparse version of it discussed below, is what is being used for further work, since it is easier to deal with in many ways and also seems to be biologically the most plausible.

Note the special case where the data are not noisy ($\beta = 0$) but each datum is stored at many noisy addresses. An example might be storing a lot of handwritten letters and then trying to identify another handwritten letter (the shape of a handwritten letter defining the address, and the name of the letter the datum).

We conclude this section by discussing the assumption that Z is approximately normally distributed. Writing $Z = \sum_t A_t$, where $A_t = \sum_{k=1}^{n} \sum_{h=1}^{M} L_{t,k,h} B_{t,k}$, we cannot claim that the A_ts are independent: An observed relatively large absolute value of a certain A_t indicates that more hard locations than expected have activated $\mathbf{Y}$, giving an increased probability for large absolute values also for the other A_ts. However, the larger the memory, the more the distribution of the number of hard locations activating $\mathbf{Y}$ is concentrated around the expected value Mr, and so the normal approximation should work for large enough memories. There are also arguments using the independence relations concerning the $L_{t,k,h}$s and $B_{t,k}$s, but we cannot go into them here. This kind of somewhat sloppy reasoning, also used in the derivation of equation (24.2) above, has been standard in the literature on SDM. It has been justified by simulations showing agreement with the theory for interesting values of the memory parameters. We plan to test the results of this paper by simulations, too.

24.2 Scaling Up the Memory

What happens to the performance of the memory, i.e. the signal-to-noise ratio ρ, when the memory gets bigger? For instance, what happens to ρ if we keep the "load" $\tau = \frac{T}{M}$ constant and let $M \to \infty$? We will consider only the case where $\eta = \beta = 0$. Putting $r = p$, $\lambda = \beta = 0$, $\kappa = \gamma = -\log_2(1 - \epsilon)$, $T = \tau M$ in equation (24.2) and simplifying, we get the following approximate equation,[4] which was already derived in Kristoferson (1995) (assuming $n = 1$):

$$(24.3) \qquad \rho^2 = \frac{Mp^{1+\gamma}}{1 - p^{1+\gamma} + \tau Mp^{1-\gamma} + \tau M^2 p^{3-\gamma}}$$

where $\gamma = -\log_2(1 - \epsilon)$.

The performance is studied in Kristoferson (1995) for different values of M and τ, always using the optimal value of p, i.e. maximizing ρ. It is shown that the optimal p satisfies the following equation:

$$(24.4) \qquad p^{3-\gamma} - \frac{\gamma}{(1-\gamma)M}p^{1-\gamma} - \frac{1+\gamma}{2(1-\gamma)\tau M^2} = 0.$$

For $\epsilon = \gamma = 0$ we get the well-known formula

$$(24.5) \qquad p = \sqrt[3]{\frac{1}{2\tau M^2}}.$$

---

[4]From now on we will approximate $M - 1$ by M without further mention.

For $\epsilon > 0$, however, only numerical methods are used in Kristoferson (1995), and no (approximate) explicit formulae for the functions $p(M, \tau)$ and $\rho(M, \tau)$ are given. Here we want to study the asymptotic behavior of p and ρ when $M \to \infty$ (with τ constant, the problem of scaling up, or with τ varying in some sensible way).[5] Then such formulae will be of interest.

To finish the case where $\epsilon = 0$, we get $\rho^2 \approx 1 \Big/ \Big[\tau \Big(1 + 3 \sqrt[3]{\frac{1}{4\tau^2 M}} \Big) \Big]$ from equations (24.3) and (24.5). Now $4\tau^2 M \gg 1$ for "normal" values of M and τ, so that

$$(24.6) \qquad \qquad \rho \approx \frac{1}{\sqrt{\tau}} \qquad \text{if } \epsilon = 0.$$

Furthermore, it is clear that for fixed τ

$$(24.7) \qquad \qquad \lim_{M \to \infty} \rho = \frac{1}{\sqrt{\tau}} \qquad \text{if } \epsilon = 0.$$

So the memory scales up when $\epsilon = 0$.

This is not the case, however, when $\epsilon > 0$, as first observed by Sjödin (1997). To prove it, consider a given $\epsilon > 0$, M and τ. Observe that

$$(24.8) \qquad \qquad \rho_\epsilon = (1 - \epsilon)^{K_\epsilon} \rho_0^* = p_\epsilon^\gamma \rho_0^* \le p_\epsilon^\gamma \rho_0,$$

where:

   p_ϵ and ρ_ϵ are the optimal values of p and ρ for the given $\epsilon > 0$, M, and τ;

   K_ϵ is the corresponding mask-length, i.e. $p_\epsilon = 2^{-K_\epsilon}$;

   ρ_0^* is the value of ρ we get if we change ϵ to 0 without changing $p = p_\epsilon$, and

   ρ_0 is the optimal value for $\epsilon = 0$, M and τ.

Now fix τ and let $M \to \infty$. Then by equation (24.4) $p_\epsilon \to 0$, and by equation (24.7) $\rho_0 \to \frac{1}{\sqrt{\tau}}$. Thus for fixed τ

$$(24.9) \qquad \qquad \lim_{M \to \infty} \rho = 0 \qquad \text{if } \epsilon > 0,$$

and the memory does not scale up.

Let us now examine in more detail how p_ϵ and ρ_ϵ depend on M and τ if $\epsilon > 0$. Substituting $p_\epsilon = \frac{k}{\sqrt{M}}$ in (24.4) and simplifying, we get

$$(24.10) \quad \phi(k) \;=\; k^{1-\gamma} \Big(k^2 - \frac{\gamma}{1-\gamma} \Big) - \frac{1+\gamma}{2(1-\gamma)\tau} M^{-\frac{\gamma+1}{2}} \;=\; 0.$$

---

[5] Observe that M shall be $\ll \binom{N}{K} 2^K$, the number of possible hard locations. This implies that N has to grow approximately like $\log M$ when $M \to \infty$.

Observe that $\phi\left(\sqrt{\frac{\gamma}{1-\gamma}}\right) < 0$. Furthermore, $\phi\left(\sqrt{\frac{1}{1-\gamma}}\right) = \left(\frac{1}{1-\gamma}\right)^{\frac{1-\gamma}{2}} - \frac{1+\gamma}{2(1-\gamma)\tau}M^{-\frac{\gamma+1}{2}} > \frac{1}{(1-\gamma)^{\frac{1-\gamma}{2}}}\left(1 - \frac{M^{-\frac{\gamma+1}{2}}}{\tau(1-\gamma)^{\frac{1+\gamma}{2}}}\right)$, which is greater than 0 if $\tau^2 M > \frac{\tau^{\frac{2\gamma}{1+\gamma}}}{1-\gamma}$.

For "normal" values of M and τ, $\tau^2 M$ is large enough for this condition to be satisfied, and then we have $\phi(k) = 0$ for some $k = k_\epsilon = k_\epsilon(M, \tau)$ between $\sqrt{\frac{\gamma}{1-\gamma}}$ and $\sqrt{\frac{1}{1-\gamma}}$, i.e.

$$(24.11) \qquad p_\epsilon = \frac{k_\epsilon}{\sqrt{M}}$$

where $0 < \sqrt{\frac{\gamma}{1-\gamma}} < k_\epsilon < \sqrt{\frac{1}{1-\gamma}}$. Substituting (24.11) in (24.3) we get, for large enough $\tau^2 M$, $\rho_\epsilon^2 \approx \frac{k_\epsilon^{2\gamma}}{(1+k_\epsilon^2)\tau M^\gamma}$. We now observe that (24.10) implies that $k_\epsilon \to \sqrt{\frac{\gamma}{1-\gamma}}$ when $\tau^2 M \to \infty$, and thus for large enough $\tau^2 M$,

$$(24.12) \qquad \rho_\epsilon \approx \frac{c_\epsilon}{\sqrt{\tau M^\gamma}},$$

where $c_\epsilon = \sqrt{\gamma^\gamma(1-\gamma)^{1-\gamma}}$ lies between $\frac{1}{\sqrt{2}}$ and 1.

This provides another proof of (24.9), and we also find the following generalization of (24.7): if $\tau = \tau_0 M^{-\gamma}$, where τ_0 is a constant, then

$$(24.13) \qquad \lim_{M \to \infty} \rho_\epsilon = \frac{c_\epsilon}{\sqrt{\tau_0}}.$$

Thus we keep the performance approximately constant when $M \to \infty$, if we take $T = \tau M$ proportional to $M^{1-\gamma}$. Values of γ around 0.5 or even higher could occur in applications of SDM; hence we would like to do better, i.e. have scaling up also for $\epsilon > 0$.

Dropping the subscript ϵ, we get $\rho \leq (1-\epsilon)^K \rho_0$ from (24.8). Recall that $p = 2^{-K}$. Since $p \to 0$ by (24.4), we have $K \to \infty$, and thus $\rho \to 0$, when $M \to \infty$, τ constant. We would like to let K be (a small) constant, but still have optimal values of p. This can be achieved by using something like Jaeckel's hyperplane design (Kanerva, 1993) with sparse addresses, as suggested by Sjödin (1997). Thus let the hard locations be defined by randomly chosen masks with a fixed number K of selected coordinates, and let the addresses be chosen randomly except that for each coordinate the probability of 1 be not $\frac{1}{2}$ as before, but some number α near 0. A hard location is activated by an address if the address has 1s in all selected coordinates. Then $p = \alpha^K$, and we assume that $\alpha = \alpha(M, \tau, \epsilon)$ is chosen so that p be optimized. Here ϵ is the probability that a bit equal to 1 in the correct address turns into 0 in the reading address (the corresponding probability for a 0 turning into 1 most likely being much lower). Let us see how this works.

We find (Kristoferson, 1995) that the stochastic variable L_t, i.e. the number of hard locations activated by both $\mathbf{Y}$ and $\mathbf{X}_t$, has the distribution $\mathrm{Bin}(M, p^2)$ for $t \geq 1$, and the distribution $\mathrm{Bin}(M, \delta p)$ for $t = 0$, where δ is the constant $(1 - \epsilon)^K$. This implies (cf. eq. 24.3)

$$(24.14) \qquad \rho^2 = \frac{M \delta p}{1 - \delta p + \frac{\tau M p}{\delta} + \frac{\tau M^2 p^3}{\delta}}.$$

By differentiation it is found that the optimal value of p is (cf. eq. 24.5)

$$(24.15) \qquad p = \sqrt[3]{\frac{\delta}{2\tau M^2}}.$$

Equations (24.14) and (24.15) imply $\rho^2 \approx \delta^2 \Big/ \left[\tau \left(1 + 3 \sqrt[3]{\frac{\delta^2}{4\tau^2 M}} \right) \right]$. Assuming $4\tau^2 M \gg 1$ we get

$$(24.16) \qquad \rho \approx \frac{\delta}{\sqrt{\tau}}$$

and, for fixed τ,

$$(24.17) \qquad \lim_{M \to \infty} \rho = \frac{\delta}{\sqrt{\tau}}.$$

So the memory scales up.[6]

We remark that the formulae (24.16) and (24.17) are not very sensitive to the value of p. They hold even if we use, e.g. $p = \sqrt[3]{\frac{1}{2\tau M^2}}$ as in Sjödin (1997).

25 A Fast Activation Mechanism for the Kanerva SDM Memory
ROLAND KARLSSON

The Kanerva sparse distributed memory (SDM; Kanerva, 1988, 1993) is a clever mechanism for storing/retrieving data in/from a memory with a huge address space. The memory addresses, also called input addresses, are N-bit vectors (N is generally large). The actual memory contains substantially fewer memory locations (called *hard locations*) than there are possible input addresses. When accessing the memory, a number of hard locations "close to" the input address are activated.

---

[6]Since M must now be $\ll \binom{N}{K} \approx \frac{N^K}{K!}$ (the number of possible hard locations), N now has to grow like $M^{\frac{1}{K}}$.

In the basic SDM, each hard location has an N-bit address, and the activation criterion is "close" according to Hamming distance (i.e. the number of mismatched address bits) between the input address and the location's address.

This paper concerns only the activation mechanism for the SDM, but briefly, the write and read operations work as follows: The contents of a hard location is a vector of integers where each integer corresponds to one bit in the input data. When writing to the memory, the data bits (from the input data vector) are added (adding -1 when the data bit is 0 and adding $+1$ when the data bit is 1) to the contents of all activated hard locations. When reading, the content vectors of the activated hard locations are summed and the sum is converted to the output data by some threshold mechanism. The key idea is that data written sufficiently "far away" (i.e. with few common activated hard locations) from the address can be considered noise that will more or less cancel out. Implementing a good threshold mechanism is somewhat involved but details can be found in Sjödin, Karlsson, and Kristoferson (1997).

Several activation mechanisms have been used, e.g. Hamming distance and the Jaeckel selected-coordinate design (Jaeckel 1989a, 1989b). The activation mechanisms have all been based on matching the input address with some "matching pattern" for each hard location. This makes the implementations impractical (except for small problems) without some massively parallel hardware support.

This paper introduces an efficient mechanism for finding the hard locations that are "close to" the input address. The proposed mechanism may be viewed as an efficient implementation of a restricted Jaeckel design. It is suitable for execution on sequential machines or machines with a moderate level of parallelism (say, tens to hundreds of processors). The implementation, apart from being much faster, yields approximately the same signal-to-noise ratio.

The rest of the paper is organized as follows. Section 25.1 describes the activation mechanism in the Jaeckel selected-coordinate design. Section 25.2 describes the activation mechanism in the new proposed design. Section 25.3 compares the performance of the Jaeckel with that of the new design. And finally section 25.4 concludes the paper.

25.1 The Jaeckel Selected-Coordinate Design

In the Jaeckel selected-coordinate design (see fig. 25.1) the activation mechanism is based on selecting an activation pattern for each hard location.

The activation pattern consists of a list of k pairs of bit-number/value. The hard location is said to be "near" the input address if the values

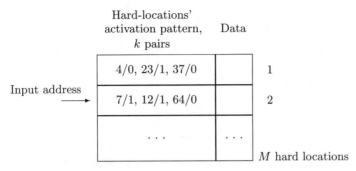

FIGURE 25.1. The Jaeckel Selected-Coordinate Design.

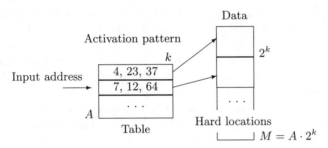

FIGURE 25.2. The new selected-coordinate design.

(of the activation bits) match exactly. In the example in figure 25.1, the first hard location is activated by an input address if the bits 4, 23, 37 in the input address have the values 0, 1, 0.

If the number of activation bits is k, the probability of activation is $p = 2^{-k}$. If the number of hard locations is M, the mean number of activations per access is $\overline{A} = M \cdot 2^{-k}$.

25.2 The New Selected-Coordinate Design

A table is used in the new selected-coordinate design (see fig. 25.2). The number of entries (A) in the table equals the number of desired activations when accessing the memory with an input address. Each entry in the table specifies a subset of k address bits. In the example in figure 25.2 the selected address bits for the first table location are 4, 23, 37. On access, the specified bits (in the input address) are used as an index to a block of 2^k hard locations. In the example this means that 3 bits in the address are used as an index to one of 8 positions in a block. The hard-location memory consists of A such blocks, and therefore the size of the hard-location memory is $M = A \cdot 2^k$.

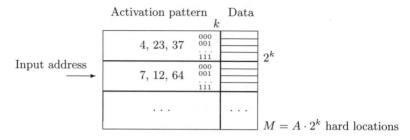

FIGURE 25.3. The new design implemented as a restricted Jaeckel design.

Compared to the earlier designs, the number of access calculations decreases by a factor 2^k. The number of bits (k) is usually in the range of 5–20, making the decrease in access time between 2 and 6 orders of magnitude.

The activation patterns in the table are substantially fewer than in the Jaeckel design (A patterns vs. M patterns). It is not a good idea to generate the activation patterns in the table at random. A bad choice of activation patterns might lead to very unsatisfactory results. To remedy this problem, a restriction is introduced for choosing bits in the activation patterns: A bit cannot be chosen if there exists any other bit that has been used fewer times. Note that this optimization is neither necessary nor used in the Jaeckel model.

The new design can be viewed as a restricted version of Jaeckel's design (see fig. 25.3), with identical (but much slower) functionality since the new design could be implemented by dividing Jaeckel's hard-location memory into A blocks each with 2^k locations, and by using in each block all combinations of 0s and 1s in a fixed subset of the address bits.

The two main advantages of the new design are (1) it is much faster and (2) the number of activations is fixed to A. The latter result is used in Sjödin, Karlsson, and Kristoferson (1997) to get better convergence. One disadvantage may be that it is less random, e.g. there may be problems with interference between the choice of activation pattern and some input data. One constraint on the basic version of the new design is that the number of hard locations is fixed to $M = A \cdot 2^k$. This can of course be remedied by not using all 2^k locations.

25.3 Results

To compare the performance of the new design with Jaeckel's design, we used an artificial benchmark. Random data patterns are written at random addresses. Then we try to retrieve those data by reading at exactly

TABLE 25.1

Retrieval Error Rates (%) for the Two Designs

Acti-		Address-bit error rate					
vations	Bits	New design			Jaeckel's design		
(A or $\overline{A}$)	(k)	0%	1%	2%	0%	1%	2%
8	10	2.6	4.6	6.8	3.6	6.0	8.4
16	9	3.5	5.4	7.6	3.7	5.6	7.7
32	8	4.7	6.5	8.4	5.2	7.0	9.0
64	7	10.3	11.9	13.8	10.0	11.9	13.8
128	6	20.0	21.6	22.7	19.8	21.4	22.9

the same input addresses or some disturbed address. Both designs were also used in a real example: trying to determine which circuit board to replace given a number of error flags.

For the artificial benchmark the tests were carried out for several sizes of hard-location memories and several numbers of stored patterns. The real example used several hard-location memory sizes. The performance of the two designs in all tests was very similar.

To get good statistics for table 25.1, we used an artificial benchmark with a small memory size. Otherwise, the execution times for the Jaeckel design become far too long. The size (M) of the hard-location memory is 8192 positions. The address and data length are both 40 bits. The number of stored patterns is 2048, or 25% of the number of hard locations. For all three runs (0, 1, 2% address-bit error rate) of the benchmark, the results for the new design and for Jaeckel's original design were comparable.

Note though that the Jaeckel results are somewhat worse for 8 activations. When the mean number of activations $\overline{A}$ is small, this is an expected result as some input addresses activate very few (sometimes even zero) hard locations. The new design always activates A hard locations.

25.4 Conclusions

A fast activation method has been found for the SDM memory. Benchmark results show that the new design has a signal-to-noise ratio comparable to that of the Jaeckel selected-coordinate design. The speed-up relative to the Jaeckel (and all older) designs is several orders of magnitude. It can be shown (Kanerva, personal communication) that the method is equivalent to the RAM-based activation of data cells in the WISARD architecture (recognition device) of Wilkie, Stonham, and Aleksander (Aleksander and Morton, 1995).

26 From Words to Understanding
JUSSI KARLGREN AND MAGNUS SAHLGREN

As was discussed in section 22, language is central to a correct understanding of the mind. Compositional analytic models perform well in the domain and subject area they are developed for, but any extension is difficult and the models have incomplete psychological veracity. Here we explore how to compute representations of meaning based on a lower level of abstraction and how to use the models for tasks that require some form of language understanding.

26.1 The Meaning of 'Meaning'

The use of vector-based models of information for the purpose of representing word meanings is an area of research that has gained considerable attention over the last decade. A number of different techniques have been suggested that demonstrate the viability of representing word meanings as semantic vectors, computed from the co-occurrence statistics of words in large text data (e.g. Deerwester et al., 1990; Schütze, 1992; Lund and Burgess, 1996). Unfortunately, the philosophical rationale for this practice has remained tacit, which is remarkable since the vector-based models purport to uncover and represent word meanings. What, one might ask, are those meanings that the words of our language apparently have? Are they perhaps some form of mental concepts that exist in the minds of language users, or are they merely the objects named by the words, and if so, how do we represent something like it in a computer system? It seems that we need to know *what* it is we want to represent before we can start thinking about *how* to represent it in a computer system. Succinctly, it seems as if the recourse to semantics demands an explanation of the meaning of 'meaning'.

Ludwig Wittgenstein suggests in *Philosophical Investigations* (1953) that we should view meaning as something founded in linguistic praxis, and that the meaning of a word is determined by the rules of its use within, as he puts it, a specific *language-game*. This suggestion led to the famous dictum "meaning is use," which is sometimes referred to as a Wittgensteinian theory of meaning. The idea is that to understand the meaning of a word, one has to consider its use in the context of ordinary and concrete language behavior. To know the meaning of a word is simply to be able to use the word in the correct way in a specific language-game or linguistic praxis. This line of reasoning thus allows us to define semantic knowledge as that which we *make use of* when successfully carrying out linguistic tasks. According to this way of thinking, meaning is the vehicle by which language travels.

Thus it is language itself and not the concept of meaning that is primary to Wittgensteinian semanticist. The question about the meaning of 'meaning' must therefore be answered "from within" a theory of language, since words do not (and in a stronger sense *cannot*) have meaning outside language. That is, it does not make any sense to ask what the meaning of a word is in isolation from its use in language, since it is only by virtue of this use that the word has meaning. The lack of rigid designations regarding the concept of meaning facilitates our understanding of language as a dynamic phenomenon. What we need in order to understand the nature of meaning is not so much a rigid definition of the concept of meaning, but rather a profound understanding of the inherent structures of natural language. In short, what we need is a structuralistic account of language.

Using such a relatively agnostic theory of meaning, we will in what follows attempt to exemplify its utility for information-access tasks, arguably the most important and applied of language-technology tasks, and one that relies crucially on some form of textual understanding.

26.2 A Case in Point: Information Access

Text is the primary repository and transmitter of human knowledge. Many other types of knowledge representation have been proposed and used for specific purposes, but for most purposes text has proven efficient, flexible, and compact for generation, storage, and access. But while accessing information in text is simple and unproblematic for a human reader, finding the right text to access may be difficult. Computer systems can be of help here, but to do this, systems must have some form of understanding of text content.

26.2.1 System View of Documents

Information-access systems view documents as carriers of topical information and hold words and terms as reasonable indicators of topic. The techniques used for analysis and organization of document collections are focused primarily on word and term occurrence statistics. Documents and information needs alike are analyzed in terms of words.

Although this simple approach has its obviously effective characteristics, it also has some drawbacks. The results provided by information-access systems of today are unimpressive: by the standard metrics defined and practiced in the field, nothing like optimal performance is delivered by any system. To some extent, this is a problem that has to do with the indeterminacy of the evaluation metrics themselves: Relevance is an ill-defined characteristic of documents. But to a great extent systems do not deliver what should and could be expected of them be-

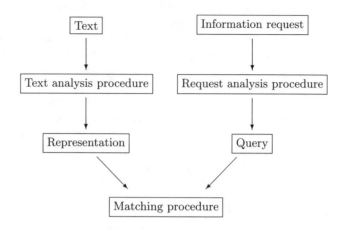

FIGURE 26.1. The standard model of information retrieval.

cause they model topic and text unsatisfactorily. Although the model is simple and designed not to rely on brittle theory, it does not reflect the underlying structure of textual information transmission sufficiently for purposes of designing useful systems for information access.

26.2.2   The Standard Model for Information Retrieval

The standard model for information retrieval and the basis for most information-system design is roughly as shown in figure 26.1. There is some body of texts; information requests are put to some system that handles this body of texts; the texts are analyzed by some procedure to yield a nontextual representation of them; the information requests are likewise analyzed by an identical or similar procedure to yield a query. The two representations are then matched. The texts with the best matches are presented as potential information sources to fulfill the request.

The point of the analysis is to facilitate matching by (1) reducing the amount of information, to make the representations manageable—it must somehow counter the variability of language and the freedom it affords language users—and (2) resolving the vagueness and indeterminacy inherent in language. The resulting representations are assumed in some way to be alinguistic and amenable to pure formal manipulation.

This quite intuitive and in many ways appealing model hides the complexity of human language use from the matching procedure, which can then be addressed using formal methods. This is not entirely to the benefit of the enterprise. The very same mechanisms that make the matching complicated—the vagueness and indeterminacy of human language—are what make human language work well as a communicative tool. Awareness of this is typically abstracted out of the search process. The major difference between using an automated information-retrieval system and consulting with a human information analyst is that the latter normally does not require the request to be transformed into some invariant and unambiguous representation; neither does the human analyst require the documents themselves to be analyzed into such a representation. A human analyst not only copes with but utilizes the flexibility of information in human language: It is not an obstacle but an asset. For nontrivial retrieval as performed by humans, concepts glide into each other painlessly and with no damage done to the knowledge representation they utilize, and documents that have previously been thought to be of some specific type or topic can be retrieved for perfectly new and unexpected purposes.

26.3 Words as Content Indicators

The basic drawback of the systems of today is their impoverished picture of text content. They treat texts as containers for words, and words as neat and useful indicators of content. But there is no exact matching from words to concepts. Words are vague, both polysemous and incomplete: every word means several things and every thing can be expressed with any one of several words. Words suffer from the combined drawback of being ambiguous and nonexclusive as indicators of content.

Any representation of content should transcend this inherent ambiguity of words—and this is how our kind of model is intended to improve matters.

26.3.1 The Distributional Hypothesis

Viewed from a structuralistic perspective, natural language may be characterized as a sequence of semantically arbitrary symbols (i.e. words). The symbols are semantically arbitrary since it is not their physical properties that determine their meaning. Rather, it is the relations between the symbols of the sequence that define them. This is to say that the meanings of the symbols in the sequence do not derive from any inherent semantic properties of the symbols.

This relational aspect of meaning can be seen if we consider a polysemous word, for example 'fly', which has a different meaning in the context of A, for example in texts referring to aerial activities, than in the context of B, for example in texts about insects. The reason the word has different meanings in these different contexts is not that it has a different inherent semantic property in the context of A than in the context of B, for that would mean that a word could change its inherent semantic properties at any time, making linguistic communication, understanding, and hence language itself virtually impossible. The reason for the different meanings of the word is rather that the context of A is different from that of B.

This characterization of natural language as a linear sequence of semantically arbitrary elements allows us to formulate a theory of meaning known as the *distributional hypothesis*. The theory originates from the work of Zellig Harris, who, in his book *Mathematical Structures of Language* (1968, p. 12), states that "the meaning of entities, and the meaning of grammatical relations among them, is related to the restriction on combinations of these entities relative to other entities."

These combinatorial restrictions can be viewed as semantic constraints that govern the distribution of entities in language. That is, if two separate entities occur in combination with the same set of other entities C, the distribution of the two separate entities are governed by the same semantic constraints that are manifested in the distributional pattern that consists in the co-occurrence with C. It is by virtue of this distributional similarity that the entities have similar meaning. This is to say that similarity in distribution implies similar values of semantic information.

The merit of this hypothesis in relation to the Wittgensteinian account of meaning is that the distributional patterns of words can be thought of as manifesting language use. That is, the use of a word is manifested by its distribution in language, which in turn is defined by the contexts in which the word occurs. This means that the context could be utilized as a measure of distribution, by which the use (and thus also the meaning) of a word could be determined. Thus, if the *meaning* of a word is determined by its *use* in language, and its use is manifested by its *distribution*, the distributional patterns as defined by the *contexts* of a word can be seen as viable tools for determining the meaning of that word.

The idea is that words are semantically similar to the extent that they share contexts. If two words w_1 and w_2, say 'beer' and 'wine', frequently occur in the same context C, say after 'drink', the hypothesis states that w_1 and w_2 are semantically related, or, stated more strongly, that they are semantically similar. The semantic similarity (or relatedness) of 'beer' and 'wine' is thus due to the similarity of usage of these words. This means that the categorization of both words as, for example, referring to alcoholic beverages is possible only because we use them in such a way; for example, after the word 'drink' and in the vicinity of the word 'drunk'. The categorization is not a *cause* of usage but a *consequence*.

In an attempt to formalize these ideas, we could say that the meaning

M of a word w is determined by its distribution D in text T. D over T can be defined as the union of the contexts C in which w occurs. Thus, if $D(w, T)$ (the distribution of w in T) determines $M(w)$ (the meaning of w), and $D(w, T)$ equals $\sum \{C \mid w \in C\}$ (the contexts in which w occurs), this can be seen as a representation of $M(w)$. This representational scheme thus justifies the claim that word meanings *can* be uncovered and represented in computer systems. It also justifies the claim that this can be done without forcing us to commit to any particular ontology about *what* these meanings are. Rather, it is because we do not demand any rigid definition of the concept of meaning that this representational scheme becomes feasible.

26.4 Latent Semantic Analysis

This representational scheme is the communal rationale for vector-based semantic analysis. The assumption that "words with similar meanings will occur with similar neighbors if enough text material is available" (Schütze and Pedersen, 1997) is central to all the various approaches. What separates them is *how* they implement the idea. The pioneering technique in this area of research, latent semantic analysis (LSA) (Landauer and Dumais, 1997), collects the text data in a words-by-documents co-occurrence matrix where each cell indicates the frequency of a given word in a given text sample of approximately 150 words. The words-by-documents matrix is normalized by using logarithms of word frequencies and entropies of words across all documents. The normalized matrix is then transformed with singular-value decomposition into a much smaller matrix. This dimension reduction appears also to accomplish inductive effects, reminiscent of human psychology, by capturing latent semantic structures in the text data. Words (or, more to the point, *concepts*) are thus represented in the reduced matrix by semantic vectors of dimensionality n (300 proving to be optimal in Landauer and Dumais's 1997 experiments).

A similar approach is taken by Schütze and Pedersen (1997), who represent the text data as a words-by-words co-occurrence matrix where each cell records the number of times that the word pair occurs in a window spanning 40 words. However, such a matrix with $v^2/2$ distinct entries, where v is the size of the vocabulary, becomes computationally intractable for large vocabularies, so they first approximate the matrix using class-based generalization in two steps and then transform it with singular-value decomposition, so that words are represented in the final reduced matrix by dense semantic vectors of dimensionality n ($n = 20$ in Schütze and Pedersen, 1997). The motivation for reducing the dimensionality of the approximated matrix with singular-value decomposition is, as in LSA, that it improves generalization and makes the representations more compact.

This kind of representational scheme where words are represented as semantic vectors that are calculated from the co-occurrence statistics of words in large text data has proven to be both computationally advantageous and cognitively justified. The drawback of singular-value decomposition is that it places heavy demands on computing time and memory, which suggests that an alternative way of achieving the inductive effects of dimension reduction might be worth considering. A number of techniques for doing so have been proposed under such names as random mapping (Kaski, 1998), random projections (Papadimitriou et al., 1998), and random indexing (Kanerva et al., 2000), and they have the same underlying mathematics.

26.5 Random Indexing

In previously reported experiments with random indexing (Kanerva et al., 2000), documents of approximately 150 words each are represented as high-dimensional random index vectors (dimensionality > 1,000) that are accumulated into a words-by-documents matrix by adding a document's index vector to the row for a given word every time the word appears in that document. The method is comparable to LSA, except that the resulting matrix is significantly smaller than the words-by-documents matrix of LSA, since the dimensionality of the index vectors is smaller than the number of documents. By comparison, assuming a vocabulary of 60,000 words in 30,000 documents, LSA would represent the data in a 60,000 × 30,000 words-by-documents matrix, whereas the matrix in random indexing would be 60,000 × 1,800 when 1,800-dimensional index vectors are used. This seems to accomplish the same inductive effects as those attained by applying singular-value decomposition to the much larger matrix, but without the heavy computational load that singular-value decomposition requires.

In the present experiment, the high-dimensional random vectors of random indexing have been used to index *words* and to accumulate a words-by-contexts matrix by means of *narrow* context windows consisting of only a few adjacent words on each side of the focus word. As an example, imagine that the number of adjacent words in the context window is set to two. This would imply a window size of five space-separated linguistic units, i.e. the focus word and the two words preceding and succeeding it. Thus the context for the word 'is' in the sentence 'This parrot is no more' is 'This parrot' and 'no more', as denoted by

[(This parrot) is (no more)].

Calculating semantic vectors using random indexing of words in narrow context windows is done in two steps. First, an n-dimensional sparse random vector called a *random label* is assigned to each word type in the text data. These labels have a small number k of randomly distributed -1s and $+1$s, with the rest set to 0. The present experiment utilized 1,800-dimensional labels with $k = 8.7$ on average, with a standard deviation of ± 2.9. Thus a label might have, for example, four -1s and six $+1$s. Next, every time a given word—the focus word f_n—occurs in the text data, the labels for the words in its context window are added to its *context vector*. For example, assuming a $2 + 2$ sized context window as represented by:

$$[(w_{n-2}w_{n-1})f_n(w_{n+1}w_{n+2})]$$

the context vector of f_n would be updated with:

$$L(w_{n-2}) + L(w_{n-1}) + L(w_{n+1}) + L(w_{n+2})$$

where $L(x)$ is the label of x. This summation has also been weighted to reflect the distance of the words to the focus word. The weights were distributed so that the words immediately preceding and succeeding the focus word get more significance in the computation of the context vectors. For the four different window sizes used in these experiments, the window slots were given weights as follows:

$1 + 1$: $[(1)\ 0\ (1)]$
$2 + 2$: $[(0.5, 1)\ 0\ (1, 0.5)]$
$3 + 3$: $[(0.25, 0.5, 1)\ 0\ (1, 0.5, 0.25)]$
$4 + 4$: $[(0.1, 0.1, 0.1, 1)\ 0\ (1, 0.1, 0.1, 0.1)]$.

The rationale for these operations is that a high-dimensional context vector, by effectively being the sum of a word's local contexts, represents the word's relative meaning. This means that we will be able to model word content with some confidence. But texts are more than words and their content.

26.6   What Is Text, from the Perspective of Linguistics?

The model described above covers much of what we want in terms of human linguistic behavior. But what we know about language and text certainly motivates a more sophisticated model than set theory on the level of word occurrences. Linguists treat linguistic expressions as being composed of words that form clauses that in turn form text or discourse. Words have predictable situation-, speaker-, and topic-*independent* structure that is described formally. Clauses have largely predictable situation-, speaker-, and topic-*independent* structure that is described formally. This is how far formal linguistic analysis takes us. Attempts at formal analysis at the next level—of text and topic structure—have been only partially successful. Texts have largely unpredictable situation-, speaker-, and topic-*dependent* structure, which cannot be handled adequately with the theoretical apparatus available to us today. Clause structure is connected only indirectly to topicality: mostly it accounts for the local organization of the clause. However, the invariant and predictable nature of clause structure certainly encourages further attempts at building theories that relate meaning to clause structure, and it would be foolish to build a text model that can take no account of recent advances in formal analysis of text structure.

26.6.1 Beyond Word Co-occurrence—Implementing Linguistics

The only property of text that is being utilized in the creation of the context vectors is the distributional patterns of linguistic entities. This comprises, however, only a small fraction of the structural complexity of large texts. There are other inherent structural relations in natural language that might be significant for uncovering semantic information. The distributional hypothesis does tell a story about the foundation of meaning, but it might not tell the *whole* story. If the overall goal of the research is to understand how meaning resides in language, and how to implement linguistic knowledge about meaning in computers, it seems unmotivated not to take these more complex linguistic features into account. Therefore, we have evaluated the method using different degrees of linguistic preprocessing of the training data, such as morphological analysis and part-of-speech tagging, with the intention of investigating whether the utilization of more sophisticated linguistic information in some way concretizes the semantic information captured in the context vectors. To ensure state-of-the art performance in linguistic analysis, we used the functional dependency grammar of English—the FDG parser— developed by Conexor to analyze the text and its words (Järvinen and Tapanainen, 1997).

26.7 The TOEFL-Test

To repeat the fundamental hypothesis of this investigation, the *raison d'être* of the high-dimensional context vectors described in above sections is that they represent the relative meaning of words, and that they therefore can be used to calculate semantic similarities between words.

We will verify this hypothesis by letting the system perform a synonym test. One such test is TOEFL (test of English as a foreign language), which is a standardized test employed, for example, by American universities to evaluate foreign applicants' knowledge of the English language. In the synonym-finding part of the test, the test taker is asked to find the synonyms to certain words. For each given word, a choice from four alternatives is provided, where one is the intended synonym and is supposed to be indicated by the person taking the test. In the present experiment, 80 test items of this type were used.

When performing the synonym test, the system simply calculates the distances (the cosine of the angle between context vectors) between the target word and the four alternatives and gives the highest-ranking alternative as its answer (i.e. the one that correlates most closely with the target word).

26.8 Experimental Set-Up

The text data used as learning material for the system was a ten-million-word corpus of unmarked English with a vocabulary of 94,000 words. In the first stage of preprocessing the number of unique word types was reduced based on frequency, by weighting the least and the most frequent words with 0 when they appeared in the context window. A frequency range of 3–14,000 was used and resulted in a vocabulary of 51,000 words. Next, a rather crude method for morphological analysis was implemented by truncating the words. The idea was to approximate word stems by simply chopping off the words at a certain predefined number of letters. In the present experiment, truncation lengths of 6, 8, 10, and 12 were used. As a comparison to the crude truncation approach to morphology, the the Conexor FDG parser was used to analyze the text initially and extract the base form of each word.

The Conexor FDG parser was also used to supply the analyzed text (the text consisting of proper word stems) with part-of-speech information in an attempt to deal with the ever-present ambiguity of languages, the problem being that the same "word" can have several meanings, and many of these orthographically identical but semantically dissimilar words belong to different parts of speech. For example, *roll* can be used as a verb or as a noun. Providing part-of-speech information by simply adding the part-of-speech tag to the beginning of each word would enable the system to detect this kind of ambiguity and to discriminate between these words. For example, the verb *roll* would become *vroll*, whereas the noun *roll* would become *nroll*.

26.9 Results and Analysis

The results of the TOEFL-test are summarized in table 26.1. The numbers in the cells are averages over five runs. The standard deviation for these results is ±1.5. All results are given in percent of correct answers to the TOEFL-test. The numbers in boldface are the results from ex-

Table 26.1

Average Results (±1.5) in Percent of Correct Answers to the TOEFL-test
Tr. means truncation length, **WS** means 'word stems', and **PoS+WS**
means 'part-of-speech tagged word stems'.

Linguistic analysis	Context window				Average (±0.73)
	1 + 1	2 + 2	3 + 3	4 + 4	
None	64.5	67.0	65.3	65.5	65.6
Tr. 6	55.0	57.5	57.3	55.3	56.3
Tr. 8	61.5	64.3	62.0	63.3	62.8
Tr. 10	66.0	68.5	66.3	66.3	66.8
Tr. 12	64.8	65.3	63.8	64.8	64.6
WS	**63.5**	**70.8**	**72.0**	**66.0**	**68.1**
PoS+WS	**66.0**	**64.5**	**65.0**	**65.5**	**65.3**
Average (±0.56)	63.0	65.4	64.5	63.8	

periments with linguistically analyzed text. By comparison, tests with LSA on the same text data, using the LSIBIN program from Telecordia Technologies, produced top scores at 600 factors of 58.75% using the unnormalized words-by-documents matrix, and 65% using a normalized one. The average result reported by Landauer and Dumais (1997) with LSA (using normalization and different text data) is 64.4%, while foreign (non-English-speaking) applicants to U.S. colleges average 64.5%.

These results indicate that high-dimensional random labeling of words in narrow context windows captures similarity relations between words just as effectively as singular-value decomposition of the words-by-documents matrix does (e.g. LSA), as measured by a standardized synonym test. Without using linguistic information, the system averages 65.6% over the four different window sizes used in these experiments. However, already when utilizing a rather naive kind of morphological analysis in the form of carefully applied truncation (using a truncation length of 10 characters), the system's average result increases to 66.8% correct, although it seems imperative not to truncate too early, since this gravely affects the results. Shortening the truncation length to eight characters decreases the result to 62.8%, and shortening it to six renders a meager 56.3%. Extending the truncation length to twelve characters also decreases the result, with a 64.6% average.

The best results were produced by proper stemming of words, which yields 68.1% correct on the average. This indicates that since the inclusion of morphology in the form of proper word-stem analysis or carefully applied truncation yields the best overall results, taking advantage of other inherent structural relations in text, in addition to the distributional patterns of linguistic entities, really might be significant for uncovering semantic information from text data. However, adding part-of-speech information did not further improve the performance. The average result when adding part-of-speech information to the morphologically analyzed text drops to 65.3%. This could be a result of the increase in the size of the vocabulary, which is the consequence of supplying part-of-speech information for each word.

Turning now to the different window sizes, the table shows that a minimal context window with just one word on each side of the focus word yields the worst average result. This might not be surprising, since it seems reasonable to assume *a priori* that a minimal context window will not provide enough contextual information for making the comparison of distributional similarity reliable. This assumption is not categorically supported by the results, however, since for the part-of-speech-tagged word stems, a 1 + 1 sized context window actually produces the best average result. The results peak in the range of two to three words on each side of the focus word, with a 2 + 2 sized context window producing the best average result of 65.4%, but with a 3 + 3 sized context window producing the best individual result of 72% using the morphologically analyzed text. A 4 + 4 sized context window is only slightly better (63.8%) than the minimal context window, and our experiments with context windows exceeding four words on each side of the focus word gave much lower scores.

26.10   Some Cognitive Implications

The results from these experiments demonstrate that the technique is capable of achieving comparatively good results on a standardized synonym test. The test is designed to measure word knowledge, which would indicate that any subject capable of performing the test with scores above the level of guessing (which statistically would yield 25% correct) possesses a certain amount of linguistic knowledge about word meanings. Therefore, the test could also be seen as a rudimentary intelligence test. Landauer et al. (1998) point out that "word-word meaning similarities are a good test of knowledge—indeed, vocabulary tests are the best single measure of human intelligence."

The results achieved in these investigations are approximately parallel to the results accomplished by foreign applicants to American universities. The question is, then, if the results, viewed from this perspective, justify the conclusion that the system has acquired and applied linguistic knowledge (about word meanings)? Do the high-dimensional random distributed representations constitute a viable model of semantic knowledge? In short: What are the cognitive implications of the accomplishments of the system?

The keyword in this discussion is *functionality*. The performance of the system could be described as *functionally* equivalent to the linguistic behavior of a human language user in carrying out the specific predefined linguistic task of picking out synonyms of a target word. This means that since the system's internal representations in the form of context vectors have been proven (by the successful execution of the TOEFL-test) to be functional for purposes pertaining to linguistic competence, we may describe the system as having acquired and applied the *computational equivalent* of the linguistic knowledge that humans possess when discriminating between word meanings.

This characterization of the system means that the relevant question is *not* whether the system's internal representations of word meanings actually *mean* anything (i.e. if they somehow correspond to how word meanings are represented in the human mind—assuming this question is meaningful), but rather whether they can be *utilized* for the purpose of modeling observable linguistic behavior. The semantic information that the context vectors carry does not reside in the vector representations alone, but rather in the relations between the vectors. The representation is relative rather than absolute, since it is only in relation to each other that the context vectors *mean* anything. The important point is therefore that the system's internal representations can produce linguistic behavioral patterns that manifest semantic knowledge—and that can be regarded a fragment of the *functionality* of a language user. In other words: It is by virtue of letting the meaning of 'meaning' remain indeterminate that we may consider the implementation of a functional pattern as an epistemic or cognitive achievement.

26.11 Implications for Information Access

More concretely, for immediate attention, if we wish to improve on information-access systems—if we use the standard architecture as delineated in the beginning of this chapter—there are three access points, points where the character of the internal text representation influences the working of the system as a whole, and points where a more adaptive and humanlike processing would make a difference:

1. the intelligent selection of document descriptors for each document;

2. the flexible internal expression of those items; and

3. the negotiable elicitation of information needs from the reader.

And this functionality should not be restricted to a single language.

26.12 Meaning in Text

The reason for using narrow context windows to calculate semantic word vectors as opposed to using whole documents, as in LSA, is the assumption that the semantically most significant context is the immediate vicinity of a word. That is, one would expect the words closest to the focus word to be more important than the words further away in the text for determining the meaning of the focus word. The intuition is that a local context is more reliable for measuring semantic similarity between words than a large context region spanning hundreds of words.

This intuition is expressed, for example, by Lin (1997), who states that "two different words are likely to have similar meanings if they occur in identical local contexts." Schütze and Pedersen (1997) argue that local co-occurrence statistics are both qualitatively and quantitatively more informative than document-based co-occurrence statistics, since the number of co-occurrence events will be higher when using a sliding window to define the co-occurrence region than when using documents, especially if the documents are long. Burgess and Lund (2000) also report on the merits of narrow context windows.

If the assumption is correct that local co-occurrence statistics give a more reliable measure of distributional similarity between words than do document-based co-occurrences, one should be able to discern an increase in performance when using narrow context windows, as opposed to documents, for calculating the semantic word vectors. The results of our experiments seem to favor this assumption. Compared to the performance of techniques based on context regions in excess of a hundred words, such as LSA, narrow context windows perform well in at least one linguistic task (TOEFL) pertaining to lexical semantic knowledge.

This improved performance raises the question of whether there might be a difference in what sort of semantic information can be extracted by considering different amounts of context. A larger context might give better clues to what a particular word is about than to what it means. The idea is that two words that are about similar things will occur in similar context regions (e.g. documents), while two words that have similar meanings will occur with similar context neighbors (i.e. words). This means that larger contexts might be more suited for tasks pertaining to topical information, such as information retrieval, than in tasks directed specifically toward lexical semantic competence. The applicability of LSA to information retrieval is well documented (e.g. Dumais et al., 1988; Deerwester et al., 1990), supporting this assumption.

The possibility of a discrepancy between the kinds of semantic information carried by different context sizes suggests that although a synonym test is a fairly reliable method for measuring one kind of semantic knowledge, other conceivable methods for measuring semantic knowledge might be worth considering. Other evaluation procedures have been reported in the literature, such as comparing vector similarities with reaction times from lexical priming studies (Lund and Burgess, 1996) or using LSA for evaluating the quality of content of student essays on given topics (Landauer et al., 1997).

Meaning, the main object of our study, is most decidedly situation-dependent. While much of meaning appears to achieve consistency across usage situations, most everything *can* be negotiated on the go. Human processing appears to be flexible and oriented toward learning from prototypes rather than learning by definition: Learning new words and adding new meanings or shades of meaning to an already known word do not require a formal retraining process. And, in fact, natural use of human languages does not make use of definitions or semantic delimitations; finding an explicit definition in natural discourse is a symptom of communicative malfunction, not of laudable explicitness.

A text model should model language *use* rather than language in the abstract. We need a better understanding of how meaning is negotiated in human language usage: Fixed representations do not seem practical and do not reflect observed human language usage. We need a more exact study of inexact expression, of the *homeosemy* ('homeo' from Greek *homoios* similar) or near and close synonymy of expressions of human language. This means we need to understand the temporality, saliency, and topicality of terms, relations, and grammatical elements—it means modeling the life cycle of terms in language, the life cycle of referents in discourse, and the connection between the two. These experiments have taken but some first steps in that direction.

References

Aleksander, I. and Morton, H. (1995). *An Introduction to Neural Computing*, second edition. London: International Thomson Computer Press.

Boden, M. B. and Niklasson, L. F. (1995). Features of distributed representation for tree structures: A study of RAAM. In L. F. Niklasson and M. B. Boden (eds.), *Current Trends in Connectionism*. Hillsdale, NJ: Erlbaum.

Burgess, C. and Lund, K. (2000). The dynamics of meaning in memory. In E. Dietrich and A. B. Markman (eds.), *Cognitive dynamics: Conceptual change in humans and machines*. Mahwah, NJ: Lawrence Erlbaum Associates.

Chalmers, D. J. (1990). Syntactic transformations on distributed representations. *Connection Science* 2(1–2):53–62.

Deerwester, S., Dumais, S. T., Furnas, G. W., Landauer, T. K., and Harshman, R. (1990). Indexing by latent semantic analysis. *Journal of the Society* for *Information Science* 41(6):391–407.

Dumais, S. T., Furnas, G. W., Landauer, T. K., and Deerwester, S. (1988). Using Latent Semantic Analysis to improve information retrieval. *Proceedings of CHI'88: Conference on Human Factors in Computing* (pp. 281–285). New York: ACM.

Durrett, R. (1995). *Probability: Theory and Examples.* 2nd ed. Belmont, Calif.: Duxbury Press, Wadsworth Publishing Co.

Eliasmith, C, and Thagard, P. (2001). Integrating structure and meaning: A distributed model of analogical mapping. *Cognitive Science* 25(2):245–286.

Fodor, J. A. and Pylyshyn, Z. W. (1988). Connectionism and cognitive architecture: A critical analysis. *Cognition* 28:3–71.

Gayler, R. W. and Wales, R. (1998). Connections, binding, unification, and analogical promiscuity. In K. Holyoak, D. Gentner, and B. Kokinov (eds.), *Advances in Analogy Research: Integration of Theory and Data from the Cognitive, Computational, and Neural Sciences* (Proc. Analogy '98 workshop, Sofia), pp. 181–190. Sofia: New Bulgarian University.

Gentner, D. (1983). Structure-mapping: A theoretical framework for analogy. *Cognitive Science* 7(2):155–170.

Gentner, D., Holyoak, K. J., and Kokinov, B. K. (eds.) (2001). *The Analogical Mind: Perspectives from Cognitive Science.* Cambridge, MA: MIT Press.

Gentner, D. and Markman, A. B. (1993). Analogy—watershed or Waterloo? Structural alignment and the development of connectionist models of analogy. In C. L. Giles, S. J. Hanson, and J. D. Gowan (eds.), *Advances in Neural Information Processing Systems 5* (NIPS '92, pp. 855–863). San Mateo, CA: Morgan Kaufmann.

Harris, Z. (1968). *Mathematical Structures of Language.* New York: Interscience Publishers.

Hinton, G. E. (1990). Mapping part-whole hierarchies into connectionist networks. *Artificial Intelligence* 46(1–2):47–75.

Hofstadter, D. R. (1984). *The Copycat Project: An Experiment in Nondeterminism and Creative Analogies.* AI Memo 755, Artificial Intelligence laboratory, Massachusetts Institute of Technology.

Hofstadter, D. R. (1985). *Metamagical Themas: Questions of the Essence of Mind and Pattern.* New York: Basic Books.

Jaeckel, L. A. (1989a). *An alternative design for a Sparse Distributed Memory.* Report RIACS TR-89.28. Research Institute for Advanced Computer Science, NASA Ames Research Center.

Jaeckel, L. A. (1989b). *A class of designs for a Sparse Distributed Memory.* Report RIACS TR-89.30, Research Institute for Advanced Computer Science, NASA Ames Research Center.

Järvinen, T. and Tapanainen, P. (1997). *Functional Dependency Grammar.* Publications of the Department for General Linguistics, University of Helsinki.

Kanerva, P. (1988). *Sparse Distributed Memory.* Cambridge, Mass.: MIT Press.

Kanerva, P. (1992). Associative-memory models of the cerebellum. In I. Aleksander and J. Taylor (eds.), *Artificial Neural Networks, 2* (Proc. ICANN '92, Brighton, UK, pp. 23–34). Amsterdam: Elsevier.

Kanerva, P. (1993). Sparse Distributed Memory and related models. In M. H. Hassoun (ed.), *Associative Neural Memories.* New York: Oxford University Press.

Kanerva, P. (1996). Binary spatter-coding of ordered K-tuples. In C. von der Malsburg, W. von Seelen, J. C. Vorbrüggen, and B. Sendhoff (eds.), *Artificial Neural Networks* (Proc. ICANN'96, Bochum, Germany, pp. 869–873). Berlin: Springer.

Kanerva, P., Kristofersson, J., and Holst, A. (2000). Random Indexing of text samples for Latent Semantic Analysis. In L. R. Gleitman and A. K. Josh (eds.), *Proceedings of the 22nd Annual Conference of the Cognitive Science Society,* p. 1036. Mahwah, New Jersey: Erlbaum.

Kaski, S. (1998). Dimensionality reduction by random mapping: Fast similarity computation for clustering. *Proceedings of the IJCNN'98, International Joint Conference on Neural Networks* (Anchorage, vol. 1, pp. 413–418). Piscataway, NJ: IEEE Press.

Kristoferson, J. (1995). *Best probability of activation and performance comparisons for several designs of Sparse Distributed Memory.* Report SICS R95:09, Swedish Institute of Computer Science.

Kristoferson, J. (1997). *Some results on activation and scaling of Sparse Distributed Memory.* Report SICS R97:04, Swedish Institute of Computer Science.

Landauer, T. K. and Dumais, S. T. (1997). A solution to Plato's problem: The Latent Semantic Analysis theory of acquisition, induction and representation of knowledge. *Psychological Review* 104(2):211–240.

Landauer, T. K., Laham, D., Rehder, B., and Schreiner, M. E. (1997). How well can passage meaning be derived without using word order? A comparison of Latent Semantic Analysis and humans. In M. G. Shafto and P. Langley (eds.), *Proceedings of the 19th annual meeting of the Cognitive Science Society,* pp. 412–417. Mawhwah, NJ: Erlbaum.

Landauer, T. K., Laham, D., and Foltz, P. W. (1998). Learning human-like knowledge by Singular Value Decomposition: A progress report. In M. I. Jordan, M. J. Kearns and S. A. Solla (eds.), *Advances in Neural Information Processing Systems* 10, pp. 45–51. Cambridge, Mass.: MIT Press.

Lin, D. (1997). Using syntactic dependency as local context to resolve word sense ambiguity. *Proceedings of ACL-97,* Madrid, Spain.

Lund, K. and Burgess, C. (1996). Producing high-dimensional semantic spaces from lexical co-occurrence. *Behavior Research Methods, Instruments & Computers* 28(2):203–208.

Mitchell, M. (1993). *Analogy-Making as Perception: A Computer Model.* Cambridge, MA: MIT Press.

Papadimitriou, C. H., Raghavan, P., Tamaki, H., and Vempala, S. (1998). Latent Semantic Indexing: A probabilistic analysis. *Proceedings of the 17th*

ACM Symposium on the Principles of Database Systems, pp. 159–168. ACM Press.

Plate, T. A. (1994). *Distributed Representation and Nested Compositional Structure.* Ph.D. Thesis. Graduate Department of Computer Science, University of Toronto.

Pollack, J. P. (1990). Recursive distributed representations. *Artificial Intelligence* 46(1–2):77–105.

Rachkovskij, D.A. and Kussul, E.M. (2001). Binding and normalization of binary sparse distributed representations by Context-Dependent Thinning. *Neural Computation* 13(2):411–452.

Rumelhart, D. E, and McClelland, J. L. (1986). On learning the past tenses of English verbs. In J. L. McClelland and D. E. Rumelhart (eds.), *Parallel Distributed Processing 2: Applications* (pp. 216–271). Cambridge, Mass.: MIT Press.

Schütze, H. (1992). Dimensions of meaning. *Proceedings of Supercomputing* (Minneapolis. pp. 787–796). Los Alamitos, CA: IEEE Computer Society Press.

Schütze, H. and Pedersen, J. O. (1997). A cooccurrence-based thesaurus and two applications to information retrieval. *Information Processing and Management* 33(3):307–318.

Sjödin, G. (1995). *Improving the capacity of SDM.* Report R95:12, Swedish Institute of Computer Science.

Sjödin, G. (1996). Getting more information out of SDM. In C. von der Malsburg, W. von Seelen, J. C. Vorbrüggen, and B. Sendhoff (eds.), *Artificial Neural Networks—Proc. ICANN '96,* 477–482. Berlin: Springer.

Sjödin, G. (1997). The Sparchunk code: A method to build higher-level structures in a sparsely encoded SDM. *Proc. 1998 IEEE International Joint Conference on Neural Networks* (IJCNN/WCCI, Anchorage, Alaska, May 1998, vol. 2, pp. 1410–1415). Pincataway, NJ: IEEE Press. Reprinted in this volume.

Sjödin, G., Karlsson, R., and Kristoferson, J. (1997). Algorithms for efficient SDM. *Proc. 1997 Real World Computing Symposium* (RWC'97, Tokyo, January 1997), 215–222. Report RWC TR-96001, Real World Computing Partnership, Tsukuba Research Center, Japan.

Smolensky, P. (1990). Tensor product variable binding and the representation of symbolic structures in connectionist systems. *Artificial Intelligence* 46(1–2):159–216.

Wittgenstein, L. (1953). *Philosophical Investigations.* Translated by G. E. M. Anscombe. Oxford: Blackwell. Swedish translation *Filosofiska undersökningar* by A. Wedberg (1992). Stockholm: Thales.

Index